REVELATIONS
— IN —
CONTEXT

The Stories behind the Sections of the Doctrine and Covenants

Edited by Matthew McBride
and James Goldberg

Including Insights from the Joseph Smith Papers

Published by
The Church of Jesus Christ of Latter-day Saints
Salt Lake City, Utah

Contents

Preface

Latter-day Saints believe in a loving God who speaks to His children "in these times as in times of old, and as well in times of old as in times to come" (1 Nephi 10:19). This fundamental principle of the restored gospel is reflected in Latter-day Saint scripture, which contains records of God's dealings with His children in the remote past, as well as His words to Joseph Smith and other latter-day prophets.

The book of Doctrine and Covenants is a witness of this outpouring of continuing revelation. Each section answers pressing questions, reveals important truths, or gives practical guidance. These revelations are the fruit of an ongoing dialogue between the Lord and His people. But in many cases, the Doctrine and Covenants contains only half of the dialogue—the Lord's revealed responses. In this way, it is unique among Latter-day Saint books of scripture. In the Bible, Book of Mormon, and Pearl of Great Price, gospel teaching is often couched in narrative. The narrative gives us clues that help us interpret the teachings and see how they influenced the lives of the men and women of the scriptures. But the Doctrine and Covenants does not contain the stories behind the revelations.

While the section headings, updated in 2013, provide some context for the revelations, instructions, and declarations in the Doctrine and Covenants, they don't tell the complete story. What were the questions that prompted the revelations? What did the Lord's responses mean to those to whom they were addressed? How did those who heard the revelations respond to new teachings? *Revelations in Context* is a collection of stories that attempts to answer these questions. Told from the point of view of people who experienced them in their immediate context, these narratives give us insight into the meaning of the revelations and help us see them with new eyes.

The stories in this collection, which treat almost all of the sections in the Doctrine and Covenants, were written by historians in the Church History Department. In telling these stories, the authors brought to bear both their faith in the restored gospel and their training and expertise in American and Mormon history. Particularly important to this series was the Joseph Smith Papers Project, which has provided a foundation of meticulous scholarship upon which all historical interpretation of Joseph Smith's life and work should build. Citations to the Joseph Smith Papers in *Revelations in Context* typically direct the reader to the documents and materials generously made available on josephsmithpapers.org.

We hope that these narratives will provide Church members not only with a clearer understanding of the revelations themselves, but a deeper appreciation for the way God speaks to His children "in their weakness, after the manner of their language, that they might come to understanding" (D&C 1:24).

The Contributions of Martin Harris

D&C 3, 5, 10, 17, 19

Matthew McBride

By 1827, Martin Harris had built a comfortable life for himself in Palmyra, New York.[1] Over the previous 14 years, he had acquired 320 acres of farmland, made them profitable through his industry and progressive ideas, and built a handsome frame home.[2] He married Lucy Walker in 1808, and the couple had five children, three of whom lived to be adults. Martin's talent and prosperity had not gone unnoticed by his neighbors, who thought of him as "an industrious, hard-working farmer, shrewd in his business calculations, frugal in his habits, and . . . a prosperous man in the world."[3]

Now at age 45 and enjoying the fruits of his labors and the respect of his peers, Martin even considered hiring someone to care for his farm for several months so he could do some travel. But just when he began to contemplate this excursion, he received a visit from Lucy Mack Smith, who bore some intriguing news.

Martin Harris knew most of the story: An angel had visited Joseph Smith and revealed to him the existence of a record on ancient metallic plates buried in a hill near his home. For three years, Joseph had watched and waited.

Now Lucy Smith had come to tell Martin that her son had, at length, obtained the plates from the angel and was intent on seeing them translated. Joseph and his family were not in a position to pay to publish the translation, but Martin Harris was. Lucy Mack Smith asked Martin if he would come visit Joseph. He agreed, and his wife, Lucy Harris, insisted she would come also.

Joseph Smith likely considered Martin Harris a friend. He had previously confided in Martin regarding his angelic visits and the existence of the plates. Martin apparently returned his friendship; he had hired Joseph Smith as a day laborer on his farm and found him to be a reliable hand.

But Martin probably harbored some doubts. He later told an interviewer that when he first heard the story of the plates, he assumed that Joseph and his money-digging friends had simply found an old brass kettle. Still, Martin was a religious man. Some even thought him superstitious in his views, disparagingly calling him a "visionary fanatic."[4] Perhaps it was this openness to the presence of the supernatural in daily life that allowed him to at least consider Joseph's claims. Lucy Harris promptly kept her promise to visit Joseph, even offering to help finance the translation of the plates herself. Martin, however, remained aloof, perhaps needing some time to think it over.

During the fall and early winter, hostile neighbors made several attempts to steal the plates from Joseph. In this precarious situation, he decided to move with his wife, Emma, to her parents' home in Harmony, Pennsylvania. Whatever the cause of Martin's earlier hesitation, he concluded that he needed to help Joseph. He met him in a tavern in Palmyra, gave him $50 in silver, and said, "I give [this] to you to do the Lords work."[5] When Joseph insisted it be considered a loan, Martin reaffirmed his desire to contribute freely to the cause.

Meanwhile, Lucy Harris had begun to doubt Joseph's story, possibly due to his insistence on keeping the plates hidden from view. This suspicion led her to resent Martin's increased interest and involvement with Joseph. Martin's relationship with his wife was already strained, and his support of Joseph Smith caused the rift between them to deepen.

"I Cannot Read a Sealed Book"

A short time after the Smiths arrived in Harmony, Martin paid them a visit and expressed his desire to assist Joseph. He proposed to journey east to New York City with a transcription of some of the characters on the plates to show them to scholars. Perhaps he wanted additional reassurance that the plates were authentic, or he may have thought a testimonial would help them borrow money to publish the translation. In any event, he insisted that the Lord had prompted him to make the trip.

At the time, neither Joseph nor Martin knew much about the language on the plates. They knew only as much as the angel Moroni had told Joseph: that it was an ancient American record. Thus, rather than seeking a scholar with a knowledge of Egyptian (Joseph later learned that the language on the plates was called "reformed Egyptian"), Martin visited several scholars with an interest in antiquities, especially American antiquities.[6]

He departed in February 1828, and en route to New York City, he stopped in Albany to visit Luther Bradish—a former Palmyra resident and family friend who had traveled extensively throughout the Near East and Egypt. Martin sought his opinion about whom to visit regarding the translation and then pressed on to New York to visit Samuel L. Mitchill, a linguist and one of the leading scholars on ancient American culture. After examining the characters, Mitchill evidently sent Martin to Charles Anthon, a young professor of grammar and linguistics at Columbia College. Anthon had been collecting American Indian stories and speeches for publication and was eager to inspect the document Martin brought him.

Martin claimed that Anthon declared the characters authentic until he learned how Joseph Smith had acquired them. He suggested Martin bring him the plates. Martin refused, and Anthon replied, paraphrasing a verse in Isaiah, "I cannot read a sealed book." Though Anthon later denied the details of Martin's account of their meeting, we do know this: Martin came away from his visits with the eastern scholars more convinced than ever that Joseph Smith was called of God and that the plates and characters were ancient. He and Joseph viewed the visit to Anthon as a fulfillment of Isaiah's prophecy (also mentioned in the Book of Mormon itself) of "a book that is sealed, which men deliver to one that is learned, saying, Read this, I pray thee: and he saith, I cannot; for it is sealed."[7]

"To Stop the Mouths of Fools"

During the spring and early summer of 1828, Martin scribed as the young seer dictated the translation. Though the process must have seemed miraculous to him, Martin was still on guard against deception. He once replaced Joseph's seer stone with another stone to see if Joseph would notice the difference. When Joseph was unable to continue translating, Martin confessed his ruse and returned the seer stone. When Joseph asked him why he had done it, Martin explained that he wanted to "stop the mouths of fools, who had told him that the Prophet had learned those sentences and was merely repeating them."[8]

Though Martin came to believe quite sincerely, his wife had turned bitterly hostile. Lucy Harris was concerned, quite understandably, that Martin might take a large financial risk to help publish the book, that her peers would mock her husband's participation in what they viewed as a fraudulent scheme, and that Martin had simply left her feelings out of his calculations. She was also stung by the way Joseph rebuffed her every attempt to see the plates, and she beleaguered Martin incessantly to show her some evidence of Joseph's ability to translate.

To ease Lucy's disquiet, Martin asked Joseph to "enquire of the Lord through the Urim and Thummin" if he might "carry the writings home and exibit them"[9] to his wife and others. Joseph wanted to please Martin because he had shown him friendship "when there seemed to be no earthly freind to succor or to sympathize."[10]

Joseph did inquire for his friend. "The answer," Joseph said, "was that he must not. [Martin] was not satisfied with this answer and desired that I would enquire again. I did so, and the answer was as before. Still he could not be contented and insisted that I should enquire once more. After much solicitation I again enquired of the Lord and permission was granted on certain conditions."[11]

Martin was to show the translated pages only to his wife, parents, brother, and sister-in-law.

Elated, Martin Harris returned home with the manuscript pages and showed them to his wife. He did not, however, handle the precious manuscript with the prescribed care, and it was soon lost. Precisely how it happened is a matter of speculation. One commonly repeated rumor was that Lucy removed the pages from Martin's bureau and burned them, though she denied any responsibility for their loss. Some, including Joseph Smith, suspected a conspiracy on the part of Lucy Harris or perhaps others.

Martin made every effort to find the manuscript, dreading the thought of confessing to Joseph what had happened. He even "ripped open beds and pillows" but to no avail. When Joseph came to his parents' home after several weeks, eager for news, Martin trudged reluctantly three miles to the Smiths' Manchester home. As he approached, he walked "with a slow and measured tread towards the house, his eyes fixed thoughtfully upon the ground. When he came to the gate, he did not open it but got upon the fence and sat some time with his hat drawn over his eyes."[12]

He at last entered, and having little appetite for the dinner they had prepared for him, he soon "pressed his hands upon his temples and cried out in a tone of deep anguish, 'Oh! I have lost my soul!'"[13] Joseph understood immediately what had happened. He demanded that Martin return and look again for the manuscript, but Martin insisted that further searching would be in vain.

Exhausted and discouraged, Joseph returned to Harmony and, walking a short distance from his home, prayed for mercy. The angel appeared and gave again to Joseph the Urim and Thummim, or interpreters, that Joseph had originally received with the plates but had lost for having "wearied the Lord in asking that Martin Harris might take the writings."[14] Using the Urim and Thummim, Joseph received the earliest of his revelations for which a text survives.

Now known as Doctrine and Covenants 3, the revelation rebuked Joseph: "How oft you have transgressed the commandments and laws of God and have gone on in the pursuasions of Men for behold you should not fear men more than God." However, it held out hope:

"Remember God is merciful. Therefore repent of that which thou hast done which is contrary to the commandment which I gave and thou art still chosen and art again called to do the work."[15]

"I Will Grant unto Him a View"

For months Martin Harris remained at his Palmyra home, haunted by the loss of the manuscript. He was also distressed to discover that his wife and others sought to discredit Joseph Smith and make him out to be a fraud who was simply after Martin's money. Longing for reconciliation and bearing news of these disturbing efforts, he visited Joseph Smith in Harmony in March 1829.

To Martin's relief, Joseph had obtained forgiveness and was preparing to resume the translation. Martin asked Joseph once again for the privilege of seeing the plates. He desired a firm witness that "Joseph hath got the things which he hath testified that he hath got," perhaps to stifle his lingering doubts and to help him persuade Lucy. Joseph received a revelation for Martin, found today in Doctrine and Covenants 5. In it, the Lord revealed that three witnesses would be called to see and give testimony of the plates. Then, to Martin Harris's delight, the Lord promised him that "if he will go out & bow down before me & humble himself in mighty prayer & faith in the sincerity of his heart then I will grant unto him a vew of the things which he desireth to vew." The revelation also indicated that the book's authenticity would be affirmed by its message rather than by the plates, and that many would not believe even if Joseph Smith were to "show them all things."[16]

Work on the translation recommenced in earnest on April 5, 1829, when newly arrived Oliver Cowdery assumed the role of scribe. Joseph and Oliver picked up where Joseph and Martin had previously left off, near the beginning of the book of Mosiah. But in May, as they approached the end of the Book of Mormon as we now have it, they wondered whether they should retranslate the lost portion. To address this question, the Lord gave Joseph Smith another revelation, now contained in Doctrine and Covenants 10. The revelation confirmed Joseph's fears of a conspiracy: "Behold, satan has put it into their hearts to alter the words which you have caused to be written." However, the Lord reassured Joseph that He had a long-prepared solution. Joseph was commanded not to retranslate the lost portion but to supplant it with a translation of "the plates of Nephi," which covered a similar time period. Thus, the Lord would frustrate the plans of the conspirators and fulfill the prayers of the ancient Nephite record keepers, who desired these writings to "come forth unto this people."[17]

"Mine Eyes Have Beheld"

As the translation neared completion, Martin, together with Oliver Cowdery and David Whitmer, begged Joseph for the privilege of being the promised witnesses of the plates. Joseph again inquired and received the revelation now contained in Doctrine and Covenants 17, promising each of the men that they would witness the plates if they would "rely upon my word" with "full purpose of heart."[18]

Martin Harris was no doubt euphoric that he would be allowed to see the plates, but in June 1829, when the three men attempted to pray and obtain a view of the plates from the angel, they were at first unsuccessful. Martin feared "his presence was the cause of our not obtaining what we wished." He retired, and shortly thereafter the angel appeared and showed Whitmer and Cowdery the plates. Joseph searched for Martin and found him some distance away. He had been praying on his own, and Joseph joined him. He soon received the manifestation he had long sought. After witnessing the plates, he shouted, "Tis enough tis enough mine eyes have beheld mine eyes have beheld."[19]

"Thou Shalt Not Covet Thine Own Property"

Bolstered by this miraculous and faith-affirming experience, Martin recommitted to provide financial support for the Book of Mormon publication. Joseph Smith had talked to several printers in Palmyra and Rochester, New York. He hoped to convince Egbert B. Grandin of Palmyra to print the book, and Martin took up the negotiations. Grandin's price was $3,000 for the unusually large printing of 5,000 copies, but he would not buy the type or begin the job until Joseph or Martin had "promised to insure the payment for the printing."[20] Martin would have to impart essentially all the property to which he had a legal right.

This moment of decision would sound the depth of Martin Harris's trust in Joseph Smith and his faith in the Book of Mormon. Seeking guidance, he spoke with Joseph, who received yet another revelation. Known today as Doctrine and Covenants 19, the revelation admonished Martin, "Thou shalt not covet thine own property, but impart it freely to the printing of the book of Mormon."[21] On August 25, 1829, he mortgaged his property to Grandin as payment for the publication. His neighbors were amazed that their sensible friend would "abandon the cultivation of one of the best farms in the neighborhood"[22] to underwrite the publication.

Initially, Martin hoped to redeem his mortgaged farm by selling copies of the Book of Mormon. In January, Joseph Smith signed an agreement with Martin, giving him "equal privilege"[23] to sell copies of the Book of Mormon until he had fully recouped the cost of printing. He began selling the book as soon as it was available in March 1830. Unfortunately, sales did not go as well as he had hoped.

Joseph Smith reportedly spotted a distraught Martin Harris late in March 1830 near Palmyra. According to Joseph Knight, Martin was carrying several copies of the Book of Mormon. He said, "The Books will not sell for no Body wants them," and told Joseph, "I Want a Commandment." Joseph's reply referred Martin to the previous revelation: "Fulfill what you have got." "But I must have a commandment," repeated Martin.[24]

He received no further commandment.[25] However, in compliance with the earlier revelation, Martin eventually sold enough of his property to pay the debt. By so doing, he secured his place as the most significant financial supporter of the Book of Mormon and thus the early Church. None among Joseph Smith's younger and poorer friends could have provided this critical contribution.

1. The author acknowledges Michael Hubbard MacKay of the Joseph Smith Papers team, whose research informed this telling of Martin Harris's story.

2. See Ronald W. Walker, "Martin Harris: Mormonism's Early Convert," *Dialogue: A Journal of Mormon Thought,* vol. 19, no. 4 (Winter 1986), 30–33.

3. Susan Easton Black and Larry C. Porter, "For the Sum of Three Thousand Dollars," *Journal of Book of Mormon Studies,* vol. 14, no. 2 (2005), 7.

4. Walker, "Martin Harris: Mormonism's Early Convert," 34.

5. Lucy Mack Smith, "Lucy Mack Smith, History, 1844–1845," book 6, page 6, josephsmithpapers.org.

6. See Lucy Mack Smith, "Lucy Mack Smith, History, 1844–1845," books 6 and 7, josephsmithpapers.org.

7. Isaiah 29:11; see also Michael Hubbard MacKay and Gerrit J. Dirkmaat, *From Darkness unto Light: Joseph Smith's Translation and Publication of the Book of Mormon* (Provo: BYU Religious Studies Center, 2015), 52.

8. Edward Stevenson, "One of the Three Witnesses: Incidents in the Life of Martin Harris," in *Latter-day Saints' Millennial Star,* vol. 44, no. 6 (Feb. 6, 1882), 87.

9. Joseph Smith, "History, circa 1841, fair copy," 14, josephsmithpapers.org; spelling standardized.

10. Lucy Mack Smith, "Lucy Mack Smith, History, 1844–1845," book 6, pages 10–11.

11. Joseph Smith, "History, circa 1841, fair copy," 14.

12. Lucy Mack Smith, "Lucy Mack Smith, History, 1844–1845," book 7, pages 5–6; punctuation standardized.

13. Lucy Mack Smith, "Lucy Mack Smith, History, 1844–1845," book 7, pages 5–6; punctuation standardized.

14. Joseph Smith, "History, circa 1841, fair copy," 14.

15. Joseph Smith, "History, circa 1841, fair copy," 15–16.

16. "Revelation, March 1829 [D&C 5]," 1–2, josephsmithpapers.org.

17. "Revelation, Spring 1829 [D&C 10]," in Book of Commandments, 22, 25, josephsmithpapers.org.

18. "Revelation, June 1829–E [D&C 17]," in Revelation Book 2, 119, josephsmithpapers.org.

19. Joseph Smith, "History, 1838–1856, volume A-1 [23 December 1805–30 August 1834]," 24–25, josephsmithpapers.org.

20. John Gilbert, as cited in "Interview with the Printer of the Bible," *New York Herald,* June 25, 1893.

21. "Revelation, circa Summer 1829 [D&C 19]," in Book of Commandments, 41, josephsmithpapers.org.

22. Stephen S. Harding, Letter to Thomas Gregg, February 1882, in Thomas Gregg, *The Prophet of Palmyra* (New York: John Alden, 1890), 37.

23. "Agreement with Martin Harris, 16 January 1830," 1, josephsmithpapers.org.

24. Joseph Knight reminiscences, undated, Church History Library, Salt Lake City.

25. Michael Hubbard MacKay, Gerrit J. Dirkmaat, Grant Underwood, Robert J. Woodford, and William G. Hartley, eds. *Documents, Volume 1: July* 1828–June 1831. Vol. 1 of the Documents series of *The Joseph Smith Papers,* edited by Dean C. Jessee, Ronald K. Esplin, Richard Lyman Bushman, and Matthew J. Grow (Salt Lake City: Church Historian's Press, 2013), 86, note 333.

Joseph Smith's Support at Home

D&C 4, 11, 23

Kay Darowski

The year 1829 dawned full of uncertainty for Joseph Smith but proved to be a remarkable period of personal growth and preparation for future events. In the aftermath of Martin Harris's loss of the first 116 pages of the Book of Mormon translation manuscript in June 1828, Joseph had not worked on the translation of the Book of Mormon for six months. He spent the winter months in Harmony, Pennsylvania, "laboring with my hands upon a small farm which I had purchased of my wife's father, in order to provide for my family."[1] In February 1829, he and his wife, Emma, received a welcome visit from his father and brother.[2]

Familial support was crucial to Joseph; for years he had shared his experiences with his parents and siblings. The day after Joseph was visited by the angel Moroni in 1823, he recounted the event to his father.[3] His mother later wrote that after that visitation, "Joseph continued to receive instructions from time to time and every evening we gathered our children togather. I think that we presented the most peculiar aspect of any family that ever lived upon the Earth all seated in a circle father Mother sons and Daughters listening in breathless anxiety to the religious teachings of a boy 19 yars of age who had never read the Bible through by course in his life."[4]

After Joseph received the golden plates, family members helped him protect them from persons whose interests ranged from the curious to the criminal.[5]

Revelation for Joseph Smith Sr.

During his visit to his son in Harmony, Joseph Smith Sr. asked for a revelation concerning his own role in the Restoration; the young prophet thus received one of his earliest revelations for another individual. When the revelation was later copied in preparation for publication, the following heading was added: "A Revelation to Joseph the Father of the Seer he desired to know what the Lord had for him to do & this is what he Received as follows."[6] The short revelation, now Doctrine and Covenants 4, is full of rich scriptural language from the Bible and Book of Mormon, anticipating a "marvelous work" and listing the attributes of those who choose to "embark in the service of God."[7]

Soon after returning to Manchester, Joseph Sr. agreed to welcome as a boarder at his home a schoolteacher named Oliver Cowdery. Joseph Sr. hesitated when Cowdery, who had heard rumors about Joseph Jr.'s visions and the plates, began to pepper him with questions. Father Smith may have been reluctant due to the harassment his family had received from neighbors and local clergy. Whatever the reason for his initial hesitation, he yielded to the revelation's mandate and served as a faithful witness to Joseph Smith's early visions.

About this same time, Joseph Smith resumed his work on the translation, assisted by Emma, his brother Samuel, and Martin Harris, each acting briefly as scribes. In early April 1829, Oliver Cowdery, his interest now piqued by his conversations with Joseph Sr., traveled to Harmony. Samuel Smith accompanied him on the journey and introduced him to Joseph.[8] Oliver felt in his "very bones" that "it is the will of the Lord that I should go and that there is a work for me to do in this thing."[9] He quickly became a full-time scribe for Joseph. With this much-needed help, work on the translation moved forward at a significantly accelerated pace.

Samuel Smith's Conversion

The following month, in May 1829, Joseph Smith and Oliver Cowdery received the authority to baptize from an angelic messenger, John the Baptist, and performed the ordinance for each other. Shortly after this event, Joseph was visited first by Samuel and then by another brother, Hyrum. During Samuel's visit, Joseph labored to convert his brother. He wrote in his history:

"About this time my brother Samuel H Smith visited us We informed him of what the Lord was about to do for the children of Men and reasoned with him, laboring to convince him of the truth of the Gospel now about to be revealed in its fulness appealing to [the] Holy Bible for the truth of the doctrines we advanced. Not being very easily convinced of these things he retired to the woods that by secret and fervent prayer he might obtain [wisdom] of a benevolent God that he might judge for himself The result was that he became convinced, by revelation, of the truth of the doctrines we presented to him In accordance with the commands of the Gospel he was babtized by O Cowdry and returned home greatly blessed praising God and being filled with the Holy Ghost."[10]

Samuel Smith would go on to serve as one of the earliest proselytizing missionaries in the Church, when in the summer of 1830 he traveled briefly to nearby Mendon, New York, to preach and sell copies of the Book of Mormon.

Revelation for Hyrum Smith

Hyrum visited Joseph shortly after Samuel. Joseph recalled, "At his earnest request I enquired of the Lord for him through the Urim and Thummin and reciev[d] for him the following Revelation."[11] This revelation is now Doctrine and Covenants 11. Although the beginning sentences reflect similar wording in other revelations given in 1829, the text continues with personal counsel, promises, and cautions that hint at Hyrum's role in the unfolding of the Lord's work.

Among other things, the Lord admonishes Hyrum, "Behold I command you, that you need not suppose that you are called to preach until you are called: wait a little longer, until you shall have my word

. . . seek not to declare my word, but first seek to obtain my word, and then shall your tongues be loosed." [12]

Shortly thereafter, in June 1829, Joseph Smith Sr., Samuel Smith, and Hyrum Smith were among the Eight Witnesses to the Book of Mormon, testifying to the world that they saw and held the plates and that they knew "of a surety" that Joseph translated them, "God bearing witness of it." [13] Once again, the loyalty and support of members of his family proved critical to Joseph in his continued labors.

"Anxious to Know . . . Their Respective Duties"

The Book of Mormon, now translated and prepared for press, was published in March 1830. On April 6, 1830, at Fayette, New York, Joseph Smith formally organized what was then called the Church of Christ. Shortly afterward, he was approached by Oliver Cowdery, Hyrum Smith, Samuel H. Smith, Joseph Smith Sr., and Joseph Knight Sr., each "being anxious to know of the Lord what might be their respective duties, in relation to this work." [14] Joseph provided each of them with a brief, personal revelation. Similar in content, length, and wording, the revelations appear to have been dictated one after the other. Acting as scribe, John Whitmer recorded each as a separate revelation, but when the revelations were published in the 1835 edition of the Doctrine and Covenants, they were combined into one section, which is now known as Doctrine and Covenants 23. [15]

Though similar, each revelation mentions the recipient by name and contains specific counsel about duties, roles, and expectations. One notable difference is that each of the first four revelations states that the recipient is "under no condemnation," as Oliver, Hyrum, Samuel, and Joseph Sr. had been baptized. The final recipient, Joseph Knight Sr., had not yet been baptized and was instead counseled that it was his "duty to unite with the true Church." [16]

The words of revelation to Hyrum hint that in the time since the earlier revelation, he had obtained the word of the Lord and that now his "tongue [was] loosed" (see D&C 23:3), and he was called to exhort. Hyrum is known to have preached the restored gospel and the Book of Mormon as early as October 1830 at his father's home in Manchester, New York. His Sabbath sermon on that occasion pricked the heart of Ezra Thayer, leading to his conversion. Thayer later recalled, "Every word touched me to the inmost soul. I thought every word was pointed to me. . . . The tears rolled down my cheeks."[17]

In the ensuing years, Joseph's family continued to demonstrate their support by serving as missionaries, by shouldering priesthood leadership roles, and through their personal sacrifice. Their paths and successes—and even hardships and failures—would unfold over time, but in 1830, as the new Church was organized, they were anxious to serve, armed with the Lord's will for them as revealed by the Prophet Joseph Smith.

1. Joseph Smith, "History, 1838–1856, volume A-1 [23 December 1805–30 August 1834]," 11, josephsmithpapers.org.

2. See Joseph Knight reminiscences, undated, 5, Church History Library, Salt Lake City; see also Joseph Smith, "History, 1838–1856, volume A-1," 11, josephsmithpapers.org.

3. Joseph Smith, "History, 1838–1856, volume A-1," 7, josephsmithpapers.org.

4. Lucy Mack Smith, "Lucy Mack Smith, History, 1844–45," book 4, page 1, josephsmithpapers.org.

5. See Lucy Mack Smith, *Biographical Sketches of Joseph Smith, the Prophet, and His Progenitors for many Generations* (Liverpool: Published for Orson Pratt by S. W. Richards, 15, Wilton Street, 1853), 102–9.

6. Historical Introduction to "Revelation, February 1829 [D&C 4]," josephsmithpapers.org.

7. "Revelation, February 1829 [D&C 4]," 1, josephsmithpapers.org.

8. See Lucy Mack Smith, *Biographical Sketches,* 128–31.

9. Lucy Mack Smith, "Lucy Mack Smith, History, 1844–1845," book 8, page 1, josephsmithpapers.org.

10. Joseph Smith, "History, circa 1841, fair copy," 36, josephsmithpapers.org.

11. Joseph Smith, "History, circa 1841, fair copy," 36, josephsmithpapers.org.

12. "Revelation, May 1829–A [D&C 11]," in Book of Commandments, 29, josephsmithpapers.org; see also Doctrine and Covenants 11:15–16, 21.

13. "Book of Mormon, 1830," 590, josephsmithpapers.org.

14. Joseph Smith, "History, 1838–1856, volume A-1," 38, josephsmithpapers.org.

15. "Revelation Book 1," 29–30, josephsmithpapers.org; see also "Doctrine and Covenants, 1835," 176–77, josephsmithpapers.org.

16. "Revelation, April 1830–E [D&C 26:6–7]," in Revelation Book 1, 30, josephsmithpapers.org; see also Doctrine and Covenants 23:7.

17. "Testimony of Brother E. Thayre Concerning the Latter Day Work," True Latter Day Saints' *Herald,* vol. 3, no. 4 (Oct. 1862), 80.

Oliver Cowdery's Gift

D&C 6, 7, 8, 9, 13

Jeffrey G. Cannon

Oliver Cowdery lay awake wondering if the stories he was hearing were true. The 22-year-old schoolteacher was boarding at the Palmyra, New York, home of Joseph Smith Sr. in the fall of 1828. Soon after he arrived in the area, he started hearing stories of the Smiths' son Joseph Jr., his encounters with angels, and his discovery of golden plates.

His curiosity piqued, he had plied his landlord with questions, eager to learn more. At first Joseph Sr. was reluctant to share, but he eventually gave way to his boarder's pleading and told him about Joseph Jr.'s experiences. Oliver needed to know if such wonderful things were true. He prayed. A peace came to him, convincing him that God had spoken and confirming the stories he had heard.[1]

He told no one of this experience, though he often spoke of the golden plates and gradually came to believe God was calling him to be a scribe for Joseph Smith as he translated.[2] When the school term ended in the spring of 1829, Oliver traveled to Harmony, Pennsylvania, where Joseph was living with his wife, Emma, farming land owned by Emma's father, Isaac Hale.

Translation of the plates had stopped for a time after Joseph's scribe Martin Harris lost the manuscript the previous summer. Despite this setback, Joseph had reassured his mother, telling her that an angel told him the Lord would send him a scribe. "And I trust his promise will be verified," Joseph said.[3] Indeed, the Lord did send a scribe, and to the surprise of Joseph's mother and father it was Oliver Cowdery, the very man they had helped prepare. Oliver arrived at Joseph and Emma Smith's home on April 5, 1829.

Joseph and Oliver wasted little time. After attending to some business on April 6, they began the work of translation together the following day.

A Revelation for Oliver

Translation continued for several days, and then Joseph received a revelation for his new scribe. Oliver's lingering doubts about Joseph Smith's prophetic gift were addressed as the words of the revelation related experiences Oliver had not shared with anyone. "Cast your mind upon the night that you cried unto me in your heart, that you might know concerning the truth of these things," the Lord reminded him. "Did I not speak peace to your mind concer[n]ing the matter?—What greater witness can you have than from God? . . . Doubt not, fear not."[4]

Oliver came to Harmony believing he had been called to write for Joseph; now he was there and wanted to know what else the Lord had in store for him. "Behold thou hast a gift," the Lord stated in revelation, "and blessed art thou because of thy gift. Remember it is sacred and cometh from above." His gift was the gift of revelation, and by it he could "find out mysteries, that [he may] bring many to the knowledge of the truth; yea, convince them of the error of their ways." The Lord also offered Oliver another gift: "If you desire of me, to translate even as my servant Joseph."[5]

In the meantime, Oliver continued to witness Joseph Smith employ his gift to translate. Sometime that same month, the two men were discussing the fate of the Apostle John—a topic of interest at the time. Joseph's history records they differed in their opinions and "mutually agreed to settle [it] by the Urim and Thummim."[6] The answer came in a vision of a parchment that Joseph translated, which is now Doctrine and Covenants 7.

Oliver Desires to Translate

As Joseph and Oliver continued their work, Oliver grew anxious to play a greater part in the translation. The Lord had promised him the opportunity to translate, and he wanted to claim it. Joseph dictated another revelation. In it, the Lord assured Oliver he could have the gift he desired. The requirements were faith and an honest heart.

The revelation continued, informing the would-be translator how the process was to work. The Lord declared: "I will tell you in your mind & in your heart by the Holy Ghost which Shall come upon you & which shall dwell in your heart." Revelation had always come in this manner. The revelation declared this was the means or "spirit by which Moses brought the children of Israel through the red Sea on dry ground."[7]

Oliver Cowdery lived in a culture steeped in biblical ideas, language, and practices. The revelation's reference to Moses likely resonated with him. The Old Testament account of Moses and his brother Aaron recounted several instances of using rods to manifest God's will (see Exodus 7:9–12; Numbers 17:8). Many Christians in Joseph Smith and Oliver Cowdery's day similarly believed in divining rods as instruments for revelation. Oliver was among those who believed in and used a divining rod.[8]

The Lord recognized Oliver's ability to use a rod: "Thou hast another gift which is the gift of working with the sprout [or rod]." Confirming the divinity of this gift, the revelation stated: "Behold there is no other power save God that can cause this thing of Nature to work in your hands for it is the work of God."[9] If Oliver desired, the revelation went on to say, the Lord would add the gift of translation to the revelatory gifts Oliver already possessed.

Though we know very few details about Oliver Cowdery's attempt to translate, it apparently did not go well. His efforts quickly came to naught. In the wake of Oliver's failure, Joseph Smith received another revelation, counseling Oliver, "Be patient my son, for it is wisdom in me, and it is not expedient that you should translate at this present time." Oliver was also told he had not understood the process. He was told: "You must study it out in your mind; then you must ask me if it be right, and if it is right, I will cause that your bosom shall burn within you."[10]

Authority Restored

While discouraged by his failed attempt to translate, Oliver dutifully resumed his role as scribe as Joseph dictated the translation from the plates. "These were days never to be forgotten," Oliver later wrote. "To [sit] under the sound of a voice dictated by the inspiration of heaven, awakened the utmost gratitude of this bosom!"[11]

When Joseph and Oliver came to the account of Jesus's personal ministry to the Nephites, they began to wonder if anyone in their day had authority to administer the true church of Christ. They were especially concerned about baptism. On May 15, 1829, they left the Smith home where they were working to find a secluded spot to pray in a wooded area nearby.

Whatever doubts Oliver Cowdery may still have entertained certainly vanished when the resurrected John the Baptist "descended in a cloud of light, and having laid his hands upon us [said,] 'Upon you my fellow servants in the name of Messiah I confer the priesthood of Aaron, which holds the keys of the ministring of angels and of the gospel of repentance, and of baptism by immersion for the remission of sins.'"[12] The experience cemented Oliver's faith. "Where was room for doubt?" Oliver later wrote of the incident. "No where; uncertainty had fled, doubt had sunk."[13]

1. Joseph Smith, "History, 1838–1856, volume A-1 [23 December 1805–30 August 1834]," 15, josephsmithpapers.org.

2. Lucy Mack Smith, "Lucy Mack Smith, History, 1844–1845," book 8, page 1, josephsmithpapers.org.

3. Lucy Mack Smith, *Biographical Sketches of Joseph Smith the Prophet and His Progenitors for Many Generations* (Liverpool, England: S. W. Richards, 1853), 126.

4. "Revelation, April 1829–A [D&C 6]," in Book of Commandments, 16–17, josephsmithpapers.org; see also Doctrine and Covenants 6:22–23, 36.

5. "Revelation, April 1829–A, [D&C 6]," in Book of Commandments, 15, 16, josephsmithpapers.org; see also Doctrine and Covenants 6:10–11, 25.

6. "History, 1838–1856, volume A-1," 15, josephsmithpapers.org.

7. "Revelation, April 1829–B [D&C 8]," in Revelation Book 1, 12–13, josephsmithpapers.org; see also Doctrine and Covenants 8:2–3.

8. See Robert C. Fuller, *Spiritual, but Not Religious: Understanding Unchurched America* (New York: Oxford University Press, 2001), 15, 17; see also Mark Ashurst-McGee, "A Pathway to Prophethood: Joseph Smith Junior

as rodsman, village seer, and Judeo-Christian prophet" (master's dissertation, Utah State University, 2000), 126–48.

9. "Revelation, April 1829–B [D&C 8]," in Revelation Book 1, 13, josephsmithpapers.org; see also Doctrine and Covenants 8:6–11. This revelation refers to Oliver Cowdery's "gift of working with the sprout." Sidney Rigdon changed "sprout" to "rod" in preparation for the revelation's publication in the Book of Commandments in 1833. The 1835 edition of the Doctrine and Covenants is the first source to call it "the gift of Aaron" (see "Book of Commandments, 1833," 19, josephsmithpapers.org; see also "Doctrine and Covenants, 1835," 161, josephsmithpapers.org). The word "sprout" meant the end of a branch or shoot (see Noah Webster, *American Dictionary of the English Language* [New York: S. Converse, 1828]).

10. "Revelation, April 1829–D [D&C 9]," in Book of Commandments, 20–21, josephsmithpapers.org; see also Doctrine and Covenants 9:3, 7–8.

11. Joseph Smith, "History, 1834–1836," 47, josephsmithpapers.org.

12. "History, 1838–1856, volume A-1," 17, josephsmithpapers.org; see also Doctrine and Covenants 13.

13. Joseph Smith, "History, 1834–1836," 49, josephsmithpapers.org.

The Knight and Whitmer Families

D&C 12, 14, 15, 16

Larry E. Morris

In the autumn of 1826, a prominent landowner by the name of Joseph Knight Sr. hired 20-year-old Joseph Smith as a laborer. Knight owned four farms, a grain mill, and two carding machines (which prepared wool, cotton, and other materials for spinning). His son Joseph Knight Jr. later wrote, "My father said Joseph [Smith] was the best hand he ever hired," adding that Joseph told him and his father "that he had seen a vision, that a personage had appeared to him and told him where there was a gold book of ancient date buried, and if he would follow the directions of the Angel he could get it. . . . My Father and I believed what he told us, I think we were the first after his father's family."[1]

A Needed Friend

The Knights proved to be loyal friends. Joseph Knight Sr. was present at the Smith home, along with another friend of the Smiths, Josiah Stowell, in Manchester, New York, on September 22, 1827—the day Joseph obtained the golden plates and the Urim and Thummim. Knight became one of the first to hear about these artifacts when Joseph pulled him aside and told him that the Urim and Thummim was "marvelous" and enabled him to "see any thing." He also said the plates, which appeared "to be Gold," were "written in Caracters" and he wanted them translated.[2]

The translation took place in Harmony, Pennsylvania, where Joseph and his wife, Emma, had purchased a house and property from Emma's parents. The Knights lived about 30 miles to the north, in Colesville, New York, and played a crucial role in the translation. Speaking of Joseph Knight Sr., Joseph wrote: "[He] very kindly and considerately brought us, a quantity of provisions, in order that we might not be interrupted in the work of translation."[3] Knight recalled providing "a Barral of Mackrel and some Lined paper for writing . . . some nine or ten Bushels of grain and some five or six Bushels taters [potatoes] and a pound of tea."[4]

Joseph Knight Jr. remembered that at one point during the translation Joseph needed $50 (apparently to make a payment on the property he and Emma had purchased). "My Father could not raise it [the money]," Knight wrote. "He then came to me, the same day I sold my house lot and sent him [Joseph Smith] a one horse wagon."[5]

About this same time, Joseph Knight Sr. became "anxious to know his duty" in the Lord's work. Joseph inquired of the Lord and received a revelation now known as Doctrine and Covenants 12. Similar to revelations dictated for Oliver Cowdery (section 6) and Hyrum Smith (section 11), this revelation instructed Knight to keep the commandments, to "seek to bring forth and establish the cause of Zion," and to "give heed with [his] might."[6]

From Harmony to Fayette

In May 1829, another family befriended Joseph Smith—the Whitmers. The Whitmer family of Fayette Township, New York (about 100 miles north of Harmony), had first heard of the "gold Bible" late in 1828, after Peter Whitmer's son David struck up a friendship with Oliver Cowdery during a visit to Palmyra. They decided to investigate the story of the plates and keep each other informed.

Oliver had stopped to see the Whitmers in the spring of 1829 when he was on his way to meet Joseph and ultimately serve as his scribe. Since then, Oliver had written letters to David telling of the miraculous translation. Like the Knights, the Whitmers became convinced they should assist in the translation, and around the end of May, David traveled to Harmony to move Joseph and Oliver to the Whitmer home. "He proposed that we should have our board free of charge," wrote Joseph. "Upon our arrival, we found Mr. Whitmer's family very anxious concerning the work, and very friendly towards ourselves. They continued so, boarded and lodged us according to proposal, and John Whitmer, in particular, assisted us very much in writing during the remainder of the work."[7] Emma arrived at the Whitmer home shortly after Joseph and Oliver and also acted as a scribe.

The month of June 1829 was a remarkable one in the history of the Church. Not only did Joseph and his scribes complete the translation, Joseph dictated at least five revelations, Oliver dictated a revelation called "Articles of the Church of Christ," and the two of them had a powerful experience "in the Chamber of Mr. Whitmer's house" in which "the word of the Lord" came unto them and instructed them regarding a series of key ordinances and meetings.[8] In addition, Joseph applied for a copyright to the Book of Mormon, and he and Martin Harris began talking to printers about publishing the book. Finally, an angel appeared and showed the plates to the Three Witnesses near the Whitmer farm in Fayette Township, and the Eight Witnesses saw and handled the plates near the Smith farm in Palmyra Township.

The Whitmers were a great support during this flurry of crucial activity. Such service brought both trials and rewards to the family. A grandson of Mary Musselman Whitmer (wife of Peter Whitmer Sr.) reported that Mary had "so many extra persons to care for" that she "was often overloaded with work." One evening, after a long day's work, she went to the barn to milk the cows and met a stranger who "showed her a bundle of plates" and "turned the leaves of the book of plates over, leaf after leaf," promising Mary that "she should be blessed" if she were "patient and faithful in bearing her burden a little longer."[9] She thus became another witness of the Book of Mormon.

Special blessings also came to Mary's sons. "David, John, and Peter Whitmer Jr became our zealous friends and assistants in the work," wrote Joseph.[10] The same can be said for Christian and Jacob

Whitmer, who joined John and Peter Jr. as four of the Eight Witnesses. When David, John, and Peter Jr. asked Joseph to inquire of the Lord concerning their duties, Joseph dictated three revelations now known as Doctrine and Covenants 14, 15, and 16. David, one of the Three Witnesses, was promised that if he asked in faith he would receive the Holy Ghost, "which giveth utterance, that you may stand as a witness of the things of which you shall both hear and see; and also, that you may declare repentance unto this generation."[11]

A declaration to both John and Peter Jr. has become one of the more memorable verses in modern scripture: "And now behold I say unto you, that the thing which will be of the most worth unto you, will be to declare repentance unto this people, that you may bring souls unto me, that you may rest with them in the kingdom of my Father."[12]

Prelude to the Organization of the Church

Even though the Book of Mormon would not be published until March 1830, these early Saints found great comfort and inspiration in reading the text. Lucy Mack Smith recalled that during the summer of 1829, one evening at the Whitmer home "was spent in reading the manuscript [of the Book of Mormon] and it would be superfluous for me to say . . . that we rejoiced exceedingly."[13]

These believers also used the yet-to-be published Book of Mormon to proclaim the gospel. Such future missionaries as Thomas B. Marsh and Solomon Chamberlain were given proof sheets of the Book of Mormon while it was being printed and became converted several months before the Church was organized. Not surprisingly, members of the Whitmer family were among those who introduced Chamberlain to the new book of scripture.

Between them, the Knight and Whitmer families constituted what became two of the first "branches" of the Church—in Colesville and in Fayette, respectively. Along with the Smith family in Palmyra (the other branch of the Church), the Whitmers and the Knights offered both spiritual and temporal support that figured prominently in the Restoration of the gospel.

1. Joseph Knight Jr., "Joseph Knight's incidents of history from 1827 to 1844[,] Aug. 16, 1862[,] compiled from loose sheets in J[oseph]. K[night].'s possession[,] T[homas]. B[ullock]," Church History Library, Salt Lake City.

2. Joseph Knight reminiscences, undated, Church History Library, Salt Lake City

3. Joseph Smith, "History, 1838–1856, volume A-1 [23 December 1805–30 August 1834]," 20, josephsmithpapers.org.

4. Joseph Knight reminiscences, undated.

5. Joseph Knight Jr., "Joseph Knight's incidents of history from 1827 to 1844."

6. "Revelation, May 1829–B [D&C 12]," in Book of Commandments, 31, josephsmithpapers.org; see also Doctrine and Covenants 12:6, 9.

7. Joseph Smith, "History, 1838–1856, volume A-1 [23 December 1805–30 August 1834]," 21–22.

8. Joseph Smith, "History, 1838–1856, volume A-1 [23 December 1805–30 August 1834]," 27.

9. Andrew Jenson, "Still Another Witness," in Andrew Jenson, ed., *Historical Record: A Monthly Periodical,* vol. 7, nos. 8–10 (Oct. 1888), 621.

10. Joseph Smith, "History, 1838–1856, volume A-1 [23 December 1805–30 August 1834]," 22.

11. "Revelation, June 1829–A [D&C 14]," in Book of Commandments, 32, josephsmithpapers.org; see also Doctrine and Covenants 14:8.

12. "Revelation, June 1829–C [D&C 15]," in Book of Commandments, 33, josephsmithpapers.org; see also Doctrine and Covenants 15:6; 16:6.

13. Lucy Mack Smith, "Lucy Mack Smith, History, 1845," 153, josephsmithpapers.org.

The Experience of the Three Witnesses

D&C 17

Larry E. Morris

More than five decades after the Book of Mormon was published, David Whitmer recalled how he first heard of the Book of Mormon: "I made a business trip to Palmyra, N. Y. [in 1828], and while there stopped with one Oliver Cowdery. A great many people in the neighborhood were talking about the finding of certain golden plates by one Joseph Smith, jr., a young man of that neighborhood. Cowdery and I, as well as others, talked about the matter." The exact details of how 23-year-old Whitmer and 22-year-old Cowdery met are unknown, but the two men quickly struck up a friendship.

"Cowdery said he was acquainted with the Smith family," Whitmer continued, "and he believed there must be some truth in the story of the plates, and that he intended to investigate the matter." Whitmer, who implied that he made more than one trip to Palmyra, conducted his own investigation and "had conversations with several young men who said that Joseph Smith had certainly golden plates. . . . These parties were so positive in their statements that I began to believe there must be some foundation for the stories then in circulation."[1]

David Whitmer, a farmer from Fayette Township, New York (about 30 miles southeast of Palmyra), and Oliver Cowdery, a Vermont native who had recently been hired by Hyrum Smith and other school trustees to teach in the Manchester area, agreed to keep each other informed of what they discovered. At this time, neither of them had met Joseph Smith, who was then living in Harmony, Pennsylvania, with his wife, Emma.

Cowdery, whose students included children of Joseph Sr. and Lucy Mack Smith, eventually boarded with the Smith family. Lucy wrote that Cowdery "soon began to importune Mr. Smith upon the subject [of the plates]; but did not succeed in eliciting any information for

[a] considerable length of time: at last he gained my husband's confidence so far as to obtain a sketch of the facts relative to the plates."

The conversation with Joseph Sr. had a powerful effect on Cowdery. "The subject . . . seems working in my very bones," he told the Smiths. "I have made it a subject of prayer, and I firmly believe that it is the will of the Lord that I should go [to Harmony to assist Joseph with the translation]."[2]

Cowdery also announced this news, apparently in a letter, to Whitmer. "Cowdery told me he was going to Harmony, Pa. . . . and see him [Joseph Smith] about the matter," Whitmer wrote. "He did go, and on his way stopped at my father's house and told me that as soon as he found out anything either truth or untruth he would let me know."

Joseph Smith and Oliver Cowdery began their translation project on April 7, 1829, and worked intensely over the next eight weeks. During that time, Cowdery wrote three letters to Whitmer discussing the translation process and offering particular information on the content of the Book of Mormon. "When Cowdery wrote me these things and told me that he had revealed knowledge concerning the truth of them, I showed these letters to my parents, and brothers and sisters," Whitmer recalled.[3]

In the last letter, Joseph Smith and Oliver Cowdery requested that Whitmer come to Harmony and help the two men move to the Whitmer home. "I had some 20 acres to plow," Whitmer wrote, "so I concluded I would finish plowing and then go." However, when he got up the next morning, he found that between five and seven acres of his land had been plowed during the night. When asked who plowed the fields, Whitmer answered, "I do not know, I cannot tell you, all I know is it was plowed. . . . It was a testimony to me that I did not have any business to put off going after Joseph. I hitched up my team and . . . started for Pennsylvania."[4]

The move to New York took place at the beginning of June, and within a month Joseph and his scribes had completed the translation of the Book of Mormon. About that same time, Joseph's parents and Martin Harris, who had received word that the translation was nearing completion, arrived from Palmyra.[5]

Lucy Mack Smith wrote that Harris "greatly rejoiced" when he heard of the progress of the translation.[6] Although Harris was quite possibly meeting both Cowdery and Whitmer for the first time, the three men bonded through their shared devotion to assist in bringing forth the Book of Mormon.

They were particularly interested in certain passages from the Book of Mormon. "In the course of the work of translation," Joseph Smith's history explains, "we ascertained that three special witnesses were to be provided by the Lord, to whom he would grant, that they should see the plates from which this work (the Book of Mormon) should be translated."

Almost immediately after this discovery was made, Joseph wrote, "It occurred to Oliver Cowdery, David Whitmer, and . . . Martin Harris . . . that they would have me enquire of the Lord, to know if they might not obtain of him to be these three special witnesses; and finally they became so solicitous, and teazed me so much, that at length I complied, and through the Urim and Thummim, I obtained of the Lord for them [a revelation]."[7]

Called to Testify

The revelation, now known as Doctrine and Covenants 17, made this promise to Cowdery, Whitmer, and Harris: "You must rely upon my word which if you do with full purpose of heart you shall have a view of the plate and also the brestplate the sword of Laban the Urim and Thumim . . . and after that you have obtained faith and have seen them with your eyes you shall testify of them by the power of God."[8]

Days later, the prophecy was dramatically fulfilled. "It was in the latter part of June, 1829," David Whitmer wrote. "Joseph, Oliver Cowdery and myself were together, and the angel showed them [the plates] to us. . . . [We were] sitting on a log when we were overshadowed by a light more glorious than that of the sun. In the midst of this light, but a few feet from us, appeared a table upon which were many golden plates, also the sword of Laban and the directors. I saw them as plain as I see you now, and distinctly heard the voice of the Lord declaring that the records of the plates of the Book of Mormon were translated by the gift and power of God."[9]

Joseph Smith and Martin Harris had a similar experience, and as the manuscript was prepared for printing, Cowdery, Whitmer, and Harris signed a joint statement that has been included in each of the more than 120 million copies of the Book of Mormon printed since then. It reads, in part: "And we declare with words of soberness, that an angel of God came down from heaven, and he brought and laid before our eyes, that we beheld and saw the plates, and the engravings thereon; and we know that it is by the grace of God the Father, and our Lord Jesus Christ, that we beheld and bear record that these things are true."[10]

1. Lyndon W. Cook, ed., *David Whitmer Interviews: A Restoration Witness* (Orem, Utah: Grandin Book, 1991), 60.

2. Lucy Mack Smith, "Lucy Mack Smith, History, 1845," 140–41, josephsmithpapers.org.

3. Cook, *David Whitmer Interviews,* 61.

4. Cook, *David Whitmer Interviews,* 41, 51.

5. See Matthew McBride, "The Contributions of Martin Harris: D&C 3, 5, 10, 17, 19," Revelations in Context series, Jan. 3, 2013, history.lds.org. Martin Harris had a long and complicated involvement with the Book of Mormon. When persecution from neighbors forced Joseph and Emma to move from Joseph Sr. and Lucy's home to Harmony late in 1827, Martin gave Joseph $50 to help with the cost of the move. The next spring, Martin left his farm to the care of others and served as Joseph's scribe for two months. But just when the translation was progressing so wonderfully, Martin borrowed

and then lost the entire 116 pages he and Joseph had translated, plunging Joseph and his family into despair and leaving Joseph to wonder if he had lost all opportunity to translate. However, in the year after the loss of the manuscript, Martin repented of his mistakes and showed renewed determination to help Joseph in whatever way he could.

6. Lucy Mack Smith, "Lucy Mack Smith, History, 1845," 153.

7. "History, 1838–1856, volume A–1 [23 December 1805–30 August 1834]," 23, josephsmithpapers.org; see additional references to the Three Witnesses in "Book of Mormon, 1830," 110–11, 548, josephsmithpapers.org.

8. "Revelation, June 1829–E [D&C 17]," in Revelation Book 2, 119, josephsmithpapers.org.

9. Cook, *David Whitmer Interviews,* 63.

10. "Testimony of Three Witnesses," Book of Mormon.

"Build Up My Church"

D&C 18, 20, 21, 22

Jeffrey G. Cannon

Standing on the shore, Joseph Smith reached down and clasped his father's hand after Oliver Cowdery raised the elder Smith from the water. "Oh! my God I have lived to see my father baptized into the true church of Jesus christ," Joseph exclaimed. His joy was too much for him. He looked for a place to get away. Friends Oliver Cowdery and Joseph Knight went after him. Knight later described Joseph as being "the most wrot upon that I ever saw any man."[1]

For years, Joseph Smith Sr. had dismissed the claims of contemporary churchmen, but now he found the truth he sought in the visions and revelations of his son, Joseph Jr. The Church of Christ was organized on April 6, 1830, and Joseph Sr. was one of the first to be baptized.

As early as the summer of 1828, Joseph Smith Jr.'s revelations had discussed establishing a church. In the aftermath of Martin Harris's loss of the first 116 pages of the Book of Mormon manuscript, Joseph dictated a revelation in which the Lord stated, "I will establish my church."[2] It was becoming clear that Joseph Smith's mission would not end with the translation of the plates. Yet even believing associates like Joseph Knight were unaware of preparations Joseph and Oliver seemed to be keeping close to the vest.

Knight later recalled that he did not learn of the impending church organization until shortly before the actual event. "Now in the Spring of 1830," he recalled, "I went with my Team and took Joseph out to Manchester to his Father. When we was on our way he told me that there must be a Church formed But did not tell when."[3]

Preparations had been underway since at least June 1829. In that month, Joseph Smith dictated the revelation for Oliver Cowdery that would become Doctrine and Covenants 18. In it Oliver was instructed to "build up my church, and my gospel, and my rock." In doing so, Cowdery was told to "rely upon the things which are written."[4] The Book of Mormon translation was nearly finished, and Cowdery indeed used the manuscript as he began to outline the polity of the new church.

Cowdery produced a document he called "Articles of the Church of Christ" in preparation for the organization of the Church. Much of this document was either a direct quotation or a close paraphrase from the Book of Mormon manuscript. Like the Nephite church, this new church would have priests and teachers. It would also have disciples, or elders. The June 1829 revelation also appointed Cowdery, along with David Whitmer, to select twelve who would serve as the Apostles sent out to spread the new church's message.

Many of those who accepted that message awaited the organization of a church. About this time, Joseph Smith announced a revelation specifying that the Church should be organized on April 6, 1830. On that day, forty or fifty men and women gathered in the small Fayette home of Peter Whitmer Sr. to observe the event. Six of them—Joseph Smith, Oliver Cowdery, and four others—served as the official organizers.[5]

They "opened the meeting by solemn prayer." Joseph and Oliver asked the other four official members if they would accept them as their spiritual teachers and whether they should proceed to organize the Church. Having the consent of the assembled believers, Joseph ordained Oliver Cowdery an elder in the Church, and Oliver did the same for Joseph. Joseph was 24 years old at the time; Oliver was 23.

With authorized men called, sustained, and ordained, it was possible for the Church to celebrate the sacrament of the Lord's supper. "We then took bread, blessed it, and brake it with them, also wine, blessed it, and drank it with them." After the sacrament, Joseph Smith's history records, "We then laid our hands on each individual member of the Church present that they might receive the gift of the Holy Ghost, and be confirmed members of the Church of Christ. The Holy Ghost was poured out upon us to a very great degree. Some prophesied, whilst we all praised the Lord and rejoiced exceedingly."

That same day, "Whilst yet together" for the organizational meeting, Joseph Smith received another revelation.[6] Now known as Doctrine and Covenants 21, the revelation instructed the newly formed church that "there Shall a Record be kept among you" in which Joseph Smith would be known as a "seer & Translater & Prop[h]et an Apostle of Jesus Christ an Elder of the Church."[7] Oliver Cowdery, acting in his role as Apostle and elder, was to perform the ordination. Though Oliver was designated the Church's Second Elder, the April 6 revelation also designated him the "first Preacher,"[8] an office he filled by preaching the Church's first public sermon on April 11.

While Joseph and Oliver's respective roles were clarified, the role Oliver's "Articles of the Church of Christ" played in the organization is unclear. Some time after Oliver had completed the articles, Joseph told him there was more. Joseph's superseding revelation, now part of Doctrine and Covenants 20, seems to have been completed after the organizational meeting in April but before the Church's first conference, held in June.[9] At the June conference, this revealed document was accepted as a statement of polity for the new church.[10] Its importance was highlighted by the fact that it was the first revelatory text published in the Church's newspaper, and it was later printed as section 2 of the 1835 edition of the Doctrine and Covenants, after the preface dictated as a revelation in 1835.[11]

During the two months between the organization of the Church and its acceptance of the new articles in June, questions arose concerning the need of believers to be baptized if they had previously been baptized in other churches. Within weeks of the first meeting of the Church, Joseph Smith received a revelation, now Doctrine and Covenants 22, emphasizing the importance of rebaptism in the new church.[12]

The new Church of Christ was more than simply another Christian denomination. After years of keeping a distance from the churches he saw around him, Joseph Smith Sr. saw in the restored Church something different: a legitimate successor to the apostolic church with prophets, apostles, revelation, and authority.

1. Lucy Mack Smith, "Lucy Mack Smith, History, 1844–1845," book 9, page 12, josephsmithpapers.org; Dean Jessee, "Joseph Knight's Recollection of Early Mormon History," *BYU Studies,* vol. 17, no. 1 (Autumn 1976), 37.

2. "Revelation, Spring 1829 [D&C 10]," in Book of Commandments, 1833, 26, josephsmithpapers.org; see also Doctrine and Covenants 10:53. The dating of this revelation remains uncertain. Convincing arguments can be made for summer 1828 or spring 1829.

3. Jessee, "Joseph Knight's Recollection," 36.

4. "Revelation, June 1829–B [D&C 18]," in Book of Commandments, 1833, 35, josephsmithpapers.org; see also Doctrine and Covenants 18:4–5.

5. Variant lists of the six organizers include Joseph Smith Jr., Oliver Cowdery, Joseph Smith Sr., Hyrum Smith, Samuel Smith, David Whitmer, John Whitmer, Peter Whitmer Sr., Peter Whitmer Jr., Christian Whitmer, and Orrin Porter Rockwell (see Richard Lloyd Anderson, "I Have a Question: Who were the six who organized the Church on 6 April 1830?" *Ensign,* June 1980, 44–45).

6. Joseph Smith, "History, 1838–1856, volume A-1, [December 1805–30 August 1834]," 37, josephsmithpapers.org.

7. "Revelation, 6 April 1830 [D&C 21]," in Revelation Book 1, 28, josephsmithpapers.org; see also Doctrine and Covenants 21:1.

8. "Revelation, 6 April 1830 [D&C 21]," 29; see also Doctrine and Covenants 21:12.

9. Based on research by Michael Hubbard Mackay and Gerrit Dirkmaat for the volume Michael Hubbard MacKay, Gerrit J. Dirkmaat, Grant Underwood, Robert J. Woodford, William G. Hartley, eds., *Documents, Volume 1: July 1828–June 1831,* vol. 1 of the Documents series of *The Joseph Smith Papers,* ed. Dean C. Jessee, Ronald K. Esplin, Richard Lyman Bushman, and Matthew J. Grow (Salt Lake City: Church Historian's Press, 2013).

10. Minutes, June 9, 1830, in Minute Book 2, 1, josephsmithpapers.org.

11. Doctrine and Covenants, 1835, 77–82, josephsmithpapers.org.

12. "Revelation, 16 April 1830 [D&C 22]," in *Painesville Telegraph,* vol. 2, no. 44 (Apr. 19, 1831), 4; josephsmithpapers.org.

"Thou Art an Elect Lady"

D&C 24, 25, 26, 27

Matthew J. Grow

In the months following the April 1830 organization of the Church of Christ (as the Church was then known), Emma Hale Smith began to understand more fully what her husband's prophetic calling would mean for her and their young family. Emma, who turned 26 years old on July 10, 1830, had married Joseph three years earlier despite the objections of her parents, Isaac and Elizabeth Hale.[1] She believed in the visions and revelations received by her husband, and those three eventful years had confirmed to her that he was indeed a prophet.

By the time of their marriage, Joseph had met with the angel Moroni once a year for three consecutive years at a hill near Palmyra, New York, to discuss the golden plates from which he would translate the Book of Mormon. In the fall of 1827, Emma went with Joseph and waited in the wagon while he received the golden plates. She soon began to assist as a scribe in the translation process. "I frequently wrote day after day," she later recalled, "often sitting at the table close by him, he sitting with his face buried in his hat, with the stone in it, and dictating hour after hour with nothing between us. . . . He had neither manuscript nor book to read from. . . . If he had had anything of the kind he could not have concealed it from me. . . . The plates often lay on the table without any attempt at concealment, wrapped in a small linen table cloth. . . . I once felt of the plates, as they thus lay on the table, tracing their outline and shape."

Decades later, she marveled at what had happened. She recalled that at the time of their marriage Joseph "could neither write nor dictate a coherent and well-worded letter; let alone dictating a book like the Book of Mormon."[2]

Emma's Trials

But these spiritual experiences had been accompanied by inconvenience and pain. Joseph and Emma first lived with the Smith family in Manchester, New York, and then moved to live with the Hales in Harmony, Pennsylvania, where Emma had grown up. During their first years of marriage, the couple moved at least four times between Harmony and upstate New York, traversing approximately 300 miles each time. In June 1828, Emma gave birth to a son, who "died the same hour" of his birth.[3] Their early years were filled with poverty. Joseph wrote that in 1829 they had become very poor—"reduced in property," he termed it—and Emma's father "was about to turn me out of doores & I had not where to go and I cried unto the Lord that he would provide for me to accomplish the work whereunto he had commanded me."[4] In their hour of need, faithful friends—such as Josiah Stowell, Martin Harris, and Oliver Cowdery—often provided Joseph and Emma with financial assistance.

Notwithstanding these challenges, Emma desired to be baptized in June 1830. Joseph and Emma traveled to Colesville, New York, where she was baptized along with several other converts, including members of the Knight family, who had also supported them financially during the translation of the Book of Mormon. However, on the evening of Sunday, June 27, opponents of the infant church destroyed a dam built for the baptisms. Early the next morning, Joseph Smith's history recounts, "we were on the alert, and before our enemies were aware we had repaired the dam, and proceeded to baptize." Oliver Cowdery baptized Emma and 12 others. Before the baptismal service had ended, "the mob began again to collect, and shortly after we had retired, they amounted to about fifty men." Joseph, Emma, and the other Church members had gone into Joseph

Knight Sr.'s home, but it was soon surrounded by men "raging with anger and apparently wishful to commit violence upon us." Joseph Smith's history continues: "Some asked us questions, others threatened us, so that we thought it wisdom to leave and go to the house of Newel Knight."[5] Nevertheless, the Saints were followed, and the harassment continued.

The Saints planned a meeting for that evening, during which Emma and the other newly baptized individuals would receive the gift of the Holy Ghost and be confirmed members of the Church. However, as they gathered, a constable arrested Joseph Smith "on charge of being a disorderly person; of setting the country in an uproar by preaching the Book of Mormon." The constable explained that the mob hoped to ambush Joseph after his arrest; however, the constable "was determined to save me from them, as he had found me to be a different sort of person from what I had been represented to him." They soon encountered the mob, but to the "great disappointment" of the vigilantes, the constable "gave the horse the whip and drove me out of their reach." After arriving in South Bainbridge in Chenango County, the constable stayed with Joseph Smith that night "in an upper room of a Tavern." To protect Joseph, the constable "slept during the night with his feet against the door, and a loaded musket by his side."[6]

Joseph Smith was tried and acquitted in South Bainbridge but then immediately arrested again to stand trial on similar charges in neighboring Broome County. The second constable initially treated Joseph harshly. When they arrived in Broome County, Joseph Smith's history records, "He took me to a tavern, and gathered in a number of men, who used every means to abuse, ridicule, and insult me." They spat on Joseph and demanded that he prophesy to them. Relatively close to their home now, Joseph asked that he "be allowed the privilege of spending the night with my wife at home," but the constable denied his request.[7]

Following a second trial the next day, Joseph was again acquitted. The constable, according to Joseph Smith's history, now "asked my forgiveness."[8] Learning of plans by the mob to tar and feather Joseph, the constable helped him escape. Joseph arrived safely at the nearby house of Elizabeth Hale Wasson, Emma's sister.

During her husband's absence, Emma had been "awaiting with much anxiety the issue of those ungodly proceedings."[9] She had gathered with other women "for the purpose of praying for the deliverance" of her husband.[10] Once reunited, Joseph and Emma traveled home to Harmony, Pennsylvania, in early July. Along with Oliver Cowdery, Joseph made one more unsuccessful trip to Colesville to confirm the newly baptized Saints but quickly returned to Harmony in the face of renewed opposition.[11]

Outpouring of Revelation

Following his return to Harmony, Joseph Smith received three revelations in July 1830. The first revelation, now known as Doctrine and Covenants 24, addressed Joseph and Oliver Cowdery, "telling them concerning their Calls." The revelation reminded them that they had been called "to write the Book of Mormon & to my ministry." Likely referring in part to their recent opposition, the revelation continued, "I have lifted thee up out of thine afflictions & have counseled thee that thou hast been delivered from all thine enemies."[12]

The revelation also spoke of Joseph Smith's material circumstances, instructing him to visit Church members in Colesville, Fayette, and Manchester after he had "sowed [his] fields." The revelation made clear that Joseph should be supported by Church members so he could "devote all [his] service in Zion." Joseph was told, "In temporal [labors] thou shalt not have strength for this is not thy calling."[13] This revelation led Joseph and Emma to understand that they would struggle financially and need to rely on support from Church members because of their dedication to the ministry.

Whatever Emma's hopes for her married life were, she could hardly have anticipated the degree to which opponents of the new church would physically intimidate and legally harass the Smiths or the way the demands of preaching and Church administration would take her husband away from their farm and family, disrupting their home life and threatening their livelihood.

In the context of these anxieties and disappointments, Joseph received a revelation for Emma, Doctrine and Covenants 25, which reiterated, "Verily I say unto thee that thou shalt lay aside the things of this world & seek for the things of a better." Through the revelation, Emma received words of consolation and instruction. She was told, "Murmur not because of the things which thou hast not seen for they are withheld from thee & the World"—perhaps a reference to the golden plates, which Emma later recalled she had handled on one occasion but not seen. The revelation called Emma "an elect lady" and told her that the "office of thy calling shall be for a comfort unto my Servant Joseph thy husband in his afflictions with consoleing words in the spirit of meekness." The revelation also spoke of Emma's work in the Church, promising that she would be "ordained" by her husband "to expound Scriptures & exhort the Church."[14] Furthermore, Emma was instructed to serve as a scribe to her husband and to compile a hymnal. Joseph Smith later explained that Emma "was ordain'd at the time, the Revelation was given, to expound the scriptures to all; and to teach the female part of community; and that not she alone, but others, may attain to the same blessings."[15]

The third revelation received by Joseph Smith in July 1830, now canonized as Doctrine and Covenants 26, instructed Joseph, along with Oliver Cowdery and John Whitmer, to dedicate their time "to the studying [of] the Scriptures & to preaching & to confirming the Church at Colesvill & to performing thy labours on the Land."[16]

In early August, a few weeks following these three revelations, Newel and Sally Knight traveled from Colesville, New York, to visit Joseph and Emma Smith in Harmony, Pennsylvania. Sally Knight had been baptized on the same day as Emma, but neither had been confirmed. As such, Joseph Smith's history recounts, "It was proposed that we should confirm them, and partake together of the sacrament, before he and his wife should leave us.—In order to prepare for this; I set out to go to procure some wine for the occasion, but had gone only a short distance when I was met by a heavenly messenger, and received the following revelation."[17]

The angel warned Joseph Smith not to "Purchase Wine neither strong drink of your enemies."[18] Joseph then returned home and "prepared some wine of our own make" for the confirmation meeting, which consisted of the Smiths, the Knights, and John Whitmer. Joseph Smith's history records, "We partook together of the sacrament, after which we confirmed these two sisters into the church, and spent the evening in a glorious manner. The Spirit of the Lord was poured out upon us, we praised the Lord God, and rejoiced exceedingly."[19] These four revelations, received between July and September 1830, provided crucial instructions to Joseph and Emma Smith, as well as other Church members, in the formative months following the Church's organization.

Emma particularly treasured the revelation addressed to her. With the assistance of William W. Phelps, she followed the Lord's instructions to compile the Church's first hymnal.[20] In 1842, Joseph Smith read the revelation to Emma at the organizational meeting of the Relief Society. He also read 2 John 1, which references the "elect lady," and explained that she was "called an Elect lady" because she was "elected to preside."[21] Joseph stated that "the revelation was then fulfilled by Sister Emma's Election to the Presidency of the Society."[22]

The revelation regarding Emma Smith, received during the tumultuous summer months of 1830, was invoked and discussed in Relief Society meetings throughout the 19th century. For example, at a jubilee celebration of the Relief Society's 50th anniversary in 1892 held in the Salt Lake Tabernacle, "Zina Y. W. Card . . . read in a very clear and distinct voice the Revelation given to Emma Smith, through Joseph the Seer . . . wherein Sister Emma is called an Elect Lady."[23] Early Relief Society general presidents were sometimes called "Elect Lady." For instance, when Zina D. H. Young became Relief Society general president, Emmeline B. Wells (who herself later served as Relief Society general president) wrote to her, "I congratulate you my beloved sister on being called, to be, according to the words of Joseph the Prophet, 'The Elect Lady.'"[24]

1. Joseph Smith III, "Last Testimony of Sister Emma," *Saints' Herald,* vol. 26, no. 19 (Oct. 1, 1879), 289.

2. Joseph Smith III, "Last Testimony of Sister Emma," 289–90.

3. Joseph Smith, "History, 1834–1836," 9, josephsmithpapers.org.

4. Joseph Smith, "Letter to William Phelps, 27 November 1832," in Joseph Smith Letterbook 1, 6, josephsmithpapers.org.

5. Joseph Smith, "History, 1838–1856, volume A-1 [23 December 1805–30 August 1834]," 43, josephsmithpapers.org.

6. Joseph Smith, "History, 1838–1856, volume A-1," 44, josephsmithpapers.org.

7. Joseph Smith, "History, 1838–1856, volume A-1," 45, josephsmithpapers.org.

8. Joseph Smith, "History, 1838–1856, volume A-1," 47, josephsmithpapers.org.

9. Joseph Smith, "History, 1838–1856, volume A-1," 47, josephsmithpapers.org.

10. "Some of the Remarks of John S. Reed, Esq., as Delivered before the State Convention," *Times and Seasons,* vol. 5, no. 11 (June 1, 1844), 551.

11. Joseph Smith, "History, 1838–1856, volume A-1," 47, josephsmithpapers.org.

12. "Revelation, July 1830–A [D&C 24]," in Revelation Book 1, 32, josephsmithpapers.org; see also Doctrine and Covenants 24:1.

13. "Revelation, July 1830–A [D&C 24]," 32–33, josephsmithpapers.org; see also Doctrine and Covenants 24:3, 7, 9.

14. "Revelation, July 1830–C [D&C 25]," in Revelation Book 1, 34–35, josephsmithpapers.org; see also Doctrine and Covenants 25:3–5, 7, 10.

15. "Nauvoo Relief Society Minute Book," 8, josephsmithpapers.org; the word "ordained" as used here corresponds to the phrase "set apart" in modern usage.

16. "Revelation, July 1830–B [D&C 26]," in Revelation Book 1, 34, josephsmithpapers.org; see also Doctrine and Covenants 26:1.

17. Joseph Smith, "History, 1838–1856, volume A-1," 51, josephsmithpapers.org.

18. "Revelation, circa August 1830 [D&C 27]," in Revelation Book 1, 35, josephsmithpapers.org; see also Doctrine and Covenants 27:3.

19. Joseph Smith, "History, 1838–1856, volume A-1," 51–52, josephsmithpapers.org. Joseph Smith's history also explains that only the first portion of the revelation "was written at this time, and the remainder [of the revelation] in the September following." Early manuscript versions only contain the first portion, while the earliest surviving copy of the later portion is found in the 1835 edition of the Doctrine and Covenants.

20. See Emma Smith, comp., "Collection of Sacred Hymns, 1835," josephsmithpapers.org.

21. "Nauvoo Relief Society Minute Book," 9, josephsmithpapers.org.

22. Joseph Smith, "Journal, December 1841–December 1842," 91, josephsmithpapers.org.

23. "Relief Society Jubilee, Exercises at the Tabernacle," *Woman's Exponent,* vol. 20, no. 18 (Apr. 1, 1892), 140.

24. Emmeline B. Wells letter to Zina D. H. Young, Apr. 24, 1888, Zina Card Brown Family Collection, Church History Library, Salt Lake City.

The Journey of the Colesville Branch

D&C 26, 51, 54, 56, 59

Joseph F. Darowski

Joseph Smith may have been alone when he experienced his First Vision and subsequently met with the angel Moroni, but he did not stand alone in his home. His mother, father, and siblings formed a supportive family network. He could confide in his parents. He could rely on his siblings. Joseph's wife, Emma, bore with Joseph the demands and strains of leadership, opposition, and persecution. Other friends, such as Martin Harris, Oliver Cowdery, and David and John Whitmer, stood with Joseph as he brought forth the Book of Mormon, organized the Church, and embarked on his quest to build a Zion society.

Equally notable among those whose connections strengthened and sustained Joseph during his many trials and travails were the extended Knight family and their neighbors in Colesville, New York. Allying themselves with the young Joseph Smith, they followed him into the budding Church, defended him, and formed the nucleus of one of the first branches of the Church. The story of the Knights and the Colesville Branch testifies of the power of kinship and friendship in the Restoration of the gospel and the building up of the Lord's kingdom.

The story of the Colesville Saints began with Joseph's visits to the region in the mid-1820s, when he began working for Josiah Stowell of neighboring South Bainbridge, New York, in a failed treasure-seeking venture. Though that quest proved unsuccessful, it yielded Joseph Smith's close friendship with Joseph Knight Sr. and his son Newel Knight. Later, Joseph Knight Sr. aided Joseph in his courtship of Emma Hale. He was present at the Smith homestead the night Joseph Smith, with Emma's help, retrieved the golden plates from the Hill Cumorah, and he provided food and writing materials to Joseph Smith during the Book of Mormon translation.

Knight family members and some of their neighbors were among the first to join the Church in 1830. Later that year they became the nucleus of one of the first (if not the first) branches organized in the Church. In July 1830, Joseph was counseled in two revelations, now found in Doctrine and Covenants 24 and 26, to visit the members in Colesville, including the Knights, to devote his time to "studying the Scriptures & to preaching & to confirming the Church at Colesvill."[1] Hyrum Smith stayed in the area in late 1830 and presided over the branch for several months. His successor was Joseph Knight Sr.'s son Newel.

The Move to Ohio

When instructions were given in December 1830 and January 1831 (see Doctrine and Covenants 37 and 38) for the New York members to move to the Ohio Valley region, the Colesville Branch members made significant financial sacrifices and prepared themselves for the move west. The families associated with the Colesville Branch included, among others, the Knights, Pecks, DeMilles, Stringhams, Culvers, Slades, Badgers, Hineses, and Carters. Everyone was expected to gather in Ohio, and the poor were not to be left behind. Setting aside their former lives and homes, the branch, under Newel Knight's leadership, began the journey to the Kirtland area in April 1831. When they arrived in May, they were advised to "remain together, and go to a neighboring town called Thompson, as a man by the name of [Leman] Copley had a considerable tract of land there which he offered to let the brethren occupy."[2]

Copley had offered his land perhaps in response to an earlier revelation (see Doctrine and Covenants 48) given to answer a key question among the Ohio Saints in early 1831: "What preperations we shall make for our Brethren from the East & when & how?"[3] The revelation answered, "Inasmuch as ye [have] lands ye shall impart to the Eastern Brethren."[4] Copley welcomed the members of the Colesville Branch, and shortly after their arrival in Thompson they began to plant and build on his ample 759-acre farm.

On May 20, Joseph Smith received another revelation, now identified as Doctrine and Covenants 51, directing those who settled in Thompson to be among the first to practice the recently revealed principles of consecration and stewardship. Newly called Bishop Edward Partridge was to "receive the properties of this People which have covenanted with me" and "appoint unto this People their portion every man alike according to their families according to their wants & their needs."[5] Although the revelation made it clear that Ohio would be a temporary gathering location, they were reminded that the "hour & the day is not given unto them" for their anticipated move to the future city of Zion. They were to "act upon this land as for years."[6]

However, the Colesville Branch members had precious little time to comply with the commandment to implement the law of consecration. Leman Copley's resolve to impart of his land was put to the test in early May when he participated in a mission to his former Shaker congregation. The experience seemed to raise doubts that weakened his testimony, and shortly after his return to Thompson he broke his agreement and evicted the Saints from his property. In June 1831, their future clouded and their lives in disarray, the Knights and other members of the Colesville Branch sought counsel and guidance from Joseph Smith as to what they should do next.

Instruction came in the form of a revelation now known as Doctrine and Covenants 54: "Take your Journeys into the regions westward unto Missorie unto the borders of the Lamanites & after you have done Journeying Behold I say unto you seek ye a living like unto men untill I prepare a place for you & again be patient in tribulation."[7] Newel Knight later described the situation: "We now understood that [Ohio] was not the land of our inheritance—the land of promise, for it was made known in a revelation that Missouri was the place chosen for the gathering of the church, and several were called to lead the way to that state."[8] Banding together once again, the Colesville members prepared for their journey. They selected Newel Knight to continue to preside over them despite his previous call, by revelation, to serve a proselytizing mission (see Doctrine and Covenants 52). In a revelation now canonized as Doctrine and Covenants 56, Knight was authorized to set aside his mission call and instead travel to Missouri as the head of the Colesville Branch.

The Move to Missouri

Leaving Thompson in early June 1831, sixty members of the branch reached Kaw Township in Jackson County, Missouri, on July 26 after a journey of about a thousand miles. Though Joseph Smith had arrived shortly before the Colesville Saints, they had the distinction of being the first branch of the Church to settle the land that had been dedicated as Zion on August 2, 1831, by Sidney Rigdon. Sadly, Joseph Knight Sr.'s wife, Polly, died a few days after their arrival. According to his later history, Joseph Smith "attended the funeral of sister Polly [Peck] Knight. . . . This was the first death in the church in this land, and I can say a worthy member sleeps in Jesus till the resurrection."[9]

That same day, Joseph received the revelation now known as Doctrine and Covenants 59, outlining how the Church was to observe the Lord's day. In that revelation, the Lord included words of comfort for Polly Knight's family and friends: "Blessed . . . are they who have come up unto this land with an eye single to my glory according to my Commandments for them that live shall inherit the earth and them that die shall rest from all their labours & their works shall follow them they shall receive a crown in the mansions of my Father which I have prepared for them."[10]

Joseph Smith visited his friends in the Colesville Branch in Missouri again in April 1832. On that occasion, Joseph sealed the members of the branch up to eternal life.[11] During the Jackson County mobbing of 1833, the Colesville Branch fled with many other Saints into neighboring Clay County. They settled together there for a time, even building a chapel. However, once the Church moved on to Caldwell County in 1836, the branch membership was scattered, and their time together as one of the first organized units in the Church came to an end.

The Knights and others from the former branch joined many of the Saints in escaping to Illinois in the aftermath of the Missouri Mormon War of 1838. The Knights settled in the Nauvoo area and remained faithful members of the Church and friends of Joseph Smith. After Joseph's martyrdom in 1844, the Knight family followed the leadership of the Quorum of the Twelve Apostles. Both Joseph Knight Sr. and his son Newel died in 1847 during the exodus from Nauvoo to the Salt Lake Valley.

1. "Revelation, July 1830–B [D&C 26]," in Revelation Book 1, 34, josephsmithpapers.org; see also Doctrine and Covenants 26:1.

2. Newel Knight, autobiography and journal, 288, Church History Library, Salt Lake City.

3. "Revelation, 9 February 1831 [D&C 42:1–72]," 6, josephsmithpapers.org.

4. "Revelation, 10 March 1831 [D&C 48]," in Revelation Book 1, 79, josephsmithpapers.org; see also Doctrine and Covenants 48:2.

5. "Revelation, 20 May 1831 [D&C 51]," in Revelation Book 1, 86, josephsmithpapers.org; see also Doctrine and Covenants 51:3.

6. "Revelation, 20 May 1831 [D&C 51]," in Revelation Book 1, 87; see also Doctrine and Covenants 51:17.

7. "Revelation, 10 June 1831 [D&C 54]," in Revelation Book 1, 90, josephsmithpapers.org; see also Doctrine and Covenants 54:8–10.

8. Newel Knight, autobiography and journal, 290.

9. Joseph Smith, "History, 1838–1856, volume A-1 [23 December 1805–30 August 1834]," 139, josephsmithpapers.org.

10. "Revelation, 7 August 1831 [D&C 59]," 1, josephsmithpapers.org; see also Doctrine and Covenants 59:1–2.

11. Dean Jessee, "Joseph Knight's Recollection of Early Mormon History," *BYU Studies,* vol. 17, no. 1 (Autumn 1976), 39.

A Mission to the Lamanites

D&C 28, 30, 32

Richard Dilworth Rust

In a revelation given before the Book of Mormon was completely translated, the Lord said that the plates were preserved "that the Lamanites might come to the knowledge of their Fathers & that they may know the Promises of the Lord that they may believe the Gospel & rely upon the merits of Jesus Christ."[1] As the principal scribe of the Book of Mormon, Oliver Cowdery knew that the book was written primarily "to the Laminates," who were "a remnant of the house of Israel."[2] It was appropriate, then, that in September 1830, six months after the Book of Mormon was published, Oliver Cowdery was the first person instructed by revelation to "go unto the Lamanites & Preach my Gospel unto them."[3]

Other early converts also expressed "a great desire" respecting "the remnants of the house of Joseph—the Lamanites residing in the west, knowing that the purposes of God were great to that people."[4] In response to those desires, Joseph Smith received another revelation, in which Peter Whitmer Jr. was called to accompany his brother-in-law Oliver Cowdery. The Lord directed him to "open thy mouth to declare my Gospel" and to "give heed unto the words & advice of thy Brother" who had been given power "to build my Church among thy Brethren the Laminates."[5]

The following month, October 1830, Parley P. Pratt and Ziba Peterson were also called to go "into the wilderness among the Lamanites." To aid them in this challenging assignment, the Lord promised that He would "go with them and be in their midst."[6]

Because of the Indian Removal Act passed in May 1830, the new territory for relocating American Indians was to be in present-day Kansas and Oklahoma. Thus, these missionaries to the Lamanites planned to go west from Independence, Missouri, into Indian Territory.

Prior to leaving on this mission, Oliver Cowdery signed a covenant to walk humbly before God and to do "this glorious work according as he shall direct me by the Holy Ghost."[7] His three companions likewise signed a covenant that they would assist Oliver Cowdery "faithfully in this thing."[8] When they departed, they carried with them numerous copies of the Book of Mormon to distribute among their listeners.

In his autobiography, Parley P. Pratt wrote that, while still in New York, the four missionaries called on "an Indian [Seneca] nation at or near Buffalo; and spent part of a day with them, instructing them in the knowledge of the record of their forefathers."[9] In retrospect, the greatest impact of their mission occurred partway through their travels. Pratt tells how they continued on their journey until they stopped in Mentor, Ohio, to call on Sidney Rigdon, Pratt's "former friend and instructor, in the Reformed Baptists Society."[10] They presented him with a copy of the Book of Mormon, which he promised to read, and then taught the restored gospel in many homes in the area. The consequence of this was that "at length Mr. Rigdon and many others . . . came forward and were baptized by us, and received the gift of the Holy Ghost by the laying on of hands."[11] Pratt tells how "the news of the discovery of the Book of Mormon and the marvellous events connected with it" created a general "interest and excitement . . . in Kirtland, and in all the region round about. The people thronged us night and day, insomuch that we had no time for rest and retirement. Meetings were convened in different neighborhoods, and multitudes came together soliciting our attendance. . . . In two or three weeks from our arrival in the neighborhood with the news, we had baptized one hundred and twenty-seven souls."[12] Among those they introduced to the gospel there were Isaac Morley, John Murdock, Lyman Wight, and Edward Partridge.

This unanticipated success in Kirtland had enormous consequences for the future of the Church. Kirtland soon became an important early gathering place for Church members and would later be the site of the Church's first temple. The group of Kirtland converts also yielded many early Church leaders. Conspicuous among these, of course, was Rigdon himself, who would later serve as a counselor to Joseph Smith. One new convert from the Kirtland area, Frederick G. Williams, joined the four missionaries on their journey.

While their primary purpose was to preach to the native tribes, Cowdery and his fellow missionaries continued to teach others they met along the way. Among these early encounters was a meeting with the Shaker community at North Union, Ohio. A second encounter with Shakers occurred at Union Village several miles north of Cincinnati. In each case, the missionaries left copies of the Book of Mormon with the Shakers, though this approach apparently met with little success: Richard McNemar, a resident of Union Village, read one of those books and noted, "Whatever benefit the Indians may derive from this book of Mormon, certain it is we can derive none."[13]

Their travel in late December and through the month of January was difficult because of what has been called "the winter of the deep snow." Parley P. Pratt described how the missionaries had to halt for a few days in Illinois on account of extended storms "during which the snow fell in some places near three feet deep." With their original plans frustrated by ice in the river, they renewed their journey on foot, traveling, as Pratt wrote, "for three hundred miles through vast prairies and through trackless wilds of snow—no beaten road; houses few and far between; and the bleak northwest wind always blowing in our faces with a keenness which would almost take the skin off the face. . . . After much fatigue and some suffering we all arrived in Independence, in the county of Jackson, on the extreme western frontiers of Missouri, and of the United States."[14]

Once the group arrived in Independence, Peter Whitmer Jr. and Ziba Peterson remained to earn money while Oliver Cowdery, Parley P. Pratt, and Frederick G. Williams went over into Indian Territory. They first preached to the Shawnees and then to the Delawares. Speaking through an interpreter, Oliver Cowdery shared the essential message of the Book of Mormon. Part of his message, as recorded by Parley P. Pratt, was that "the Lord commanded Mormon and Moroni, their last wise men and prophets, to hide the Book in the earth, that it might be preserved in safety, and be found and made known in the latter day to the pale faces who should possess the land; that they might again make it known to the red man; in order to restore them to the knowledge of the will of the Great Spirit and to His favor."[15]

The Delaware Indians were receptive, and the chief requested that the missionaries return in the spring when "you shall read to us and teach us more concerning the Book of our fathers and the will of the Great Spirit."[16] However, because of an order by a federal agent, the missionaries were expelled from Indian Territory. Seeking unsuccessfully to get authorization from William Clark, the superintendent of Indian affairs in the area, the missionaries were no longer able to proselytize in Indian Territory.[17]

Although the Lamanite mission thus ended, it helped chart the course the fledgling Church would follow during the coming decade. The missionaries had established the Church in the Kirtland area, and they prepared the way for Joseph Smith to go to Ohio in early 1831 and then call for the Saints in the east to move there as well. Later in 1831, Joseph himself traveled to Jackson County, where he identified the location of the New Jerusalem and, on August 3, 1831, near the Independence courthouse, laid a cornerstone for the temple.[18]

1. "Revelation, July 1828 [D&C 3]," in Revelation Book 1, 2, josephsmithpapers.org; see also Doctrine and Covenants 3:19–20. Early Church members considered all American Indians to be direct descendants of Book of Mormon peoples. The introduction to the Book of Mormon clarifies that Lamanites were "among the ancestors of the American Indians."

2. Title page of the Book of Mormon.

3. "Revelation, September 1830–B [D&C 28]," in Revelation Book 1, 41, josephsmithpapers.org; see also Doctrine and Covenants 28:8.

4. "History, 1838–1856, volume A-1 [23 December 1805–30 August 1834]," 60, josephsmithpapers.org.

5. "Revelation, September 1830–D [D&C 30:5–8]," in Revelation Book 1, 42, josephsmithpapers.org; see also Doctrine and Covenants 30:5–6.

6. "Revelation, October 1830–A [D&C 32]," in Revelation Book 2, 84, josephsmithpapers.org; see also Doctrine and Covenants 32:2–3.

7. "Covenant of Oliver Cowdery and Others, 17 October 1830," 1, josephsmithpapers.org; published in the *Ohio Star,* vol. 1, no. 49 (Dec. 8, 1831), 1.

8. "Covenant of Oliver Cowdery and Others," 1.

9. *The Autobiography of Parley Parker Pratt; One of the Twelve Apostles of The Church of Jesus Christ of Latter-Day Saints,* ed. Parley P. Pratt Jr. (Chicago: Law, King, and Law, 1888), 49. Cowdery and company would later preach to the Wyandot Indians near Sandusky, Ohio.

10. *The Autobiography of Parley Parker Pratt,* 49.

11. *The Autobiography of Parley Parker Pratt,* 50.

12. *The Autobiography of Parley Parker Pratt,* 50.

13. Quoted in Christian Goodwillie, "Shaker Richard McNemar: The Earliest Book of Mormon Reviewer," *Journal of Mormon History,* vol. 37, no. 2 (Spring 2011), 144; punctuation standardized.

14. *The Autobiography of Parley Parker Pratt,* 54–55.

15. *The Autobiography of Parley Parker Pratt,* 58.

16. Quoted in *The Autobiography of Parley Parker Pratt,* 44.

17. See Leland H. Gentry, "Light on the 'Mission to the Lamanites,'" *BYU Studies,* vol. 36, no. 2 (1996–97), 229.

18. A revelation given on July 20, 1831, indicated that "the place which is now called Independence is the centre place, & the spot for the Temple is lying westward upon a lot which is not far from the court-house" ("Revelation, 20 July 1831 [D&C 57]," in Revelation Book 1, 93, josephsmithpapers.org; see also Doctrine and Covenants 57:3).

"All Things Must Be Done in Order"

D&C 28, 43

Jeffrey G. Cannon

In the summer of 1830, Oliver Cowdery wrote to Joseph Smith from the home of Peter Whitmer, where the Church had been organized earlier that year: "I command you in the name of God to erase those words, that no priestcraft be amongst us."[1] His passion was clear, but what had so alarmed the Church's Second Elder that he would be so forceful in his communication with the Prophet?

Under divine commission, Oliver had written a document called the "Articles of the Church of Christ" that was later superseded by a second document written by Joseph, titled "Articles and Covenants of the Church of Christ." Joseph's document used much of the same language but added significant passages clarifying and expanding on Oliver's original. Joseph's later document was accepted by the Church at its June 1830 conference as binding. Notwithstanding the Church's acceptance, Oliver disapproved of a phrase in the list of requirements for baptism: "And truly manifest by their works that they have received of the Spirit of Christ unto the remission of their sins."[2]

Perhaps Oliver felt his involvement in the document's development entitled him to make demands concerning the text. Joseph, however, disagreed, insisting that the requirement had come by revelation. In his response, Joseph asked "by what authority he [Oliver] took upon him to command me to alter, or erase, to add or diminish to or from a revelation or commandment from Almighty God."[3]

A few days later, Joseph began a journey from his home in Harmony, Pennsylvania, to see Oliver at the Whitmer home in Fayette, New York. Joseph's history records, "I found the [Whitmer] family in general [favor] of his [Oliver's] opinion . . . and it was not without both labor and perseverance that I could prevail with any of them to reason calmly on the subject." In the end, "I succeeded of bringing not only the Whitmer family, but also Oliver Cowdery also to acknowledge that they had been in error."[4]

With the benefit of several years' experience, Joseph later reflected on the incident, writing, "And thus was this error rooted out, which having its rise in presumption and rash judgement, was the more particularly calculated (when once fairly understood) to teach each and all of us the necessity of humility, and meekness before the Lord, that he might teach us of his ways; that we might walk in his paths, and live by every word which proceedeth forth from his mouth."[5]

The lesson, however, does not seem to have been so easily learned. Within months, Joseph again needed to assert his authority as the mouthpiece of revelation. Persecution around his home in Harmony, Pennsylvania, had forced Joseph and his wife, Emma, to take up residence with the Whitmers in August 1830. Upon arriving, Joseph found that Hiram Page, the husband of one of the Whitmers' daughters, had used a stone to receive two revelations concerning the Church.[6]

Perhaps remembering his success persuading Oliver Cowdery and the Whitmers of their error concerning the "Articles and Covenants," Joseph intended to reason with them until a conference that was to be convened in September. He soon discovered, however, that belief in Hiram Page's supposed revelations was more widespread than he had thought, so he sought a revelation on the matter.[7]

The revelation was addressed to Oliver Cowdery. Oliver was assured his voice would be heard but was warned that "no one shall be appointed to Receive commandments & Revelations in this

Church excepting my Servent Joseph for he Receiveth them even as Moses & thou shalt be obedient unto the things which I shall give unto him." [8]

Oliver was to be to Joseph as Aaron was to Moses, serving as a teacher and spokesman. His first assignment in that role was to convince Hiram Page of his error concerning the revelations from his stone. Second, he was to undertake a mission to the American Indians. [9]

When the conference convened in late September, Joseph Smith's retrospective history records, "The subject of the stone above mentioned, was discussed, and after considerable investigation, Brother Page, as well as the whole church who were present, renounced the said stone, and all things connected therewith, much to our mutual satisfaction and happiness." [10] Oliver Cowdery's brief minutes record that Joseph Smith "was appointd by the voice of the Conference to receive and write Revelations & Commandments for this Church." [11]

Joseph frequently received revelations and commandments, but most of them remained unpublished for several years, limiting their availability among Church members. At the same time, the Church's missionary efforts produced a large number of new proselytes. Many members either were unaware of, misunderstood, or chose to disregard the revelations that clarified Joseph Smith's role, and spurious claims to revelation for the Church continued on occasion.

Not long after the Church's relocation to Kirtland, Ohio, a "woman by the name of Hubble" came forward claiming her own revelations. [12] Once again, a revelation (now known as Doctrine and Covenants 43) confirmed that Joseph was the one "appointed unto you to receive commandments & Revelations from my hand" and added "that none else shall be appointed unto this gift except it be through him." [13]

The Saints' doctrine of renewed, New Testament–like manifestations of the Holy Ghost invited members to seek the gift of revelation for themselves. For the Church as a whole, however, the developing structure and practice designated Joseph Smith's as the lone voice of authority to pronounce revelation that would be binding on all Church members. "For," as the September 1830 revelation told Oliver Cowdery, "all things must be done in order." [14]

1. Joseph Smith, "History, 1838–1856, volume A-1 [23 December 1805–30 August 1834]," 51, josephsmithpapers.org.

2. Joseph Smith, "History, 1838–1856, volume A-1 [23 December 1805–30 August 1834]," 51.

3. Joseph Smith, "History, 1838–1856, volume A-1 [23 December 1805–30 August 1834]," 51.

4. Joseph Smith, "History, 1838–1856, volume A-1 [23 December 1805–30 August 1834]," 51.

5. Joseph Smith, "History, 1838–1856, volume A-1 [23 December 1805–30 August 1834]," 51.

6. See Joseph Smith, "History, 1838–1856, volume A-1 [23 December 1805–30 August 1834]," 53–54.

7. See Joseph Smith, "History, 1838–1856, volume A-1 [23 December 1805–30 August 1834]," 54.

8. "Revelation, September 1830–B [D&C 28]," in Revelation Book 1, 40, josephsmithpapers.org; see also Doctrine and Covenants 28:2.

9. See "Revelation, September 1830–B [D&C 28]," in Revelation Book 1, 40–41.

10. Joseph Smith, "History, 1838–1856, volume A-1 [23 December 1805–30 August 1834]," 58.

11. "Minutes, 26 September 1830," in Minute Book 2, 2, josephsmithpapers.org.

12. "John Whitmer, History, 1831–circa 1847," 18, josephsmithpapers.org. This was likely Louisa Hubbell, a convert from the Disciples of Christ who rejoined the Disciples in May 1831. An alternate possibility is Laura Hubbell, another Ohio convert.

13. "Revelation, February 1831–A [D&C 43]," in Revelation Book 1, 67, josephsmithpapers.org.

14. "Revelation, September 1830–B [D&C 28]," in Revelation Book 1, 41.

The Faith and Fall of
Thomas Marsh

D&C 31, 112

Kay Darowski

Few stories from Church history have been used as a cautionary tale as often as that of Thomas B. Marsh. The first to serve as President of the Quorum of the Twelve Apostles, Marsh left the Church in 1838 and later repented, returning to full fellowship in 1857. His importance in the early Church is evidenced by his being the sole recipient of two revelations in the Doctrine and Covenants and having been specifically instructed in four others.[1]

Marsh "ran away" from home at age 14 and supported himself with various jobs in Vermont and New York until his early 20s. After he married, he settled in Boston and found work in a type foundry for several years. He studied the Bible and religious sects, but he felt impressed that "a new church would arise, which would have the truth in its purity."[2]

In 1829, Marsh "believed the Spirit of God dictated me to make a journey west." With a friend, he traveled to western New York and stayed for three months. At one point, a woman asked if he had "heard of the Golden Book found by a youth named Joseph Smith." Marsh "became very anxious to know concerning the matter" and visited Palmyra. He found Martin Harris at E. B. Grandin's printing office, where the first 16 pages of the Book of Mormon had just come off the press. Because Joseph Smith was in Harmony, Pennsylvania, Harris took Marsh to Oliver Cowdery, "who gave me all the information concerning the book I desired."

"Highly pleased" with all he learned, Marsh returned home to Boston and shared his new knowledge with his wife, who also believed it to be from God. "From this time for about one year I corresponded with Oliver Cowdery and Joseph Smith, jun., and prepared myself to move west,"[3] Marsh wrote.

"Learning by letter that the Church of Jesus Christ had been organized on the 6th day of April, 1830," he continued, "I moved to
Palmyra, Ontario co., in September following, and landed at the
house of Joseph Smith, sen., with my whole family. During this
month I was baptized by David Whitmer, in Cayuga lake, and in a
few days I was ordained an Elder by Oliver Cowdery with six Elders,
at Father Whitmer's house."[4]

Later that same month, the second conference of the Church was
held in Fayette, New York. During the proceedings, Joseph Smith
received revelations for four individuals, including one for Thomas
Marsh, now Doctrine and Covenants 31.[5]

The revelation is rich in content—some wording is similar to other
early revelations, and some promises and instructions are personal
for Marsh and his family. Marsh was told that he and his family,
"yea thy little ones," would be blessed. At that time, he had three
sons, the oldest being nine years old. Marsh was called to serve
as a missionary and was told that his sins were forgiven. He was
counseled to be patient, to revile not, to pray always, and to give
heed to the Comforter.

The revelation contains an intriguing promise: "Behold I say unto
you that thou shalt be a P[h]ysician unto the Church but not unto
the World for they will not receive thee."[6] What does the title mean?
Was he recognized as a medical doctor, to aid members with medical
needs, or was the meaning perhaps more religious in nature, as one
called to spiritually minister or heal? There are only two mentions
of Marsh helping members with physical ailments,[7] and he had no
special medical training. The term "physician of the soul" is as old
as Socrates, and other churches have used the terms "doctor to the
church" or "doctor of the church" for hundreds of years. The latter
part of the verse, "but not unto the world, for they will not receive
you," adds to the ambiguity.

A Faithful Servant

There is every indication that for several years Thomas Marsh
humbly followed the counsel he received. He was ordained a high
priest in 1831 and served missions in 1831 and 1832. He moved

his family to "Zion" (Jackson County, Missouri) in 1832, settled on the Big Blue River, and served as branch president of the Big Blue branch. Along with other members of the Church, he was forced out of Jackson County in 1833 and moved to Lafayette County for the winter and then on to Clay County. He was called to the high council in Missouri in 1834 and named, with others, to receive an endowment of spiritual power in the house of the Lord in Kirtland, Ohio, which was then under construction.[8]

"Agreeable to revelation," Marsh left for Kirtland in January 1835, preached along the way, and arrived in April.[9] Unbeknownst to him during his travels, he had been called to the newly organized Quorum of the Twelve Apostles in February.[10] Shortly after his arrival in Kirtland, he was ordained to the Quorum.[11] By seniority and revelation, he was named president of the quorum, even though he was still a relatively young man of about 35 years.[12]

The next month, Marsh and other members of the Twelve left on a mission to the eastern states, returning in September. That fall and winter, he attended the Elders' School and Hebrew school in Kirtland and participated in spiritual preparations for the endowment of power anticipated with the dedication of the house of the Lord in Kirtland. Marsh attended the dedication on March 27, 1836, as well as the solemn assembly three days later. The following month he began a trek back to his family in Missouri, preaching as he traveled. From July through September, he visited branches of the Church in Illinois, Kentucky, and Tennessee.

Troubles Arise

By the following year, relationships among the Twelve Apostles had deteriorated significantly. It was a time of intensifying conflicts and dissatisfaction within the Church in Kirtland. Among the Twelve, youth and inexperience, a lack of precedence, and disagreements about their role and purpose and the bounds of their authority caused disharmony.[13] These difficulties were compounded by distance and communication struggles, as some resided in Kirtland and some in Missouri, and quorum members from both places were often called to serve missions elsewhere.

Hoping to bolster quorum unity, Marsh returned to Kirtland in July, only to find that some Apostles had left for a mission to Great Britain and several others had apostatized. Seeking counsel, Marsh visited Joseph Smith, who dictated a revelation for him (now Doctrine and Covenants 112). The revelation was a source of great guidance and comfort to Marsh, as well as stern admonition. Marsh was told that "all thy sins are forgiven" and that "I, the Lord, have a great work for thee to do." The Lord also told Marsh, "I know thy heart and have heard thy prayers. . . . Thou art the man whom I have chosen to hold the keys of my kingdom (as pertaining to the twelve)" and "how great is your calling." Yet Marsh was also told there were a few things in his life "with which I, the Lord, was not well pleased." Marsh was counseled to "be ye faithful before me," and for he and the Twelve to "exalt not yourselves; rebel not against my servant Joseph" but to "purify your hearts" and "cleanse your hearts" in preparation for proclaiming the gospel. The revelation also included the oft-quoted promise "Be thou humble, and the Lord thy God shall lead thee by the hand and give thee an answer to thy prayers."[14]

Relationships among the Twelve improved for a season, and in July, Marsh, Joseph Smith, and others departed for a mission to Canada.[15] Returning to Far West, Missouri, Marsh continued his efforts to strengthen the Church and show support for Joseph Smith.[16] A heavy blow to Marsh's family fell the following May, when his second son, James, died suddenly at the age of 14 after a short illness.[17] Joseph Smith preached his funeral sermon.

A Falling Away

Within a few months, Marsh fell prey to a spirit of apostasy, as had many others. He was among several Latter-day Saints who became disturbed by the increasingly violent relationship between Church members and their Missouri neighbors. Also contributing to his deepening dissatisfaction was the infamous "cream strippings" incident, which occurred in August or September 1838, involving Marsh's wife, Elizabeth, and Lucinda Harris, the wife of George W. Harris. According to George A. Smith, the women had agreed to exchange milk from their cows for making cheese. But counter to their agreement, Elizabeth allegedly kept the cream strippings—the richer part of the milk that rises to the top—before sending the rest of the milk to Lucinda. According to Smith, the matter went before the teachers quorum, then the bishop, and then the high council, all of whom found Elizabeth to be at fault. Marsh, not satisfied, appealed to the First Presidency, who agreed with the earlier decisions. Further hurt by this chain of events, the already frustrated Marsh was said to have declared "that he would sustain the character of his wife, even if he had to go to hell for it."[18]

Sometime in the fall of 1838, Marsh left Far West with his family and began actively opposing the Saints. He swore out an affidavit in October 1838 that detailed his concerns about acts of violence and destruction he believed were being planned or carried out by members of the Church against their neighbors in Caldwell and Daviess Counties. The affidavit also stated his fear that "all the Mormons who refused to take up arms, if necessary in difficulties with the citizens, should be shot or otherwise put to death" and that "no Mormon dissenter should leave Caldwell county alive."[19] Orson Hyde added his signature in support of Marsh's statements.

Although Marsh's affidavit was just one piece of evidence against the Saints presented to Missouri officials, George A. Smith later declared, "That affidavit brought from the government of Missouri an extermination order, which drove some 15,000 Saints from their homes and habitations, and some thousands perished through suffering the exposure consequent on this state of affairs."[20] Spurned by his former friend and supporter, Joseph Smith harshly characterized Marsh's two-page affidavit as containing "all the vilest calumnies, aspersions, Lies and slanders, towards myself and the Church that his wicked heart could invent."[21]

Marsh's bitter feelings toward the Church kept him away for almost two decades. At some point in the mid-1850s, having lost his wife and suffering from health problems, Marsh determined to reunite with the Church. His regret and repentance appeared to be humble and genuine. Writing to Heber C. Kimball in Salt Lake City, Marsh lamented, "The Lord could get along very well without me and He has lost nothing by my falling out of the ranks; But O what have I lost?!" Marsh further explained that he had "met with G W. Harris and a reconsiliation has taken place with us."[22]

After Marsh's arrival in Salt Lake City in September 1857, Brigham Young allowed him to address the Saints. In a weakened voice, Marsh explained his apostasy and asked for forgiveness:

"I have frequently wanted to know how my apostacy began, and I have come to the conclusion that I must have lost the Spirit of the Lord out of my heart.

"The next question is, 'How and when did you lose the Spirit?' I became jealous of the Prophet, and then I saw double, and overlooked everything that was right, and spent all my time in looking for the evil; and then, when the Devil began to lead me, it was easy for the carnal mind to rise up, which is anger, jealousy, and wrath. I could feel it within me; I felt angry and wrathful; and the Spirit of the Lord being gone, as the Scriptures say, I was blinded, . . . I got mad, and I wanted everybody else to be mad."[23]

After Marsh spoke, Brigham Young asked for a vote receiving Thomas B. Marsh back into full fellowship as a member of the Church, and not a hand was raised in opposition.[24]

1. See "Revelation, September 1830–F [D&C 31]" and "Revelation, 23 July 1837 [D&C 112]," josephsmithpapers.org; see also Doctrine and Covenants 31; 112; 56:5; 75:31; 118:2.

2. Thomas B. Marsh, "History of Thos. Baldwin Marsh, Written by himself in Great Salt Lake City, November, 1857," *Deseret News*, vol. 8, no. 3 (Mar. 24, 1858), 18.

3. Marsh, "History of Thos. Baldwin Marsh," 18.

4. Marsh, "History of Thos. Baldwin Marsh," 18.

5. "Revelation, September 1830–F [D&C 31]," in Revelation Book 1, 43–44, josephsmithpapers.org.

6. "Revelation, September 1830–F [D&C 31]," 44; spelling standardized; see also Doctrine and Covenants 31:10.

7. See Marsh, "History of Thos. Baldwin Marsh," 18; references include "I was sent for by them about midnight, to doctor them, . . . and soon found br. Blackslee, but too late to do him any good. He died the next day. . . .

I was invited by br. Joseph Knight, who was very sick with the bloody flux. I attended him faithfully and my wife nursed him; he succeeded in overcoming the disease and soon got well." Both of these incidents appear to have occurred in 1832.

8. See "Minute Book 2," 42, josephsmithpapers.org.

9. Marsh, "History of Thos. Baldwin Marsh," 18.

10. See "Record of the Twelve, 14 February–28 August 1835," 1, josephsmithpapers.org.

11. See "Record of the Twelve," 5, josephsmithpapers.org.

12. "Verily I say unto you my servant Thomas, thou art the man whom I have chosen to hold the keys of my kingdom (as pertaining to the twelve) abroad among all nations" ("Revelation, 23 July 1837 [D&C 112]," 73, josephsmithpapers.org; see also Doctrine and Covenants 112:16).

13. Discord and opposition reached such levels that nine of the original Twelve

Apostles left the Church at various times, and some never returned. For a discussion of these issues, see Ronald K. Esplin, *The Emergence of Brigham Young and the Twelve to Mormon Leadership, 1830–1841* (Provo, Utah: Joseph Fielding Smith Institute for Latter-day Saint History and BYU Studies, 2006).

14. "Revelation, 23 July 1837 [D&C 112]," in Joseph Smith, Journal, March–September 1838, 72–74, josephsmithpapers.org; punctuation standardized.

15. Marsh, "History of Thos. Baldwin Marsh," 18.

16. See Esplin, *The Emergence of Brigham Young and the Twelve to Mormon Leadership,* 324, which reads, "Even though most of the dissidents in Missouri had not yet openly broken with Smith, those Missouri leaders faithful to the Prophet were not unaware of the undercurrents. Led by Thomas Marsh, they determined to hold the line against rebellion until Joseph Smith arrived."

17. *Elders' Journal,* July 1838, 48, josephsmithpapers.org.

18. See George A. Smith, in *Journal of Discourses,* 3:283–84; George A. Smith gave the only full account of this oft-repeated story in Salt Lake City on April 6, 1856. He prefaced it by saying, "Sometimes it happens that out of a small matter grows something exceedingly great."

19. Marsh's affidavit further stated, "The plan of said Smith, the prophet, is to take this State, and he professes to his people to intend taking the United States, and ultimately the whole world" (*Document Containing the Correspondence, Orders, &c. in Relation to the Disturbances with the Mormons; and the Evidence Given before the Hon. Austin A. King, Judge of the Fifth Judicial Circuit of the State of Missouri, at the Court-House in Richmond, in a Criminal Court of Inquiry, Begun November 12, 1838, on the Trial of Joseph Smith, Jr., and Others, for High Treason and Other Crimes against the State* [Fayette, Missouri: Boon's Lick Democrat, 1841], 57–59).

20. George A. Smith, in *Journal of Discourses,* 3:284.

21. "History, 1838–1856, volume B-1 [1 September 1834–2 November 1838]," 838, josephsmithpapers.org.

22. Thomas B. Marsh letter to Heber C. Kimball, May 5, 1857, Church History Library, Salt Lake City; see also Lyndon W. Cook, " 'I Have Sinned Against Heaven, and Am Unworthy of Your Confidence, But I Cannot Live without a Reconciliation': Thomas B. Marsh Returns to the Church," *BYU Studies,* vol. 20, no. 4 (Summer 1980), 389–400.

23. Thomas B. Marsh, in *Journal of Discourses,* 5:206–7.

24. Brigham Young, in *Journal of Discourses,* 5:209.

Ezra Thayer:
From Skeptic to Believer
D&C 33
Matthew McBride

In the fall of 1830, Ezra Thayer was living in the township of Farmington, New York, with his wife, Elizabeth,[1] and their children.[2] He was in his late thirties and had spent several years in the area building bridges, dams, and mills.[3]

The Skeptic

Earlier that year, some of the workmen he employed told him of rumors circulating about Joseph Smith and his translation of the Book of Mormon. Thayer rejected the story as blasphemy and "was filled with wrath about it."

His brusque reaction was due in part to the fact that he knew the Smiths, having previously employed Joseph, his father, and his brothers to work on projects near Palmyra. The idea of Joseph translating and publishing a book of scripture was totally incongruous with what Thayer knew of the uneducated young man.

Thayer was perturbed to discover that several members of his family began to take an interest in the Book of Mormon. While he was away for a few days, his half brother and nephew rode his horses to hear Hyrum Smith preach. When Thayer returned, he chastised them, demanding that they "not take [his] horses again to hear those blasphemous wretches preach." They maintained "that there was something in it, and that [Thayer] had better go and hear him."[4]

Thayer remained unconvinced, but his brother soon came to visit from Auburn, New York, about 40 miles to the east. He, too, desired to learn more about the Book of Mormon and demanded that Thayer go with him to hear the Smiths preach. "I will not be found going after such a delusion," Thayer retorted. His brother insisted there could be no harm in going to listen—after all, Ezra did know the Smith family. Thayer reluctantly agreed to go.

The Believer

On a Sunday in early October,[5] the two brothers traveled roughly 12 miles to the Smith farm in Manchester, just south of Palmyra. When they arrived, they encountered "a large concourse of people" filling the lot around Joseph Smith Sr.'s log home and spilling out into the road.

Intent on hearing what was said, Thayer jostled through the crowd to get a place near the stand at the front. As Hyrum Smith began to preach, Thayer's resistance melted away. He later wrote about his experience that day: "Every word touched me to the inmost soul. I thought every word was pointed to me. . . . The tears rolled down my cheeks, I was very proud and stubborn. There were many there who knew me. . . . I sat until I recovered myself before I dare look up."[6]

After the sermon, Hyrum showed Thayer a copy of the Book of Mormon. As he took and opened it, he was instantly filled with "exquisite joy." Closing the cover, he asked, "What is the price of it?" He paid the 14 shillings and took the book. When Martin Harris, who was standing by, affirmed that the book was true, Thayer replied "that he need not tell me that, for I knew that it is true as well as he."[7]

Upon arriving home, Thayer realized that although he was thoroughly convinced, it would be another matter to help his family, friends, and neighbors understand, let alone believe as he did. Word spread among his neighbors that Ezra Thayer, respectable businessman, was now Ezra Thayer, believer in Joseph Smith and his "gold Bible."

Thayer's house was soon thronged with neighbors anxious to dissuade him. He recalled, "They filled my house all day, and men made my wife believe that I was crazy and would lose my friends and all my property." When Thayer endeavored to reason with a Methodist couple regarding his new faith, they curtly dismissed his argument, leaving Thayer's wife, Elizabeth, to despair. "My wife began to cry," he wrote, "and said that I was crazy, and it would ruin me, and she would leave me."[8] He succeeded in calming her fears, but his newfound faith would soon undergo further attacks.

He took his Book of Mormon to the nearby town of Canandaigua, where his friends, unimpressed by it, took turns giving him their opinions. When they asked if he still believed it, he countered, "I could not say that I believed it, I knew it." A local newspaper editor "said that he could tell me that I knew nothing concerning God if I had not had a liberal education."[9] Thayer demonstrated his simple faith and testified of God and of the Book of Mormon.

The Revelation

In the wake of these encounters, he experienced a vision or dream in which "a man came and brought me a roll of paper and presented it to me, and also a trumpet and told me to blow it. I told him that I never blowed any in my life. He said you can blow it, try it. I put it in my mouth and blowed on it, and it made the most beautiful sound that I ever heard."[10] The meaning of the dream for Thayer would soon become apparent.

The following Sunday, Thayer returned to Manchester to meet with other believers. This time, he met Joseph Smith and related to him his experience with the Book of Mormon. He accepted Joseph's invitation to be baptized and traveled a few miles to a millpond, where Parley P. Pratt baptized him and others, including a man named Northrop Sweet. Joseph Smith confirmed them.

Shortly after their baptism, Thayer and Sweet were called to the ministry in a revelation (now Doctrine and Covenants 33) dictated by Joseph Smith in nearby Fayette, New York. In it, the voice of God commanded them, "Lift up [your] voices as with the sound of a Trump to declare my Gospel unto a Crooked & a perverse generation."[11] This passage reminded Thayer of his dream. He concluded, "The roll of paper was the revelation on me and Northrop Sweet. Oliver [Cowdery] was the man that brought the roll and trumpet."[12]

The Missionary

"Open thy mouth," the revelation intoned, admonishing the newly called missionaries to "spare not." But Ezra Thayer and Northrop Sweet responded in markedly different ways to this injunction. Sweet soon parted ways with Joseph Smith to form what he called "the Pure Church of Christ." He and five others began to hold meetings, but this early schism grew no further.[13]

Thayer, on the other hand, immediately began to assist in the spread of his new faith. He arranged to have Joseph Smith come preach at his barn and encouraged his family, friends, and neighbors to attend. On the appointed day, his 50-by-18-foot barn was filled to overflowing, and the onlookers heard sermons from Joseph and Hyrum Smith as well as four other recently called missionaries: Oliver Cowdery, Parley P. Pratt, Peter Whitmer Jr., and Ziba Peterson.

In December,[14] Thayer arranged another meeting, this time in Canandaigua. At first he attempted to secure a Methodist meetinghouse as the venue but was rebuffed, so he reserved the courthouse. That evening, Sidney Rigdon and others met Thayer at his home, and Thayer accompanied them to Canandaigua and "attended the door" while Rigdon preached.

Because of the deeply spiritual experiences that led to his conversion, Thayer acted on the revelation's call to share his belief in spite of risks to his reputation and livelihood. He later wrote, "When God shows a man such a thing by the power of the Holy Ghost he knows it is true. He cannot doubt it."[15]

1. Some historians have mistakenly identified the Ezra Thayer of this story with another Ezra Thayre from Massachusetts. Consequently, his wife is often listed as Polly Wales. See Michael Hubbard MacKay, Gerrit J. Dirkmaat, Grant Underwood, Robert J. Woodford, William G. Hartley, eds., *Documents: July 1828–June 1831,* vol. 1 of the Documents series of The Joseph Smith Papers, edited by Dean C. Jessee, Ronald K. Esplin, and Richard Lyman Bushman. Salt Lake City: Church Historian's Press, 2013.

2. The 1830 New York Census counts nine members of the household, including seven children. It is unlikely that all seven children were Thayer's, as he had a half brother and nephew living with him for at least part of that year.

3. Frederick B. Blair, comp., *The Memoirs of W. W. Blair* (Lamoni, IA: Herald House, 1908), 39.

4. "Testimony of Brother E. Thayre Concerning the Latter Day Work," *True Latter Day Saints' Herald,* vol. 3, no. 4 (Oct. 1862), 79–80.

5. Possibly October 10.

6. "Testimony of Brother E. Thayre," 80.

7. "Testimony of Brother E. Thayre," 80.

8. "Testimony of Brother E. Thayre," 80–81.

9. "Testimony of Brother E. Thayre," 82.

10. "Testimony of Brother E. Thayre," 82.

11. Revelation, October 1830–B, [D&C 33]," in Revelation Book 1, 44, josephsmithpapers.org.

12. "Testimony of Brother E. Thayre," 82.

13. George A. Smith, Nov. 15, 1864, in *Journal of Discourses* (Liverpool: Latter-day Saint Book Depot, 1853-81), 11:4.

14. "Book of Mormon," *Buffalo [NY] Patriot,* Dec. 28, 1830.

15. "Testimony of Brother E. Thayre," 80.

Orson Pratt's Call to Serve

D&C 34

Matthew McBride

Orson Pratt was an inquisitive, seeking child. He recalled that at an early age he "had many serious impressions in regard to God and a future state."[1] Though they did not affiliate with any particular church, his parents, Jared and Charity Pratt, encouraged their son to read the Bible for answers to his many questions. His reading only spurred more questions.

The family was, as Pratt would later put it, "numbered among the poor of this world." He recalled, "A succession of misfortunes kept them down in the low vales of poverty."[2] Due to their meager circumstances, Pratt's parents sent him at age 11 to work the fields of other farmers in exchange for room and board. For nearly nine years, Pratt worked as a hired hand for a succession of farmers stretching from Ohio to Long Island. Though he felt "tossed about without any permanent abiding-place," he noted that the "early impressions of morality and religion instilled into [his] mind by [his] parents, always remained with [him]"[3] and served as an anchor.

He continued to feel "a great anxiety to be prepared for a future state," but it wasn't until the fall of 1829 that Pratt began to earnestly pray for spiritual direction in his life. He later wrote, "In the silent shades of night, while others were slumbering upon their pillows, I often retired to some secret place in the lonely fields or solitary wilderness, and bowed before the Lord, and prayed for hours." He summarized his feelings at that time: "The greatest desire of my heart was for the Lord to manifest His will concerning me."[4]

An Unexpected Visit

He persisted in his prayers while working on farms for room and board near his family's home in Canaan, New York, until September 1830. That month he received a visit from his older brother Parley.

Just a few weeks earlier, Parley P. Pratt had encountered the Book of Mormon and become converted to the Church restored by Joseph Smith. Newly baptized and ordained to preach, Parley traveled east to Canaan, intent on sharing his enthusiasm for his new faith with his family. While his parents believed "in part," Parley later noted, "My brother Orson, a youth of nineteen years, received it with all his heart."[5]

What Orson Pratt heard in his brother's message satisfied his spiritual longings, and he was baptized on September 19, his 19th birthday. Within a few weeks of his baptism, he started for Fayette, New York, eager to meet Joseph Smith.

A Call to Preach

After a journey of more than 200 miles, Orson Pratt arrived at the home of Peter Whitmer Sr., where Joseph Smith then resided. He there met Joseph and learned that his brother Parley had been called by revelation to "go forth unto the Lamanites, to proclaim glad tidings of great joy unto them."[6] Orson, still anxious to know the Lord's will for him, asked Joseph "whether he could not ascertain what his mission was."[7] Was there a revelation for him as there had been for his brother?

Joseph Smith invited Orson Pratt and John Whitmer upstairs into the chamber where Joseph had recently completed the translation of the Book of Mormon.[8] In this more private space, Joseph asked Orson if he would be willing to write the revelation down as he spoke it. "Being then young and timid and feeling his unworthiness," Orson asked if John Whitmer might act as scribe in his place.

Joseph Smith agreed and "produced a small stone called a seer stone, and putting it into a Hat soon commenced speaking."[9]

In the revelation, the Lord commended Orson for his faith and called him to the ministry: "Blessed are ye because ye have believed & more blessed are ye because ye are called of me to Preach my Gospel."[10] Orson Pratt later described his feelings upon hearing the Lord speak to him through Joseph: "I thought that was a very great and important calling, and I felt altogether incompetent unless the Lord qualified me by his Spirit."[11]

On December 1, Joseph Smith ordained him an elder, and Orson immediately made preparations to embark. Though the revelation had not specified where he should go, it was decided he should preach in Colesville, New York.[12] Orson was relying on this promise in the revelation: "Lift up thy voice & spare not for the Lord God hath spoken therefore Prophecy & it shall be given by the power of the Holy Ghost."[13] He later reflected, "I thought to myself, that unless the Lord shall pour out his Spirit upon me more fully than anything I ever yet have experienced, I never can perform these duties acceptably in his sight."[14]

Carrying a letter of introduction signed by Joseph Smith,[15] Orson arrived in Colesville, where he obediently "commenced to open [his] mouth in public meetings, and teach the things of God as the Holy Ghost gave [him] utterance." The small branch of the Church in Colesville received him warmly,[16] and he returned to Fayette later that month.

Pratt confessed that he "felt oftentimes to tremble and shrink, for fear [he] never should be able to fulfill and accomplish so great a work."[17] However, the revelation made the Lord's will clear to him, and he went on to serve as a missionary and Apostle for more than 60 years in response to that call.

1. Orson Pratt, "History of Orson Pratt," *Latter-day Saints' Millennial Star,* vol. 27, no. 3 (Jan. 21, 1865), 39.

2. Orson Pratt, "History of Orson Pratt," *Latter-day Saints' Millennial Star,* vol. 27, no. 3 (Jan. 21, 1865), 39.

3. Orson Pratt, "History of Orson Pratt," *Latter-day Saints' Millennial Star,* vol. 27, no. 4 (Jan. 28, 1865), 55.

4. Orson Pratt, "History of Orson Pratt," *Latter-day Saints' Millennial Star,* vol. 27, no. 4 (Jan. 28, 1865), 55.

5. *The Autobiography of Parley Parker Pratt; One of the Twelve Apostles of The Church of Jesus Christ of Latter-day Saints,* ed. Parley P. Pratt Jr. (Chicago: Law, King, and Law, 1888), 45.

6. "Covenant of Oliver Cowdery and Others, 17 October 1830," 1, josephsmithpapers.org.

7. Lyndon W. Cook, ed., *David Whitmer Interviews: A Restoration Witness* (Orem, Utah: Grandin Book, 1991), 239–40. The author is indebted to Michael Hubbard Mackay and Gerrit Dirkmaat, whose research for the Joseph Smith Papers called this source to my attention.

8. See Orson Pratt, in *Journal of Discourses,* 7:311.

9. Cook, *David Whitmer Interviews,* 239–40.

10. "Revelation, 4 November 1830 [D&C 34]," in Revelation Book 1, 45, josephsmithpapers.org; see also Doctrine and Covenants 34:4–5.

11. Orson Pratt, in *Journal of Discourses,* 7:311.

12. See Orson Pratt, "History of Orson Pratt," *Latter-day Saints Millennial Star,* vol. 27, no. 4 (Jan. 28, 1865), 55.

13. "Revelation, 4 November 1830 [D&C 34]," 46, josephsmithpapers.org; see also Doctrine and Covenants 34:10.

14. Orson Pratt, in *Journal of Discourses,* 7:311.

15. See Joseph Smith, "Letter to the Church in Colesville, 2 December 1830," in Newel Knight, History, 196, josephsmithpapers.org.

16. See Newel Knight, "Newel Knight Journal," in *Scraps of Biography, Tenth Book of the Faith-Promoting Series (Salt Lake City:* Juvenile Instructor, 1883), 46–69.

17. Orson Pratt, in *Journal of Discourses,* 7:311.

"Go to the Ohio"

D&C 35, 36, 37, 38

Elizabeth Maki

Not long after the second conference of the young Church of Christ concluded in late September 1830, four missionaries—Oliver Cowdery, Peter Whitmer Jr., Parley P. Pratt, and Ziba Peterson—set out from New York to preach to the American Indians in Missouri. After a brief visit with Seneca Indians near Buffalo, New York, the group followed Pratt's inclination along Lake Erie to Mentor, Ohio, home of his former spiritual leader, Sidney Rigdon.

Sidney Rigdon's Conversion

Then a preacher with two Reformed Baptist congregations, Rigdon was influential enough that those in his flock were known by many as Rigdonites.[1] Recognizing his influence, Pratt and Cowdery called on Rigdon on October 28, but his reaction to their message was not a positive one. He skeptically accepted a copy of the Book of Mormon, and one congregant remembered that he "partly condemned it."[2] Nevertheless, he agreed to read it.

The missionaries preached a sermon in Mentor to little effect and soon moved on to Kirtland and the Isaac Morley farm, arriving November 2. Also a Reformed Baptist, Isaac Morley was the "spiritual father of a large communal family"—composed mostly of members of Rigdon's congregations—living at his farm. As a group, the "family" sought to reestablish the gospel of Jesus Christ as described in the Bible. The missionaries found a warm reception for their message among the members of the "family" at the Morley farm and baptized many of them.

The next day, November 4, Rigdon came to Kirtland to perform a marriage and then joined the missionaries as they traveled the area preaching the message of the restored gospel. Seventeen more people were baptized the next day, and though Rigdon was not among them, within another day he had joined in the preaching and, according to one observer, was "much affected and shedding tears" at the meeting.[3]

By Sunday, November 7, the preaching drew a crowd so large that listeners spilled outside and someone pulled boards off the building so the overflow crowd could hear. Parley P. Pratt taught from the Book of Mormon and then invited others to speak—an invitation Sidney Rigdon quickly accepted. Rigdon stood and announced that after hearing the missionaries' message, he "should never try to preach again" and urged listeners not to contend against what they had heard.

Rigdon had become convinced that the missionaries did, indeed, have authority previously not found on the earth. He desired to be baptized and discussed the matter with his wife, Phebe, warning her of how their lives might change if they obeyed the gospel:

"'My dear, you have once followed me into poverty; are you again willing to do the same?' She answered, 'I have weighed the matter; I have contemplated . . . the circumstances in which we may be placed; I have counted the cost, and I am perfectly satisfied to follow you. Yea, it is my desire to do the will of God, come life or come death.'"[4]

Trip to New York to Visit Joseph

Knowing that the cost of their conversion would probably include their home and their living, both Sidney and Phebe Rigdon were baptized in November 1830. Rigdon gave up preaching and worked briefly on Morley's farm but soon left for New York with "much anxiety to see Joseph Smith Jr. the Seer whom the Lord had raised up in these last days."[5] Rigdon was accompanied on his journey by one of his former parishioners, Edward Partridge, whose wife, Lydia, believed the missionaries' message. Still skeptical, Partridge desired to meet Joseph before he would be baptized.

The two men met Joseph in New York in early December 1830, and Rigdon was soon "desirous to have the Seer enquire of the Lord, to know what the will of the Lord was concerning him."[6] In response, Joseph dictated the revelation now known as Doctrine and Covenants 35. Rigdon was praised for his work in his ministry in Ohio and charged to be Joseph's companion and scribe for the ongoing translation of the Bible. He was told that as he did so, "the scriptures shall be given even as they are in mine own bosom to the salvation of mine own elect."[7] Accordingly, Rigdon stayed in Fayette with Joseph and began his service as scribe.

Upon his arrival in New York, Partridge spoke with the Smiths' neighbors about the family's character. Fully satisfied with what he learned, he requested baptism, and Joseph promised to baptize him after Partridge had rested from his journey. Joseph Smith soon received a revelation for Partridge as well, in which Partridge was commissioned to "preach the everlasting gospel among the Nation."[8] After his baptism, Partridge traveled east to share his new faith with his family.

The Call to Gather

Rigdon and Partridge's arrival in New York brought with it word of how deeply the restored gospel had taken root in Ohio.[9] And even as the number of converts in Ohio rapidly grew, the Church in New York faced increasing opposition. A few months previously, Joseph Smith had received a revelation declaring that the Church should be gathered in one place, though that location had not yet been revealed (see D&C 29:7–8).

Joseph's mother, Lucy, later remembered that Joseph had received word that the fledgling congregations in Ohio were badly in need of direction, as the number of converts had ballooned to 300.[10] Then, as Joseph and Sidney Rigdon traveled from Fayette to Canandaigua, New York, in late December, they received a revelation directing the Church to "go to the Ohio."[11] In the revelation, the men were also directed to temporarily stop working on the Bible revision in order to strengthen the congregations in New York in preparation for the move.

Three days later, the third conference of the Church convened in Fayette, and Joseph announced to the members the Lord's charge to leave their homes and gather in Ohio. In connection with the announcement, Joseph dictated another revelation that elaborated on the command to gather and promised members that in Ohio they would receive God's "law & there you shall be endowed with power from on high."[12]

Newel Knight later wrote that the members present were "instructed as a people, to begin the gathering of Israel, and a revelation was given to the Prophet on this subject."[13] Though some Church members balked at the commandment to abandon their homes and gather to a new place, after a night of fasting and prayer, the young Church committed to obey the charge.[14]

1. For more on the early Church in Ohio, see Mark Lyman Staker, *Hearken, O Ye People: The Historical Setting of Joseph Smith's Ohio Revelations* (Draper, Utah: Greg Kofford Books, 2009).

2. M.S.C. (Matthew S. Clapp), "Mormonism," *Painesville Telegraph,* vol. 2, no. 35 (Feb. 15, 1831).

3. Josiah Jones, "History of the Mormonites," *The Evangelist,* June 1, 1831, 132–36.

4. Joseph Smith, "History, 1838–1856, volume A-1 [23 December 1805–30 August 1834]," 75, josephsmithpapers.org; punctuation and capitalization standardized.

5. "John Whitmer, History, 1831–circa 1847," 1, josephsmithpapers.org.

6. "John Whitmer, History, 1831–circa 1847," 2, josephsmithpapers.org.

7. "Revelation, 7 December 1830 [D&C 35]," in Revelation Book 1, 47, josephsmithpapers.org; see also Doctrine and Covenants 35:20.

8. "Revelation, 9 December 1830 [D&C 36]," in Revelation Book 1, 48, josephsmithpapers.org; see also Doctrine and Covenants 36:5.

9. See Staker, *Hearken, O Ye People,* 60–61.

10. Lucy Mack Smith letter to Solomon Mack, Jan. 6, 1831, Church History Library, Salt Lake City, Utah.

11. "Revelation, 30 December 1830 [D&C 37]," in Revelation Book 1, 49, josephsmithpapers.org; see also Doctrine and Covenants 37:1.

12. "Revelation, 2 January 1831 [D&C 38]," in Revelation Book 1, 52, josephsmithpapers.org; see also Doctrine and Covenants 38:32.

13. Newel Knight autobiography, circa 1871, 268–69, Church History Library, Salt Lake City, Utah.

14. Letter to the editor, Jan. 26, 1831, in *The Reflector* [Palmyra, New York], Feb. 1, 1831, 95.

James Covel and the "Cares of the World"

D&C 39, 40

Jed Woodworth

Of all the parables of Jesus, none illustrates the precariousness of Christian discipleship more powerfully than the parable of the sower (see Matthew 13:3–23). All the seeds in the story start out with great potential for growth, but not all are planted in soil nourishing enough to develop that potential. Seeds that fall into good ground get the nutrients required to develop a deep and extensive root system and thus push aside threats to their growth. Other seeds are not so fortunate. Some fall by the wayside; God's word is never truly understood, and the wicked one snatches the seeds away. Still others fall on stony ground and, lacking adequate roots, wither in the scorching sun of tribulation. Finally, other seeds fall among thorns. Jesus likens the plight of these seeds to those who hear the word but are choked by the deceitfulness of riches and the "care of this world" (Matthew 13:22).

Doctrine and Covenants 39 and 40 mirror the language of this parable in the telling of the story of James Covel, a Methodist minister who showed intense but fleeting interest in the Church. Covel, like the seeds in the story, started out with great potential. Born the son of a Baptist-minister father and a Methodist mother in Chatham, Massachusetts, in about 1770, Covel became an itinerant preacher in the Methodist Episcopal Church in 1791. He traveled the circuit in and around Litchfield, Connecticut, and eventually married and settled in Poughkeepsie, New York.[1]

Covel was recognized in Methodist circles as a steady and reliable man. By the 1820s, he had become a leader in the Methodist reform movement. (The reformed Methodists arose to contest the worldliness they saw entering their church when mainstream Methodism started to abandon the exercise of spiritual gifts.) Before converting to Mormonism, Brigham Young, Wilford Woodruff, and John Taylor, among others, saw themselves as reformed Methodists. In 1826, Covel was named president of the New York Conference of the Methodist Society, a group of dissenting Methodists who brought together a number of small offshoots. He later served as book agent in New York City for the literature published by reformers in the movement.

Covel was preaching in the Richmond circuit, 45 miles east of Fayette, New York, when he attended a conference of Latter-day Saints at Fayette in early January 1831. The Church was on its way out of New York then, the call to settle in Ohio having already come through revelation (see D&C 37:3).

Covel was more impressed with the teachings of the Church than with the call to move. In fact, he seemed poised to convert. He lingered a few days, talking with Church leaders, and covenanted with God to obey the call to repent and be baptized.[2]

On January 5, 1831, a revelation came through Joseph Smith, calling Covel to join the Saints in their move to Ohio. "Thou art called to Labour in my Vineyard & to build up my Church," the revelation said.[3] Such language would have comforted any Methodist preacher, but the next verse was troubling: "Verily I say unto you thou art not called to go unto the Eastern countries but thou art called to go to Ohio."[4] For 40 years, Covel had preached east of upstate New York. Now he was being asked to go the opposite direction to preach.

The January 5 revelation warned Covel that in times past he had rejected the Lord. Like the seed that falls among thorns, Covel had let "the cares of the world" choke the seed the Lord had wanted to plant.[5]

Covel must have known that moving west would mean cutting ties with the deep and extensive associations he had built up over his career. Two of his sons were Methodist preachers, and his years spent working in New York City had put him in contact with the movement's most powerful voices. All the prestige he had accumulated over the course of a lifetime would have to be abandoned. It took Covel less than 48 hours to decide that he would not move to Ohio. A follow-up revelation made clear that Covel had rejected the Lord's call: Covel, it said, "Received the word with Gladness but

Straitway Satan came & tempted him & the fear of persecution & the cares of the world caused him to reject the word."[6]

After his fleeting interest in the Church, Covel returned to his former position. He preached and gained converts for Methodism in upstate New York until 1836, when he moved back to New York City. He remained there until his death in February 1850. By then the Saints had moved still farther west, beyond the Rocky Mountains to the arid Great Basin.

1. The biographical details found in this article are taken from Christopher C. Jones, "Mormonism in the Methodist Marketplace: James Covel and the Historical Background of Doctrine and Covenants 39–40," *BYU Studies Quarterly,* vol. 51, no. 1 (2012), 67–98.

2. See "Revelation, 6 January 1831 [D&C 40]," in Revelation Book 1, 60, josephsmithpapers.org.

3. "Revelation, 5 January 1831 [D&C 39]," in Revelation Book 1, 59, josephsmithpapers.org.

4. "Revelation, 5 January 1831 [D&C 39]," 59.

5. "Revelation, 5 January 1831 [D&C 39]," 59; the original wording "be cause of the world" has been changed to "the cares of the world" in modern publications (see Doctrine and Covenants 39:9).

6. See "Revelation, 6 January 1831 [D&C 40]," 60.

"A Bishop unto the Church"

D&C 41, 42, 51, 54, 57

Sherilyn Farnes

In the fall of 1830, four young men in their late teens or early twenties appeared at the door of Edward Partridge's hat shop in Painesville, Ohio. As Partridge listened to the men's extraordinary tale of a restoration of authority and a revelation of new scripture, he called them imposters and sent them away. Yet after they left, Partridge sent one of his employees after the men in order to purchase a copy of the book they carried, the Book of Mormon.[1]

Partridge and his wife, Lydia, were searching for a church that taught the New Testament gospel in its plainness and provided proof of divine authority to lead the church. Upon learning of the missionaries' message, Lydia recognized the truth she knew from the Bible in their teachings and was baptized.[2] Edward Partridge remained unconvinced, but after traveling to New York to meet the Prophet Joseph, he, too, was baptized.

About this same time, Joseph Smith received a revelation in which the Lord promised Edward Partridge, "thou shalt Receive my spirit, the Holy Ghost, even the comforter, which shall teach you the peacible things of the Kingdom." With this reassurance, the Lord called Partridge "to preach my Gospel as with the voice of a Trump."[3] Partridge left to share his newfound faith with his parents and siblings in Massachusetts. Although his family members were for the most part unreceptive to his message, Partridge fulfilled his commission to preach the gospel to them.[4]

On February 4, 1831, upon Partridge's return to Ohio, Joseph Smith received a revelation (now Doctrine and Covenants 41) calling Edward Partridge as the first bishop in the 10-month-old Church. The office of bishop was one of the first priesthood offices restored in this dispensation, and, like other offices, an understanding of the duties of a bishop came line upon line. Unlike bishops today, Partridge was instructed to not only be "ordained a bishop unto the Church" but also to "leave his merchandise & spend all his time in the labours of the Church."[5]

With no handbook and no living precedents, Partridge may have wondered what exactly were the "labours of the Church" he was to perform. Fortunately, a few days later, Joseph received a revelation (called "the Law" by early Church members) that contained further information about Partridge's duties as bishop.

In this revelation (now found in Doctrine and Covenants 42), the Lord commanded the Saints to consecrate all their properties to Him through the bishop and his counselors "with a covena[n]t and Deed which cannot be broken." Then, the one consecrating would receive a stewardship from the bishop "sufficient for him self and family." The bishop was charged to maintain any remaining property in a storehouse to "administer to the poor and needy," to purchase lands, and to build Zion.[6]

Partridge faced one of his first major tasks as bishop with the arrival in Ohio of the Saints who had been commanded to flee New York. Partridge was charged with settling them upon lands for their inheritances. Early Church member Leman Copley offered to let the Saints from Colesville, New York, settle on his 759-acre property in Thompson, Ohio, about 20 miles from Kirtland, and Partridge needed more specific revelation about how to organize the Colesville Saints on Copley's property. In response, the Lord gave instructions to Partridge through Joseph Smith. These instructions are now found in Doctrine and Covenants 51. The Lord taught Partridge that as he divided the land for the Colesville Saints, he was to "appoint unto this People their portion every man alike according to their families according to their wants & their needs." Although Partridge still owned property in Painesville and did not need land, he was told in the revelation that in return for sacrificing his full-time job as a hatter to serve as bishop, he was to draw upon the supplies in the storehouse to support his family.[7]

Living the law of consecration was to be considered a privilege.[8] Yet not everyone viewed it that way. Copley soon rescinded his offer and evicted the Colesville Saints from his land, leaving them wondering where to turn.[9] On June 10, a revelation (now Doctrine and Covenants 54) addressed their concern in a surprising way: it called them to move permanently to Missouri, more than 800 miles away.[10]

At about the same time, Joseph Smith, Edward Partridge, and others were also preparing to depart on a trip to Missouri, the anticipated location of the future city of Zion.[11] Partridge left, assuming he would return in a few months. But upon the elders' arrival in Independence, Missouri, a frontier town in the far western part of the state, Joseph Smith received a revelation (now found in Doctrine and Covenants 57) declaring that Independence was to be the center of latter-day Zion. The revelation also contained a daunting imperative: "It is wisdom that the land should be purchased by the saints & also every tract lying westward even unto the [western border of Missouri,] And also every tract bordering by the Prairies." The Lord further instructed, "Let my servant Edward [Partridge] stand in the office which I have appointed him to [divide] unto the saints their inheritance even as I have commanded." The Lord then called several individuals to remain in Missouri and build up Zion. Contrary to his plans, Partridge was among those who were to "be planted in the Land of Zion as speedily as can be with their families to do these things even as I have spoken."[12]

In a letter to Lydia written a few days later, Partridge broke the news that he wouldn't be returning to Ohio that summer and instead asked that she and their five daughters join him on the Missouri frontier. Additionally, instead of being able to return to Ohio to help them move that fall, he wrote, "Brother Gilbert or I must be here to attend the sales in Dec. & not knowing that he can get back by that time I have thought it advisable to stay here for the present contrary to [my] expectations." He also warned that once she joined him in Missouri, "We have to suffer & shall for some time many privations here which you & I have not been much used to for year[s]." Following the direction given to counsel between themselves and the Lord, he made suggestions about how she and the girls could make the journey, then suggested that she proceed as she thought best.[13] Lydia willingly obeyed the revelation to move, packing her home and gathering her five daughters to travel west to a place she had never seen before.

In Missouri, anticipating the imminent arrival of the Colesville Saints and many others to follow, Partridge followed the Lord's direction to prepare "to [divide] unto the saints their inheritance," beginning to purchase land within two weeks of his arrival in Missouri. As Partridge settled the Saints on their land there, he followed the instructions given to him in May that "when he shall appoint a man his portion give unto him a writing that shall secure unto him his portion."[14]

In response to this revelation, Partridge printed consecration deeds that had two parts. In the first part, he carefully recorded the property and goods that an individual Saint or family "laid before the Bishop." In return, Partridge carefully recorded on the second part of the deed the property or goods that each member had steward-ship over—usually the same as what they had consecrated. Each member was then appointed "a Steward over his own property, or that which he hath received [by consecration]."[15]

Partridge served as the Lord's representative for many Saints who chose to live the law of consecration and accept the Lord's invitation to act upon principles of stewardship, agency, and accountability. Yet once again, not everyone wished to live the law. Some purchased land on their own. Some, as had Copley and another man named Bates, donated property or money then changed their minds and demanded it back. Partridge was called upon to help lift and encourage the recalcitrant as well as the receptive Saint. After the law of consecration was received, John Whitmer wrote: "The Bishop Edward Partridge visited the church in its several branches, there were some that would not receive the Law."[16]

Of the difficulties of dealing with imperfect Saints, Partridge's daughter Emily Dow Partridge later remembered, "When I look back and remember the great responsibility that rested upon my father as first Bishop—his poverty and privations, and the hardships that he had to endure, the accusations of false brethren, the fault-finding of the poor, and the persecutions of our enemies—I do not wonder at his early death."[17] Partridge's own patriarchal blessing warned him, "Thou shalt stand in thy office untill thou art weary of it and shall desire to resign it that thou mayest rest for a little season."[18]

In addition to dealing with the human weaknesses of others, Partridge faced the reality of his own fallen nature. When faced with the challenge of building Zion with few visible resources, Partridge apparently doubted the possibility of success. In response, the Lord warned him, "But if he repent not of his sins which is unbelief & blindness of heart let him take heed lest he fall."[19] Partridge's August 1831 letter to Lydia revealed his own insecurities in his position. "You know I stand in an important station," he wrote, "& as I am occasionally chastened I sometimes feel as though I must fall, not to give up the cause, but I fear my station is above what I can perform to the acceptance of my heavenly father." He then pled with his wife, "Pray for me that I may not fall."[20]

Two years later, in July 1833, a mob of angry men entered Partridge's home, where he was sitting with his wife and three-week-old son and namesake, Edward Partridge Jr. They dragged him to the center square of Independence, where they beat and tarred and feathered him. Unafraid, three days later Partridge, along with five other men, offered their lives as a ransom for the rest of the Saints in an attempt to prevent further violence towards the Saints. Their offer was refused, and the men instead were forced to agree to leave Jackson County. A few weeks later, Partridge wrote to his friends in Ohio, "I feel willing to spend and be spent, in the cause of my blessed Master."[21]

The revelations calling Partridge as bishop and outlining his duties in that office shaped the remainder of his life. He continued to serve as bishop throughout the Saints' time in Missouri and into the Illinois period. In the spring of 1840, while building a home for his family in Nauvoo, Partridge fell sick. He died on May 27, 1840, leaving a wife and five children ages 6 to 20.

When Partridge was called as bishop, the Lord described him as one whose "heart is pure before me for he is like unto Nathaniel of old in whome there is no guile."[22] Early Church member David

Pettigrew described Partridge as "a Gentleman, filling that high Office which he Occupied, with great dignity, Such as the New Testament States, that a man filling the Office of a Bishop Should be His appe[a]rance was grave, and thaughtful, yet pleasant and agreeable, his family like himself verry agreeable."[23] W. W. Phelps wrote of Partridge that "few will be able to wear his mantle with such simple dignity. He was an honest man, and I loved him."[24] Eight months after Partridge's death, the Lord revealed that the faithful first bishop of the restored Church was with Him.[25]

1. Edward Partridge Jr., "Genealogical Record," 5, Church History Library, Salt Lake City.

2. Edward Partridge Jr., "Genealogical Record," 5.

3. "Revelation, 9 December 1830 [D&C 36]," in Revelation Book 1, 48, josephsmithpapers.org; punctuation standardized; see also Doctrine and Covenants 36:1.

4. Edward Partridge, Misc. Papers, Church History Library, Salt Lake City. Partridge noted a few years later that his brother James Harvey had joined the Church.

5. "Revelation, 4 February 1831 [D&C 41]," in Revelation Book 1, 62, josephsmithpapers.org; see also Doctrine and Covenants 41:9.

6. "Revelation, 9 February 1831 [D&C 42:1–72]," 3, josephsmithpapers.org; see also Doctrine and Covenants 42:30, 32, 34–35.

7. "Revelation, 20 May 1831 [D&C 51]," in Revelation Book 1, 86–87, josephsmithpapers.org; see also Doctrine and Covenants 51:2.

8. "Revelation, 20 May 1831 [D&C 51]," in Revelation Book 1, 87; see also Doctrine and Covenants 51:15.

9. Joseph Knight autobiographical sketch, 1832, 1862, Church History Library, Salt Lake City.

10. See "Revelation, 10 June 1831 [D&C 54]," in Revelation Book 1, 90, josephsmithpapers.org; see also Doctrine and Covenants 54:8.

11. See "Revelation, 6 June 1831 [D&C 52]," in Revelation Book 1, 87, josephsmithpapers.org; see also Doctrine and Covenants 52:3, 24.

12. "Revelation, 20 July 1831 [D&C 57]," in Revelation Book 1, 93–94, josephsmithpapers.org; see also Doctrine and Covenants 57:4–5, 7, 14; "Revelation, 1 August 1831 [D&C 58]," in Revelation Book 1, 96, josephsmithpapers.org; Doctrine and Covenants 58:24.

13. Letter, Aug. 5, 1831, in Edward Partridge letters, 1831–1835, Church History Library; see also Doctrine and Covenants 58:24.

14. "Revelation, 20 May 1831 [D&C 51]," in Revelation Book 1, 86; see also Doctrine and Covenants 51:4.

15. "Revelation, 9 February 1831 [D&C 42:1–72]," 3; see also Doctrine and Covenants 42:31–32.

16. "John Whitmer, History, 1831–circa 1847," 17, josephsmithpapers.org.

17. Emily Dow Partridge Young, "Autobiography of Emily D. P. Young," *Woman's Exponent,* Mar. 1, 1885, 145.

18. Patriarchal blessing, May 4, 1835, in Edward Partridge papers, 1818–39, Church History Library, Salt Lake City.

19. "Revelation, 1 August 1831 [D&C 58]," in Revelation Book 1, 95, josephsmithpapers.org; see also Doctrine and Covenants 58:15.

20. Letter, Aug. 5, 1831, in Edward Partridge letters.

21. Edward Partridge, "Dear Friends and Neighbors," *Latter Day Saints' Messenger and Advocate,* vol. 1, no. 4 (Jan. 1835), 61. The letter itself is dated Aug. 31, 1833.

22. "Revelation, 4 February 1831 [D&C 41]," in Revelation Book 1, 62; see also Doctrine and Covenants 41:11.

23. David Pettigrew, "A History of David Pettegrew," journal, 12, Church History Library, Salt Lake City.

24. "Extract of a Letter from W.W. Phelps," *Times and Seasons,* vol. 1, no. 12 (Oct. 1840), 190.

25. See "Revelation, 19 January 1841 [D&C 124]," in Book of the Law of the Lord, 4, josephsmithpapers.org; see also Doctrine and Covenants 124:19.

"I Quit Other Business":
Early Missionaries
D&C 42, 75, 79, 80, 84, 99
Lisa Olsen Tait

John Murdock began preaching the gospel immediately after his baptism in November 1830, one of the scores of converts taught by Oliver Cowdery, Parley P. Pratt, Ziba Peterson, and Peter Whitmer Jr. when they stopped in the Kirtland, Ohio, area during the Church's first organized missionary effort.[1] "Being thronged with inquiries, I quit other business," Murdock recorded, "and gave my full time to the ministry." Within four months, he was responsible for adding "about seventy souls" to the Church.[2] By April 1834, when he joined Zion's Camp, Murdock had been gone from home almost continuously for three years, preaching the gospel.

In January 1831, Jared Carter, a 29-year-old tanner in Chenango, New York, set off on a business trip, expecting to be gone for several weeks. Along the way, he heard of the Book of Mormon. It caused him "much astonishment," but he read it and prayed earnestly that the Lord would "show [him] the truth of the book." Immediately, he became convinced that it was a revelation of God. "It had such an influence on my mind," he later wrote, "that I had no mind to persue my business. . . . I found I was completely unqualified for any business until I should go and assist the Church of Christ."[3]

Three months later, Carter moved his family to the Kirtland area.[4] Feeling as though "it was [his] indispensable duty to preach the gospel," he departed in September of that year on the first of several missions to the eastern United States that would occupy him almost continuously for the next three years.[5]

Jared Carter and John Murdock were not unique. As other men embraced the new message of the Restoration, they accepted the call to preach as their "indispensable duty." The missionary mandate originated in revelation as a "calling and commandment": "Every man which will embrace it with singleness of heart may be ordained and sent forth," the Lord declared.[6]

Just as revelation called for missionary work, missionary work led to further revelation. The Doctrine and Covenants shows how the Lord built on what early Church members already knew about missionary work to give His Church an increasingly distinctive missionary system over time.

The 19th-Century Preaching Culture

In the early 19th century, unprecedented spiritual fervor swept the English-speaking world, diffused through numerous churches and religious movements. Especially on the American frontier, missionaries of various stripes were a common sight. Unnumbered preachers, seekers, evangelists, and lay ministers labored relentlessly to bring their gospel message to the people.[7] The Methodists—a sect to which many early Latter-day Saints belonged at one time—were especially prolific, building their success on an extensive system of itinerant preaching.[8] Many other believers, whether on their own initiative or representing a group, set out with little but a burning desire to proclaim the gospel as they understood it.

Most of these multitudinous preachers followed a New Testament pattern, traveling "without purse, and scrip,"[9] seeking food and shelter along with listening ears. Many offered baptism; some simply preached the necessity of spiritual reform or religious restoration. Their messages were biblical and urgent, sometimes welcome and sometimes not. For local people, a preaching meeting was an occasion for entertainment and socializing, regardless of how interested they were in the message. If sparks could fly between the visiting messenger and the local minister, that was all the more exciting.

Latter-day Saints knew these patterns well and adopted or adapted many of them. But they knew they had something more to offer: new revelation, new scripture, and divinely restored authority. That burning testimony prompted scores of men such as Jared Carter and John Murdock to "quit other business" and devote their time to the ministry, converting scores of others who, in turn, helped spread the word.

Revelatory Foundations

Though early Latter-day Saint missionaries drew in part on the practices of other churches, several revelations provided the foundation for their missionary efforts in the early 1830s. The revelation sometimes called the "law of the Church" (Doctrine and Covenants 42) addressed the "elders of [the] church" and established basic procedures.[10] "Ye shall go forth in the power of my Spirit, preaching my gospel, two by two, in my name, lifting up your voices as with the sound of a trump, declaring my word like unto angels of God," the Lord commanded.[11]

The elders were to declare repentance and baptize and thus "build up [the Lord's] church in every region." They were to teach "the principles of [the] gospel" from the Bible and the Book of Mormon and follow the "covenants and church articles" (that is, the guidelines found in Doctrine and Covenants 20). Most importantly, they were to teach "as . . . directed by the Spirit": the Lord taught, "If ye receive not the Spirit ye shall not teach."[12] Another revelation to the "elders of [the] church," Doctrine and Covenants 43, reiterated the command: "Lift up your voices and spare not." The elders were to be "taught from on high," and they were to deliver an urgent message of warning: "Prepare yourselves for the great day of the Lord."[13] In the fall of 1832, an important revelation on priesthood, now Doctrine and Covenants 84, gave more extensive instructions for missionaries—setting forth the New Testament pattern they were to follow, expounding on the messages they were to deliver, and assuring them of God's power and protection.[14]

John Murdock's Missions to Missouri

The June 1831 conference of the Church, held at Kirtland, yielded a dramatic opportunity for many elders to apply revealed patterns. Twenty-eight men, in addition to Joseph Smith and Sidney Rigdon, were commanded by revelation (now Doctrine and Covenants 52) to make their way, "two by two," to Missouri. The next conference of the Church would be held there, and the specific location for the city of Zion would be made known.[15] John Murdock was assigned to travel with Hyrum Smith by way of Detroit.[16]

This call came at a time of great sorrow for Murdock. Just five weeks earlier, his wife, Julia, had died shortly after giving birth to twins, a boy and a girl. Emma Smith had given birth to a set of twins on the same day, but the babies had not survived. Joseph Smith asked Murdock to let him and Emma raise the motherless newborns.[17] But that poignant decision still left Murdock with three small children to raise—two boys and one girl, six years old and younger—in the midst of his pressing commitment to missionary work. When the call to Missouri came, he arranged for other Church members to care for his children and departed, likely without realizing that he would not return for almost a year.

That year was one of extreme hardship for Murdock. He traveled through territory that was essentially a wilderness. One day, he recorded, they "waded through Mudy creek waist deep in mud 2 inches of water on the top of the mud and snakes in the water 4 Rods acrost it and prickly vines runing in the mud which cut our legs." When the men finally got out of the creek, they had to travel half a mile before they found enough water to wash the mud off their feet and legs so they could attend to their wounds.[18] Crossing the Mississippi, Murdock "got [his] feet wet" and soon became very sick. Murdock was still ill when he and his companions met up with Joseph Smith in Jackson County; he suffered for the remainder of his mission, and his bad health delayed his return to Kirtland.[19] Nonetheless, he recorded that he did much preaching and baptizing.

Murdock and his fellow missionaries also experienced plenty of rejection and human opposition. Once Murdock spent "half of the day trying to get up a meeting" in Detroit but "could find nobody willing to hear." One man, Murdock wrote, "turned me out of his door for preaching Repentance to him."[20] He also noted several instances of unfriendly ministers who challenged the elders to debate, sometimes angrily.

When he returned to his children in June 1832, Murdock found that all was not well. The family caring for his eldest son had left the Church and demanded payment for keeping the boy, the family keeping his other son had moved to Missouri, and the family caring for his daughter "would keep her no longer" and also demanded payment. His "little daughter Julia," one of the twins, was thriving in the care of Emma and Joseph, but not her brother. "My little son Joseph was dead," Murdock recorded. "When the Prophet was halled out of bed by the mob in Hyrum, the child having the mezles lay in bed with him." Though targeting the prophet, the mob had harmed the baby. "At the time they stripped the cloth off the child he took cold and died. They are in the Lord's hands," Murdock added, referring to the members of the mob.[21]

Murdock was home for two months, "confirming and strengthening the church and regaining [his] health," before departing again to fulfill the call received by revelation in August 1832 to "go into the eastern countries" and proclaim the gospel.[22] But first, the Lord instructed Murdock to see that his children were "provided for, and sent up kindly unto the bishop of Zion."[23] This time it would be two years before Murdock and his children were reunited. Sadly, just after his arrival in Missouri, Murdock received word that his six-year-old daughter, Phebe, had come down with cholera. "I had seen all my children in good health," he recorded, "but the destroyer commenced his work." John cared for his little girl for several days, but she died on July 6.[24] Within a few months, he left on yet another mission, this time bound for Ohio.

John Murdock's experiences illustrate the combination of individual initiative and divine mandate that spurred early Mormon missionary work. Sometimes men left their business and set out to preach on the basis of individual desire, prompting from the Spirit, or obedience to the general expectation that elders would "lift up [their] voices"; at other times they were commissioned through revelation that called them by name and specified a field of labor. Many of those revelations, such as Doctrine and Covenants 75, 79, 80, and 99, are part of the scriptures today.

Jared Carter: "To the East"

Like John Murdock, Jared Carter went on missions both by formal calling and out of personal initiative. In the fall of 1831, while John Murdock was lying sick in Missouri, Carter set out with a companion on a "mission to the east," and soon reached his hometown of Benson, Vermont. In another pattern typical of Latter-day Saint missionaries, his intention was to share his newfound faith with his "connections"—his relatives and friends.[25] Arriving in Benson in late October, Jared immediately "commenced holding meetings" and exhorting the people "to pray earnestly to the Lord to know the truth of this work." Most people made light of his message and opposed his efforts, but, Jared recorded, "those that continued to call on the name of the Lord soon became convinced that the work was true and were baptized."[26] The 27 people converted through Jared Carter's efforts had been members of the Free Will Baptist sect to which the Carter kin belonged. Their substantial stone meetinghouse with a vaulted ceiling soon became a Latter-day Saint meeting place.[27]

Carter labored in the area for nearly three months. His journal records several instances of miraculous "healing manifestations" after his administration to the sick.[28] This was another pattern in early Latter-day Saint missionary work. Elders testified that the gifts of the Spirit were active in the new Church and demonstrated the Lord's promise that He would show "miracles, signs, and wonders, unto all those who believe on [His] name."[29] Those gifts also benefited the elders themselves, often providing specific guidance in their work. In January—in the dead of a New England winter—Jared began traveling again, following the Spirit's promptings regarding what direction to take. Having followed an impression to go to a certain town, Jared was surprised to meet up with his own brother, saving himself a 50-mile detour.[30]

Jared returned home to Ohio on the last day of February 1832, "having been gone on this mission five months and upwards."[31]

A few weeks later he visited Joseph Smith "to inquire [about] the will of the Lord concerning my ministry the ensuing season."[32] The resulting revelation, Doctrine and Covenants 79, instructed him to "go again into the eastern countries, from place to place, and from city to city, in the power of the ordination wherewith he has been ordained."[33] He departed on April 25 and was gone for six months, laboring extensively in Vermont and New York with some success. The Lord has "blessed me with sheaves and with health and blessed be his name," Carter wrote.[34]

Women's Efforts

Because it was men who were ordained to go forth and preach, women's contributions to early missionary work may be less visible. But those efforts too were vital. An incident from Jared Carter's second mission to Vermont illustrates this point. In July 1832, he recorded that he visited his brother-in-law Ira Ames, "in which time [Ames] became convinced of the truth of the Book of Mormon and was willing to be baptized."[35]

But there was more to the story. Ira Ames had heard of the gospel two years earlier from his mother. In August 1830, Ames received a letter from his mother, Hannah, informing him that she and several relatives (including Jared Carter) had been baptized. Ames had already heard of the Mormons from other sources and felt some interest, but the letter from his mother had a powerful effect. "When reading over my Mothers letter it ran through me like lightning, it roused every feeling of my mind, the effect was powerful," he remembered. These feelings prompted him to pray for a witness "whether the letter and the matter of it was true or false." In response, a "clear calmness" entered his mind.[36] Jared Carter's visit almost two years later provided Ira his first opportunity to act on that testimony.

Many Latter-day Saint women likewise reached out to family members and friends, often in letters such as the one from Hannah Ames, testifying of their faith and inviting loved ones to join them. "I can say that did you know of the things of God and [could you] receive the blessings that I have from the hand of the Lord you would not think it a hardship to come here," wrote Phebe Peck from Independence, Missouri, in August 1832, to an "Affectionate Sister." She continued, "The Lord is revealing the misteries of the heavenly Kingdom unto his Children."[37] Rebecca Swain Williams testified to her family that she had heard the testimonies of the Smith family and "from the three witnesses them selves" concerning the Book of Mormon.[38] Such testimonies surely found receptive ears on many occasions, and Jared Carter was likely not the only Mormon elder to harvest seeds planted by women.

1. See Doctrine and Covenants 28:8–10; 30:5–8; 32:1–5.

2. John Murdock journal, typescript, 1, Church History Library, Salt Lake City; spelling and punctuation modernized.

3. Jared Carter journal, typescript, 1, Church History Library, Salt Lake City; spelling modernized. Some errors in the typescript have been corrected by reference to the handwritten originals.

4. Carter consistently refers to Kirtland as "Kirkland" in his journal.

5. Jared Carter journal, typescript, 4.

6. Doctrine and Covenants 36:4, 7.

7. Nathan O. Hatch, *The Democratization of American Christianity* (New Haven, Connecticut: Yale University Press, 1989) 1–16.

8. John H. Wigger, *Taking Heaven by Storm: Methodism and the Rise of Popular Christianity in America* (New York City: Oxford University Press, 1998), 48–79.

9. Luke 22:35.

10. At this time, priesthood offices and terminology were still developing. The office of elder was the only office in what we now call the Melchizedek Priesthood. The Articles and Covenants (Doctrine and Covenants 20) treated the office of elder as the highest in the Church, since elders could ordain men to all other offices and were designated as being the preferred authorities to conduct meetings (see Doctrine and Covenants 20:38–60). This revealed statement of the Church's initial structure did not speak of the Melchizedek or Aaronic or "greater" or "lesser" priesthoods.

11. Doctrine and Covenants 42:6.

12. Doctrine and Covenants 42:6–14.

13. Doctrine and Covenants 43:1, 16, 20.

14. Doctrine and Covenants 84:62–120.

15. Doctrine and Covenants 52:2, 5, 9–10.

16. Doctrine and Covenants 52:8–9. Jared Carter, newly arrived in Kirtland, was not called to go; the revelation instructed that he be ordained a priest (see Doctrine and Covenants 52:38).

17. Emma Smith requested that John not tell the children they had been adopted. He complied with the request for many years and then corresponded with his daughter Julia when she was grown and he was 67, identifying himself as her birth father and offering her a blessing before he died if they could find a way to meet (see Marjorie Newton, "Father of Joseph's Daughter: John Murdock," *Journal of Mormon History,* vol. 18, no. 2 [1992], 189–93).

18. John Murdock journal, typescript, 4.

19. Murdock does not describe his illness in detail, but subsequent entries mention ague, shaking, and other symptoms that recurred intermittently, suggesting that it was malaria or something similar.

20. John Murdock journal, June 15, 1831, page 3, Church History Library, Salt Lake City.

21. John Murdock journal, typescript, 11; punctuation modernized.

22. Doctrine and Covenants 99:1.

23. Doctrine and Covenants 99:6.

24. John Murdock journal, typescript, 36.

25. Jared Carter journal, typescript, 6–7.

26. Jared Carter journal, typescript, 7; spelling modernized.

27. Erik Barnouw, "The Benson Exodus of 1833: Mormon Converts and the Westward Movement," *Vermont History,* vol. 54, no. 3 (Summer 1986), 142.

28. Jared Carter journal, typescript, 7–8.

29. Doctrine and Covenants 35:8.

30. Jared Carter journal, typescript, 8. He does not name this brother.

31. Jared Carter journal, typescript, 9.

32. Jared Carter journal, typescript, 9.

33. Doctrine and Covenants 79:1.

34. Jared Carter journal, typescript, 9.

35. Jared Carter journal, typescript, 18.

36. Ira Ames autobiography and journal, image 16, Church History Library, Salt Lake City.

37. Phebe Peck letter to Anna Pratt, Aug. 10, 1832, Church History Library, Salt Lake City; also published in Janiece Johnson, "'Give Up All and Follow Your Lord': Testimony and Exhortation in Early Mormon Women's Letters, 1831–1839," *BYU Studies,* vol. 41, no. 1 (2002), 92–93.

38. Rebecca Williams letter to Isaac Swain, in Johnson, "'Give Up All and Follow Your Lord,'" 100.

The Law

D&C 42

Steven C. Harper

"We have received the laws of the Kingdom since we came here," Joseph Smith wrote to Martin Harris in February 1831, "and the Disciples in these parts have received them gladly."[1]

Joseph had been in Ohio less than a month when he wrote those words to Martin Harris, who was still in Palmyra, New York. Prior to Joseph's own move from New York, the Lord gave him a commandment to gather the Church in Ohio and promised: "There I will give unto you my law."[2] Shortly after Joseph's arrival in Kirtland, he received the promised revelation, which in early manuscripts was entitled "The Laws of the Church of Christ." It is now canonized as Doctrine and Covenants 42:1–73.

The Church's need for the revelation at this time was acute. When he arrived in Ohio, Joseph found the Saints there to be sincere but confused about the biblical teaching that early Christians "were of one heart and of one soul: neither said any of them that ought of the things which he possessed was his own; but they had all things common" (Acts 4:32).

Many of the Church's converts in Ohio were members of "the Family," a communal group that shared the home and farm of Lucy and Isaac Morley in an effort to be true Christians. While their intentions were in keeping with the account Joseph himself had recently received of Enoch's Zion, where the people had achieved the ideal "of one heart and one mind" and completely eliminated poverty (Moses 7:18), the Prophet found the Ohio converts following practices that undermined personal agency, stewardship, and account-ability—though they were "striving to do the will of God, so far as they knew it."[3] As a result, the converts were, in the words of Joseph Smith's history, "going to destruction very fast as to temporal things: for they considered from reading the scripture that what belonged to a brother belonged to any of the brethren."[4]

Very shortly after Joseph arrived in Ohio, the Lord revealed that "by the prayer of your faith ye shall receive my law that ye may know how to govern my Church."[5] A few days later, Joseph gathered several elders and in "mighty prayer" asked the Lord to reveal His law as promised.[6]

"Consecrate of Thy Properties"

The revelation Joseph received in response upheld the first great commandment, loving God wholeheartedly, as the motivation for keeping all the others, including the law of consecration, suggesting that love for God is the reason for the practice. To consecrate, the early Saints were taught, meant to make their property sacred by using it for the Lord's work, including purchasing land on which to build New Jerusalem and crowning it with a temple. The law revealed that consecration was as much about receiving as it was about giving, since the Lord promised that each faithful Saint would receive "sufficient for him self and family" here and salvation hereafter.[7]

The law clarified that consecration did not envision communal ownership of property. Rather, it required the willing to acknowledge that the Lord was the owner of all and that each of the Saints was to be a hardworking "Steward over his own property"[8] and thus accountable to the actual owner, the Lord, who required that the Saints freely offer their surplus to His storehouse to be used to relieve poverty and build Zion.[9]

The Ohio converts' faith in Joseph's revelations led them to align their practices with the Lord's revealed plan. As Joseph's history put it, "The plan of 'common stock,' which had existed in what was called 'the family,' whose members generally had embraced the ever lasting gospel, was readily abandoned for the more perfect law of the Lord."[10]

As time went on, Bishop Edward Partridge implemented the law as best he could, and willing Saints signed deeds consecrating their property to the Church. But obeying the law was voluntary, and some Saints refused. Others were untaught, and many were scattered.[11] Some rebellious Saints even challenged the law in court, leading to refinements in its language and changes in practice.

Other early Saints understood that the eternal principles of the law—agency, stewardship, and accountability to God—could be applied in changing situations, as when Leman Copley decided not to consecrate his farm in Thompson, Ohio, sending the Saints gathered there on to Missouri to live the law, or again when a mob drove Church members from Jackson County in 1833, ending the bishop's practice of giving and receiving consecration deeds but not the law itself. Just as the law of consecration, though revealed in February 1831, did not begin then, it did not end when some refused to obey and others were thwarted in their attempts. President Gordon B. Hinckley taught that "the law of sacrifice and the law of consecration have not been done away with and are still in effect."[12]

Answers to Various Questions

In addition to expounding the law of consecration, the revelation answered many questions of importance to the Church at that time. Joseph and the elders who gathered in February 1831 in pursuit of the revelation first asked if the Church should "come to gether into one place or continue in separate establishments." The Lord answered with what are now essentially the first 10 verses of Doctrine and Covenants 42, calling on the elders to preach the gospel in pairs, declare the word like angels, invite all to repent, and baptize all who were willing. By gathering Saints into the Church from every region, the elders would prepare for the day when the Lord would reveal the New Jerusalem. Then, "ye may be gathered in one," the Lord said.[13]

The Lord then answered a question that had troubled Christianity for centuries: was Christ's Church an orderly, authoritative institution or an unfettered outpouring of the Spirit and its gifts? Some people made extreme claims to spiritual gifts, and others responded with an equal and opposite reaction, stripping away the spontaneity of the Spirit, completely in favor of rigid rules. This dilemma existed in the early Church in Ohio, and the Lord responded to it with several revelations, including His law. The law did not envision the Church as either well ordered or free to follow the Spirit; rather, it required that preachers be ordained by those known to have authority, that they teach the scriptures, and that they do it by the power of the Holy Ghost.[14]

Other portions of the law restated and commented on the commandments revealed to Moses[15] and included conditional promises of more revelation depending on the Saints' faithfulness to what they had received, including sharing the gospel.[16]

"How," the elders wondered, should they care for "their families while they are proclaiming repentance or are otherwise engaged in the Service of the Church?"[17] The Lord answered with what has become verses 70–73, then elaborated further in later revelations, now found in Doctrine and Covenants 72:11–14 and 75:24–28. The concept was further clarified in the 1835 edition of the Doctrine and Covenants.

Early versions of the law also include short answers to two additional questions: Should the Church have business dealings— especially get into debt—with people outside the Church, and what should the Saints do to accommodate those gathering from the East? The answers have been left out of later versions of the text, perhaps because Doctrine and Covenants 64:27–30 answers the first question, while the answer to the second is so specific to a past place and time that it may have been considered unimportant for future generations.[18]

"How to Act upon the Points of My Law"

During that same month (February 1831), Joseph received what became Doctrine and Covenants 43, which commanded him to assemble a counsel to "instruct and edify each other, that ye may know how to act, and direct my church how to act upon the points of law and commandments, which I have given."[19] With that commandment in mind, Joseph convened a meeting of seven Church elders to determine how to act on disciplinary cases regarding the law of chastity revealed in the law[20] and how the Church should enact the law in situations ranging from murder to meanness. These additional regulations were added to published versions of the law and now comprise verses 74–93 of Doctrine and Covenants 42.

The law, together with the Church's founding "Articles and Covenants" (now Doctrine and Covenants 20), organized the rapidly growing Church under one set of regulations and unified the various budding congregations in their teaching and practice. It shows how the Lord has revealed, does reveal, and will yet reveal His will to the Saints. From clarifying parts of the law given to Moses and specifying how the Saints in 1831 should apply it in their circumstances, to promising further revelation as sought and needed in the future, this living document continues to serve as a law of the Church of Jesus Christ.

1. Joseph Smith letter to Martin Harris, Feb. 22, 1831, 1, josephsmithpapers.org.

2. "Revelation, 2 January 1831 [D&C 38]," in Revelation Book 1, 52, josephsmithpapers.org; see also Doctrine and Covenants 38:32.

3. Joseph Smith, "History, 1838–1856, volume A-1 [23 December 1805–30 August 1834]," 93, josephsmithpapers.org.

4. "John Whitmer, History, 1831–circa 1847," 11, josephsmithpapers.org.

5. "Revelation, 4 February 1831 [D&C 41]," in Revelation Book 1, 61, josephsmithpapers.org; see also Doctrine and Covenants 41:3.

6. "John Whitmer, History, 1831–circa 1847," 12.

7. "Revelation, 9 February 1831 [D&C 42:1–72]," 3, josephsmithpapers.org; see also Doctrine and Covenants 42:32.

8. "Revelation, 9 February 1831 [D&C 42:1–72]," 3.

9. See "Revelation, 9 February 1831 [D&C 42:1–72]," 3, 4.

10. Joseph Smith, "History, 1838–1856, volume A-1 [23 December 1805–30 August 1834]," 93.

11. See "John Whitmer, History, 1831–circa 1847," 17.

12. Gordon B. Hinckley, *Teachings of Gordon B. Hinckley* (Salt Lake City: Deseret Book, 1997), 639.

13. "Revelation, 9 February 1831 [D&C 42:1–72]," 1–2.

14. See "Revelation, 9 February 1831 [D&C 42:1–72]," 2.

15. See "Revelation, 9 February 1831 [D&C 42:1–72]," 2–3.

16. See "Revelation, 9 February 1831 [D&C 42:1–72]," 4–5.

17. "Revelation, 9 February 1831 [D&C 42:1–72]," 5.

18. One question read, "How far it is the will of the Lord that we Should have dealings with the wo[r]ld & how we Should conduct our dealings with them?" The answer was, "Thou shalt contract no debts with them & again the Elders & Bishop shall Council together & they shall do by the directions of the spirit as it must be necessary." The other question was, "What preperations we shall make for our Brethren from the East & when [another manuscript asks where] & how?" The Lord answered, "There shall be as many appointed as must needs be necessary to assist the Bishop in obtaining places that they may be together as much as can be & is directed by the holy Spirit" ("Revelation, 9 February 1831, [D&C 42:1–72]," 6).

19. Joseph Smith, "History, 1838–1856, volume A-1 [23 December 1805–30 August 1834]," 101; see also Doctrine and Covenants 43:8–9.

20. See "Revelation, 9 February 1831 [D&C 42:1–72]," 2–3.

Joseph Smith's Bible Translation

D&C 45, 76, 77, 86, 91

Elizabeth Maki

As Joseph Smith translated the Book of Mormon in the late 1820s, he learned more than the history of the Lamanites and Nephites.

More than once, the Book of Mormon text indicated that "many plain and precious parts" of the Bible had been lost.[1] In the summer of 1830, just a few short months after the Book of Mormon was published, Joseph Smith began a new translation of the Bible intended to restore some of those plain and precious parts. This effort defied the prevailing opinion of the day that the Bible contained the inerrant word of God as contained in the revered text of the King James Version.

Joseph's translation was not carried out in the traditional sense. He didn't consult Greek and Hebrew texts or use lexicons to create a new English version. Rather, he used the King James Version of the Bible as his starting point and made additions and changes as he was directed by the Holy Ghost.

Although Joseph made many minor grammatical corrections and modernized some language, he was less concerned with these technical improvements than he was with restoring, through revelation, important truths not included in the contemporary Bible. Historian Mark Lyman Staker characterized the translation as one of "ideas rather than language."[2]

Joseph Smith worked diligently on his translation from the summer of 1830 until July 1833. He considered this project a divine mandate, referring to it as a "branch of my calling."[3] Yet while portions were printed in Church publications before his death, Joseph Smith's complete translation of the Bible was not published during his lifetime.

Even so, the effort the Prophet poured into that work is evident in the pages of the Doctrine and Covenants; the translation process served as the direct catalyst for many revelations contained in that book, which includes more than a dozen sections that arose directly from the translation process or contain instructions for Joseph and others pertaining to it.[4]

The Translation Process

It was while the Book of Mormon was being printed at E. B. Grandin's print shop in October 1829 that Oliver Cowdery purchased from Grandin the King James Bible that Joseph Smith used in the translation.

In June 1830, Joseph received a revelation that he described as the "visions of Moses."[5] This revelation may have served as a catalyst to Joseph's work on the translation. This revelation now appears as the first chapter in the book of Moses in the Pearl of Great Price. The earliest manuscripts of the Bible translation, beginning with Genesis 1 (now Moses 2), were created in Harmony, Pennsylvania, about one month later, with Oliver Cowdery and John Whitmer acting as scribes. Shortly thereafter, in a revelation addressed to Joseph's wife, Emma Hale Smith, the Lord instructed that Emma serve as Joseph's scribe[6] for the translation, which she apparently did for a brief time.[7] Over the next few months, the translation progressed through the book of Genesis.

In December of that year, after Sidney Rigdon was baptized in Ohio and traveled to Fayette, New York, to meet the leader of his new faith, Joseph Smith received a revelation directing Rigdon to serve as his scribe: "Thou shalt write for him & the scriptures shall be given even as they are in mine own bosom to the salvation of mine own elect."[8]

Rigdon commenced to serve as scribe, and shortly after he and Joseph recorded the story of Enoch, Joseph was instructed to cease translating for a time and take the Church to Ohio. He did so, and soon after he was settled in Kirtland, the translation again became one of his primary tasks. In early February 1831, Joseph received a revelation instructing that a home be built in which he could "live & translate."[9] A few days later, another revelation assured Joseph that as he asked, the "scriptures shall be given."[10]

Doctrine and Covenants 45

The earliest work of the translation focused on the text of Genesis, but a March 7, 1831, revelation soon changed Joseph's course. In the revelation, canonized as Doctrine and Covenants 45, Joseph was instructed to put aside the Old Testament for a time and instead focus on translating the New Testament.

"I give unto you that ye may now Translate it," he was told, "that ye may be prepared for the things to come for Verily I say unto you that great things await you."[11]

Accordingly, Joseph and Sidney began the next day to work on the New Testament translation. They continued until leaving for Missouri that summer and then resumed the translation in the fall, after Joseph and Emma moved roughly 30 miles south of Kirtland to Hiram, Ohio, to live in the home of John Johnson. The move was, in part, Joseph's attempt to find a place "to work in peace and quiet on the translation of the Bible."[12] Joseph Smith later recalled that the bulk of his time after arriving at the Johnson home was spent in preparing to continue his translation work.

Joseph also set about overseeing the Church and preaching in the area, and then in January 1832 he received a revelation that directed him to once again focus his work on the translation "untill it be finished."[13] It was while he and Sidney Rigdon did so that, on February 16, they received a landmark revelation in the Johnson home. While working to translate the book of John, the men's inquiries led to a vision of the kingdoms of glory that was a source of significant new doctrines for the young Church. Today, that vision is contained in Doctrine and Covenants 76.

Sections 77 and 86

Similarly, an explanation of passages in the book of Revelation, now Doctrine and Covenants 77, also arose directly from the Bible translation. Taking the form of a series of questions and answers, it was considered an inspired text and was included in an early revelation book.

Joseph and Emma left the Johnson farm and returned to Kirtland in September 1832. Over the next few months, Joseph continued to work diligently on the translation, now with the help of Frederick G. Williams as scribe. In December, another revelation arising from the translation was received, this time explaining the parable of the wheat and tares found in Matthew 13. The revelation, now Doctrine and Covenants 86, designates the body of the priesthood in the latter days as "a saviour unto my people Israel."[14]

In July 1832, Joseph wrote to W. W. Phelps that "we have finished the translation of the New testament."

"Great and glorious things are revealed," he wrote, adding that they were "making rapid strides in the old book and in the strength of God we can do all things according to his will."[15]

Work on the translation of the Old Testament continued, and Joseph recorded in January 1833 that "this winter was spent in translating the scriptures; in the school of the prophets; and sitting in conferences. I had many glorious seasons of refreshing."[16] In March 1833, Joseph received instruction that when the translation was finished, he should "thence forth preside over the affairs of the church."[17] So he eagerly pushed ahead.

Doctrine and Covenants 91

Joseph Smith soon came to a section in his King James Bible containing a collection of 14 books known as the Apocrypha. While most Bibles in Joseph Smith's day contained these books, there was a growing movement at the time that questioned their status as scripture.[18] Given this dispute, Joseph wanted to know if he should seek to translate the books and took the question to the Lord. The resulting revelation, now Doctrine and Covenants 91, taught Joseph that while "there are many things contained therein that are true and it is mostly translated correct—there are many things contained therein that are not true which are interpelations by the hands of men varely I say unto you that it is not needful that the Apocrypha should be translated."[19]

Skipping that section, Joseph continued to labor over the Old Testament translation for several more months until, on July 2, 1833, a letter from the First Presidency (including Joseph Smith, Sidney Rigdon, and Frederick G. Williams) in Kirtland to the Saints in Zion recorded that they "this day finished the translating of the Scriptures, for which we returned gratitude to our heavenly father."[20]

The Translation's Legacy

After Joseph's death, his widow, Emma, retained the translation manuscripts, which were published by the Reorganized Church of Jesus Christ of Latter Day Saints in 1867. For the modern LDS Church, Joseph Smith's translation supplies portions of the Pearl of Great Price (the book of Moses and Matthew 24) and informs many footnotes in the Latter-day Saint edition of the King James Version of the Bible.

But the translation also had a significant influence on the Church in the way it shaped the content of the Doctrine and Covenants. More than half of the current Doctrine and Covenants consists of revelations received during the three-year period in which Joseph Smith labored over the Bible translation.[21] Many revelations were received as direct answers to questions Joseph was inspired to ask as his understanding of the gospel expanded during the effort to restore plain and precious parts of the Bible.

1. See 1 Nephi 13:28; 14:23; Mormon 8:33.

2. Mark Lyman Staker, *Hearken, O Ye People: The Historical Setting of Joseph Smith's Ohio Revelations* (Salt Lake City: Greg Kofford Books, 2009), 313. For more on the nature of the changes Joseph Smith made, see Scott H. Faulring, Kent P. Jackson, and Robert J. Matthews, eds., *Joseph Smith's New Translation of the Bible: Original Manuscripts* (Provo, Utah: Religious Studies Center, Brigham Young University, 2004).

3. Joseph Smith, "History, 1838–1856, volume A-1 [23 December 1805–30 August 1834]," 175, josephsmithpapers.org.

4. See Doctrine and Covenants 35, 37, 41, 42, 45, 73, 76, 77, 86, 93, 91, 94, 124.

5. "Visions of Moses, June 1830 [Moses 1]," 1, josephsmithpapers.org.

6. See "Revelation, July 1830–C [D&C 25]," in Revelation Book 1, 34, josephsmithpapers.org; see also Doctrine and Covenants 25:6.

7. "Emma and the Joseph Smith Translation," *Insights,* Aug. 1996, 2.

8. "Revelation, 7 December 1830 [D&C 35]," in Revelation Book 1, 47, josephsmithpapers.org; see also Doctrine and Covenants 35:20.

9. "Revelation, 4 February 1831 [D&C 41]," in Revelation Book 1, 62, josephsmithpapers.org; see also Doctrine and Covenants 41:7.

10. "Revelation, 9 February 1831 [D&C 42:1–72]," 4, josephsmithpapers.org; see also Doctrine and Covenants 42:56.

11. "Revelation, circa 7 March 1831 [D&C 45]," in Revelation Book 1, 75, josephsmithpapers.org; see also Doctrine and Covenants 45:61–62.

12. Staker, *Hearken, O Ye People,* 310.

13. "Revelation, 10 January 1832 [D&C 73]," 1, josephsmithpapers.org; see also Doctrine and Covenants 73:4.

14. "Revelation, 6 December 1832 [D&C 86]," in Revelation Book 2, 32, josephsmithpapers.org; see also Doctrine and Covenants 86:11.

15. Joseph Smith, "Letter to William W. Phelps, 31 July 1832," 5, josephsmithpapers.org.

16. Joseph Smith, "History, 1838–1856, volume A-1 [23 December 1805–30 August 1834]," 270, josephsmithpapers.org.

17. "Revelation, 8 March 1833 [D&C 90]," 2, josephsmithpapers.org.

18. Steven C. Harper, *Making Sense of the Doctrine and Covenants: A Guided Tour through Modern Revelations* (Salt Lake City: Deseret Book, 2008), 340.

19. "Revelation, 9 March 1833 [D&C 91]," 55, in Revelation Book 2, josephsmithpapers.org; see also Doctrine and Covenants 91:1–3.

20. "Letter to Church Leaders in Jackson County, Missouri, 2 July 1833," in Joseph Smith Letterbook 1, 51, josephsmithpapers.org.

21. See Robert J. Matthews, "Joseph Smith Translation of the Bible (JST)," in Daniel H. Ludlow, ed., *Encyclopedia of Mormonism,* 5 vols. (New York: Macmillan, 1992), 2:767.

Religious Enthusiasm among Early Ohio Converts

D&C 46, 50

Matthew McBride

Levi Hancock was 27 years old in 1830 and lived in New Lyme, Ohio, about 30 miles east of Kirtland. During his childhood, his mother had instilled in him a deep interest in spiritual matters. Hancock believed that God often intervened in daily life and spoke to men and women through dreams.[1]

Arrival of the First Missionaries

In the early part of November 1830, Hancock's brother Alvah brought him word of the Book of Mormon: "Four men have come and have brought a book with them that they call [a] history and a record of the people that once inhabited this land." His interest stirred, Hancock expressed a desire to hear these preachers. "Tomorrow they are to hold a meeting at Mr. Jackson's in Mayfield," his brother said, adding, "They lay hands on those they baptize and bestow on them the Holy Ghost."

Hancock described his reaction: "At these last words . . . there seemed to fall on me something pleasant and delightful[.] It seemed like a wash of something warm took me in the face and ran over my body which gave me that feeling I cannot describe. The first word I said was, 'It is the truth, I can feel it. I will go and hear for myself tomorrow.'"

The four men Hancock went to hear preach were Oliver Cowdery, Parley P. Pratt, Peter Whitmer Jr., and Ziba Peterson. They passed through northeastern Ohio as missionaries in the fall of 1830 en route to Missouri. During their brief stay, they created quite a stir. Preaching the restoration of the Church of Christ in preparation for the Second Coming of Jesus, they proclaimed that, among other things, the Lord had restored the gifts of the spirit spoken of in the New Testament.

Levi Hancock was one of more than a hundred baptized as a result of their visit. But the missionaries' stay was short-lived; they soon departed for Missouri, leaving the small band of converts near Kirtland without experienced leadership. Several prominent figures among the new converts left about the same time (including Sidney Rigdon and Edward Partridge, who went to New York to meet Joseph Smith).

The Second Great Awakening

In the early 1800s, New York and Ohio were awash in religious fervor. It began as early as the 1790s, when many Christians became concerned by the way increasing rationalism and skepticism had encroached upon their religious life. They thirsted for more from religion than their churches then offered, some seeking a return to primitive Christianity as described in the New Testament. This popular stir in religious zeal, later called the Second Great Awakening, led to numerous revivals, a surge in conversions, and even the founding of new Christian sects.

One characteristic of this revivalist culture was an increased interest in spiritual manifestations and gifts. The ardent preaching of Charles Finney, Lorenzo Dow, George Lane, and others elicited passionate responses from their audiences, including prophesying, crying, shouting, dancing, shaking, and rolling on the ground. Some groups, such as the United Society of Believers in the Second Coming of Jesus Christ (Shakers), even made some of these practices a formal part of their worship.

This style of worship was not without detractors. In fact, many mainstream Christians frowned upon this so-called enthusiasm. By 1830, the surge in religious excitement began to subside. However, there were still many who believed these manifestations were authentic expressions of the spirit. The Mormon missionaries' message that spiritual gifts had returned to the Church thus appealed to many of those they taught in Ohio.

Strange Spiritual Manifestations

After the departure of the missionaries, the converts had little experience, few copies of the Book of Mormon, and no copies of Joseph Smith's other revelations to consult in practicing their new faith. Flush with zeal, some of them began to introduce elements of enthusiastic worship—or "spiritual operations" as they sometimes called them—into their meetings. However, it was not always clear which manifestations were inspired and which were spurious.

In early January 1831, Levi Hancock met three young men named Edson Fuller, Heamon Bassett, and Burr Riggs, who introduced themselves as elders of the Church of Christ. According to Hancock, these young elders engaged in "all manner of doings" during worship services. Burr Riggs would "jump up from the floor, strike his head against the joist . . . swing some minutes, then fall like he was dead." He would then rise and relate visions he had while unconscious. "Edson Fuller would fall and turn black in the face. He[a]mon Bassett would behave like a baboon."

These strange behaviors perplexed Hancock. After all, he himself had experienced feelings, impressions, and dreams he believed were spiritual communications. The young men seemed "so honest and sincere I was led to believe all [they] said." He even worried that "perhaps I was not as pure as those young men." However, their actions were very different from the spiritual feelings he had experienced.

These three young practitioners of enthusiastic worship were not alone. Many converts from diverse religious backgrounds contributed to a wave of enthusiasm in the Church in Ohio in early 1831. A man known as Black Pete, a former slave and new convert, brought his experience with the slave shout tradition, including perhaps the practice of speaking in tongues.[2] Others introduced innovations peculiar to their groups: "Some would fancy to themselves that they had the sword of Laban, and would wield it as expert as a light dragoon . . . some would slide or scoot and [on] the floor, with the rapidity of a serpent, which the[y] termed sailing in the boat to the Lamanites."[3]

Word that local Mormon worship services often featured these curious manifestations drew the ridicule of many observers. A newspaper in nearby Painesville reported contemptuously that after the missionaries left, "a scene of the wildest enthusiasm was exhibited, chiefly, however, among the young people."[4] John Corrill, a January 1831 convert, later wrote, "It was but a very few of the church who were exercised in that way," and there were many, he added, that "were suspicious that it was from an evil source."[5]

Joseph Smith's Arrival

Still in New York, Joseph Smith became concerned about the lack of leadership among the new Ohio converts and sent John Whitmer to Kirtland with copies of the revelations to "strengthen my brethren in that land."[6] When Whitmer arrived in mid-January 1831, he was surprised by the variety of spiritual operations he witnessed.

Shortly after his own arrival in Kirtland in February, Joseph Smith set about to check these displays of enthusiasm. He wrote to his brother Hyrum (then in Colesville, New York) on March 3 reporting, "I hav been ingageed in regulating the Churches here as the deciples are numerous and the devil had made many attempts to over throw them."[7]

But there were important questions that remained to be answered. If the Book of Mormon promised the presence of spiritual gifts in the Church, what was wrong with these practices? Had not Joseph himself been blessed with miraculous manifestations of the spirit? And what of the Book of Mormon stories of Alma and Lamoni, who fell, apparently unconscious, while the spirit spoke to them? Just how was one to distinguish the gifts of God from human inventions or the influence of evil?

A revelation (now Doctrine and Covenants 46) given on March 8 in response to Joseph's inquiries about how to conduct sacrament meetings shed some light on these questions. In it the Lord reminded the elders that they should be "guided by the Holy Spirit" in directing their meetings. The revelation sanctioned the presence of spiritual gifts in the Church, even encouraged the members to "seek ye earnestly the best gifts always remembering for what they are given." It cautioned, however, "Some are of men & others of Devils[.] Wherefore beware lest ye are deceived."

The revelation listed a number of gifts the faithful could expect to find in the Church, including faith, miracles, knowledge, healing, and speaking in tongues. This list is similar to those found in the New Testament and the Book of Mormon (see 1 Corinthians 12:4–11; MoronI 10:8–18). The Lord also promised that bishops, elders, and others with the appointment to "watch over the Church" would have the gift "to decern all those gifts lest there shall be any prophecying among you & yet not be of God."[8]

A Revelation on Discerning Spirits

When Parley P. Pratt returned from Missouri in March, he too noted the continued displays of enthusiasm as he visited the congregations scattered about the Kirtland area. He later wrote, "Feeling our weakness and inexperience, and lest we should err in judgment concerning these spiritual phenomena, myself, John Murdock, and several other Elders, went to Joseph Smith, and asked him to inquire of the Lord concerning these spirits or manifestations."[9]

They met on May 9, and after they prayed together, Joseph Smith received the revelation now found in Doctrine and Covenants 50. Pratt described what he witnessed: "Each sentence was uttered slowly and very distinctly, and with a pause between each, sufficiently long for it to be recorded, by an ordinary writer, in long hand. . . . There was never any hesitation, reviewing, or reading back, in order to keep the run of the subject."[10] In this revelation, the Lord spoke "as touching the Church & the spirits which have gone abroad in the Earth." He indicated that many of these were "false spirits" and that "Satan hath sought to deceive you that he might overthrow you." He cautioned that some of the practices exhibited by the enthusiasts were "abominations" and that "there are hypocrites among you & have deceived some which have given the adversary power."[11]

The Lord reasoned in mercy with this earnest but inexperienced young group of disciples, reminding them that the Holy Ghost is the "spirit of truth" and that anything "which doth not edify is not of God & is darkness." It also taught them of the corollary "That which is of God is light." The revelation proceeded to give instructions on how to detect manifestations inspired of God as opposed to those coming from other sources: "If ye behold a spirit manifested that ye cannot understand & you receive not that spirit ye shall ask of the father in the name of Jesus & if he give not unto you that spirit then ye may know that it is not of God." The elders were to rebuke false spirits with a loud voice, and the Lord promised they would be given power to resist evil influences so long as they remained humble.[12]

Setting Things in Order

With these revelations, Joseph and the Kirtland elders were better equipped to understand and discern the many spiritual manifestations they encountered. But establishing order in the various congregations would require several weeks, as Joseph and others needed time to put into practice the revelation's instructions.

On June 4, Joseph Smith met with several elders of the Church in a log schoolhouse on Isaac Morley's farm near Kirtland. Levi Hancock attended this meeting and witnessed the way Joseph Smith responded to the Lord's counsel. When several elders began to exhibit the influence of unknown spirits, Hyrum Smith said, "Joseph, that is not of God." Joseph prayed as the revelation directed, and a moment later stood and rebuked the spirits.

Parley P. Pratt and Joseph Wakefield went "forth among the churches" as the revelation directed, "rebuking the wrong spirits which had crept in among them, setting in order things that were wanting."[13] Jared Carter was also among the growing number who felt newly empowered by the revelation, and he contested a false manifestation during a meeting in Amherst, Ohio.

Reflecting on his experience as a witness to this early wave of spiritual enthusiasm, Levi Hancock said he felt ashamed he had believed it "like a fool." He gratefully embraced the new revelation and was a faithful member of the Church for the rest of his life.

Joseph Smith's history summarizes the events of these tumultuous weeks: "Some strange notions and false spirits had crept in among them. With a little caution, and some wisdom, I soon assisted the brethren and sisters to overcome them. . . . The false spirits were easily discerned and rejected by the light of revelation."[14]

1. Unless otherwise noted, quotes in this article are taken from Levi Hancock autobiography (1803–1836), unpublished typescript, L. Tom Perry Special Collections, Harold B. Lee Library, Brigham Young University, Provo, Utah.

2. See Mark Lyman Staker, *Hearken, O Ye People: The Historical Setting of Joseph Smith's Ohio Revelations* (Salt Lake City: Greg Kofford Books, 2009), 71–86.

3. "John Whitmer, History, 1831–circa 1847," 26, josephsmithpapers.org.

4. "Mormonism," *Telegraph* [Painesville, Ohio], Feb. 15, 1831.

5. John Corrill, "Brief History," Manuscript, circa 1838–1839, 23, josephsmithpapers.org.

6. "John Whitmer, History, 1831–circa 1847," 10.

7. "Letter to Hyrum Smith, 3–4 March 1831," 1, josephsmithpapers.org. The author is indebted to Michael Hubbard Mackay and Gerrit J. Dirkmaat for this interpretation of Joseph Smith's letter.

8. "Revelation, circa 8 March 1831–A [D&C 46]," in Revelation Book 1, 76–78, josephsmithpapers.org; see also Doctrine and Covenants 46:2, 7–8, 27.

9. *The Autobiography of Parley Parker Pratt; One of the Twelve Apostles of The Church of Jesus Christ of Latter-day Saints,* ed. Parley P. Pratt Jr. (Chicago: Law, King, and Law, 1888), 65.

10. *The Autobiography of Parley Parker Pratt,* 65–66.

11. "Revelation, 9 May 1831 [D&C 50]," in Revelation Book 1, 82, josephsmithpapers.org.

12. "Revelation, 9 May 1831 [D&C 50]," in Revelation Book 1, 84.

13. *The Autobiography of Parley Parker Pratt,* 70.

14. Joseph Smith, "History, 1838–1856, volume A-1 [23 December 1805–30 August 1834]," 93, josephsmithpapers.org.

The Book of John Whitmer

D&C 47, 69

Brian Reeves

John Whitmer was born in Pennsylvania in 1802. His family later moved to New York, eventually settling "with other German families near Fayette," a sparsely populated township about 30 miles southeast of Palmyra.[1] Through his family's friendship with Oliver Cowdery, John Whitmer learned about Joseph Smith and his in-progress translation of an ancient scriptural record, the Book of Mormon.[2]

The Whitmers became very interested in Joseph's work, and in June 1829 arrangements were made for the young prophet and his scribe Oliver Cowdery to stay at the Whitmer home as they finished the translation. John's brother David traveled to Harmony, Pennsylvania, to help move Joseph and Oliver to the Whitmer home in Fayette, New York. David also proffered "the assistence of one of his brothers," John, as a scribe. Joseph accepted and resided with the Whitmers "until the translation was finished." As promised, John assisted "very much in writing during the remainder of the work."[3]

Soon after Joseph arrived in Fayette, 26-year-old John Whitmer was baptized in Seneca Lake. He became one of the Eight Witnesses, who saw the Book of Mormon plates, and he later declared, "I handled those plates; there were fine engravings on both sides."[4]

When the Church was organized at the Whitmer home on April 6, 1830, the Lord instructed Joseph Smith, "There Shall a Record be kept among you."[5] To comply with this commandment, Oliver Cowdery was appointed the first Church historian.[6]

Joseph's revelations formed a significant part of the historical record. John Whitmer wrote that during the early days of the Church, "the Lord blessed his disciples greatly, and he gave Revelation after Revelation, which contained doctrine, instructions, and prophecies."[7] In July 1830, the Prophet "began to arrange and copy the revelations that he had received thus far," with Whitmer acting as scribe.[8]

John Whitmer as Historian and Recorder

In the fall of 1830, Oliver Cowdery embarked on a mission to the Lamanites. In his stead, John Whitmer was appointed "by the voice of the Elders to keep the Church record," Whitmer wrote. "Joseph Smith Jr. said unto me you must also keep the Church history."[9]

Whitmer was comfortable transcribing Joseph Smith's revelations but hesitant to embrace the unfamiliar role of historian. He told Joseph, "I would rather not do it," but he agreed to accept the assignment if the Lord willed it—in which case, Whitmer continued, "I desire that he would manifest it through Joseph the Seer."[10]

In the resulting revelation (now Doctrine and Covenants 47), dated March 8, 1831, the Lord affirmed Whitmer's twofold assignment to "write & keep a regula[r] history & assist my servent Joseph in Transcribing all things which shall be given him."[11] Responding to Whitmer's insecurity about his writing skills, the Lord promised, "It shall be given thee by th[e] comforter to write these things."[12] Three months later, Whitmer began his history, "The Book of John Whitmer."[13]

A few months after that, Church leaders took steps to publish Joseph Smith's revelations, a hymnal, a Church newspaper, and other works.[14] A November 1831 revelation (now Doctrine and Covenants 69) directed Oliver Cowdery and John Whitmer to carry the manuscript revelations to Independence, Missouri, to have them published where W. W. Phelps had set up a printing press.[15] The revelation further instructed that missionaries who were "abroad in the Earth should send forth their accounts to the Land of Zion" and enlarged Whitmer's duties as Church historian, telling him to "travel many times from place to place & from Church to Church that he may the more easily obtain knowledge Preaching & expounding writing cop[y]ing & selecting & obtain[in]g all things which shall be for the good of the Church & for the rising generations which shall grow up on the Land of Zion."[16]

In July 1832, Joseph Smith encouraged Whitmer to "remember the commandment to him to keep a history of the church & the gathering."[17] Later that year, the Prophet received another revelation that expanded John Whitmer's historical charge: "It is the duty of the lord['s] clerk whom he has appointed to keep a hystory and a general church reccord of all things that transpire in Zion . . . and also [the] manner of life and the faith and works and also of all the apostates."[18]

Whitmer thus kept his record of the young Church for the duration of his membership, which ended in 1838. According to one group of historians, the history John Whitmer created "illuminates many important concerns of the early church, including property issues, church discipline," the New Jerusalem, "the treatment of dissidents, and the establishment of a priesthood leadership hierarchy. . . . Whitmer's work is particularly significant for the revelations, petitions, and letters that form a large part of his history."[19]

What Became of John Whitmer and His History?

In 1834, Joseph Smith appointed a presidency for the Church in Missouri, with John Whitmer and W. W. Phelps serving as counselors to David Whitmer. John Whitmer and Phelps were later accused of financial wrongdoing in connection with their positions there and were subsequently excommunicated from the Church in March 1838.

Whitmer wrote in his history: "Some temeral movements, have not proved satisfactory to all parties has also terminated in the expulsion of [many] members, among whom is W. W. Phelps and myself.

"Therefore I close the history of the church of Latter Day Saints, Hoping that I may be forgiven of my faults, and my sins be bloted out and in the last day be savd in the kingdom of God notwithstanding my presnt situation."[20]

Joseph Smith arrived in Far West just days after the excommunications. A newly appointed clerk called on Whitmer to obtain his history, but Whitmer refused to surrender the document.[21] He temporarily left Far West during the Mormon difficulties of 1838–39, but he returned a short time later and resided there for the rest of his life.[22]

After John Whitmer's death in 1878, his history passed to his brother David,[23] and in 1903 the Reorganized Church of Jesus Christ of Latter Day Saints obtained the history from a David Whitmer descendant. Eventually, in 1974, the LDS Church obtained a microfilmed copy of the manuscript in an exchange of historical materials with the RLDS Church.[24] In 2012, John Whitmer's history was published as part of the LDS Church's Joseph Smith Papers project.[25]

1. Scott C. Esplin, "'A History of All the Important Things' (D&C 69:3): John Whitmer's Record of Church History," in *Preserving the History of the Latter-day Saints,* ed. Richard E. Turley Jr. and Steven C. Harper (Provo, Utah: Religious Studies Center, Brigham Young University, 2010), 51.

2. Stanley R. Gunn, *Oliver Cowdery, Second Elder and Scribe* (Salt Lake City: Bookcraft, 1962), 33.

3. "History of Joseph Smith," *Times and Seasons,* vol. 3, no. 20 (Aug. 15, 1842), 884–85.

4. B. H. Roberts, *A Comprehensive History of the Church,* 3:307–8.

5. "Revelation, 6 April 1830 [D&C 21]," in Revelation Book 1, 28, josephsmithpapers.org; see also Doctrine and Covenants 21:1.

6. Howard C. Searle, "Historians, Church," in *Encyclopedia of Mormonism,* ed. Daniel H. Ludlow, 5 vols. (New York: Macmillan, 1992), 2:589.

7. "John Whitmer, History, 1831–circa 1847," 22, josephsmithpapers.org.

8. Lyndon W. Cook, *The Revelations of the Prophet Joseph Smith: A Historical and Biographical Commentary of the Doctrine and Covenants* (Salt Lake City: Deseret Book, 1985), 37–38.

9. "John Whitmer, History, 1831–circa 1847," 24.

10. "John Whitmer, History, 1831–circa 1847," 24.

11. "Revelation, circa 8 March 1831–B [D&C 47]," in Revelation Book 1, 79, josephsmithpapers.org; see also Doctrine and Covenants 47:1.

12. "Revelation, circa 8 March 1831–B [D&C 47]," in Revelation Book 1, 80; see also Doctrine and Covenants 47:4.

13. "John Whitmer, History, 1831–circa 1847," 25.

14. Lyndon W. Cook, "Literary Firm," in Arnold K. Garr, Donald Q. Cannon, and Richard O. Cowan, eds., *Encyclopedia of Latter-day Saint History* (Salt Lake City: Deseret Book, 2000), 670.

15. Cook, *The Revelations of the Prophet Joseph Smith,* 113.

16. "Revelation, 11 November 1831–A [D&C 69]," in Revelation Book 1, 122, josephsmithpapers.org; see also Doctrine and Covenants 69:5, 7–8. The revelations that Cowdery and Whitmer took to Independence were being typeset by William W. Phelps as the Book of Commandments when, on July 20, 1833, a mob destroyed the printing press. By that time Phelps had printed 160 pages containing 65 revelations.

17. Historical Introduction to "John Whitmer, History, 1831–circa 1847."

18. "Letter to William W. Phelps, 27 November 1832," in Letterbook 1, 1, josephsmithpapers.org; see also Doctrine and Covenants 85:1–2.

19. Historical Introduction to "John Whitmer, History, 1831–circa 1847."

20. "John Whitmer, History, 1831–circa 1847," 85. Whitmer subsequently lined through much of this text, beginning with "among whom is W. W. Phelps and myself."

21. See Roberts, *A Comprehensive History of the Church,* 3:8–9, 13–15.

22. See Richard L. Anderson, *Investigating the Book of Mormon Witnesses* (Salt Lake City: Deseret Book, 1981), 131.

23. See Esplin, "'A History of All the Important Things' (D&C 69:3)," 57.

24. See Esplin, "'A History of All the Important Things' (D&C 69:3)," 73.

25. See "John Whitmer, History, 1831–circa 1847," josephsmithpapers.org. In 1995, Bruce N. Westergren published an annotated transcription of John Whitmer's history: *From Historian to Dissident: The Book of John Whitmer,* ed. Bruce N. Westergren (Salt Lake City: Signature Books, 1995).

Leman Copley and the Shakers
D&C 49
Matthew McBride

In the spring of 1831, a prosperous farmer named Leman Copley joined the fledgling Church of Christ (as the Church was then known). His farm in Thompson, Ohio, was only a few miles northeast of the village of Kirtland, which had recently been established as the Church's new headquarters.

Copley had been a member of the United Society of Believers in Christ's Second Appearance for many years before his conversion. Members of this sect were commonly known as Shakers because their worship included a form of ecstatic dancing. The many similarities between Shaker and Mormon doctrines no doubt appealed to Copley: The two faiths shared a belief in a general apostasy, modern prophecy, the agency of man, and the ideal of a communal life. They differed dramatically, however, on other important points.

Shakers did not consider baptism—or any other ordinance—essential for salvation. They believed Jesus Christ had already made His Second Coming in the form of Mother Ann Lee (1736–84), an early Shaker leader. Some practiced vegetarianism. Mormons and Shakers also diverged in their views of marriage and sexual relations; devout Believers (as Shakers called themselves) insisted upon absolute celibacy, which they referred to as "taking up the cross."

These two religious groups had first crossed paths during the previous winter, when a group of Mormon missionaries, which included Oliver Cowdery and Parley P. Pratt, stopped briefly in the Shaker settlement of North Union, Ohio, en route to Missouri. The North Union community was situated a mere 15 miles southwest of Kirtland.

Cowdery introduced himself to the Shaker leader, Ashbel Kitchell, as "an assistant in the translation of the golden Bible" and as one of three who had witnessed an angel bear testimony of its truthfulness. Kitchell allowed Cowdery to share his message at one of the community's gatherings.[1]

After two nights in North Union, Cowdery and his companions went on their way, but not before leaving seven copies of the Book of Mormon with Kitchell. The missionaries had complete confidence "in the virtue of their Books, that whoever would read them, would feel thoroughly convinced of the truth of what they contained." Following this early encounter, the Shakers and Mormons in Ohio remained on good terms, engaging in "trade and other acts of good neighborship," according to Kitchell. Their friendly interchange, however, was about to be put to the test.

A Revelation for the Shakers

Before joining the Church, Leman Copley associated with the North Union Shakers, perhaps attending their meetings, though he did not immerse himself fully in their austere communal life. The fact that he lived 35 miles from the community and remained married gives some indication of his level of commitment to Shaker principles. While clearly attracted to some of their teachings and perhaps their mode of worship, he was not a full participant. In fact, Kitchell chided Copley for rejecting a life of celibacy and for having "taken up with Mormonism as the easier plan."

Like all early Mormon converts, Copley brought with him traditions and attitudes shaped by his previous religious experience. Joseph Smith spoke to Copley shortly after his conversion and noted that he was "apparently honest hearted, but still retaining ideas that the Shakers were right in some particulars of their faith."[2] John Whitmer further noted that Copley "was anxious that some of the elders should go to his former brethren and preach the gospel." He even "teased to be ordained to preach himself."[3]

Copley decided to visit Joseph Smith—who was then living at the home of his friend Isaac Morley near Kirtland—on Saturday, May 7, 1831.[4] Though we have no record of their conversation, Copley likely hoped for clarification about certain Shaker beliefs and perhaps suggested the idea of a mission to North Union. As a result of this meeting, Joseph received the revelation now canonized as Doctrine and Covenants 49. This revelation authoritatively addressed the doctrinal differences between the two faiths. It began by rebuking the Shakers: "They desire to know the truth in Part," it read, "but not all for they are not right before me & must needs repent."

Reaffirming that baptism is indispensible, the revelation proceeded to denounce several of the Shakers' dearly held beliefs, declaring that marriage is ordained of God, that animals were given to man for food and clothing, and that "the son of man cometh not in the form of a woman neither of a man traveling on the earth."[5]

In the revelation, the Lord called Copley—along with Sidney Rigdon and Parley P. Pratt—to preach the gospel to his brothers and sisters at North Union. While all three of them were acquainted with Shaker principles, Copley was much less seasoned as a preacher and missionary than either of his companions. His apparent interest in preaching to his Shaker friends meant he would be calling to repentance the very people who scorned him for what they felt was his lack of religious commitment. Perhaps he hoped to demonstrate the true substance of his new faith. In any event, Copley agreed to comply faithfully with the revelation's commandment to "reason with" the Shakers.[6]

The Mission to North Union

So, with revelation in hand, Rigdon and Copley set out for North Union almost immediately. They arrived in North Union later that day and were received cordially by Kitchell and his associates. They spent the evening together, debating the relative merits of their religions, each likely feeling they had gotten the best of the debate.

The next morning, Kitchell proposed to Rigdon and Copley that neither side should "force their doctrine on the other at this time."

Rigdon had planned to read the revelation to the Shakers at their Sabbath service that day but decided to keep his peace for the moment and "subject himself to the order of the place."

Just before the meeting began, Parley P. Pratt arrived at North Union on horseback. Upon hearing of Rigdon's submissive response to Kitchell's proposal, the fiery Pratt insisted they "pay no attention to [him], for they had come with the authority of the Lord Jesus Christ, and the people must hear it."

The missionaries sat in silence until the meeting was complete. As the people stood to leave, Rigdon "arose and stated that he had a message from the Lord Jesus Christ to this people; could he have the privilege of delivering it?" With Kitchell's permission, he read the revelation in its entirety and asked if they might be allowed to continue preaching as the revelation dictated.

Kitchell, keeping his indignation in check, responded that he did not accept the message and "would release them & their Christ from any further burden about us, and take all the responsibility on myself." Rigdon countered, "This you cannot do; I wish to hear the people speak." But when Kitchell allowed others present to speak their minds, they too affirmed "that they were fully satisfied with what they had."

Rigdon stoically set the revelation aside, resigned that their mission had been unfruitful. Pratt, on the other hand, was not finished so easily. He arose, Kitchell recounted, and shook the dust from his coattail "as a testimony against us, that we had rejected the word of the Lord Jesus." In so doing, Pratt was following Jesus's injunction to His disciples in the Gospels.

But Kitchell would not tolerate it. His forbearance at its limit, the Shaker leader denounced Pratt in full sight of his congregation: "You filthy Beast, dare you presume to come in here, and try to imitate a man of God by shaking your filthy tail; confess your sins and purge your soul from your lusts, and your other abominations before you ever presume to do the like again."

Kitchell then turned his wrath to Copley, who had begun weeping, and gave this stinging rebuke: "You hypocrite, you knew better;— you knew where the living work of God was; but for the sake of indulgence, you could consent to deceive yourself."

The Aftermath

Kitchell promptly dismissed the congregation. The frustrated Pratt mounted his horse and returned to Kirtland immediately. He later summed up their visit: "We fulfilled this mission, as we were commanded, in a settlement of this strange people, near Cleveland, Ohio; but they utterly refused to hear or obey the gospel."[7] Following this incident, contact between the Church and the Shakers was rare and usually tense.

Rigdon stayed for supper before returning to Kirtland that evening, leaving a copy of the revelation with Kitchell. Copley, meanwhile, remained at North Union that night and made for his farm the next day, his hopes of converting some of his former brethren sadly dashed. The encounter had shaken him such that upon his return to Thompson, he backed out of an agreement he had made to permit Church members from Colesville, New York, to live on his farm.

The vacillating Copley continued to teeter in his devotion to the restored Church for many years after his mission to the Shakers. He finally broke company with the Church permanently around 1838 and remained in Ohio the rest of his life.

1. Lawrence R. Flake, "A Shaker View of a Mormon Mission," *BYU Studies,* vol. 20, no. 1 (Fall 1979), 95. Unless otherwise cited, the quotations in this narrative are found in an excerpt from Ashbel Kitchell's diary, as transcribed in Lawrence R. Flake's article.

2. Joseph Smith, "History, 1838–1856, volume A-1 [23 December 1805–30 August 1834]," 112, josephsmithpapers.org.

3. "John Whitmer, History, 1831–circa 1847," 26, josephsmithpapers.org.

4. This date for the revelation is based on research by Gerrit Dirkmaat for the volume Michael Hubbard MacKay, Gerrit J. Dirkmaat, Grant Underwood, Robert J. Woodford, and William G. Hartley, eds., *Documents, Volume 1: July 1828–June 1831,* vol. 1 of the Documents series of *The Joseph Smith Papers,* ed. Dean C. Jessee, Ronald K. Esplin, Richard Lyman Bushman, and Matthew J. Grow (Salt Lake City: Church Historian's Press, 2013).

5. "Revelation, 7 May 1831 [D&C 49]," in Revelation Book 1, 80–81, josephsmithpapers.org; see also Doctrine and Covenants 49:2, 15, 19, 22.

6. "Revelation, 7 May 1831 [D&C 49]," 80, josephsmithpapers.org; see also Doctrine and Covenants 49:4.

7. *The Autobiography of Parley Parker Pratt; One of the Twelve Apostles of The Church of Jesus Christ of Latter-Day Saints,* ed. Parley P. Pratt Jr. (Chicago: Law, King, and Law, 1888), 65.

The Center Place

D&C 52, 57, 58

Jed Woodworth

Across the long span of Western history, Christians of all kinds have longed for a new heaven and a new earth. John the Revelator's breathtaking vision of "the holy city, new Jerusalem, coming down from God out of heaven," preparing the way for the return of Jesus Christ as Lord and King, has stirred the hopes and the aspirations of many.[1] What was the New Jerusalem? Was it, as St. Augustine contended, a metaphor for the blessed "immortality and eternity of the saints"?[2] Or was it something more literal, as the 17th-century American Puritans believed when they imagined their colony as a source of religious regeneration, a "New" England?[3]

The restored Church of Jesus Christ was still in its infancy—not yet six months old—when Latter-day Saints began to envision the New Jerusalem in their own way.[4] Joseph Smith's early revelations described this entity not as a metaphor or a colony. It was, rather, a city the Saints must build. The New Jerusalem, also called Zion, was to be a refuge, a place of peace, a "center place."[5]

Two questions came to mind immediately for the Saints. The first was where the Lord would have the New Jerusalem built. The second was who would be welcome in the city. A revelation given to Joseph Smith in August 1830 offered preliminary answers, directing Oliver Cowdery, Parley P. Pratt, and several others to head west while preaching along the way. "You shall go unto the Lamanites," the Lord commanded, referring to the name the early Saints used for the American Indians, "and preach my gospel unto them . . . [and] cause my church to be established among them."[6] The site for the city, the revelations said, would be "among the Lamanites."[7]

Cowdery's group preached in and around Kirtland, Ohio, converting many there. They then traveled hundreds of miles south and west, ending up at the far western boundary of the United States, on the border between the state of Missouri and Indian Territory. They preached to several tribes but were soon ordered off the territory by federal agents charged with managing relations between whites and Indians.[8] This was discouraging news, but Joseph Smith was undaunted, backed as he was by the voice of God. In a revelation now known as Doctrine and Covenants 52, given in June 1831, the Lord commanded Joseph Smith to travel to Missouri, "the land which I will consecrate unto my people."[9] There the site for the city of Zion would be made known.

As He had done with the land of Canaan millennia before, God had identified the land as sacred before His covenant people settled there, and like Canaan before it, Missouri was not empty when the covenant people arrived.[10] The site where the Saints had been called to gather had a long and complicated history of occupancy.

Contested Boundaries

Once he arrived in Missouri, Joseph Smith learned through revelation that the site for the city of Zion was on land situated below a bend in the Missouri River, about 10 miles east of the Missouri-Indian territory line (currently the Missouri-Kansas border). For generations this area of western Missouri was home to Central Siouan tribes. As late as the 1600s, Indians from this language group migrated south from the Ohio River Valley, down the Mississippi River, and westward across the lower Missouri, settling on the rich and fertile bluffs between the woodlands on the east and the Great Plains on the west.[11]

Following a century of turbulence in which European diseases ravaged native peoples, the Central Siouan peoples reorganized into different tribes. The *Wah-haz-he* ("the upstream people")—which the French abbreviated to Osage—emerged as the main residents of the lower Missouri River. Described as a "tall, robust, broad shouldered people resembling giants," the Osage built permanent settlements between the Osage River in north central Missouri and the Missouri River near present-day Independence.[12] Their lodges, located on high bluffs overlooking the countryside, were constructed by bending saplings over ridgeposts to form the arch of a roof and sometimes measured 100 feet in length. This hunter-gatherer society with a complex sociopolitical structure and an elaborate kinship organization dominated the lower Missouri River region for centuries.[13]

The area near Independence, Missouri, was not the "center place" of Osage society, as it became for the Latter-day Saints. As late as 1800, the Osage controlled perhaps one-half of modern-day Missouri, Oklahoma, Arkansas, and Kansas. The core of their empire was in south central Missouri, not the western border of the state.[14]

Other groups rivaled the Osage for the land the Mormons would later call New Jerusalem. The vast size of the North American wilderness fueled grandiose dreams of empire on the part of several European nations. The Spanish staked their claim on the entire interior of North America in 1539, and not to be outdone, the French claimed in 1682 all of North America between the Appalachian Mountains on the east and the Rocky Mountains on the west. These claims took little account of Indian tribes like the Osage, paying scant attention to the remote lands along the Missouri River near Independence.[15] Europe's great interest was on the margins of their empires, in the places with lucrative industry and easy shipping access—along the Saint Lawrence River, in what would become Canada, and on the islands of the Caribbean.

The French called the massive continental tract they staked for themselves Louisiana, after the French king. The land eventually passed into Spanish possession and then back to the French, who sold it to the United States in the Louisiana Purchase of 1803. With that purchase came the future site for the city of Zion.

The Louisiana Purchase brought new settlers as U.S. citizens moved into Missouri, which became a state in 1821.[16] The same forms of government found in other states were imported to Missouri.

Citizens along the western border petitioned the Missouri legislature for county organization, and in 1827, the legislature created Jackson County. The newly settled town of Independence, located just south of the Missouri River along a trade road called the Santa Fe Trail, became the county seat.

Doctrine and Covenants 57, given soon after Joseph Smith arrived in western Missouri, oriented the Saints within this sociopolitical space. The "center place" for Zion, the revelation said, would be located at "the place which is now called Independence," which at the time had no more than a few hundred residents.[17] White settlers at this time often squatted on land, imagining it unpossessed before later registering their claim in the county courthouse. The revelation mentioned this courthouse—a temple, the revelation said, should be built to the west of it. At the time the revelation was given, most of the land had already been claimed by settlers, requiring the Saints to negotiate with the land's legal possessors. The revelation implied that the Latter-day Saints would not contend for the holy land by force as the Israelites had done in Canaan millennia before. "It is wisdom that the land should be purchased by the saints," the Lord said.[18]

Sacred Peoples

For generations, a small number of Europeans—mainly Spanish and French traders—lived among the Indians along the Missouri River, intermarried, and entered into commerce with them.[19] But as white families pushed westward, settling in lands then occupied by Indians, they overwhelmingly rejected these cultural exchanges. Whites demanded that all Indian tribes be removed from the state. Between 1824 and 1830, tribes who had lived within Missouri's borders for centuries ceded virtually all of their territory. The mighty Osage sold their lands in 1825 and migrated further west to Kansas and Oklahoma.[20] By the time the Latter-day Saints arrived in Jackson County in 1831, Indians had vacated their settlements and evacuated beyond a newly established line dividing Indian and white territories.

Doctrine and Covenants 57 observed the existence of this settlement line without endorsing it. The revelation noted that Zion should be built along "the line running directly between Jew and Gentile," or the line separating the state of Missouri from Indian Territory to the west.[21] The revelation resisted the usual categories, however, primarily through its curious use of the terms *Jew* and *Gentile*. The standard terms then used by Americans—*white* and *Indian* or *white* and *red*—suggested a racial and cultural divide. The two groups were worlds apart, and white people often deployed the terminology to emphasize this incompatibility.[22]

The categories of Jew and Gentile, however, indicated a distinction between groups but not an incompatibility between them. According to the Book of Mormon, both Jew and Gentile had a vital role in God's unfolding plan. God invited them to work together. The gospel in ancient times would go from the Jews, God's ancient covenant people, unto the Gentiles, who would be grafted into the covenant. In the latter days the relationship would be reversed—the gospel would proceed from the Gentiles unto the Jews, who would come to recognize Jesus as the Messiah.[23] Doctrine and Covenants 57 echoes this covenantal structure by designating Indians as Jews, in this way recognizing the group as part of God's covenant people.[24] The Indians were of the house of Israel, chosen, beloved, and remembered by God.[25]

At the time when Indian removal—the separation of one race from another—had become a national policy of the U.S. government, Joseph Smith's revelations moved in another direction.[26] Rather than marginalizing Indians, pushing them to the outskirts of civilization, the revelations brought Zion to them, putting God's holy city in their midst. Zion was to be found between Jew and Gentile, between the races.[27] In this arrangement, people of multiple races could play an essential role in God's work. People on every compass point of the center, if they were willing, could become "the pure in heart" and dwell in Zion in safety and peace.[28]

Doctrine and Covenants 58, given while Joseph Smith was still in Missouri, conveyed the breadth of this vision. The revelation said nothing about Indians and whites. Not even Jews and Gentiles were mentioned this time. Instead, the revelation spoke of "the inhabitants of the earth," putting all of God's children together.[29] Zion, the revelation explained, was a place where "all nations shall be invited."[30]

The word *nations* would have resonated with readers in the 1830s, for it was the word both Indians and whites used to describe the largest unit of their political organization. The revelation went on to speak of Zion including "the rich and the learned, the wise and the noble"—people with political and social power. But it was also to include people who had traditionally lacked such power, those who had been traditionally forgotten and marginalized: "the poor, the lame, and the blind, and the deaf."[31] Ultimately, all of God's children were to have a seat at the same table. Bound in covenant relation, all were to share in God's sacred space.

Conclusion

Within two years of these Jackson County revelations, Zion was in flames, its inhabitants on the run from persecutors. The Saints retreated from Jackson County, but not from the task of creating Zion along the line between Jew and Gentile, first in Nauvoo and then, later, in the deserts of the Great Basin. Wherever the Saints settled, they invited people everywhere to join with them.[32] Even today the vision of a Zion society where "all nations shall be invited" to live in refuge and peace inspires Latter-day Saints. The aspiration, promise, and hope of the early Missouri revelations live on.

1. Revelation 21:2–5, 7.

2. For this and other conceptions, see David Lyle Jeffrey, ed., *A Dictionary of Biblical Tradition in English Literature* (Grand Rapids, MI: William B. Eerdmans, 1992), "New Jerusalem," 546–48.

3. John Winthrop, "Model of Christian Charity" [1630], *Collections of the Massachusetts Historical Society,* vol. 7 (1838), 47; spelling modernized; Francis J. Bremer, *Building a New Jerusalem: John Davenport, a Puritan in Three Worlds* (New Haven, CT: Yale University Press, 2012), 174–79.

4. The New Jerusalem was mentioned in the Book of Mormon, and revelations began talking about a specific location as early as February 1831 (see 3 Nephi 21:23–24; Ether 13:3–6; Doctrine and Covenants 42:35, 62).

5. Doctrine and Covenants 45:66–71; 57:3.

6. Doctrine and Covenants 28:8; see also Ronald E. Romig, "The Lamanite Mission," *John Whitmer Historical Association Journal,* vol. 14 (1994), 25–33.

7. "Revelation, September 1830–B [D&C 28]," in Revelation Book 1, 41, josephsmithpapers.org. The passage was later revised to read "on the borders by the Lamanites" (see Book of Commandments [1833] 30:9 [Doctrine and Covenants 28:9]).

8. These tribes included the Shawnee and the Delaware, who had been displaced from the east. See *Documents, Volume 1: July 1828–June 1831,* vol. 1 of the Documents series of *The Joseph Smith Papers,* ed. Dean C. Jessee, Ronald K. Esplin, and Richard Lyman Bushman (Salt Lake City: Church Historian's Press, 2013), 288–94.

9. Doctrine and Covenants 52:2–3.

10. Numbers 33:53; 34:2.

11. Tanis C. Thorne, *The Many Hands of My Relations: French and Indians on the Lower Missouri* (Columbia: University of Missouri Press, 1996), 13–14, 16–17, 20; Louis F. Burns, *A History of the Osage People* (Tuscaloosa: University of Alabama Press, 2004), 3, 22.

12. William E. Parrish, Charles T. Jones, and Lawrence O. Christensen, *Missouri: The Heart of the Nation,* 3rd ed. (Wheeling, IL: Harlan Davidson, 2004), 13.

13. Willard H. Rollings, *The Osage: An Ethnohistorical Study of Hegemony on the Prairie-Plains* (Columbia: University of Missouri Press, 1992), 23–26, 45–66; Gilbert C. Din and A. P. Nasatir, *The Imperial Osages: Spanish-Indian Diplomacy in the Mississippi Valley* (Norman: University of Oklahoma Press, 1983), 11–14.

14. Burns, *History of the Osage People,* 25–28, 30, 46.

15. The Independence area was neither named nor noticed on 18th-century maps. See Din and Nasatir, *The Imperial Osages,* 40–41, 64, 288–89, 338–39.

16. The name *Missouri* dates to the 1670s, when the French missionary Jacques Marquette sketched a map with the name *Ou-Missouri* near the river that bears its name, his transliteration of the tribe who lived along the river. The Osage generally took the land to the south of the river, the Missouri the lands to the north.

17. Doctrine and Covenants 57:3.

18. Doctrine and Covenants 57:4. The courthouse was the highest point in the area. By locating the temple nearby, the revelation implicitly compared the temple of New Jerusalem to the temple of Jerusalem, which was also located on a high point. Mark Roscoe Ashurst-McGee, "Zion Rising: Joseph Smith's Early Social and Political Thought" (PhD diss., Arizona State University, 2008), 233.

19. Thorne, *Many Hands,* 76–86, 96–97, 135–76.

20. These tribes included, besides the Osage, the Missouri, Sac, Fox, Ioway, Delaware, and Shawnee, among others. The Missouri did not cede the last of their lands in the state until 1854. See Billy J. McMahon, "'Humane and Considerate Attention': Indian Removal from Missouri, 1803–1838" (master's thesis, Northwest Missouri State University, 2013), 7–8, 75–83; John P. Bowes, *Exiles and Pioneers: Eastern Indians in the Trans-Mississippi West* (New York: Cambridge University Press, 2007); Charles J. Kappler, comp., *Indian Affairs: Laws and Treaties* (Washington, D.C.: Government Printing Office, 1904), 217–21.

21. Doctrine and Covenants 57:4.

22. See, for example, Nancy Shoemaker, *A Strange Likeness: Becoming Red and White in Eighteenth-Century North America* (New York: Oxford University Press, 2004).

23. 1 Nephi 15:13–17; 22:8–9; 3 Nephi 21:2–5.

24. The revelations elsewhere spoke of "the Jew, of whom the Lamanites are a remnant" (Doctrine and Covenants 19:27). On the multiple meanings of the term *Jew* in modern scripture, see Victor L. Ludlow, "Jew(s)," in Dennis L. Largey, ed., *Book of Mormon Reference Companion* (Salt Lake City: Deseret Book, 2003), 463–64; Thomas R. Valetta, "Jew(s)," in Dennis L. Largey and Larry E. Dahl, eds., *Doctrine and Covenants Reference Companion* (Salt Lake City: Deseret Book, 2012), 315–16.

25. At least as early as Thomas Thorowgood's *Jewes in America* (1650), English and American Puritans had postulated that the Indians were descended from the lost tribes of Israel. Such conceptual schemes tended to be short-lived. Joseph Smith's revelations overturned the standard 19th-century narrative about indigenous peoples as a "vanishing" people by giving "the remnant of Jacob" a saving role in the latter days of earth's history. See Jared Hickman, "The Book of Mormon as Amerindian Apocalypse," *American Literature,* vol. 86, no. 3 (Sept. 2014), 429–61; see also Andrew Delbanco, *The Puritan Ordeal* (Cambridge, MA: Harvard University Press, 1989), 110.

26. Under the Indian Removal Act, Indian removal became a federal policy in 1830. See Ronald N. Satz, *American Indian Policy in the Jacksonian Era* (Norman: University of Oklahoma Press, 2002).

27. Doctrine and Covenants 57:4.

28. Doctrine and Covenants 97:21.

29. Doctrine and Covenants 58:48.

30. Doctrine and Covenants 58:9.

31. Doctrine and Covenants 58:8, 10–11. The passage reinterpreted Jesus's parable of the marriage of the king's son (see Matthew 22:1–14) in a modern context.

32. Although the Latter-day Saints did not always live up to their ideals in their interactions with Indians, the unique role given to native peoples in the revelations often tempered the ways white Latter-day Saints treated Indians. See Ronald W. Walker, "Seeking the 'Remnant': The Native American During the Joseph Smith Period," *Journal of Mormon History,* vol. 19, no. 1 (1993), 1–33; "Peace and Violence among 19th-Century Latter-day Saints," Gospel Topics, topics.lds.org.

Ezra Booth and Isaac Morley

D&C 57, 58, 60, 61, 62, 63, 64, 71, 73

Matthew McBride

For early members of the Church, the summer of 1831 began with high expectations. An important conference was held during the first week of June in the schoolhouse on Isaac Morley's farm near Kirtland. The room was crowded, and many sat just outside the open windows, straining to hear. The summer breeze carried the fragrance of freshly harvested mint, planted by the acre in the nearby fields. Joseph Smith opened the conference with prayer.

At this gathering, the first ordinations to the "high priesthood" were performed.[1] Several of the elders experienced spiritual manifestations, including the casting out of evil spirits. Then, near the close of the four-day conference, Joseph Smith received a revelation that spoke to the dearest hopes of the faithful.

Ever since they had first read the Book of Mormon, believers had wondered how, where, and when the book's prophecies would be realized. When would the Lamanites—then believed to be the North American Indians—be converted and join Church members in building a New Jerusalem in the Americas? These early members knew the site for the city would be "among the Lamanites."[2] They had even dispatched Oliver Cowdery and three other missionaries to the far western reaches of the United States to preach to American Indians near Missouri.

Now, in this new revelation, the Lord declared that Missouri was indeed "the land which I will consecrate unto my People." Speaking of the New Jerusalem, He promised that He would "hasten the City in its time." The revelation also called Joseph Smith, Sidney Rigdon, and 13 other pairs of missionaries to travel two by two to Missouri, where the next conference was to be held. It also told them that if they were faithful, the Lord would reveal "the land of [their] inheritance."[3]

The pairs of missionaries departed for Missouri with high hopes. They believed the day of Jesus's return to earth was very near and that they were traveling to locate and build a temple city in which they would gather to receive the Lord when He came. Rumors rippled that Oliver Cowdery and his fellow missionaries were on the verge of converting many American Indians.[4] The missionaries anticipated that in Missouri "the objects of faith and hope, were to become the objects of knowledge and fruition."[5]

The Journey to Missouri

Isaac Morley and Ezra Booth were among the missionaries called. They had both attended the conference and had been ordained, and they were now designated to travel as companions.

Isaac Morley had been among the first converts to the Church in Ohio. At the time of his conversion, Morley; his wife, Lucy; his family; and several friends lived on his farm, sharing a communal lifestyle. They were trying the best they could to live as the early Christians mentioned in the book of Acts, who had "all things common" (Acts 4:32).

Ezra Booth had been a respected Methodist preacher in northeastern Ohio.[6] His conversion created a small stir among his friends and acquaintances, who lamented his joining the "Mormonites."[7] Booth had felt strongly prompted to join the new faith. "The impressions of my mind were deep and powerful," he recalled, "and my feelings were excited to a degree to which I had been a stranger."[8]

But by the time of his departure in June 1831, Booth had begun to doubt. The spiritual manifestations at the conference did not meet his expectations, and he was upset that Joseph Smith and Sidney Rigdon left for Missouri on a wagon, while he and Isaac were called to walk the entire distance in the summer heat, preaching along the way.

The journey was inconvenient for others as well. Joseph Smith departed just weeks after he and Emma lost twins shortly after birth. He left his grieving wife, who would have to care for herself and the newly adopted Murdock twins (whose mother, Julia, had died in late April and whose father, John, would also make the trip to Missouri).

When Ezra Booth finally arrived in Missouri, he felt deflated. He and others "expected to find a country abounding with the necessaries and comforts of life." Instead, he looked around and noted that "the prospect appeared somewhat gloomy."[9] Booth remembered Joseph Smith confidently asserting before the trip that the Church in Missouri would be large and growing, but when they arrived they found only seven new members.

Joseph Smith himself might have been disappointed initially when he arrived in Missouri. The area around Independence was mostly open prairie with a few scattered trees. Far from inspiring visions of a millennial capital, the frontier town itself was "a century behind the times."[10] For most of the elders, the reality on the ground in Missouri was a disappointment. But they would deal with that disappointment in different ways.

A Prayer for Guidance

Was this really the place and time to try to build up Zion? On July 20, anxious to understand God's timing and intentions, Joseph turned to the Lord. "When will the wilderness blossom as the rose?" he prayed. "When will Zion be built up in her glory, and where will thy Temple stand?"[11] These questions prompted a revelation—now Doctrine and Covenants 57—that finally designated the site for the city and temple.

A further revelation on August 1 (Doctrine and Covenants 58) instructed the missionaries to dedicate the land but hinted that Zion would be built up only "after much tribulation." The revelation chastised those who, like Ezra Booth, had murmured complaints. "They say in their hearts this is not the work of the Lord for his promises are not fulfilled." It warned that "their reward lurketh beneath & not from above."[12]

In spite of disappointment and the enormity of the city building project, Joseph was determined to make a start. Together with Sidney Rigdon and others, he set to work. They consecrated the land near Independence for a place of gathering, laid the first log for a house in Zion, and set the northeast cornerstone for a temple.

Some of the elders, like Reynolds Cahoon, saw exciting possibilities in these symbolic beginnings. "There my mortal eyes beheld grate and marvilous things," he wrote, "such as my eyes once never even contemplated of seeing in this world."[13] But Ezra Booth was unimpressed by the meager start. It was "a curiosity," he said, "but not worth going to Missouri to see."[14]

The Return to Ohio

Though a few of the missionaries had been chosen to remain in Missouri, the August 1 revelation commanded the rest of the missionaries to return to their homes, indicating that "the time has not yet come for many years for them to receive their inheritance in this land."[15]

Another revelation, now Doctrine and Covenants 60, instructed the returning missionaries to travel on the Missouri River east to St. Louis.[16] There Joseph and Sidney Rigdon would travel speedily to Cincinnati, Ohio, to preach, while the others were to travel "two by two & preach the word not in haste among the congregations of the wicked."[17]

They embarked in canoes for St. Louis on August 8. The Missouri River was notoriously difficult to navigate. Steamboat captains dreaded the sawyers, or fallen trees lurking in the river, that frequently wrecked their vessels. The elders would later tell Elizabeth Marsh that the river's roiling current "look[ed] mad as if it had been cursed."[18]

The journey was a contentious one for the elders. Exhaustion, heat, and the treacherous Missouri River frayed their nerves. On their third day on the water, some of the canoes nearly became entangled in the sawyers, which threatened to capsize the canoes, endangering the lives of those who could not swim.

After they made it safely to shore, they continued bickering. Though certainly capable of contention himself, Ezra Booth had little tolerance for it in others. He later observed sarcastically, "These are the leaders of the church, and the only church on earth the Lord beholds with approbation."[19]

Joseph Smith received another revelation the following morning on the riverbank (Doctrine and Covenants 61), in which the Lord warned them of danger upon the water but said, "It mattereth not unto me . . . whether they go by water or by land."[20]

Joseph proceeded on land the next day with a part of the group. They encountered his brother Hyrum and others who had been delayed and had yet to visit the site for Zion. A revelation (Doctrine and Covenants 62) admonished them, "Continue your Journey, assemble yourselves upon the land of Zion, & hold a meeting & rejoice together & offer a sacrament unto the most high."[21]

Ezra Booth, on the other hand, decided to get back as quickly as possible rather than preach by the way according to the earlier revelation. He and a few companions traveled the remainder of the journey to Ohio by boat and coach.

"Confound Your Enemies"

Shortly after his return to Ohio, Ezra Booth parted ways with the Church in a very public fashion. Because his experience did not match his expectations of how Zion should look or how Joseph Smith should behave, he first wavered and then abandoned his faith. Beginning that October, the *Ohio Star,* a newspaper located in Ravenna, Ohio, began publishing a series of letters Booth penned, heavily criticizing Joseph Smith and the Church.

By December his letters had even started to hinder missionary work, and Joseph Smith received two revelations in December 1831 and January 1832, now found in Doctrine and Covenants 71 and 73. They challenged Booth and other dissidents such as Symonds Ryder to "bring forth their strong reasons against the Lord." They also encouraged Joseph and Sidney Rigdon to preach actively: "Confound your enemies; Call upon them to meet you both in publick and in private."[22]

Though Sidney Rigdon challenged Booth and Ryder to public debate, they declined, perhaps aware of Rigdon's reputation as a fierce debater. Rigdon preached in Ravenna, Ohio, and in other locations, refuting Booth's claims. Although Booth's letters had a dampening effect on missionary work, that effect was short-lived.

Tragically, Booth's cynicism had driven a wedge not only between him and the restored Church but also between him and his earlier spiritual experiences. He ultimately "abandoned Christianity and became an agnostic."[23]

Isaac Morley's Test

While Ezra Booth's experiences in traveling to Missouri turned him away from the Church, Isaac Morley's ultimately drew him closer. During the trip, Morley evidently shared, at least to a degree, in Ezra Booth's cynicism. A revelation received on September 11 (Doctrine and Covenants 64) chastised both Booth and Morley: "They condemned for evil that thing in which there was no evil." Any second thoughts Morley may have had about his mission were short-lived. Unlike Ezra Booth, Isaac Morley had ceased his criticisms and changed his outlook. The revelation continued in the Lord's own voice: "I have forgiven my Servant Isaac."[24]

But the Lord had additional sacrifices in mind for Isaac Morley. He was asked to relinquish his large landholdings in Kirtland and return to Missouri with his family. In a revelation given shortly after Joseph Smith's return to Kirtland (Doctrine and Covenants 63), the Lord instructed Morley's brother-in-law Titus Billings to "dispose of" Morley's farm.[25] In the revelation given on September 11, the Lord explained that he commanded the farm be sold, "that my servant Isaac may not be tempted above that which he is able to bear."[26]

Isaac and Lucy Morley willingly made the sacrifice. In October 1831, Titus Billings sold much of Morley's farm. Morley took his family back to Independence, as he was commanded, and set to work once again to establish a foundation for the temple city. Having persevered through his doubts, he went on to serve as a bishop and a patriarch. He passed away in Utah in 1865.[27]

1. These ordinations to the "high priesthood" refer to what later became known as the office of high priest within the Melchizedek Priesthood.

2. "Revelation, September 1830–B [D&C 28]," in Revelation Book 1, 41, josephsmithpapers.org.

3. "Revelation, 6 June 1831 [D&C 52]," josephsmithpapers.org.

4. Ezra Booth mentions these rumors. See also "Letter from Oliver Cowdery, 8 April 1831," josephsmithpapers.org.

5. Ezra Booth, in Eber D. Howe, *Mormonism Unvailed* (Painesville, Ohio: By the author, 1834), 192. Ezra Booth's letters were originally

published between September and December 1831 in the *Ohio Star* (Ravenna) and were later reprinted in Howe's book.

6. "Booth, Ezra," josephsmithpapers.org.

7. This was a term commonly used to refer to early members of the Church. See Mark Lyman Staker, *Hearken, O Ye People: The Historical Setting of Joseph Smith's Ohio Revelations* (Salt Lake City: Greg Kofford Books, 2009), 73–74.

8. Ezra Booth, in Howe, *Mormonism Unvailed*, 176.

9. Ezra Booth, in Howe, *Mormonism Unvailed*, 199.

10. "History, 1838–1856, volume A-1 [23 December 1805–30 August 1834]," 127, josephsmithpapers.org.

11. "History, 1838–1856, volume A-1 [23 December 1805–30 August 1834]," 127; punctuation modernized.

12. "Revelation, 1 August 1831 [D&C 58]," josephsmithpapers.org.

13. Reynolds Cahoon diaries, 1831–32, images 10–11, Church History Library, Salt Lake City.

14. Ezra Booth, in Howe, *Mormonism Unvailed,* 194–95.

15. "Revelation, 1 August 1831 [D&C 58]."

16. The group likely consisted of Joseph Smith, Sidney Rigdon, Oliver Cowdery, Sidney Gilbert, W. W. Phelps, Reynolds Cahoon, Samuel Smith, Ezra Booth, Frederick G. Williams, Peter Whitmer Jr., and Joseph Coe.

17. "Revelation, 8 August 1831 [D&C 60]," josephsmithpapers.org.

18. Elizabeth Godkin Marsh letter to Lewis Abbott and Ann Abbott, Sept. 1831, Abbott Family Collection, Church History Library, Salt Lake City, as quoted in Matthew C. Godfrey, Mark Ashurst-McGee, Grant Underwood, Robert J. Woodford, and William G. Hartley, eds., *Documents, Volume 2: July 1831–January 1833*. Vol. 2 of the Documents series of *The Joseph Smith Papers,* ed. Dean C. Jessee, Ronald K. Esplin, Richard Lyman Bushman, and Matthew J. Grow (Salt Lake City, Church Historian's Press, 2013), 39.

19. Ezra Booth, in Howe, *Mormonism Unvailed,* 205.

20. "Revelation, 12 August 1831 [D&C 61]," josephsmithpapers.org.

21. "Revelation, 13 August 1831 [D&C 62]," josephsmithpapers.org; punctuation modernized.

22. "Revelation, 1 December 1831 [D&C 71]," josephsmithpapers.org; punctuation modernized.

23. J. N. Fradenburgh, *History of Erie Conference,* 2 vols. (Oil City, Pennsylvania: Derrick Publishing Company, 1907), 1:346.

24. "Revelation, 11 September 1831 [D&C 64]," josephsmithpapers.org.

25. "Revelation, 30 August 1831 [D&C 63]," josephsmithpapers.org.

26. "Revelation, 11 September 1831 [D&C 64]."

27. "Morley, Isaac," josephsmithpapers.org.

William McLellin's
Five Questions
D&C 1, 65, 66, 67, 68, 133

Matthew C. Godfrey

Within two months of his baptism on August 20, 1831, William E. McLellin, a former schoolteacher, became deeply involved in the restoration story. Following his conversion, McLellin was ordained an elder and preached the gospel with Hyrum Smith for a few weeks before traveling to Orange, Ohio, in late October for a general conference of the Church. McLellin noted in his journal that it was at this conference that he "first saw brother Joseph the Seer, also brothers Oliver [Cowdery], John [Whitmer] & Sidney [Rigdon] and a great many other Elders." At the conference, McLellin was ordained a high priest and heard Joseph teach about the powers and duties of that office. "This conference was attended by me with much spiritual edification & comfort to my heart," he declared.[1]

Doctrine and Covenants 66

After the conference, McLellin traveled to Kirtland and, in the course of his journey, "stepped off of a large log and strained my ankle very badly"—so much so that he petitioned Joseph to heal him. "He laid his hands on" the ankle, McLellin wrote in his journal, "and it was healed although It was swelled much and had pained me severely."[2] Just a few days later, McLellin decided to test Joseph Smith's calling. After going to Joseph's home in Hiram, Ohio, on October 29, McLellin "went before the Lord in secret, and on my knees asked him to reveal the answer to five questions through his Prophet." Without letting Joseph know what these five questions were, McLellin asked Joseph to provide to him God's will. The resulting revelation—now known as Doctrine and Covenants 66—answered McLellin's five questions to his "full and entire satisfaction." Even after he later fell away from the Church, McLellin stated that he still considered this revelation an evidence of Joseph's prophetic calling, "which," he said, "I cannot refute."[3]

Doctrine and Covenants 65

Just a day after this revelation was given, McLellin attended a Church meeting at John Johnson's home, where Joseph was living, and spoke to those in attendance for an hour and a half. "And it was not I but the spirit and power of God which was in me," he explained.[4] At the same meeting, Joseph received another revelation, now canonized as Doctrine and Covenants 65. The revelation proclaimed that "the keys of the kingdom of God" were again "committed unto man on the Earth" and that the gospel would "roll forth unto the ends of the Earth . . . untill it hath filled the whole Earth."[5]

Doctrine and Covenants 68

Two days later, on November 1, McLellin attended a conference of elders convened in Hiram, Ohio. Even though he had already received a revelation by Joseph providing the Lord's will for him, McLellin joined three other men at the conference—Orson Hyde, Luke Johnson, and Lyman Johnson—in petitioning Joseph to reveal "the mind & will of the Lord" pertaining to their responsibilities.[6] McLellin later recollected that when he was ordained a high priest, he "did not understand the duties of the office."[7] Perhaps that lack of understanding led in part to his request, for the revelation that followed—now Doctrine and Covenants 68—provided McLellin and his companions with information about the duties of high priests and elders to preach the gospel to all the earth.[8]

Doctrine and Covenants 1

Given that responsibility to preach, and given that the October 30 revelation stated that the gospel would "roll forth unto the ends of the earth,"[9] it was imperative that the revelations Joseph had already received should be published. McLellin later recollected that "hours were spent" at the conference discussing whether to publish the revelations before "it was finally decided to have them printed."[10] According to McLellin's recollections, he, Oliver Cowdery, and possibly Sidney Rigdon had been appointed to draft a preface for the Book of Commandments. Yet when the men presented the preface to the conference, its participants "picked it all to pieces" and "requested Joseph to enquire of the Lord about it." After bowing in prayer with the conference, Joseph, according to McLellin, "dictated by the Spirit the preface," doing so as he sat by "a window of the room in which the conference was sitting." McLellin remembered that "Joseph would deliver a few sentences and Sydney [Rigdon] would write them down, then read them aloud, and if correct, then Joseph would proceed and deliver more." According to McLellin, "by this process the preface"—now Doctrine and Covenants 1—"was given."[11]

Doctrine and Covenants 67

Joseph Smith also desired that the participants in the conference provide their testimony of the divine origin of the revelations. Some were reluctant to do so, leading to the dictation of another revelation, now Doctrine and Covenants 67. In this revelation, the Lord provided a way for the elders to determine whether the revelations were from God: "If there be any among you that shall make one like unto" the revelations, it stated, "then ye are Justified in saying that ye do not know that is true," but if no one could "make one like unto it ye are under condemnation if ye do not bear that it is true."[12]

According to one account, McLellin volunteered to try to write his own revelation but failed miserably.[13] Thereafter, McLellin, along with other conference attendees, affixed his name to a testimony, prepared by Joseph, stating that "god hath born record to our souls through the

Holy Ghost shed forth upon us that these commandments are given by inspiration of God & are profitable for all men & are verily true."[14]

Doctrine and Covenants 133

After the conference concluded, McLellin stayed with Joseph Smith for another two weeks, copying revelations and preparing for an upcoming mission with Samuel H. Smith to the eastern states.[15] He may even have been present on November 3 when Joseph received what would become known as the appendix to the Book of Commandments, which appears in the current Doctrine and Covenants as section 133.

Like Doctrine and Covenants 1, it warned the inhabitants of the earth of Christ's imminent return and the need to repent and accept God's direction as provided in the revelations He had given to Joseph. Bolstered by the word of God, McLellin departed for his mission with Samuel Smith on November 16 and preached the gospel for several weeks thereafter.[16]

McLellin would eventually be called as one of the initial members of the Quorum of the Twelve Apostles.[17] Unfortunately, he did not remain true to his testimony; he fell away from the Church and even participated in the persecution of the Saints in Missouri.[18] Yet for a few short weeks in the fall of 1831, he was an eyewitness to Joseph Smith's prophetic calling, witnessing several revelations, including ones addressed directly to him, and participating in the decision to publish the revelations as the Book of Commandments. McLellin, together with other participants in another November 1831 conference, declared that these revelations were "worth to the Church the riches of the whole Earth" and that they contained "the Keyes of the mysteries of the Kingdom, & the riches of Eternity to the church."[19]

1. *The Journals of William E. McLellin, 1831–1836,* ed. Jan Shipps and John W. Welch (Chicago: University of Illinois Press, 1994), 44–45; see also "Minutes, 25–26 October 1831," in Minute Book 2, 10, josephsmithpapers.org.

2. Shipps and Welch, *The Journals of William E. McLellin,* 45.

3. William E. McLellin, *The Ensign of Liberty of the Church of Christ,* vol. 1, no. 4 (Jan. 1848), 61.

4. Shipps and Welch, *The Journals of William E. McLellin,* 47.

5. "Revelation, 30 October 1831 [D&C 65]," in Revelation Book 1, 112, josephsmithpapers.org; see also Doctrine and Covenants 65:2.

6. "Revelation, 1 November 1831–A [D&C 68]," in Revelation Book 1, 113, josephsmithpapers.org.

7. W. E. McLellin, M.D., letter to Davis H. Bays, May 24, 1870, in *Saints' Herald,* Sept. 15, 1870, 553–57.

8. See Doctrine and Covenants 68:1–12.

9. "Revelation, 30 October 1831 [D&C 65]," in Revelation Book 1, 112, josephsmithpapers.org.

10. William E. McLellin, "From a Letter dated Dec. 14th, 1878," in John L. Traughber Papers, J. Willard Marriott Library, University of Utah, Salt Lake City, Utah.

11. Wm. H. Kelley, "Letter From Elder W. H. Kelley," *Saints' Herald,* vol. 29, no. 5 (Mar. 1, 1882), 67.

12. "Revelation, circa 2 November 1831 [D&C 67]," in Revelation Book 1,

115, josephsmithpapers.org; see also Doctrine and Covenants 67:6–8.

13. "History, 1838–1856, volume A-1 [23 December 1805–30 August 1834]," 162, josephsmithpapers.org; see also Mark R. Grandstaff, "Having More Learning Than Sense: William E. McLellin and the Book of Commandments Revisited," *Dialogue: A Journal of Mormon Thought,* vol. 26, no. 4 (Winter 1993), 26. McLellin himself never mentioned such an incident.

14. "Testimony, circa 2 November 1831," in Revelation Book 1, 121, josephsmithpapers.org.

15. See Shipps and Welch, *The Journals of William E. McLellin,* 47.

16. See Shipps and Welch, *The Journals of William E. McLellin,* 47.

17. See "Minute Book 1," 149, josephsmithpapers.org.

18. See Shipps and Welch, *The Journals of William E. McLellin,* 325–27.

19. "Minute Book 2," 18, josephsmithpapers.org.

Newel K. Whitney and the United Firm

D&C 70, 78, 82, 92, 96, 104

Matthew C. Godfrey

In April 1834, Newel K. Whitney, the bishop of the Church in Kirtland, Ohio, and a prominent businessman, forgave over $3,600 in debts owed to him by several individuals, including Joseph Smith, Sidney Rigdon, and Oliver Cowdery. The debts had accumulated over two years as these men worked together, in an administrative body called the United Firm, to direct and finance the temporal operations of the Church. Now, after two tumultuous years, the United Firm was to be dissolved. "Joseph said it was the will of the Lord" that the accounts be balanced "in full without any value rec[eived]," Whitney declared. Whitney then said that he would do what Joseph asked.[1]

From the beginning of the Church's Restoration, the Lord gave Joseph Smith tasks that required temporal means to accomplish. For example, with Martin Harris's financial help, the young prophet published the Book of Mormon. As the Church grew in numbers, the scope of its revealed mission grew as well. Building Zion communities required land and resources. Proclaiming the revealed gospel to the world required access to a printing press. The United Firm was established to coordinate and fund these ambitious efforts.

Just as he was present at the United Firm's dissolution, Newel K. Whitney was present at its formation. As a bishop, Whitney attended a meeting of high priests in Kirtland in March 1832. At that meeting, the Prophet Joseph Smith received a revelation (now Doctrine and Covenants 78) that instructed Joseph, Sidney Rigdon, and Bishop Whitney to travel to Missouri to oversee the formation of "an organization of the Literary and Merchantile establishments of my church."[2] At the time, Sidney Gilbert, an agent of Bishop Edward Partridge in Independence, Missouri, operated a store on behalf of the Church, and Whitney's store in Kirtland was also designated as a Church storehouse.

In addition, William W. Phelps, the Church's printer, had established a printing shop in Independence, where he was printing a newspaper and preparing to publish a compilation of Joseph Smith's revelations in a book called the Book of Commandments. To oversee the publication of the Book of Commandments, a November 1831 revelation—now Doctrine and Covenants 70—had appointed Joseph Smith, Sidney Rigdon, Oliver Cowdery, John Whitmer, Martin Harris, and William W. Phelps "stewards over the revelations," declaring that they would be compensated for their work out of the profits of the book's sales.[3] Now, in March 1832, the Lord told Joseph Smith and others that the operations of the printing establishment and the storehouses needed to be coordinated.

During the first week of April 1832—just days after a mob attacked Joseph Smith and Sidney Rigdon, leading to the death of Joseph's adopted son, Joseph Murdock—Joseph Smith, Newel K. Whitney, Sidney Rigdon, and several others departed for Independence to fulfill this commandment.[4] On April 26, shortly after arriving in Missouri, the Prophet convened a council of high priests. At this meeting, Sidney Rigdon read the March 1832 revelation to the council, stating that it gave "the reason why we were commanded to come to this land & sit in council with the Highpriests here." A revelation was then given to Joseph, further outlining what they were to do.[5]

This revelation, in its original form, stated that it was "expedient" for Joseph Smith, Sidney Rigdon, Newel K. Whitney, Edward Partridge, Sidney Gilbert, John Whitmer, Oliver Cowdery, William W. Phelps, and Martin Harris to "be bound together by a bond & Covenant that cannot be broken in your several Stewartships to manage the literary & Mercantile concerns & the Bishopricks both in the Land of Zion & in the Land of Kirtland."[6] The revelation—now Doctrine and Covenants 82—also stated that these nine individuals were "to have equal claims on the properties for the benefits of managing the concerns of your stewartship." It declared that the Lord had appointed this "firm" to be "an everlasting firm unto you & unto your Successor."[7]

In addition, the revelation told the men to "bind" themselves together by a covenant "according to the Laws of the Land."[8] Essentially, this revelation stated that those members of the firm would receive sustenance for themselves and their families out of the mercantile and publishing establishments that they were commanded to manage and that they were to enter into a legal bond that would join them together in terms of their obligations for the firm's debts.

The council met again the next day and directed that the two main branches of the firm be Gilbert, Whitney & Co. (the mercantile partnership of Newel K. Whitney and Sidney Gilbert in Independence) and N. K. Whitney & Co. (Whitney's Kirtland firm). They also appointed Phelps and Gilbert to draft the bond that the members of the firm needed to enter as instructed by the revelation.[9] Just a few days later, around May 1, 1832, the United Firm held its first regular meeting, with all of its members in attendance except Martin Harris. At this meeting, Whitney and Gilbert were "appointed agents to act in the name of this Firm" and the firm was directed to secure a loan of $15,000 through N. K. Whitney & Co.[10]

For the next two years, the United Firm played a key role in administering the Church. In addition to supervising the storehouses and printing office, its members served as a de facto board of directors for Joseph Smith. For example, when Joseph, who remained in Ohio, wanted information about what was occurring in Missouri, where the city of Zion was being established, he addressed letters to members of the firm.[11] Likewise, the firm's assets became essential for financing Church projects and for providing members of the firm and their families with the necessities of life.

In 1833, two additional members were added to the firm, both by revelation. A March 1833 revelation—now Doctrine and

Covenants 92—directed that Frederick G. Williams be received "into the firm" and that he be "a lively member."[12] Then, in June 1833, another revelation—now Doctrine and Covenants 96—commanded that John Johnson "become a member of the firm that he may assist in bringing forth my word unto the children of men."[13] Williams, a member of the Church's governing presidency, had large land-holdings in Ohio, as did Johnson. The United Firm drew on these men's holdings to manage its stewardships.

Newel K. Whitney, meanwhile, continued his involvement in the firm. In addition to operating his store in Kirtland as a Church storehouse, Whitney became responsible for debts owed on a large parcel of land purchased in Kirtland where Church leaders planned to construct the house of the Lord.[14] Through the means of his store, Whitney also provided financing and goods for the sustenance of Joseph Smith and others, generating the debts that Whitney would forgive in April 1834.

However, the United Firm was on shaky financial ground by 1834. When the Saints were driven from Jackson County, Missouri, in the fall of 1833, the Church lost two vital components of the firm: Phelps's printing office and Gilbert's storehouse. In addition, the United Firm had debts due to the purchase of goods for the storehouses, a new printing press in Kirtland, and land for Kirtland's development.

On January 11, 1834, six members of the firm, including Whitney, prayed that the Lord "would provide, in the order of his Providence, the bishop of this Church with means sufficient to discharge every debt that the Firm owes, in due season."[15] But by April 1834, Whitney noted that he was $8,000 in debt because of his role in the firm. He needed at least $4,000 that month to help pay the debts, the balance of which needed to be repaid by September 1834.[16] Facing this bleak financial picture, the Prophet Joseph held a meeting of the United Firm on April 10, 1834, during which it was decided that "the firm should be desolvd and each one have their stewardship set off to them."[17]

Less than two weeks later, on April 23, 1834, the Lord gave Joseph Smith a revelation—now Doctrine and Covenants 104—that assigned these stewardships to the different members of the firm.

The stewardships were specific pieces of property that individual members of the firm became responsible for. For example, Newel K. Whitney was given his houses and store, the lots on which they were located, and the lot on which his ashery was located. Others were given land and buildings resting on properties owned by Frederick G. Williams and John Johnson.[18] Although the revelation itself intimated that the United Firm would continue after this distribution of stewardships and a reorganization of the firm, the firm essentially ceased to function thereafter. Instead, the Kirtland high council, formed in February 1834, took on the role of governing the Church's mercantile and publishing efforts.[19]

In later editions of the Doctrine and Covenants, the United Firm was called the "United Order," and code names were inserted in place of the participants' names. In addition, language about the firm's purpose was changed so that it referred more vaguely to meeting the needs of the poor. This was done to protect the identity of those involved in the firm and to keep its purposes confidential. The names of the individuals were restored to the revelations in the 1980s, but the firm is still referred to as the United Order in the 2013 edition of the Doctrine and Covenants.[20]

Newel K. Whitney's participation in the United Firm left him with increased indebtedness, but he never showed any bitterness towards Joseph Smith or the Lord because of this. Whitney did not record his feelings about forgiving the large sum of $3,600, but his forgiveness of the debts showed his willingness to follow the Prophet even in temporal matters. His role in the firm gave him an opportunity to work closely with Joseph Smith and other Church leaders in providing the Church with means to carry out its mission. The United Firm played a vital role in the administration of the Church from 1832 to 1834—just as Whitney played a vital role in the firm itself.

1. "Balance of Account, 23 April 1834," josephsmithpapers.org.

2. "Revelation, 1 March 1832 [D&C 78]," 1, josephsmithpapers.org; see also Doctrine and Covenants 78:3–4, 9–11. When this revelation was published in the 1835 edition of the Doctrine and Covenants, "organization of the Literary and Merchantile establishments" was changed to "organization of my people, in regulating and establishing the affairs of the storehouse for the poor of my people." This wording remains in the revelation today.

3. "Revelation, 12 November 1831 [D&C 70]," in Revelation Book 1, 124, josephsmithpapers.org; see also Doctrine and Covenants 70:1–8.

4. Joseph Smith, "History, 1838–1856, volume A-1 [23 December 1805–30 August 1834]," 209, josephsmithpapers.org.

5. Minutes, 26–27 April 1832, in Minute Book 2, 24–25, josephsmithpapers.org.

6. "Revelation, 26 April 1832 [D&C 82]," in Revelation Book 1, 128, josephsmithpapers.org; see also Doctrine and Covenants 82:11–12. When this revelation was published in the 1835 edition of the Doctrine and Covenants, the wording "to manage the literary & Mercantile concerns & the Bishopricks" was changed to "to manage the affairs of the poor, and all things pertaining to the bishopric," and that wording remains in the revelation today.

7. "Revelation, 26 April 1832 [D&C 82]," in Revelation Book 1, 129, josephsmithpapers.org; see also Doctrine and Covenants 82:17, 20. Note that "firm" was changed to "order" in the 1835 edition of the Doctrine and Covenants and remains "order" in the Doctrine and Covenants today.

8. "Revelation, 26 April 1832 [D&C 82]," in Revelation Book 1, 129, josephsmithpapers.org; see also Doctrine and Covenants 82:15.

9. Minutes, 26–27 April 1832, in Minute Book 2, 25, josephsmithpapers.org.

10. Minutes, circa 1 May 1832, in Minute Book 2, 26, josephsmithpapers.org.

11. See, for example, Joseph Smith, "Letter to Edward Partridge and Others, 30 March 1834," in Oliver Cowdery Letterbook, 30–38, josephsmithpapers.org.

12. "Revelation, 15 March 1833 [D&C 92]," in Revelation Book 2, 55; see also Doctrine and Covenants 92:1–2. Note that "firm" was changed to "order" when this revelation was published and remains so today.

13. "Revelation, 4 June 1833 [D&C 96]," in Revelation Book 2, 61, josephsmithpapers.org; see also Doctrine and Covenants 96:6–8. Note that "firm" was changed to "order" when this revelation was published and remains so today.

14. See Geauga Co., Ohio, Deed Records, 1795–1921, vol. 17, 360–61, microfilm 20,237, U.S. and Canada Record Collection, Family History Library, Salt Lake City; see also "Revelation, 27–28 December 1832 [D&C 88:1–126]," in Revelation Book 2, 45–46, josephsmithpapers.org; see also Doctrine and Covenants 88:119.

15. "Prayer, 11 January 1834," in Joseph Smith, Journal, Nov. 1832–Dec. 1834, 43–45, josephsmithpapers.org.

16. Newel K. Whitney, "Order from Newel K. Whitney, 18 April 1834," josephsmithpapers.org.

17. Joseph Smith, "Journal, 1832–1834," Apr. 10, 1834, page 71, josephsmithpapers.org.

18. "Revelation, 23 April 1834 [D&C 104]," in Book of Commandments Book C, 25–29, josephsmithpapers.org.

19. See Max H Parkin, "Joseph Smith and the United Firm: The Growth and Decline of the Church's First Master Plan of Business and Finance, Ohio and Missouri, 1832–1834," *BYU Studies,* vol. 46, no. 3 (2007), 33–34.

20. David J. Whittaker, "Substituted Names in the Published Revelations of Joseph Smith," *BYU Studies,* vol. 23, no. 1 (Winter 1983), 103–12.

"The Vision"
D&C 76

Matthew McBride

While traveling east on a mission during the early spring of 1832, Samuel H. Smith and Orson Hyde stopped for dinner at the home of recent convert Lincoln Haskins.[1] Haskins, who lived in the far-western reaches of New York, had just returned from a journey to Ohio, where he met Joseph Smith.[2] The timing of Haskins's late-February visit to Kirtland and Hiram was providential: Just days earlier, the Prophet and Sidney Rigdon had experienced a momentous vision.

"Great and Marvelous Things"

Haskins likely heard about this vision from Joseph or one of the few other men who were present when it occurred on February 16 at the home of John Johnson in Hiram. Joseph Smith and Sidney Rigdon were there working on a revision of the New Testament. Earlier revelations made it "apparent that many important points, touching the Salvation of man, had been taken from the Bible." According to Joseph's history, the two men were pondering the significance of a passage on the Resurrection found in John 5:29 when "the Lord touched the eyes of our understandings" and they witnessed the vision.[3]

"Not a sound nor motion [was] made by anyone but Joseph and Sidney," recalled Philo Dibble, one of those present. "I saw the glory and felt the power, but did not see the vision."[4] Dibble and as many as 12 others listened as Joseph Smith and Sidney Rigdon described aloud what they saw.

"The Vision," as it became known, contained a sweeping description of what awaited humankind after death. It outlined varying degrees of glory divided into three kingdoms as the inheritances for the vast majority of God's children; revealed that consignment to eternal punishment would be the fate of only a small few; and explained that the righteous would receive the Father's fulness: "Wherefore as it is writen they are Gods even the sons of God wherefore all things are theres."[5]

Haskins shared his elation over this expansive vision with his guests during their visit to his home. "He told us that he had seen Joseph & Sidney & that they had had a vision & that they had seen great & marvilous things," Samuel Smith wrote in his journal.[6]

A few days after their visit with Haskins, the missionaries "had the privlidge of reading" a written account of "the Vision" when they met Seth and Joel Johnson, two Church members who carried with them a precious handwritten copy they had made while in Kirtland.[7] These exchanges demonstrate the excitement with which some early converts treated "the Vision." But not everyone shared their enthusiasm.

Universalism

The view of the afterlife laid out in "the Vision" contrasted starkly with the beliefs of most Christians at the time. A majority believed in a strict heaven-and-hell theology of the world to come: those obedient to the gospel of Jesus Christ would be saved, but the wicked would be consigned to eternal punishment.[8] However, there were a growing number who felt that this view was inconsistent with other biblical teachings about God's mercy, justice, and power to save.

For example, a young Congregationalist named Caleb Rich became troubled when his minister taught that Christ would have a mere few "trophies of his Mission to the world, while his antagonist would have countless millions." Rich feared that his own spiritual "situation appeared more precarious than a ticket in a lottery."[9] He eventually rejected his minister's doctrine and embraced what is known as Universalism. Simply put, Universalists believed that God would not eternally punish sinners but that all would eventually be saved in God's kingdom. Joseph Smith's father and his grandfather Asael Smith held Universalist views.[10]

Most Christians felt that Universalism went too far, that its teaching of universal salvation removed all incentive to keep God's commandments and would lead to an immoral, dissolute life. Many early converts to the Church agreed and may have felt confirmed in their view by certain Book of Mormon passages.[11] However, Joseph Smith's vision of the afterlife appeared to some of these converts to advocate Universalist teachings. Consequently, as people like Lincoln Haskins and Joel and Seth Johnson began to carry word of "the Vision" to the scattered branches of the Church, it created a stir.

Many Stumbled at It

Some outside observers scoffed at the newly revealed doctrine. One Christian newspaper responded to "the Vision" by sarcastically claiming that Joseph Smith sought to "*disgrace* Universalism by professing . . . the salvation of all men."[12] But more disconcerting to the Prophet were the reactions of some Church members.

"It was a great trial to many," Brigham Young remembered. "Some apostatized because God . . . had a place of salvation, in due time, for all."[13] Young himself had difficulty accepting the idea: "My traditions were such, that when the Vision came first to me, it was directly contrary and opposed to my former education. I said, Wait a little. I did not reject it; but I could not understand it."[14] His brother Joseph Young also confessed, "I could not believe it at first. Why the Lord was going to save every body."[15]

Perhaps in a knee-jerk reaction to what seemed to be hints of Universalism, some early members overlooked the subtle beauty of "the Vision." Avoiding the extremes of Universalism and the orthodox view of heaven and hell, it suggested that the sufferings of the disobedient would indeed ultimately end but that the Lord also held out the promise of unimaginable rewards for those who are "valient in the testamony of Jesus."[16]

Many of those who stumbled at the vision simply needed some time to ponder it or the patient explanation of a missionary or spiritual leader. Joseph Young remembered, "After I had prayed over it and Joseph had explained it I could see it was nothing but good sense accompanying the power of God."[17] Brigham Young had to "think and pray, to read and think, until [he] knew and fully understood it for [himself]."[18]

In May or June 1832, missionary John Murdock encountered resistance to the ideas in "the Vision" while in Orange, Ohio (near Cleveland): "The brethren had just received the Revilation called the vision & were stumbling at it." Murdock acted the part of spiritual mentor: "I called them togather & confirmed them in the truth."[19]

Later, Murdock and fellow missionary Orson Pratt encountered a Brother Landon in Geneseo, New York, who "said the vision was of the Devil." Landon had influenced his branch to reject the new revelation as well. The missionaries spent a few days with the branch. "Br Orson led in explination of the vision & other revelation followed by my self & Br Lyman," wrote Murdock. Landon soon "acknowledged what we taught to be true."[20]

Joseph Smith sent the branch in Geneseo a letter admonishing them to have faith in the revelation. He warned, "Where there are contentions, and unbelief in the sacred things communic[ated] to the saints by revelation, that discord, hardness, jealousies, and numberless evils will inevitably issue."[21]

"Remain Silent"

The prophet learned from this experience just how delicate the testimonies of many new converts could be and counseled missionaries to take a milk-before-meat approach to teaching gospel principles (see 1 Corinthians 3:2). Prior to the departure of the Twelve Apostles to England, Joseph Smith urged them to "remain silent concerning the gathering, the vision, and the Book of Doctrine and Covenants until such time as the work was fully established."[22]

However, it proved difficult for some members to contain their enthusiasm for the new revelation.

Heber C. Kimball, echoing Joseph Smith's counsel, encouraged his fellow missionaries to keep to the introductory principles of the gospel. Kimball had helped convert a minister, Timothy Matthews, in Bedford, England, and established an appointment for his baptism. But another elder, John Goodson, "contrary to [Kimball's] counsel and positive instructions, and without advising with any one, read to Mr. Matthews, the vision . . . which caused him to stumble." Matthews failed to keep his appointment and never joined the Church.[23]

"It Came from God"

While a few early Church members struggled to accept "the Vision," many embraced it unreservedly. William W. Phelps, Church printer in Missouri, published it in the Church-owned periodical *The Evening and the Morning Star* in July 1832, calling it "the greatest news that was ever published to man."[24]

Wilford Woodruff, who joined the Church in 1833, recalled, "When I read the vision . . . it enlightened my mind and gave me great joy. It appeared to me that the God who revealed that principle unto man was wise, just, and true—possessed both the best of attributes, and good sense, and knowledge. I felt He was consistent with both love, mercy, justice, and judgment; and I felt to love the Lord more than ever before in my life."[25]

Perhaps some of those who embraced "the Vision" were predisposed by their past beliefs.[26] Some, like Joseph Smith's father, may have had Universalist leanings. But while this new vision shared some similarities with the thought and writings of the Universalists, it departed from and expanded upon these ideas in new and inspired ways. Joseph Smith's history concluded, "Nothing could be more pleasing to the Saint . . . than the light which burst upon the world, through the foregoing vision. . . . The sublimity of the ideas; the purity of the language; the scope for action; the continued duration for completion, in order that the heirs of salvation, may confess the Lord and bow the knee; The rewards for faithfulnes & the punishments for sins, are so much beyond the narrow mindedness of men, that every honest man is constrained to exclaim; It came from God." [27]

1. Orson Hyde diary, Mar. 21, 1832, Church History Library, Salt Lake City.

2. While in Ohio, Haskins was baptized and became the subject of a revelation that commanded him to "go forth and proclaim my gospel" (see "Revelation, 27 February 1832," in Revelation Book 2, 10, josephsmithpapers.org).

3. Joseph Smith, "History, 1838–1856, volume A-1 [23 December 1805–30 August 1834]," 183, 185, josephsmithpapers.org.

4. Philo Dibble, "Recollections of the Prophet Joseph Smith," *Juvenile Instructor,* vol. 27, no. 10 (May 15, 1892), 303–4. This account was the last of three that Dibble gave of "the Vision," and it differs somewhat from his earlier versions. In one earlier account, he claimed not to have arrived until the vision was ending (see "Record of Sunday Meetings," Jan. 7, 1877, in Payson [UT] Ward general minutes, 137, Church History Library, Salt Lake City).

5. "Vision, 16 February 1832 [D&C 76]," in Revelation Book 2, 6, josephsmithpapers.org; see also Doctrine and Covenants 76:58.

6. Samuel H. Smith diary, Mar. 21, 1832, Church History Library, Salt Lake City.

7. Samuel H. Smith diary, Mar. 27, 1832.

8. The Westminster Confession of Faith, which served as the basis of orthodox belief for most early Americans, states that following the judgment "shall the righteous go into everlasting life, and receive that fullness of joy and refreshing, which shall come from the presence of the Lord; but the wicked, who know not God, and obey not the gospel of Jesus Christ, shall be cast into eternal torments, and be punished with everlasting destruction."

9. Nathan O. Hatch, *The Democratization of American Christianity* (New Haven, CT: Yale University Press, 1989), 172. For more on Universalism, see Milton V. Backman, *American Religions and the Rise of Mormonism* (Salt Lake City: Deseret Book Company, 1970), 216–23.

10. See Casey Paul Griffiths, "Universalism and the Revelations of Joseph Smith," in Andrew H. Hedges, J. Spencer Fluhman, and Alonzo L. Gaskell, eds., *The Doctrine and Covenants, Revelations in Context* (Salt Lake City: Deseret Book, 2008), 168–87.

11. For example, in the Book of Mormon, a man named Nehor is condemned for teaching "that all mankind should be saved at the last day" (Alma 1:4).

12. "Changes of Mormonism," *Evangelical Magazine and Gospel Advocate,* vol. 3, no. 11 (Mar. 17, 1832); emphasis in original.

13. Brigham Young, in *Journal of Discourses,* 26 vols. (London: Latter-Day Saints' Book Depot, 1854–86), 16:42.

14. Brigham Young, in *Journal of Discourses,* 6:281.

15. Joseph Young, "Discourse," *Deseret News* (Mar. 18, 1857), 11.

16. "Vision, 16 February 1832 [D&C 76]," in Revelation Book 2, 7.

17. Joseph Young, "Discourse," 11.

18. Brigham Young, in *Journal of Discourses,* 6:281.

19. "John Murdock journal and autobiography, circa 1830–1867," 18, Church History Library, Salt Lake City.

20. "John Murdock journal and autobiography, circa 1830–1867," 27–28.

21. Joseph Smith, "Letter to Church Leaders in Geneseo, New York, 23 November 1833," 1–2, josephsmithpapers.org.

22. Joseph Smith, "History, 1838–1856, volume B-1 [1 September 1834–2 November 1838]," 762, josephsmithpapers.org.

23. Orson F. Whitney, "Life of Heber C. Kimball," *Juvenile Instructor,* 1888, 162. Kimball wrote to Willard Richards, "The hearts of the people are closed up in Bedford, by Elder Goodson preaching those things he was commanded to let alone" (72).

24. "Items for the Public," *The Evening and the Morning Star,* vol. 1, no. 2 (July 1832), 25; "the Vision" itself is published on pages 27–30.

25. Wilford Woodruff, in *Journal of Discourses,* 5:84.

26. Alexander Campbell, a leader of the Disciples of Christ (a movement with which many early Ohio converts were previously affiliated), expounded a theory of "Three Kingdoms" a few years earlier in the *Christian Baptist,* vol. 6, no. 1 (Aug. 4, 1828), 97–99. Campbell's ideas bore only a vague resemblance to those contained in "the Vision" but may have resonated with some of Campbell's former followers (see Mark Lyman Staker, *Hearken, O Ye People: The Historical Settings of Joseph Smith's Ohio Revelations* [Salt Lake City: Greg Kofford Books, 2009], 322–28). Campbell may have been influenced by the writings of the Swedish mystic, Emanuel Swedenborg (see J. B. Haws, "Joseph Smith, Emanuel Swedenborg, and Section 76: Importance of the Bible in Latter-day Revelation," in Hedges, Fluhman, and Gaskill, *The Doctrine and Covenants, Revelations in Context,* 142–67).

27. Joseph Smith, "History, 1838–1856, volume A-1 [23 December 1805–30 August 1834]," 192.

Jesse Gause:
Counselor to the Prophet
D&C 81

Robin Scott Jensen

The early Church underwent significant changes to its organization in a relatively short period of time. Many of these changes can be tracked by reading the early revelations given to individuals in the Doctrine and Covenants. For modern readers, some of the earliest revelations reference lesser-known organizations or individuals. One such revelation, given on March 15, 1832 (now Doctrine and Covenants 81), was given to a relatively unknown figure from Church history: Jesse Gause.[1] Born in 1784, Jesse Gause was raised in Pennsylvania and lived for a time in Delaware. He joined the Society of Friends (the Quakers) in 1806, married Martha Johnson in 1815, and had moved to Ohio by the following year. Five years later, he returned to Delaware. After the death of his first wife in 1828, he moved closer to his extended family—who were members of the United Society of Believers in Christ's Second Appearing (the Shakers)—for help in supporting his children. By 1829, he had joined the Shaker faith. He remarried in 1830 to Minerva Eliza Byram and settled in a Shaker community in North Union, Ohio, just 15 miles from Kirtland, Ohio.[2]

Exactly how Jesse came to be baptized is unknown, but he quickly gained Joseph Smith's trust and rose to prominence in the Church. On March 8, 1832, at Hiram, Ohio, Gause and Sidney Rigdon were appointed counselors to Joseph Smith in the newly formed presidency of the high priesthood.[3] Joseph's own appointment as president of the high priesthood had taken place in January.[4] This presidency was the forerunner to the First Presidency of the Church.

Gause not only acted as a counselor to Joseph Smith, but he also served a mission, traveled to Missouri on Church business, and served as a scribe on the Bible revision project, later known as the Joseph Smith Translation. Like many other members of the early Church, he showed his dedication to his new faith through his labors in helping the cause of Zion.

Sidney Rigdon, who had been baptized in Ohio in late 1830 and had served as a scribe for Joseph Smith, had already been the subject and recipient of several revelations. The revelation that is now Doctrine and Covenants 81, however, was the first one to address Jesse Gause directly. While it is unclear whether Gause specifically requested a revelation from Joseph Smith, the text gives important clarification of Gause's duties, not just as a member of the Church but as a counselor to Joseph Smith.

The revelation informed Gause (and future readers) that the "keys of the kingdom" belong to the office of the presidency of the high priesthood—in this case, to Joseph Smith himself. It also said that Gause would be blessed if he was "faithful in counsel, in the office" to which he was appointed.

Gause was to "do the greatest good unto [his] fellow beings," including praying publicly and preaching the gospel to members and nonmembers alike. This, he was told, would "promote the glory of him who is your Lord." And if he remained "faithful unto the end," he would receive a "crown of Immortality." [5]

Perhaps surprisingly, Gause was excommunicated from the Church less than a year after the revelation admonished him to endure to the end.[6] His virtual disappearance from the historical records following his missionary labors with Zebedee Coltrin in August 1832 make it difficult to understand why he left.[7] Given his background in both the Quaker and Shaker faiths, it is possible that he came to have theological disagreements with Joseph Smith or other Church members—particularly as Joseph continued to update the doctrine of the Church through revelations.

Modern-day readers of Doctrine and Covenants 81 will find Jesse Gause's name only in the section heading. By the time the revelation was published in the 1835 edition of the Doctrine and Covenants, Gause's name had been replaced with that of the man called to take his place: Frederick G. Williams. Subsequent editions of the Doctrine and Covenants retained Williams as the recipient of this revelation. Williams, who replaced Gause as a counselor in January 1833, had been an early convert and supporter of Joseph Smith. Like Gause and Rigdon, Williams also acted as a scribe and clerk to Joseph Smith.

The written records of Joseph Smith's early revelations underwent changes when early leaders of the Church prepared those revelatory texts for publication in the Doctrine and Covenants in 1835.[8] The changes were logical because some of the revelations no longer reflected the current state of Church organization or doctrinal understanding. As the editors prepared the revelations for print, they likely viewed the revelation in Doctrine and Covenants 81 not merely as counsel to an individual, but rather as a more general revelation to a counselor who was to support Joseph Smith. And because Jesse Gause had left the Church, it is understandable that the editors would have substituted the name of Williams instead.

In some ways, the early revelations were snapshots in time, providing modern readers with a window to the way continuing revelation shaped the early Church. In other ways, the revelations have broader applications. Doctrine and Covenants 81 can be read today not only as an intimate revelation to an early member of the Church, but also as counsel to anyone who is willing to support the prophet.

1. The name of the recipient of this revelation was changed later. See discussion below.

2. See Erin B. Jennings, "The Consequential Counselor: Restoring the Root(s) of Jesse Gause," *Journal of Mormon History,* vol. 34, no. 2 (Spring 2008), 182–227.

3. Joseph Smith, "Note, 8 March 1832," josephsmithpapers.org; Matthew C. Godfrey, Mark Ashurst-McGee, Grant Underwood, Robert J. Woodford, and William G. Hartley, eds., *Documents, Volume 2: July 1831–January 1833,* vol. 2 of the Documents series of *The Joseph Smith Papers,* ed. Dean C. Jessee, Ronald K. Esplin, Richard Lyman Bushman, and Matthew J. Grow (Salt Lake City: Church Historian's Press, 2013), 201–4.

4. Minutes for this January 1832 conference do not survive. See "Minutes, 26–27 April 1832," josephsmithpapers.org.

5. "Revelation, 15 March 1832 [D&C 81]," josephsmithpapers.org; *Documents,*

Volume 2: July 1831–January 1833, 207–8.

6. Joseph Smith, "Journal, 1832–1834," Dec. 3, 1832, josephsmithpapers.org; Dean C. Jessee, Mark Ashurst-McGee, and Richard L. Jensen, eds., *Journals, Volume 1: 1832–1839,* vol. 1 of the Journals series of *The Joseph Smith Papers,* ed. Dean C. Jessee, Ronald K. Esplin, and Richard Lyman Bushman (Salt Lake City: Church Historian's Press, 2008), 10.

7. Zebedee Coltrin journal, folder 0002, image 41, Church History Library, Salt Lake City.

8. See the historical introduction to "Doctrine and Covenants, 1835," josephsmithpapers.org; see also Robin Scott Jensen, Richard E. Turley Jr., and Riley M. Lorimer, eds., *Revelations and Translations, Volume 2: Published Revelations,* vol. 2 of the Revelations and Translations series of *The Joseph Smith Papers,* ed. Dean C. Jessee, Ronald K. Esplin, and Richard Lyman Bushman (Salt Lake City: Church Historian's Press, 2011), 301–10.

Peace and War

D&C 87

Jed Woodworth

A few days before Christmas 1832, Latter-day Saints in Kirtland came in from the cold, damp air to sit by the light of their warm, flickering fires. They opened up their local paper, the *Painesville Telegraph,* to find alarming news. Seven hundred miles to the south, the legislature of South Carolina, a state within the United States, had declared "null and void" taxes placed on imported goods by the federal government. This move created a "nullification crisis" that challenged the right of the federal government to enforce its own laws. War loomed on the horizon.[1]

These tariffs had been established to protect northern manufacturers from foreign competition. Southern farmers found them unfair. Why should they pay more for goods their region did not produce?[2] Andrew Jackson, the president of the United States, issued a proclamation in which he warned that South Carolina's rejection of federal tariffs was an act of rebellion that could end in bloodshed. South Carolina promptly responded by preparing for war.[3] Compromise seemed nowhere in sight. The accounts read by Kirtland residents sounded the war drum: "Let one menacing Federal bayonet glitter upon our borders," one account read, and it will be a "war of *sovereigns*."[4]

The Christmas Day Revelation

Joseph Smith followed this conflict closely through the newspapers that passed into Kirtland. He appended a note in his history about the people of South Carolina "declaring their state, a free and Independent Nation" and the "proclamation against this rebellion" given by President Jackson.[5] And then, following these lines, Joseph inserted what he called "a prophecy on war," a revelation he dictated to his clerk Frederick G. Williams on Christmas Day 1832, just days after the startling news appeared in the Kirtland papers. That revelation is known today as Doctrine and Covenants 87.

Without ever mentioning President Jackson by name, the prophecy on war made the president's conditional promises inevitable. President Jackson had predicted that armed conflict would result if South Carolina continued to insist on its own sovereignty. According to President Jackson, South Carolina had said through its actions: "Peace and prosperity we will deface; this free intercourse we will interrupt; these fertile fields we will deluge with blood."[6] Yet, if South Carolina backed down, the deluge could be avoided. In Joseph Smith's prophecy, however, bloodshed was a foregone conclusion. "The wars that will shortly come to pass beginning at the rebellion of South Carolina," the revelation said, "will eventually terminate in the death and misery of many souls."[7] The revelation foreshadowed no peaceful resolution.

Destruction was not a new theme in Joseph Smith's revelations. The Lord had already warned of a time when famine, pestilence, and tempests would befall the world's inhabitants.[8] The revelations taught that widespread destruction would precede the Lord's Second Coming, and the frequency of references to destruction in the revelations prompted many Latter-day Saints to conclude that the Second Coming must be imminent.[9]

Doctrine and Covenants 87 only heightened expectations that the Second Coming was not far away. Other revelations located destruction in an indeterminate time and place: Destruction would happen "before this great day," referring to the Second Coming, or would occur among "all nations."[10] War and rumors of war would be "in your own lands," the revelations said, and "in foreign lands."[11]

Doctrine and Covenants 87, by contrast, tied destruction to specific places and events in a contemporary landscape: South Carolina and its rebellion were singled out by name. Conflict involved more than just warring nations. It would also involve oppressed groups—"slaves" and "remnants"—rising up against their masters and overseers.[12]

The reference to slaves inserted Doctrine and Covenants 87 directly into the conflict over federal power. In the run-up to the crisis, South Carolinians had argued that the federal tariffs were intentionally designed to subvert the slave-labor farming economy that dominated the American South. States that stood to benefit from the tariffs, including Ohio, had all made slavery illegal. Joseph Smith's prophecy on war recognized these geopolitical rifts and tied them to the wars inevitably to follow: "The Southern States shall be divided against the Northern States, and the Southern States will call on other nations, even the nation of Great Britain."[13] In 1832, Europe depended on southern cotton for its textile industries. Great Britain seemed a likely ally for South Carolina's cause.

Crisis Averted

To the great surprise of all, the nullification crisis ended almost before it began. In February 1833, President Jackson orchestrated a lowered, compromise tariff, asserting the rights of the federal government while satisfying the demands of states-rights secessionists. Crisis was averted, peace had returned to the land, and President Jackson basked in what may have been his greatest triumph as president.[14]

The peaceful resolution of the crisis pleased everyone but the most ardent firebrands. As a follower of Christ, Joseph Smith loved peace and welcomed compromise, and he looked forward to the return of the Prince of Peace and His peaceful millennial reign. But the dire predictions contained in the prophecy on war, tied as they were to contemporary events, must have puzzled Joseph. The death and misery of many souls did not occur. The Southern states continued to be divided against the North over the question of slavery, but the slaves did not rise up against their masters, and South Carolina did not call on Great Britain for help.[15] Anyone looking for the fulfillment of the revelation in 1833 would have been disappointed.

Joseph Smith seemed reluctant to spread news of his prophecy on war too widely. Even before the crisis had been averted, he told a newspaper editor that he was sure "not many years shall pass away before the United States shall present such a scene of bloodshed as has not a parallel in the history of our nation."[16] But he did not get any more specific than that. He did not mention South Carolina in his later teachings and sermons. When he compiled his revelations for publication in 1835, Joseph withheld Doctrine and Covenants 87 from the collection. After the nullification crisis ended peacefully, it seemed best to set the revelation aside during his lifetime.[17]

Joseph was sure of his prior revelations. He had felt the voice of God speak through him before and had seen those words come to pass. He must have wondered if this revelation was a case of false prophecy. Or, if the prophecy was true, what would God have Joseph do now that peace, even if temporary, had been achieved?

Holy Places

Doctrine and Covenants 87 did not radically reorient Joseph Smith's approach to life. He did not hide in a bunker or otherwise drop out from public view, waiting for the end. Even before President Jackson's successful resolution of the crisis, when war still looked likely, Joseph quietly opened a school for elders who would soon go out into the world as missionaries. The School of the Prophets, as Joseph called it, met with a small group of Latter-day Saint men in the Newel K. Whitney storehouse in Kirtland.

In the school, Joseph taught students how to "speak in the name of God."[18] He encouraged the men to purify themselves so that God's Spirit could help them find and teach the elect. Those who kept the Word of Wisdom, Joseph taught, would run and not be weary and walk and not faint.[19] President Jackson had sought to avert destruction through diplomacy. Joseph taught that the "destroying angel" could be avoided through righteous living.[20]

Joseph never shied away from warning the world of the cataclysms to come. But that was not the point of his message. He was not

161

a doomsayer prophet, content with predicting only misery and woe.[21] At the end of Doctrine and Covenants 87, the Lord told the Saints how to respond to such troubling prophecies. They were not to live in fear or abandon their current endeavors. They were to "stand . . . in holy places and be not moved."[22]

A few days after Doctrine and Covenants 87 was received, Joseph Smith received another revelation, in which the Lord commanded the Saints to build a temple in Kirtland (Doctrine and Covenants 88). This revelation, like the prophecy on war, spoke of the destructions to come. Yet it also spoke of an important work the Saints were to perform. They were not to sit passively, awaiting Christ's return while the world fell apart all around them. Nor were they simply to preach, as the doomsayers did. They were to build new structures, new institutions, new "holy places." Always obedient to his revelations, Joseph opened the School of the Prophets, as the revelation enjoined him to do. Later that summer he would break ground for the temple.

Down to the end of Joseph's life, it would be the "holy places," temples and schools, that would most capture his attention. Experience taught him to put little faith in the power of diplomacy, as Andrew Jackson did. Joseph knew from the all-too-frequent moves the Saints were forced to undertake how tenuous peace could be. Despite the conflict that surrounded them, the Saints could always find peace in the process of creating and inhabiting holy places.

Conclusion

Three decades after Doctrine and Covenants 87 was received, South Carolina rebelled again. Convinced that Abraham Lincoln's election as U.S. president spelled trouble for the institution of slavery, the state legislature voted to secede from the United States. South Carolina's move triggered a war between North and South. Much death and misery resulted. Southerners called on Great Britain for help. Slaves rose up against their masters. All the while, the Saints, now in their new mountain home in the West, toiled away on the foundations of yet another holy place—the Salt Lake Temple.

1. See William W. Freehling, ed., *The Nullification Era: A Documentary Record* (New York: Harper Torchbooks, 1967). The news of South Carolina's rebellion against federal tariffs had been reported before this time, but not until December 21 did the *Painesville Telegraph* report the speech of the governor of South Carolina supporting the actions of the legislature.

2. The U.S. Constitution gave the federal government power to regulate commerce, and for the first two decades of the country's existence, tariffs were set low in order to stimulate revenue. The higher tariff rates came in response to the large-scale British manufacturing of the 1810s and '20s (see Paul P. Abrahams, "Tariffs," in Paul S. Boyer, ed., *The Oxford Companion to United States History* [New York: Oxford University Press, 2001], 761).

3. Andrew Jackson, Proclamation, Dec. 10, 1832, in James D. Richardson, comp., *A Compilation of the Messages and Papers of the Presidents,* 11 vols. (New York: Bureau of National Literature, 1897), 3:1203–19. The South Carolina legislature authorized $200,000—an enormous sum—for munitions and gave its governor authority to call out the militia (see Robert V. Remini, *Andrew Jackson and the Course of American Democracy, 1833–1845* [New York: Harper & Row, 1984], 26). Proponents of nullification naturally greeted President Jackson's proclamation with contempt, viewing it as a means of intimidating South Carolina Whigs into submission by fomenting the opponents of nullification within the state. For these radical nullifiers, President Jackson's proclamation amounted to a "declaration of war" ("South Carolina," *Alexandria [Virginia] Gazette,* Dec. 25, 1832, 2).

4. "The Charleston Mercury," *Painesville Telegraph,* Dec. 21, 1832, 3, column 2. James Hamilton, the outgoing governor of South Carolina, seemed almost to invite war in a widely reported speech given on December 10. "A large majority of our people," he said, "would rather have every house on the surface of our Territory razed to the ground, and every blade of grass burnt, than surrender to the despotism and injustice of that system of Government against which we have unalterably taken our stand" ("South Carolina," *American Traveller* [Boston], Dec. 25, 1832, 3).

5. Joseph Smith, "History, 1838–1856, volume A-1 [23 December 1805–30 August 1834]," 244, josephsmithpapers.org.

6. Richardson, *A Compilation of the Messages and Papers of the Presidents,* 3:1217.

7. "Revelation, 25 December 1832 [D&C 87]," in Revelation Book 2, 32, josephsmithpapers.org; spelling modernized; see also Doctrine and Covenants 87:1.

8. See "Revelation, September 1830–A [D&C 29]," in Revelation Book 1, 37–38, josephsmithpapers.org; see also Doctrine and Covenants 29:14–19.

9. On Mormon millennialism, see Grant Underwood, *The Millenarian World of Early Mormonism* (Urbana: University of Illinois Press, 1986). For millennialism generally, the classic works include James West Davidson, *The Logic of Millennial Thought: Eighteenth-Century New England* (New Haven: Yale University Press, 1977) and Ernest R. Sandeen, *The Roots of Fundamentalism: British and American Millenarianism, 1800–1930* (Chicago: University of Chicago Press, 1970).

10. "Revelation, September 1830–A [D&C 29]," 37; "Revelation, 4 November 1830 [D&C 34]," in Revelation Book 1, 46, josephsmithpapers.org; see also Doctrine and Covenants 29:14; 34:8–9.

11. "Revelation, circa 7 March 1831 [D&C 45]," in Revelation Book 1, 73, 75; see also Doctrine and Covenants 45:26, 63.

12. "Revelation, 25 December 1832 [D&C 87]," 32–33; see also Doctrine and Covenants 87:1.

13. "Revelation, 25 December 1832 [D&C 87]," 33; capitalization and punctuation modernized; see also Doctrine and Covenants 87:3.

14. Merrill D. Peterson, *Olive Branch and Sword—The Compromise of 1833* (Baton Rouge: Louisiana State University Press, 1982); William W. Freehling, *Prelude to Civil War: The Nullification Controversy in South Carolina, 1816–1836* (New York: Harper & Row, 1966), 293. Scholars are divided on President Jackson's handling of the nullification crisis. Older scholarship tends to be more laudatory and celebratory, but more recent scholars have argued that

compromise constituted a serious embarrassment that hurt President Jackson politically in the years to come (see Richard E. Ellis, *The Union at Risk: Jacksonian Democracy, States' Rights, and the Nullification Crisis* [New York: Oxford University Press, 1987], 181–82).

15. Slave rebellions had occurred prior to 1832, but they tended to be isolated and short-lived events. See, for example, Stephen B. Oates, *The Fires of Jubilee: Nat Turner's Fierce Rebellion* (New York: Harper & Row, 1975).

16. Joseph Smith letter to Noah C. Saxton, Jan. 4, 1833, in Joseph Smith Letterbook 1, 17–18, josephsmithpapers.org; spelling modernized.

17. Although missionaries had carried handwritten copies of the revelation for decades, it was not published until 1851 (see Scott C. Esplin, "'Have We Not Had a Prophet among Us?': Joseph Smith's Civil War Prophecy," in *Civil War Saints,* ed. Kenneth L. Alford [Salt Lake City: Deseret Book, 2012], 41–59).

18. "Revelation, 1 November 1831–B [D&C 1]," in Revelation Book 1, 126, josephsmithpapers.org; see also "Revelation, 27–28 December 1832 [D&C 88:1–126]," in Revelation Book 2, 46, josephsmithpapers.org; Doctrine and Covenants 1:20; 88:122.

19. See Jed Woodworth, "The Word of Wisdom: D&C 89," history.lds.org; see also Doctrine and Covenants 89:20–21.

20. "Revelation, 27 February 1833 [D&C 89]," in Revelation Book 2, 51, josephsmithpapers.org; spelling modernized; see also Doctrine and Covenants 89:21.

21. See Susan Juster, *Doomsayers: Anglo-American Prophecy in the Age of Revolution* (Philadelphia: University of Pennsylvania Press, 2003).

22. "Revelation, 25 December 1832 [D&C 87]," 33; see also Doctrine and Covenants 87:8.

"A House for Our God"
D&C 88, 94, 95, 96, 97, 109, 110, 137

Lisa Olsen Tait and Brent Rogers

On June 1, 1833, Joseph Smith received a revelation that contained a stern rebuke. "Ye have sinned against me a very grievous sin," the Lord declared, "in that ye have not considered the great commandment in all things that I have given unto you concerning the building of mine house."[1] That "great commandment" had come five months earlier in a lengthy revelation Joseph called the "olive leaf" (now Doctrine and Covenants 88). It had directed the Saints to "organize [themselves]" and establish "an house of prayer, an house of fasting, an house of faith, an house of learning, an house of glory, an house of order, an house of God."[2]

Taken together with instructions to "teach one another" and "seek learning even by study and also by faith," Joseph Smith and the elders in Kirtland understood this revelation to deliver a twofold mandate.[3] They were to "build an house of God, & establish a school for the Prophets."[4] Joseph Smith and the Saints in Kirtland began acting on this instruction almost immediately, but, as the June 1 revelation indicated, they still had only a dim understanding of what it would ultimately mean or of the enormous sacrifices it would require.

"Ye Have Not Considered"

Within weeks of the olive leaf revelation, the School of the Prophets was well under way, with as many as 25 men meeting in a small room above the Newel K. Whitney Store (see Nathan Waite, "A School and an Endowment: D&C 88, 90, 95, 109, 110," on page 174 of this book). The school adjourned for the season by April 1833, and Joseph and the brethren turned their attention to the practical aspects of fulfilling the revelation. Land purchases were soon finalized, and men were appointed to oversee the various industries on those properties.[5] On May 4, a conference of high priests met to consider "the necessity of building a school house for the purpose of accommodating the Elders who should come in to receive their education for the ministry." Hyrum Smith, Jared Carter, and Reynolds Cahoon were appointed "a committee to obtain subscriptions [donations], for the purpose of Erecting such a building."[6]

Though the building would come to be known as the Kirtland Temple, the Saints in 1833 did not yet know they were building a temple. They had read of temples in the Bible and the Book of Mormon, but they still knew little about them. Two years earlier, a revelation had indicated that a temple would be built in Jackson County, Missouri.[7] Joseph Smith himself had helped set the cornerstone in 1831, but almost no progress had been made, and further revelations gave only a faint view of what the purpose of temples was to be.

The records from the spring of 1833 show that the Saints were thinking of the Kirtland "house" primarily as a "school house," not necessarily connecting their command with the temple in Zion. Now the June 1 revelation declared that Joseph Smith and the Saints had not sufficiently "considered" the urgency or the importance of the commandment.

That revelation (now Doctrine and Covenants 95) gave some indication of the bigger picture. It revealed that in the "house" the Lord would "endow those whom I have chosen with power from on high"[8]—connecting the construction of the house with a promised endowment of power.[9] It specified the interior dimensions of the building—55 feet wide by 65 feet long—and described the functions of the upper and lower floors of the "inner court," a phrase that evoked images of the biblical temple in Jerusalem. The revelation also promised further instruction. The house was to be built "not after the manner of the world," but "after the manner which I shall show unto three of you, whom ye shall appoint and ordain unto this power."[10]

Joseph Smith and his counselors, Sidney Rigdon and Frederick G. Williams, were duly appointed "to obtain a draft or construction of the inner court of the house."[11] Williams later described the ensuing vision. "We went upon our knees," he remembered, "called on the Lord, and the Building appeared within viewing distance: I being the first to discover it. Then all of us viewed it together. After we had taken a good look at the exterior, the building seemed to come right over us." The finished building, he said, "seemed to coincide with that I there saw to a minutia."[12]

One fundamental question settled by this vision was the matter of what materials to use in building the house. Lucy Mack Smith remembered a council meeting in which it was decided that a frame building would be too expensive; a log house was proposed instead. Joseph Smith reminded them "that they were not making a house for themselves or any other man but a house for God." He said, "And shall we, brethren, build a house for Our God of logs? No, brethren, I have a better plan than that. I have the plan of the house of the Lord given by himself." Lucy remembered Joseph saying that this plan would show them "the difference between our calculations and his Ideas." The brethren were "delighted" when Joseph described the full plan, which envisioned a stone structure.[13]

A Plan for a "City of the Stake of Zion"

These events expanded the vision of Joseph Smith and the Saints regarding the physical appearance of the house of the Lord to be built in Kirtland; other revelations contributed to an understanding of Zion and its geography. In June, three weeks after the presidency received their assignment to obtain the Lord's will regarding the design of the house of the Lord in Kirtland, they produced a plat map for the proposed city of Zion in Missouri that placed the temple at the center and included a sketch of its size, form, and dimensions.[14] The presidency directed Missouri leaders to build according to these patterns "immediately in Zion."[15]

Meanwhile, a revelation of June 4, 1833 (now Doctrine and Covenants 96), instructed that Bishop Newel K. Whitney take charge of the property on which the house of the Lord was to be built in Kirtland. Kirtland would be the "city of the stake of Zion"—a secondary gathering place patterned after the center place in Missouri. As directed in a revelation dated August 2, 1833 (now Doctrine and Covenants 94), it would be laid out similar to the plan for Missouri, with the house of the Lord at the center, much as the temple was the focus of the envisioned city of Zion. The revelation also called for the construction of two additional buildings—a "house" for the presidency and another for a printing operation—to be built alongside the temple in the city's center.[16] Also on August 2, a revelation (Doctrine and Covenants 97) reiterated the command that a "house" be built in Zion (Missouri), "like unto the pattern which I have given you." It was to be "built speedily" for a place of thanksgiving and instruction.[17]

Guided by the revelations, the presidency drew a Kirtland plat map and revised the plat for the city of Zion in Missouri.[18] They sent the revised plans and copies of the revelations to leaders in Missouri, but by the time the letter arrived, mob violence had broken out. Within months, Church members were forced to vacate Jackson County and put on hold any plans to build a temple there.

Joseph Smith's efforts at city planning were not unique in 19th-century America. They have been called "one flake in a blizzard of town plans" during that era of rapid westward expansion and urban development.[19] The plans for the city of Zion also appeared similar to those of many other towns—drawn up in a grid pattern and carefully laid out in the cardinal directions, with wide streets and spacious lots. But there was a crucial difference: Zion was centered on temples, not markets. It was a place of gathering, where converts came to live in sacred space and from which missionaries fanned out to preach the gospel—which led more people to gather. This spiritual and geographical pattern established in the summer of 1833 would shape Latter-day Saint communities for the rest of the century and beyond.[20]

"One Mainspring to All Our Thoughts"

After the violence in Missouri, efforts to build the house of the Lord in Kirtland began to accelerate. Responding to the aforementioned revelations, the previously appointed committee of Hyrum Smith, Reynolds Cahoon, and Jared Carter was now called the "building committee," and its mandate was expanded from fundraising to construction. They were to "proceed immediately to commence building the House or obtaining materials, Stone Brick Lumber &c."[21] On June 7, Hyrum Smith recorded in his diary, "This day commenced making preparations for the Building of the House of the Lord."[22]

Building the temple would be a huge challenge for the Saints. In the summer of 1833, there were only 150 members of the Church living in the area.[23] None of them had the traditional qualifications to oversee such an ambitious construction project—there was not a single architect or engineer among them, or even an experienced draftsman to draw up the plans.[24] Money was already tight, and the construction of the large, distinguished building, at an estimated cost of $40,000, stretched the Church's financial resources beyond capacity over the next three years.[25]

While the building's dimensions and functions and some aspects of its appearance were specified by revelation, other elements were left up to the leaders and workers on the site. The building's design shows that they drew on their own experience and assumptions about what a church building should look like. Its shape reflects the popular Greek Revival style. Like many builders of the time, they also borrowed an eclectic mix of features from standard building manuals.[26] The Gothic windows were widely associated with religious buildings, and the tower and steeple had become iconic features of New England churches.

By that fall, stone foundation walls were in place, but construction soon ground to a halt.[27] Workers at the Church-owned brickyard had not been able to produce enough bricks of sufficient quality for use in construction.[28] A decision was made to "discontinue the building of the temple for the winter for want of materials and to prepare and get all things ready to recommence it early in the spring."[29]

The next major phase of construction began with the arrival in April 1834 of Artemus Millet, a convert and experienced masonry builder from Canada. Millet's crucial contribution was the suggestion to use a rubblework-and-stucco building technique instead of the more expensive brick construction.[30] Following his counsel, the Saints built the walls of rough stone, hauled in from the nearby sandstone quarry, which was then faced with stucco to give it a finished look.

The spring and summer of 1834 were difficult seasons for construction on the temple because most of the men in the community went with Joseph Smith to Missouri in the Camp of Israel, hoping to aid the Saints who had been driven by mob violence from their homes. With the men gone, women carried on the labor. Some did masonry, others drove cattle and hauled rock, and still others sewed, spun, and knit to make clothing for workers.[31]

The return of Joseph Smith and most of the men from the Camp of Israel meant constructing the temple once again became the primary focus of activity in Kirtland. Joseph himself "acted as foreman in the temple stone quarry" and labored on the building "when other duties would permit."[32] By February 1835, the walls were in place and work had begun on the roof. A meeting was held on March 7, 1835, at which Joseph Smith expressed appreciation to those "who had distinguished themselves Thus far by consecrating to the upbuilding of said house as well as laboring [on its construction]." Sidney Rigdon then gave blessings to 120 individuals who had assisted in building the house of the Lord through their work and consecration.[33]

By that fall, there was even greater urgency to finish the temple. Lucy Mack Smith expressed the dedication of Church members to the effort. "There was but one main spring to all our thoughts," she said, "and that was building the Lords house."[34] Truman Angell, a carpenter's apprentice from Providence, Rhode Island, took the lead on the carpentry work in the upper level.[35] Brigham Young and his brother Joseph employed their expert craftsmanship to build and install the windows.[36] Another Young brother, Lorenzo, worked with Artemus Millet on the exterior stucco, a challenging job in the cold winter weather. The plastering of the interior was overseen by Jacob Bump, a skilled carpenter who had also built the pulpits and crafted the beautiful woodwork in the lower court. Stoves were strategically placed to warm the interior and aid in the drying of the plaster.[37]

Women worked on the veils that would be hung from the ceiling to subdivide the lower hall and made other furnishings for the temple. Joseph Smith later "pronounced a blessing upon the Sisters for the liberality in giving their servises so cheerfully to make the veil for the Lord's house."[38] Children even helped by gathering broken dishes and glassware, which were added to the stucco to help it glisten in the sun.[39]

"A Place to Manifest Himself"

The interior of the temple was completed in stages, and as rooms were completed, Church leaders and members began to use them for various purposes. Meanwhile, Joseph Smith labored relentlessly to prepare the Saints spiritually for the manifestations promised in the revelations. "I returned to my house being weary with continual anxiety & labour in puting all the Authorities in [order] & in striving to purify them for the solemn assembly according to the commandment of the Lord," he recorded in his journal on January 30, 1836.[40] Just a few days earlier, in the midst of such preparations, Joseph had received a vision of the celestial kingdom (Doctrine and Covenants 137); other spiritual outpourings during this period offered a glimpse of even greater experiences to come.

The dedication of the house of the Lord was a moment of celebration and satisfaction for the early Saints. The revelations of three years earlier had taken shape through immeasurable sacrifices of labor and resources. In the dedicatory prayer, now found in Doctrine and Covenants 109, Joseph Smith pleaded, "We ask thee, O Lord, to accept of this house, the workmanship of the hands of us, thy servants, which thou didst command us to build; for thou knowest that we have done this work through great tribulation: and out of our poverty we have given of our substance to build a house to thy name, that the Son of Man might have a place to manifest himself to his people."[41]

The promised manifestations did come. The Savior appeared and declared his acceptance of the temple, and other heavenly beings committed priesthood keys to Joseph Smith and Oliver Cowdery.[42]

Those manifestations opened the way for future temple revelations and ordinances. Having shown their willingness to build the Lord a house, the Latter-day Saints had only just begun to learn the purpose of temples.

1. "Revelation, 1 June 1833 [D&C 95]," 59, josephsmithpapers.org; spelling modernized; see also Doctrine and Covenants 95:3.

2. "Revelation, 27–28 December 1832 [D&C 88:1–126]," 45–46, josephsmithpapers.org; punctuation and capitalization modernized; see also Doctrine and Covenants 88:119.

3. "Revelation, 27–28 December 1832 [D&C 88:1–126]," 45; punctuation and capitalization modernized; see also Doctrine and Covenants 88:118.

4. Joseph Smith letter to William W. Phelps, Jan. 11, 1833, in Letterbook 1, page 19, josephsmithpapers.org.

5. On April 2, for example, Frederick G. Williams was appointed to oversee brickmaking work on a newly purchased property and to serve as agent in renting the farmland. See Joseph Smith, "History, 1838–1856, volume A-1 [23 December 1805–30 August 1834]," josephsmithpapers.org. See also "Minutes, 23 March 1833–A," josephsmithpapers.org.

6. Minute Book 1, May 4, 1833, page 20, josephsmithpapers.org; spelling modernized.

7. See "Revelation, 20 July 1831 [D&C 57]," 93, josephsmithpapers.org; Doctrine and Covenants 57:2–3; see also "Revelation, 2 August 1833–A [D&C 97]," 1–2; Doctrine and Covenants 97:10–17.

8. "Revelation, 1 June 1833 [D&C 95]," 59–60, josephsmithpapers.org; see also Doctrine and Covenants 95:8.

9. See "Revelation, 2 January 1831 [D&C 38]," 52, josephsmithpapers.org; "Revelation, February 1831–A [D&C 43]," 68, josephsmithpapers.org; see also Doctrine and Covenants 38:32, 38; 43:16.

10. "Revelation, 1 June 1833 [D&C 95]," 60, josephsmithpapers.org; see also Doctrine and Covenants 95:13–17.

11. "Minutes, circa 1 June 1833," in Minute Book 1, page 12, josephsmithpapers.org; Doctrine and Covenants 95:14.

12. Truman O. Angell autobiography, photocopy of typescript, 4, Church History Library, Salt Lake City.

13. Lucy Mack Smith, "Lucy Mack Smith, History, 1844–1845," book 14, page 1, josephsmithpapers.org; punctuation modernized.

14. "Plan of the House of the Lord, between 1 and 25 June 1833," josephsmithpapers.org. On this drawing, Williams noted that "the size form and deme[n]sions were given us of the Lord."

15. "'Explanation of the Plat of the City of Zion,' circa 25 June 1833," 38–41, josephsmithpapers.org.

16. See "Revelation, 2 August 1833–B [D&C 94]," 1, josephsmithpapers.org; see also Doctrine and Covenants 94:1. In early editions of the Doctrine and Covenants, this revelation was incorrectly dated May 6, 1833. The date was corrected in the 2013 edition. See the explanation for changes in section headings based on manuscript historical sources.

17. "Revelation, 2 August 1833–B [D&C 94]," 2–3; see also Doctrine and Covenants 94:3–12. The two buildings were never built, since all of the Church's resources were required to construct the temple.

18. See "Revelation, 2 August 1833–A [D&C 97]," 1, josephsmithpapers.org; see also Doctrine and Covenants 97:10–13.

19. Gerrit J. Dirkmaat, Brent M. Rogers, Grant Underwood, Robert J. Woodford, and William G. Hartley, eds., *Documents, Volume 3, February 1833–March 1834,* vol. 3 of the Documents series of *The Joseph Smith Papers,* ed. Ronald K. Esplin and Matthew J. Grow (Salt Lake City: Church Historian's Press, 2014), 208–21; see also "Revised Plat of the City of Zion, circa Early August 1833," josephsmithpapers.org.

20. Richard Lyman Bushman, "Making Space for the Mormons," in Richard Lyman Bushman, *Believing History: Latter-day Saint Essays,* ed. Reid L. Neilson and Jed Woodworth (New York: Columbia University Press, 2004), 179.

21. Bushman, "Making Space for the Mormons," 181–84.

22. "Minutes, 6 June 1833," in Minute Book 1, page 21, josephsmithpapers.org.

23. Hyrum Smith, Diary and Account Book, Nov. 1831–Feb. 1835, Hyrum Smith Papers, ca. 1832–1844, L. Tom Perry Special Collections, Harold B. Lee Library, Brigham Young University, Provo, Utah. Historical records give some conflicting accounts of the beginning of construction. See also "Notes for JS History, circa 1843," in Revelation Book 2, page 1, josephsmithpapers.org; Lucy Mack Smith, "Lucy Mack Smith, History, 1844–1845," book 14, pages 1–2, josephsmithpapers.org.

24. Joseph Smith and others, "Letter to Church Leaders in Jackson County, Missouri, 25 June 1833," josephsmithpapers.org.

25. Elwin C. Robison, The First Mormon Temple: Design, Construction, and Historic Context of the Kirtland Temple (Provo, Utah: Brigham Young University Press, 1997), 4, 9–16.

26. John Corrill, a former leader and Church historian, gave the cost as "nearly forty thousand dollars" and stated that the Church was "thirteen or fourteen thousand dollars in debt" after the temple's construction. "John Corrill, 'Brief History,' Manuscript, circa 1838–1839," 33–34, josephsmithpapers.org. In 1837 Sidney Rigdon said that close to $13,000 in debt remained unpaid. See "Anniversary of the Church of Latter-day Saints," Latter Day Saints' Messenger and Advocate, vol. 3, no. 7 (Apr. 1837), 488.

27. Robison, The First Mormon Temple, 16; see also C. Mark Hamilton, Nineteenth-Century Mormon Architecture and City Planning (New York: Oxford University Press, 1995), 37–38.

28. Ira Ames, who arrived in Kirtland around the beginning of October 1833, found that the temple "was raised up to the first floor." Ira Ames autobiography and journal, image 20, Church History Library, Salt Lake City.

29. Robison, The First Mormon Temple, 33.

30. Frederick G. Williams, "Frederick G. Williams to 'Brethren,' 10 October 1833," in Letterbook 1, pages 57–58, josephsmithpapers.org.

31. Robison, The First Mormon Temple, 33.

32. Aroet L. Hale reminiscences, Church History Library, Salt Lake City; see also "Extracts from H. C. Kimball's Journal," Times and Seasons, vol. 6 (Apr. 15, 1845), 867.

33. Joseph Smith, "History, 1838–1856, volume B-1 [1 September 1834–2 November 1838]," 553, josephsmithpapers.org.

34. "Minutes and Discourses, 7–8 March 1835," in Minute Book 1, pages 192–95, josephsmithpapers.org. Fifteen more individuals received blessings the next day following Church services.

35. Lucy Mack Smith, "Lucy Mack Smith, History, 1844–1845," book 14, page 3, josephsmithpapers.org.

36. Truman O. Angell autobiography, 4; see also Robison, The First Mormon Temple, 66–68.

37. Robison, The First Mormon Temple, 78.

38. Joseph Smith, "History, 1838–1856, volume B-1 [1 September 1834–2 November 1838]," 684, josephsmithpapers.org. For more information on the use of stoves, see William W. Phelps letter to Sally Phelps, Dec. 18, 1835, in Bruce A. Van Orden, ed., "Writing to Zion: The William W. Phelps Kirtland Letters (1835–1836)," BYU Studies, vol. 33, no. 3 (1993), 571.

39. Joseph Smith, "Journal, 1835–1836," Feb. 23, 1836, josephsmithpapers.org.

40. The story that Saints intentionally broke dishes to add to the stucco is not supported by historical documents but may have been inspired by this reuse of fragments from discard piles. See discussion in Robison, First Mormon Temple, 79.

41. Joseph Smith, "Journal, 1835–1836," Jan. 30, 1836, josephsmithpapers.org.

42. "Prayer of Dedication, 27 March 1836 [D&C 109]," 1, josephsmithpapers.org; see also Doctrine and Covenants 109:4–5.

43. "Revelation, 3 April 1836 [D&C 110]," 192–93, josephsmithpapers.org; see also Doctrine and Covenants 110:7, 11–16.

A School and an Endowment

D&C 88, 90, 95, 109, 110

Nathan Waite

In spring 1834, at a meeting of all priesthood bearers in Kirtland, Ohio, Joseph Smith shared the vision he had of the Church's destiny. It was more than any of those in attendance could imagine; he said, "You know no more concerning the destinies of this Church and kingdom than a babe upon its mother's lap." Then he prophesied: "It is only a little handfull of Priesthood you see here tonight, but this Church will fill North and South America—it will fill the world." [1]

To the men in the room, this must have been a thrilling thought but a daunting one. They had already accomplished much in the mission field, baptizing Church members in parts of the United States and Canada. Thinking of taking the gospel to all the earth, though, they surely felt their own limitations. What would have to happen to expand from a handful of Church members to a worldwide faith? How would the elders of the Church help fulfill the Lord's vision?

A Promise of Divine Help

In the New Testament, Jesus promised His Apostles heavenly assistance as they went forth to "preach the gospel to every creature." He instructed them to "tarry . . . in the city of Jerusalem, until ye be endued with power from on high." [2] The Lord had similarly promised the Saints in 1831 that after gathering to Ohio, they would be "endowed with power from on high" and then sent out to spread the gospel message. [3] In later years, this endowment came to be understood as a specific set of ceremonies performed in the Nauvoo Temple and later temples, but in the 1830s it was understood to be a spiritual outpouring similar to what happened on the day of Pentecost, a literal endowment or bestowal of miraculous power on those who went to spread the gospel. [4]

In a revelation received in late December 1832 and early January 1833, now Doctrine and Covenants 88, the Lord elaborated on what the elders should do to "be prepared in all things when I shall send you again" to testify and to warn the people of the earth.[5] The revelation commanded Church members to organize themselves and "teach one another" and to build a "house of God." Echoing Jesus's command in the New Testament, the revelation told the elders to "tarry" in Kirtland, where they were to be instructed and empowered at the school, "that [they] may be perfected in [their] ministry to go forth among the Gentiles for the last time."[6]

Learning in the School of the Prophets

Acting on the revelation, the Saints began work to "establish a school for the Prophets" in Kirtland.[7] The concept of a school of the prophets was not unique to the Latter-day Saints. In the 17th and 18th centuries, Harvard and Yale were seminaries for training clergy, and both were referred to at times as schools of the prophets. Later, reform movements associated with the Second Great Awakening—a widespread religious revival movement in the United States in the early 19th century—established private ministerial schools under the same name.[8]

The early Latter-day Saints did not have the resources or educational background of most school founders, but they went forward in faith. Not yet having a house of the Lord to meet in, the School of the Prophets was officially organized on January 22 and 23, 1833, in a small room above Newel K. Whitney's store in Kirtland. Though both men and women attended the January 22 portion of the meeting, the school itself was reserved for men ordained to the priesthood. Those in attendance at the first meeting received "the divine manifestation of the Holy Spirit," including speaking in tongues.[9]

Unlike a conventional school, with semesters and set schedules in a fixed location, the School of the Prophets was intermittent and moved around. In farming communities such as Kirtland, winter months provided more time for such activities as schooling. The first session lasted about three months and closed in April.[10] Subsequent sessions, called variously the "school of the prophets," the "school of mine apostles," and "Elders school," were held that summer in Missouri and again in Kirtland in fall 1834 and winter

1835–36 in the Church's printing office or in the attic floor of the unfinished Kirtland Temple.[11]

The December 1832 revelation had given specific instructions for the school's course of study, which was to include both religious and secular topics. Students were to become well versed in the "theory, principle, doctrine, and the law of the gospel," and they were also to learn about the earth itself—what was above it, on it, and under it. They were to learn history and current events, with perspective on the future through prophetic revelation. They were to learn about foreign countries. The School of the Prophets was to be instructed both by an officially appointed teacher and by the participants themselves learning from one another, with each having a turn to speak "that all may be edified of all."[12]

A revelation on March 8, 1833, now Doctrine and Covenants 90, gave the newly appointed First Presidency of the Church the "keys" to administer the School of the Prophets, and it appears that Joseph Smith took the lead in spiritual subjects, assisted by Sidney Rigdon. The School of the Prophets was the venue in which the seven lectures on theology now known as the Lectures on Faith were delivered. These lectures were included in early editions of the Doctrine and Covenants. They were the first part of the book, designated "Doctrine," while the second part was the "Covenants," or revelations. The Lectures on Faith endure as an important theological contribution of the early 1830s.[13]

Language studies were a major part of the more traditional schooling, beginning with English grammar. For the most part, the elders in attendance were not well educated and could say with Joseph Smith that as children of poor parents, they had been "mearly instructtid in reading and writing and the ground rules of Arithmatic."[14] Though Orson Hyde had been orphaned as a child and received little formal education, he had a gift for learning and was appointed teacher.[15] On several occasions, Joseph Smith went home in the evening and gathered his family around him to teach them the very grammar lessons he had learned that day in the School of the Prophets.[16] A course in Hebrew, taught by a Jewish professor from a nearby college, was given in 1836 and was attended by many students of the School of the Prophets.

Becoming Clean and Unified

The School of the Prophets allowed the early Saints to reach for more education than they had access to previously. But it also served purposes that went beyond learning facts and concepts. The first generation of Latter-day Saints grew up in a culture where personal reputation was highly valued and where it was normal and even encouraged to react forcefully to real or perceived slights. The revealed order of the School of the Prophets was designed in part to help members rise above these shortcomings of their culture. Ritual practices underscored the need to become clean and unified.

To become "clean from the blood of this generation" and to set themselves apart from the world, the elders participated in ritual washings.[17] After each elder washed his own face, hands, and feet, Joseph Smith washed the feet of each, following the example set by Jesus in John 13:4–17 and instructions in Doctrine and Covenants 88:138–41. Joseph washed the feet of each new member of the school and repeated the ceremony at other meetings of the School of the Prophets.[18] Later washings and anointings, including foot washing, were part of preparations for the solemn assembly held in the newly dedicated Kirtland Temple, and these washings featured prominently in the solemn assembly itself.

A more mundane concern with cleanliness also played a role in the School of the Prophets. One participant remembered that before each school day, "we washed ourselves and put on clean linen."[19] And Emma Smith's complaints about the filth caused by the school members' chewing tobacco led to the revelation known as the Word of Wisdom.[20]

In addition to symbolizing purification, the washing of feet was also intended to help unify the elders. Revelations urged them again and again to "love one another" and to "cease to find fault with one another," warning, "If ye are not one ye are not mine."[21] Joseph Smith taught that unity was a prerequisite to being endowed and was part of the definition of Zion.[22] Harmony between Church leaders in Ohio and Missouri was something Joseph Smith continually strived for, and he taught that in addition to spiritual cleansing, the washing of feet was "calculated to unite our hearts, that we may be one in feeling and sentiment."[23]

The prescribed greeting when entering the school was also intended to promote harmony, even in a culture of contention. The president or teacher was to enter first and greet each participant by raising his hands to heaven and saying, "Art thou a brother or brethren? I salute you in the name of the Lord Jesus Christ, in token or remembrance of the everlasting covenant, in which covenant I receive you to fellowship, in a determination that is fixed, immovable, and unchangeable, to be your friend and brother through the grace of God in the bonds of love, to walk in all the commandments of God blameless, in thanksgiving, forever and ever. Amen." The student seeking to enter the school would repeat back the covenant or simply reply, "Amen."

Participants in the School of the Prophets also partook of the sacrament together—but in portions that perhaps resembled the Last Supper more than the morsel of bread and sip of water that Latter-day Saints are accustomed to today. As Zebedee Coltrin recalled, "Warm bread to break easy was provided and broken into pieces as large as my fist and each person had a glass of wine and sat and ate the bread and drank the wine."[24]

Working toward the Promises

In spite of these unifying ordinances, harmony proved elusive. The first session was wrapped up in April 1833 at the time of several mission calls, and a revelation in June (Doctrine and Covenants 95) made it clear that the term ended on a dissonant note: "Contentions arose in the school of the prophets," the Lord said, "which was very grievous unto me." The same revelation reprimanded the Saints for not yet starting work on the house of the Lord and reiterated that it was the place for the "school of mine apostles." This revelation promised that the long-anticipated "endowment" would come at a "solemn assembly" within the walls of the new temple.

Beginning in 1834, Church leaders from both Missouri and Ohio gathered in Kirtland to attend the school and otherwise prepare for the solemn assembly where they would receive the endowment.

The two sets of leaders had a history of not getting along, however, and lapses of unity characterized the period. Around the same time, Orson Hyde sent a scathing letter to Joseph Smith about a dispute with another Apostle, Joseph's brother William Smith.[25] Hyde refused to attend the school until the matter was settled. Though Hyde's concerns were soon resolved, other disputes continued to trouble the group. "The adversary is bringing into requisition all his subtlety," Joseph Smith said, "to prevent the Saints from being endowed by causing devision among the 12, also among the 70, and bickerings and jealousies among the Elders."[26]

Fortunately, the winter of 1835–36 brought a long hoped-for period of reconciliations and harmony in the Church. Joseph Smith and his brother William mended a damaged relationship, one that had been characterized by the occasional throwing of fists.[27] A major disagreement between the First Presidency and Quorum of the Twelve ended with an emotional reconciliation and covenant making that hearkened back to the greeting of the School of the Prophets.[28] Regarding a Church meeting shortly thereafter at which the newly unified Church leaders spoke, Joseph Smith's journal reports, "The Lord poured out his spirit upon us, and the brethren began to confess their faults one to the other and the congregation were soon overwhelmed in tears and some of our hearts were too big for utterance, the gift of toungs, come upon us also like the rushing of a mighty wind, and my soul was filled with the glory of God."[29] Thus unified, and with such manifestation of God's approval, they were readying themselves to receive the promised endowment.

Spiritual Outpourings

Miraculous spiritual manifestations occurred at various times over the course of the School of the Prophets as the elders worked to live up to God's vision for them and prepare for the endowment.[30] Joseph Smith said such manifestations were "a prelude of those joys that God will pour out" at the solemn assembly.[31]

When the Kirtland Temple was finally ready for dedication in March 1836, Joseph Smith sought guidance in preparing a prayer for the monumental occasion. The prayer, given by revelation and now published as Doctrine and Covenants 109, touched on many of the themes that had occupied the School of the Prophets over the long preparation for the endowment of power. It spoke of learning, of spiritual cleanliness, of organization and unity, and of missionary work.

At the long-awaited solemn assembly in the temple, many people experienced powerful spiritual experiences that they affirmed as an endowment of power. Joseph Smith recorded, "The Saviour made his appearance to some, while angels minestered unto others, and it was a penticost and enduement indeed, long to be remembered for the sound shall go forth from this place into all the world, and the occurrences of this day shall be handed down upon the pages of sacred history to all generations, as the day of Pentecost." Further manifestations and visions accompanied the dedication of the Kirtland Temple that same week.[32]

On Sunday, April 3, 1836, as Joseph Smith and Oliver Cowdery prayed at the temple pulpits, they were visited by Jesus Christ and many angelic messengers. Christ pronounced them clean, accepted the house they had built for Him, and affirmed "the endowment with which my servants have already been endowed." Immediately thereafter, they received from Moses himself "the keys of the gathering of Israel from the four parts of the Earth," as well as receiving other keys from other ancient prophets.[33] In their eyes, the promises had been fulfilled and the elders did not need to tarry in Kirtland any longer.

To All Nations

Over the following months, missionaries departed from Kirtland to preach the gospel. In 1837, Orson Hyde and Heber C. Kimball went to England. This mission and ensuing missions in the British Isles brought thousands of people into The Church of Jesus Christ of Latter-day Saints and changed the course of its history. In 1844, Joseph Smith reported, "Missionaries of this church have gone to the East Indies, to Australia, Germany, Constantinople, Egypt, Palestine, the Islands of the Pacific, and are now preparing to open the door in the extensive dominions of Russia."[34] These missionary efforts, undertaken in great part by those educated in the School of the

Prophets and endowed with power in the Kirtland Temple, marked the beginnings of the restored gospel going forth to fill all the world.

1. Wilford Woodruff, in Conference Report, Apr. 1898, 57.

2. Mark 16:15; Luke 24:47–49; see also Matthew 28:18–20.

3. "Revelation, 2 January 1831 [D&C 38]," josephsmithpapers.org.

4. John Corrill and others believed that this promise was fulfilled when individuals were first ordained to the high priesthood in June 1831. Several reported spiritual manifestations, but it was soon understood that a greater endowment would be coming (see John Corrill, *Brief History of the Church of Christ of Latter Day Saints [Commonly Called Mormons]* [St. Louis, Missouri: printed by author, 1839]; Karen Lynn Davidson, Richard L. Jensen, and David J. Whittaker, eds., *Histories, Volume 2: Assigned Histories, 1831–1847,* vol. 2 of the Histories series of *The Joseph Smith Papers,* ed. Dean C. Jessee, Ronald K. Esplin, and Richard Lyman Bushman [Salt Lake City: Church Historian's Press, 2012], 145).

5. "Revelation, 27–28 December 1832 [D&C 88:1–126]," josephsmithpapers.org; punctuation modernized.

6. "Revelation, 27–28 December 1832 [D&C 88:1–126]."

7. Joseph Smith, "Letter to William W. Phelps, 11 January 1833," josephsmithpapers.org.

8. See Joseph F. Darowski, "Schools of the Prophets: An Early American Tradition," *Mormon Historical Studies,* vol. 9, no. 1 (Spring 2008), 1–13.

9. "Minutes, 22–23 January 1833," 7, josephsmithpapers.org.

10. Joseph Smith, "History, 1838–1856, volume A-1 [23 December 1805–30 August 1834]," 287, josephsmithpapers.org.

11. The name "school of mine apostles" appears in Doctrine and Covenants 95:17. "Elders school" appears in Joseph Smith, "History, 1838–1856, volume B-1 [1 September 1834–2 November 1838]," 562, josephsmithpapers.org.

12. "Revelation, 27–28 December 1832 [D&C 88:1–126]."

13. Historical introduction for "Doctrine and Covenants, 1835," josephsmithpapers.org.

14. Joseph Smith, "History, circa Summer 1832," 1, josephsmithpapers.org.

15. Orson Hyde apparently had a gift for languages and later memorized the Bible in English, German, and Hebrew (see Orson Hyde, "The Marriage Relations," in *Journal of Discourses,* 26 vols. [1854–86], 2:81).

16. Joseph Smith, "Journal, 1835–1836," Nov. 4, 5, 11, 1835, josephsmithpapers.org.

17. Doctrine and Covenants 88:138.

18. Zebedee Coltrin reminiscences, in Minutes, Salt Lake City School of the Prophets, Oct. 3, 1883; boap.org/LDS/Early-Saints/ZebC.html.

19. Zebedee Coltrin reminiscences, in Minutes, Salt Lake City School of the Prophets, Oct. 3, 1883.

20. Jed Woodworth, "The Word of Wisdom: D&C 89," history.lds.org.

21. Doctrine and Covenants 88:123–24; 38:27.

22. Joseph Smith, "Journal, 1835–1836," Jan. 16, 1836; Dean C. Jessee, Mark Ashurst-McGee, and Richard L. Jensen, eds., *Journals, Volume 1: 1832–1839,* vol. 1 of the Journals series of *The Joseph Smith Papers,* ed. Dean C. Jessee, Ronald K. Esplin, and Richard Lyman Bushman (Salt Lake City: Church Historian's Press, 2008), 157.

23. Joseph Smith, "Journal, 1835–1836," Nov. 12, 1835.

24. Zebedee Coltrin reminiscences, in Minutes, Salt Lake City School of the Prophets, Oct. 3, 1883.

25. "Letter from Orson Hyde, 15 December 1835," josephsmithpapers.org. For the resolution of Orson Hyde's concerns, see Joseph Smith, "Journal, 1835–1836," Dec. 17, 1835.

26. Joseph Smith, "Journal, 1835–1836," Jan. 1, 1836.

27. Joseph Smith, "Journal, 1835–1836," Jan. 1, 1836.

28. Joseph Smith, "Journal, 1835–1836," Jan. 16, 1836.

29. Joseph Smith, "Journal, 1835–1836," Jan. 17, 1836.

30. Zebedee Coltrin reminiscences, in Minutes, Salt Lake City School of the Prophets, Oct. 3, 1883. Many of the features of this preparation and endowment, such as washing and anointing, instruction, and coming into the presence of God, would play a central role in the endowment ceremony as revealed in Nauvoo.

31. Joseph Smith, "Journal, 1835–1836," Nov. 12, 1835.

32. Joseph Smith, "Journal, 1835–1836," Mar. 30, 1836.

33. "Revelation, 3 April 1836 [D&C 110]," josephsmithpapers.org.

34. Joseph Smith, "Latter Day Saints," 409, josephsmithpapers.org. This essay was published in Israel Daniel Rupp, ed., *He Pasa Ekklesia* (1844).

The Word of Wisdom
D&C 89
Jed Woodworth

Like many other revelations in the early Church, Doctrine and Covenants 89, also known today as the Word of Wisdom, came in response to a problem. In Kirtland, many men in the Church were called to preach in various parts of the United States. They were to cry repentance unto the people and gather in the Lord's elect. To prepare these recent converts for their important labors, Joseph Smith started a training school called the School of the Prophets, which opened in Kirtland on the second floor of the Newel K. Whitney mercantile store in January 1833.[1]

Every morning after breakfast, the men met in the school to hear instruction from Joseph Smith. The room was very small, and about 25 elders packed the space.[2] The first thing they did, after sitting down, was "light a pipe and begin to talk about the great things of the kingdom and puff away," Brigham Young recounted. The clouds of smoke were so thick the men could hardly even see Joseph through the haze. Once the pipes were smoked out, they would then "put in a chew on one side and perhaps on both sides and then it was all over the floor."[3] In this dingy setting, Joseph Smith attempted to teach the men how they and their converts could become holy, "without spot," and worthy of the presence of God.[4]

Tobacco

This episode in the Whitney store occurred in the middle of a massive transformation within western culture. In 1750, personal cleanliness and hygiene were infrequent, haphazard practices, mostly the concern of the wealthy and aristocratic. By 1900, regular bathing had become routine for a large portion of the population, especially the middle classes, who had adopted gentility as an ideal.[5] Tobacco spitting shifted from being a publicly acceptable practice among most segments of the population to becoming seen as a filthy habit beneath the dignity of polite society. In the midst of this cultural shift, at the very moment when everyday people started to concern themselves with their own cleanliness and bodily health, the Word of Wisdom arrived to light the way.

The scene in the School of the Prophets would have been enough to give any non-tobacco user like Joseph Smith cause for concern.[6] Joseph's wife, Emma, told him that the environment concerned her. He and Emma lived in the Whitney store, and the task of scrubbing the spittle from the hardwood fell upon her. She may have complained of being asked to perform this thankless task, but there was also a more practical consideration: "She could not make the floor look decent," Brigham Young recalled.[7] The stains were impossible to get out. The whole situation seemed less than ideal for those who were called of God as these elders were, especially when we remember that the room with the filthy floor was Joseph's "translation room," the same place where he received revelations in the name of God. Joseph began inquiring of the Lord about what could be done, and on February 27, scarcely a month after the school started, he received the revelation later canonized as Doctrine and Covenants 89. The answer was unequivocal: "Tobacco is not for man but is for bruises & all sick cattle; to be used with judgement & skill."[8]

Strong Drinks

Tobacco was just one of a host of substances pertaining to bodily health and cleanliness whose merits were hotly debated on both sides of the Atlantic Ocean at the time the Word of Wisdom was received. Discussion was so frequent because abuse was so widespread. Frances Trollope, a British novelist, reported disdainfully in 1832 that in all her recent travels in the United States, she hardly ever met a man who was not either a "tobacco chewer or a whisky drinker."[9]

Drinking, like tobacco chewing, had clearly gotten out of hand. For centuries nearly all Americans had consumed large quantities of alcoholic beverages, much like their European counterparts. The Puritans called alcohol the "Good Creature of God," a blessing from heaven to be imbibed in moderation. Alcohol was consumed at virtually every meal, in part because the unpurified water of the time was so unhealthy. Home-brewed beer was a favorite, and after 1700, British-American colonists drank fermented peach juice, hard apple cider, and rum either imported from the West Indies or distilled from molasses made there. By 1770, per capita consumption of distilled spirits alone—to say nothing of beer or cider—stood at 3.7 gallons per year.[10]

The American Revolution only exacerbated this reliance on alcohol. After molasses imports were cut off, Americans sought a substitute for rum by turning to whiskey. Grain farmers in western Pennsylvania and Tennessee found it cheaper to manufacture whiskey than to ship and sell perishable grains. As a consequence, the number of distilleries grew rapidly after 1780, boosted by settlement of the corn belt in Kentucky and Ohio and the vast distances to eastern markets. To the astonishment of observers like Trollope, Americans everywhere—men, women, and children—drank whiskey all day long. American consumption of distilled spirits climbed precipitously, from two and a half gallons a person in 1790 to seven gallons in 1830, the highest amount of any time in American history and a figure three times today's consumption rate.[11]

This elevated alcohol consumption offended religious sensibilities. As early as 1784, both Quakers and Methodists were advising their members to abstain from all hard liquor and to avoid participation in its sale and manufacture.[12] A more aggressive temperance movement took hold among the churches in the early decades of the 19th century. Alcohol became viewed more as a dangerous tempter and less as a gift from God. In 1812, the Congregational and Presbyterian churches in Connecticut recommended strict licensing laws limiting the distribution of alcohol. Lyman Beecher, a leader in this reform movement, advocated even more extreme measures, endorsing full abstinence from alcoholic beverages. The idea soon became a central plank of the American Temperance Society (ATS), organized in Boston in 1826. Members of the organization were encouraged to sign a temperance pledge not just to moderate their alcohol intake but to abstain altogether. A capital "T" was written next to the names of those who did so, and from this the word "teetotaler" was derived. By the mid-1830s, the ATS had grown to well over a million members, many of them teetotalers.[13]

Encouraged by the ATS, local temperance societies popped up by the thousands across the U.S. countryside. Kirtland had its own temperance society, as did many small towns.[14] Precisely because alcohol reform was so often discussed and debated, the Saints needed a way of adjudicating which opinions were right. Besides rejecting the use of tobacco, the Word of Wisdom also came down against alcoholic beverages: "Inasmuch as any man drinketh wine or Strong drink among you behold it is not good, neither mete in the sight of your Father."[15]

Nevertheless, it required time to wind down practices that were so deeply ingrained in family tradition and culture, especially when fermented beverages of all kinds were frequently used for medicinal purposes. The term "strong drink" certainly included distilled spirits such as whiskey, which thereafter the Latter-day Saints generally shunned. They took a more moderate approach to milder alcoholic beverages like beer and "pure wine of the grape of the vine, of your own make."[16] For the next two generations, Latter-day Saint leaders taught the Word of Wisdom as a command from God, but they tolerated a variety of viewpoints on how strictly the commandment should be observed. This incubation period gave the Saints time to develop their own tradition of abstinence from habit-forming substances. By the early 20th century, when scientific medicines were more widely available and temple attendance had become a more regular feature of Latter-day Saint worship, the Church was ready to accept a more exacting standard of observance that would eliminate problems like alcoholism from among the obedient. In 1921, the Lord inspired President Heber J. Grant to call on all Saints to live the Word of Wisdom to the letter by completely abstaining from all alcohol, coffee, tea, and tobacco. Today Church members are expected to live this higher standard.[17]

Hot Drinks

American temperance reformers succeeded in the 1830s in no small part by identifying a substitute for alcohol: coffee. In the 18th century, coffee was considered a luxury item, and British-manufactured tea was much preferred. After the Revolution, tea drinking came to be seen as unpatriotic and largely fell out of favor—the way was open for a rival stimulant to emerge. In 1830, reformers persuaded the U.S. Congress to remove the import duty on coffee. The strategy worked. Coffee fell to 10 cents a pound, making a cup of coffee the same price as a cup of whiskey, marking whiskey's decline. By 1833, coffee had entered "largely into the daily consumption of almost every family, rich and poor." The *Baltimore American* called it "among the necessaries of life."[18] Although coffee enjoyed wide approval by the mid-1830s, including within the medical community, a few radical reformers such as Sylvester Graham and William A. Alcott preached against the use of any stimulants whatsoever, including coffee and tea.[19]

The Word of Wisdom rejected the idea of a substitute for alcohol. "Hot drinks"—which Latter-day Saints understood to mean coffee and tea[20]—"are not for the body or belly," the revelation explained.[21] Instead, the revelation encouraged the consumption of basic staples of the kind that had sustained life for millennia. The revelation praised "all wholesome herbs" and explained that "all grain is for the use of man & of beasts to be the staff of life . . . as also the fruit of the vine that which beareth fruit whether in the ground or above ground." In keeping with an earlier revelation endorsing the eating of meat, the Word of Wisdom reminded the Saints that the flesh of beasts and fowls was given "for the use of man with thanksgiving," but added the caution that meat was "to be used sparingly" and not to excess.[22]

"I Will Pour Out My Spirit upon All Flesh"

Latter-day Saints who learn of the American health reform movements of the 1820s and 1830s may wonder how these movements relate to the Word of Wisdom. Did Joseph Smith simply draw upon ideas already existing in his environment and put them forward as revelation?

Such concerns are unwarranted. Remember that many early Latter-day Saints who took part in temperance societies viewed the Word of Wisdom as inspired counsel, "adapted to the Capacity of the weak & the weakest of Saints who are or can be called Saints."[23] Moreover, the revelation has no exact analog in the literature of its day. Temperance reformers often tried to frighten their hearers by linking alcohol consumption with a host of horrific diseases or social ills.[24] The Word of Wisdom offered no such rationale. Strong drink, the revelation says simply, is "not good." Similarly spare explanations are given for the injunctions against tobacco and hot drinks.[25] The revelation can be understood more as an arbiter and less as a participant in the cultural debate.

Instead of arguing from a position of fear, the Word of Wisdom argues from a position of confidence and trust. The revelation invites hearers to trust in a God who has the power to deliver great rewards, spiritual and physical, in return for obedience to divine command. Those who adhere to the Word of Wisdom, the revelation says, shall "receieve health in their navel and marrow to their bones & shall find wisdom & great treasures of wisdom & knowledge even hidden treasures."[26] These lines link body to spirit, elevating care for the body to the level of a religious principle.[27]

In the end, some overlap between the Word of Wisdom and the health reform movement of the 19th century is to be expected. This was a time of "refreshing" (Acts 3:19), a moment in history where light and knowledge were pouring down from heaven. On the night Joseph Smith was visited by the angel Moroni for the first time, in the fall of 1823, the angel quoted a line from the book of Joel and said it was about to be fulfilled: "I will pour out my spirit upon *all flesh*," the passage read (Joel 2:28; emphasis added). Insofar as temperance reform made people less dependent on addictive substances, prompting humility and righteous action, the movement surely was inspired by God. "That which is of God inviteth and enticeth to do good continually," the Book of Mormon stated (Moroni 7:13).[28] Rather than concerning themselves with cultural overlap, Latter-day Saints can joyously contemplate how God's Spirit touched so many, so widely, and with such force.

Soon after receiving the Word of Wisdom, Joseph Smith appeared before the elders of the School of the Prophets and read the revelation to them. The brethren did not have to be told what the words meant. They "immediately threw their tobacco pipes into the fire," one of the participants in the school recalled.[29] Since that time, the inspiration in the Word of Wisdom has been proven many times over in the lives of the Saints, its power and divinity cascading down through the years. In some ways, the American health reform movement has faded from view. The Word of Wisdom remains to light our way.

1. See Milton V. Backman Jr., "School of the Prophets and School of the Elders," in *Joseph: Exploring the Life and Ministry of the Prophet,* ed. Susan Easton Black and Andrew C. Skinner (Salt Lake City: Deseret Book, 2005), 165–75.

2. Orson Hyde was the main instructor that first term, but Joseph Smith seems to have had a regular presence. See Steven R. Sorensen, "Schools of the Prophets," in Daniel H. Ludlow, ed., *Encyclopedia of Mormonism,* 4 vols. (New York: Macmillan, 1992), 3:1269; Lyndon W. Cook, *The Revelations of the Prophet Joseph Smith: A Historical and Biographical Commentary on the Doctrine and Covenants* (Salt Lake City: Deseret Book, 1985), 191–92.

3. Brigham Young, Discourse, December 2, 1867; February 8, 1868, Papers of George D. Watt, shorthand transcribed by LaJean Purcell Carruth, Church History Library, Salt Lake City. The former sermon is unpublished. For a published version of the latter sermon, see Brigham Young, "Remarks," *Deseret News: Semi-Weekly,* Feb. 25, 1868, 2.

4. See "Revelation, 2 January 1831 [D&C 38]," in Revelation Book 1, 51, josephsmithpapers.org.

5. The "civilizing" process had been going on for centuries but accelerated up and down the social structure during the 19th century. See Norbert Elias, *The History of Manners,* trans. Edmunds Jephcott (New York, 1978); Georges Vigarello, *Concepts of Cleanliness: Changing Attitudes in France since the Middle Ages,* trans. Jean Birrell (Cambridge: Cambridge University Press and Editions de la Maison des Sciences de l'Homme, 1988); Richard L. Bushman and Claudia L. Bushman, "The Early History of Cleanliness in America," *Journal of American History,* vol. 74 (Mar. 1988), 1213–38; Richard L. Bushman, *The Refinement of America: Persons, Houses, Cities* (New York: Knopf, 1992); Dana C. Elder, "A Rhetoric of Etiquette for the 'True Man' of the Gilded Age," *Rhetoric Review,* vol. 21, no. 2 (2002), 155, 159.

6. On Joseph Smith's non-use of tobacco, see Brigham Young, Discourse, Feb. 8, 1868, Papers of George D. Watt, transcribed by LaJean Purcell Carruth, Church History Library, Salt Lake City.

7. Brigham Young, Discourse, Feb. 8, 1868. The published version changes the wording to reflect complaint more than consternation: "the complaints of his wife at having to clean so filthy a floor" ("Remarks," 2).

8. See "Revelation, 27 February 1833 [D&C 89]," in Sidney Gilbert, Notebook, 113, josephsmithpapers.org; punctuation standardized; see also Doctrine and Covenants 89:8.

9. Frances Trollope, *Domestic Manners of the Americans,* 2 vols. (London, 1832), 2:101. By 1800, tobacco was known to cure a long list of ailments: abdominal pain, snake bites, scurvy, piles, "madness," and dozens of more ills. But the spread of middle-class refinement in the early decades of the 19th century brought a new round of public critics. Tobacco came to be known as the "filthy weed," and words like "disgusting" and "annoying" increasingly became associated with it. See Lester E. Bush Jr., "The Word of Wisdom in Early Nineteenth-Century Perspective," *Dialogue,* vol. 14 (Fall 1981), 56; "For the Evening Post," *New York Evening Post,* June 27, 1829, [2].

10. See W. J. Rorabaugh, *The Alcoholic Republic: An American Tradition* (New York: Oxford University Press, 1979), 25–57; W. J. Rorabaugh, "Alcohol in America," *OAH Magazine of History,* vol. 6 (Fall 1991), 17–19; Peter C. Mancall, "'The Art of Getting Drunk' in Colonial Massachusetts," *Reviews in American History,* vol. 24 (Sept. 1996), 383.

11. See Gordon Wood, *Empire of Liberty: A History of the Early Republic, 1789–1815* (New York: Oxford University Press, 2009), 339; Joseph F. Kett, "Temperance and Intemperance as Historical Problems," *Journal of American History,* vol. 67 (Mar. 1981), 881; Rorabaugh, "Alcohol in America," 17.

12. See Mark Edward Lender and James Kirby Martin, *Drinking in America: A History,* rev. and exp. ed. (New York: Free Press, 1987), 35.

13. See Ian R. Tyrrell, *Sobering Up: From Temperance to Prohibition in Antebellum America, 1800–1860* (Westport, Connecticut: Greenwood Press, 1979); James R. Rohrer, "The Origins of the Temperance Movement: A Reinterpretation," *Journal of American Studies,* vol. 24 (Aug. 1990), 230–31; Lyman Beecher, *Six Sermons on the Nature, Occasions, Signs, Evils, and Remedy of Intemperance* (New York: American Tract Society, 1827), 194; Daniel Walker Howe, *What Hath God Wrought: The Transformation of America, 1815–1848* (New York: Oxford University Press, 2007), 166–68. The American Temperance Society adopted a formal pledge of abstinence from all alcoholic beverages in 1831. See Robert H. Abzug, *Cosmos Crumbling: American Reform and Religious Imagination* (New York: Oxford University Press, 1994), 98.

14. See Christopher G. Crary, *Pioneer and Personal Reminiscences* (Marshalltown, Iowa: Marshall Printing, 1893), 25. I am indebted to Andy Hedges for drawing this source to my attention.

15. See "Revelation, 27 February 1833 [D&C 89]," in Sidney Gilbert, Notebook, 113; see also Doctrine and Covenants 89:5. The term "strong drink" is a biblical phrase applying to wine, but temperance reformers often gave the term a more expansive definition that included distilled spirits. See Addison Parker, Address Delivered before the Southbridge Temperance Society, on the Evening of Dec. 1, 1830 (Southbridge: Josiah Snow, 1830), 7–8; Fifth Report of the American Temperance Society, Presented at the Meeting in Boston, May 1832 (Boston: Aaron Russell, 1832), 47, 95, 112.

16. Doctrine and Covenants 89:6; see also "Revelation, 27 February 1833 [D&C 89]," in Sidney Gilbert, Notebook, 113.

17. Moderation rather than abstinence was applied to virtually all of the "do nots" of the Word of Wisdom until the early 20th century. On the tightening up of Word of Wisdom observance, see Thomas G. Alexander, *Mormonism in Transition: A History of the Latter-day Saints, 1890–1930* (Urbana: University of Illinois Press, 1986), 258–71; Paul H. Peterson and Ronald W. Walker, "Brigham Young's Word of Wisdom Legacy," *BYU Studies,* vol. 42, nos. 3–4 (2003), 29–64.

18. Rorabaugh, *Alcoholic Republic,* 99–100.

19. See Bush, "The Word of Wisdom in Early Nineteenth-Century Perspective," 52.

20. See Paul H. Peterson, "An Historical Analysis of the Word of Wisdom" (master's thesis, Brigham Young University, 1972), 32–33; "The Word of Wisdom," *Times and Seasons,* vol. 3 (June 1, 1842), 800.

21. See "Revelation, 27 February 1833 [D&C 89]," in Sidney Gilbert, Notebook, 113; "City Marshall's Department," *City Gazette and Commercial* [Charleston, South Carolina], Apr. 18, 1823, 3; "Gaming," *Berks and Schuylkill Journal* (Reading, Pennsylvania), Jan. 8, 1825, 3.

22. "Revelation, 27 February 1833 [D&C 89]," in Sidney Gilbert, Notebook, 114; see also "Revelation, 7 May 1831 [D&C 49]," in Revelation Book 1, 81, josephsmithpapers.org.

23. See "Revelation, 27 February 1833 [D&C 89]," in Sidney Gilbert, Notebook, 113.

24. In the words of one authority, alcohol "stupefies their feelings, benumbs their moral sensibilities, weakens the powers of digestion, and in course brings on dispepsia, than which a more formidable disease hardly afflicts the human race" ("On Drunkenness," *Connecticut Herald,* Feb. 21, 1826, 1). For other such arguments, see "Twenty Dollars Reward," *Daily National Intelligencer,* Sept. 23, 1823, 4; "Rev. Isaac McCoy," *New Hampshire Repository,* vol. 6 (May 3, 1824), 70; "From the Times and Advertiser," *Times and Hartford Advertiser,* Jan. 3, 1826, 4.

25. This is not to say that all health pro-posals of the time relied on elaborate argumentation. See, for example, Samuel Underhill's propositions in Mark Lyman Staker, *Hearken, O Ye People: The Historical Setting for Joseph Smith's Ohio Revelations* (Salt Lake City: Greg Kofford Books, 2009), 110. For other ways the Word of Wisdom may have departed from accepted wisdom, see Steven C. Harper, *Making Sense of the Doctrine and Covenants: A Guided Tour through Modern Revelations* (Salt Lake City: Deseret Book, 2008), 332–33. In the 20th century, some Latter-day Saints sought to isolate the offending chemicals in the substances prohibited in the Word of Wisdom, but such analysis was never accepted as Church doctrine and went beyond the reasoning of the revelation itself. See John A. Widtsoe and Leah D. Widtsoe, *The Word of Wisdom: A Modern Interpretation* (Salt Lake City: Deseret Book, 1950).

26. "Revelation, 27 February 1833 [D&C 89]," in Sidney Gilbert, Notebook, 114–15.

27. See Harper, *Making Sense of the Doctrine and Covenants,* 328.

28. By 1840, per capita consumption in America had fallen to about three gallons, the steepest 10-year drop in American history. See Lender and Martin, *Drinking in America,* 71–72; Tyrrell, *Sobering Up,* 225–51.

29. Zebedee Coltrin reminiscence, in Salt Lake School of the Prophets, Minutes, Oct. 3 1883, Church History Library, Salt Lake City.

"Man Was Also in the Beginning with God"

D&C 93

Matthew McBride

From late January until April 1833, Joseph Smith and 15 to 20 other men attended the School of the Prophets in Newel K. Whitney's store in Kirtland, Ohio. In their meetings, they sang, prayed, studied a variety of subjects from the mundane to the sacred, and exercised spiritual gifts. During one of these sessions, held on February 27—the same day the Word of Wisdom was revealed—David W. Patten was moved by the Holy Ghost to sing a hymn in an unknown tongue. Someone present, perhaps Sidney Rigdon, interpreted Patten's hymn for the others. The hymn was about Enoch's vision as found in Joseph Smith's revision of Genesis.[1]

Enoch's vision was probably familiar to most of the men in the school. Penned about two years earlier and published in the *Evening and Morning Star* (an early Church newspaper) in August 1832, the vision gave a grand overview of human history—in the words of Patten's interpreted hymn, Enoch was shown "what had passed and then was and is present and to come."[2] The vision also gave Church members one of the earliest glimpses of the idea of a premortal existence.[3] "I made the world, and men before they were in the flesh," the Lord told the ancient prophet (Moses 6:51). The interpretation of the hymn given in the schoolroom echoed the revealed text: "He saw the time when Adam his father was made and he saw that he was in eternity before a grain of dust in the ballance was weighed."[4]

Joseph Smith's revisions of the Bible, including the vision of Enoch, contained profound ideas about premortal life and human-kind's relationship to the divine. But they were only hinted at, not explained in detail. We can sense in the interpreted hymn the excitement these early members felt as they contemplated what these hints might mean. But we can only guess what questions these hints may have planted in the minds of Joseph Smith and his companions in the school.

On May 6, a few weeks after the school adjourned for the warm season, Joseph Smith received a revelation giving further details about a premortal existence. Now found in Doctrine and Covenants 93, the revelation departed from traditional Christian ideas about the nature of humankind, opening startling new vistas on our premortal past, our future potential, and our relationship to God.

Since the fifth century, Christian orthodoxy had imposed an almost impassable gulf between the Creator and His creations.[5] Humankind, Christians came to believe, was created from nothing. God was not a craftsman who refashioned existing materials but wholly different and apart from His creation—mysterious and unknowable. The Bible's parent-child description of God's relationship to us was understood largely as a metaphor instead of a literal kinship. To suggest otherwise, in the estimation of most Christian thinkers, blasphemously lessened God or dangerously elevated humankind.

The May 6 revelation was bold and new, yet also ancient and familiar. As with so many of Joseph Smith's revelations, it recovered lost truths that were apparently known to biblical figures, in this case the Apostle John. It declared that as Christ "was in the begining with the father," so "man was also in the begining with God." It dismissed the long-held belief in creation out of nothing: "Inteligence or the Light of truth was not created or made neither indeed can be."[6] In other words, the spirits of mortal men and women were as eternal as God Himself.

The revelation provided additional truth about God and human nature. It echoed both the text of the Book of Mormon and David Patten's hymn by defining truth as "knowledge of things as they are and as they were and as they are to come." These insights into past, present, and future were given "that you may understand and know how to worship and know what you worship."[7] The revelation dealt in particular with God's past and humanity's potentially glorious future. Jesus Christ, Joseph was told, had progressed to become like His Father. He "received not of the fulness at the first" but "continued from grace to grace" until He received His Father's fulness. Likewise, humankind had godlike potential. Men and women who keep God's commandments "receive grace for grace" until they, too, "shall receive of his fulness and be glorified in me as I am glorified in the father."[8] These flashes of insight into "things as they [really] are" recovered an ancient understanding of the relationship of God and His children and narrowed the yawning gap between Creator and creation that Mormons had inherited from the Christian tradition.

Joseph Smith spent the rest of his life pondering the implications of these stunning revelatory teachings. Years later in Nauvoo, he gave these truths their most complete expression in his last conference sermon. Echoing the words of the revelation, he taught that men and women were co-eternal with God and could become like Him by "going from a small capacity to a great capacity," until eventually they dwell "in everlasting burnings." Speaking with revealed assurance, he taught: "The soul, the mind of man, whare did it come from? The learned says God made it in the beginning, but it is not so. I know better. God has told me so."[9]

1. A broadside published after Patten's death identifies the singer as Patten and the interpreter as Rigdon. "Mysteries of God, as revealed to Enoch, on the Mount Mehujah," [After 1838], Church History Library, Salt Lake City. The hymn has also been attributed to Frederick G. Williams (see Frederick G. Williams, "Singing the Word of God: Five Hymns by President Frederick G. Williams," *BYU Studies*, vol. 48, no. 1 [2009], 6488).

2. Robin Scott Jensen, Robert J. Woodford, and Steven C. Harper, eds., *Revelations and Translations, Volume 1: Manuscript Revelation Books,* vol. 1 of the Revelations and Translations series of *The Joseph Smith Papers,* edited by Dean C. Jessee, Ronald K. Esplin, and Richard Lyman Bushman (Salt Lake City: Church Historian's Press, 2011), 525–27; josephsmithpapers.org.

3. Alma 13:3–4 in the Book of Mormon has been interpreted as referring to a premortal life. There is no evidence, however, that Joseph Smith or his contemporaries viewed Alma 13 in this way (see Terryl L. Givens, *When Souls Had Wings: Premortal Existence in Western Thought* [New York: Oxford University Press, 2010], 360, note 21).

4. "Revelation Book 2," 48, josephsmithpapers.org. The interpreted hymn was mailed to Independence, Missouri, where W. W. Phelps published it in the Church's newspaper. Sometime before it was printed, the text was adapted into a song with meter and rhyming. This passage was printed: "With God [Enoch] saw his race began, / And from him emanated man, / And with him did in glory dwell, / Before there was an earth or hell" ("Songs of Zion," *Evening and Morning Star,* vol. 1, no. 12 [May 1833], 192).

5. The Council of Chalcedon in A.D. 451 condemned the doctrine of premortal existence and defined Christ's nature as both God and man, these two natures being indivisible and unchangeable (see Historical Introduction to "Revelation, 6 May 1833 [D&C 93]," josephsmithpapers.org).

6. "Revelation, 6 May 1833 [D&C 93]," 3, josephsmithpapers.org; see also Doctrine and Covenants 93:21, 29.

7. "Revelation, 6 May 1833 [D&C 93]," 3, josephsmithpapers.org; see also Doctrine and Covenants 93:19, 24.

8. "Revelation, 6 May 1833 [D&C 93]," 2–3, josephsmithpapers.org; see also Doctrine and Covenants 93:12–13, 20.

9. "Discourse, 7 April 1844, as Reported by Wilford Woodruff," 135, 137, josephsmithpapers.org; punctuation modernized.

Waiting for the Word of the Lord

D&C 97, 98, 101

David W. Grua

On July 20, 1833, leaders of a mob in Jackson County, Missouri, called a meeting with William W. Phelps and other Church leaders. The mob leaders had a number of complaints about the Saints. They felt threatened by the Saints' belief that Jackson County was a promised land that they called Zion. They objected to the large number of people, many of them poor, who had come to their county over the previous two years to build up Zion. And because of an article Phelps had recently published in the *Evening and the Morning Star*[1]—discussing the legal requirements designed to inhibit the immigration of free blacks to Missouri—the mob was afraid that free black Church members would soon begin gathering to Zion, disrupting the racial dynamics in their slaveholding state.

In a follow-up editorial, Phelps tried to diffuse tension between the Saints and Jackson County leaders, but nothing he wrote changed their minds about the Saints' intentions. As far as the mob was concerned, the time for explanations was over. They gave Phelps and his fellow Church leaders 15 minutes to agree to move the whole Mormon community away by the next spring—or suffer the consequences.[2]

Phelps and other Church leaders hesitated. Revelation to Joseph Smith had declared Jackson County to be "the place for the City of Zion." Revelation had called Phelps to move his family there, set up a print shop, and "be established as a Printer unto the Church."[3] The Saints had sacrificed a great deal to build Zion. Could they simply leave it?

Without a promise that the Saints would leave, the mob began a campaign of violent intimidation. They battered down the door of Phelps's house, threw the printing press out of the second story onto the street below, and then destroyed the building.[4] The Phelps family was left to seek shelter that night in an abandoned stable.[5] Other Saints also suffered that day: Bishop Edward Partridge and Charles Allen were tarred and feathered, and Sidney Gilbert's store was attacked. Three days later, Partridge, Phelps, and other Church leaders, seeing no alternative, formally agreed that all the Saints would evacuate the county by April 1834.[6]

"In our present situation I have nothing to write," the ordinarily verbose Phelps wrote to the Prophet Joseph Smith in Kirtland, Ohio, a few days later. Phelps wanted to fulfill his calling to build up Zion but could not see how he could do so under the current conditions. "I wait for the word of the Lord," Phelps stated, hoping that Joseph would seek revelatory answers for why the Lord had allowed these things to happen to Zion. "If the Lord will yet speak to his children, it may be well to inquire every matter concerning the destruction of the printing office," he suggested. In the meantime, Phelps tried to see his trials in a positive light. "I know from the experience I have had," he assured the Saints in Kirtland in a letter, "that it is a good thing to have our faith thoroughly tried."[7]

Receiving Divine Guidance

Joseph Smith did not receive detailed news of these events until August 9, 1833, when Oliver Cowdery—the Missouri Saints' emissary—arrived in Kirtland after a two-and-a-half-week journey.[8] The 900 miles that separated Independence from Kirtland ensured that written accounts sent through the mail or published in newspapers did not reach Ohio until mid-August.[9] In the meantime, Joseph Smith had received two revelations (Doctrine and Covenants 97 and 98) in early August that, although they did not address the specific difficulties experienced by Church members in Jackson County on July 20, nevertheless offered words of divine consolation and guidance that Phelps and the other Missouri Saints could later use to help them make sense of their experiences and sufferings.

On August 2, 1833, Joseph Smith dictated the first revelation, now Doctrine and Covenants 97. In it, the Lord commended the Church's school in Jackson County and reiterated the command that "an house should be built unto me in the land of Zion." The revelation stated that "if Zion do these things she shall prosper and spread herself and become very glorious. . . . Let Zion rejoice (for this is Zion the pure in heart)." However, the Lord warned that "vengence cometh speedily upon the ungodly." Zion would escape these calamities only "if she observe to do all things whatsoever I have commanded her." If not, "I will visit her according to all her works, with sore afflictions." [10]

Joseph Smith received the second revelation, now Doctrine and Covenants 98, on August 6, 1833. Although the Lord encouraged the Saints to support the U.S. Constitution and the rule of law, the revelation warned that "when the wicked rule the people mourn." Anticipating coming persecutions, the revelation commanded Church members to "renounce war and proclaim peace." When they suffered abuse from enemies of the Church, the Saints were commanded to "bear it patiently," forgive their oppressors, and allow the Lord to avenge the wrong.[11] These revelations were sent in a letter to the Missouri Saints on August 6, three days before Cowdery's arrival in Kirtland.[12] When received in Jackson County around the beginning of September, the revelations were doubtless a source of comfort and direction for Saints such as Phelps, who had been waiting to receive divine guidance.

"After Much Tribulation Cometh the Blessing"

Taking counsel from Joseph's revelations, Missouri Church leaders worked to find legal protection from the mob and from its demand that they leave by spring. In September and October 1833, they sought redress from state officials and hired attorneys to represent the Mormons' cause in the courts. The Saints' legal actions had convinced the mob that Church members wouldn't leave unless driven out. Before their case could be heard in court, mob violence broke out again.

In late October and early November, Jackson County vigilantes threatened the Saints and then drove them from their homes. Although Church members made some effort to defend themselves, they evidently sought to follow the Lord's counsel in the August 6 revelation (Doctrine and Covenants 98) to endure their persecutions patiently.[13] On November 6 and 7, while living as a refugee in Clay County, just north of Jackson County, Phelps wrote the first detailed account to Joseph Smith of the violence, describing beatings of Church members, destruction of their houses, and even bloodshed on both sides. He signed it, "Yours in affliction."[14] Over the next week, as Phelps continued to think about what had happened, a passage from the New Testament came to his mind. "The Savior said, Blessed are ye when ye are hated of all men for my name's sake," he wrote on November 14, "and I think we have come to that."[15]

As this letter and other reports of the expulsion trickled into Kirtland in late November and early December, Joseph Smith prayerfully sought the revelatory guidance that Phelps and other Saints desperately desired. In a December 10 letter, Joseph reminded Church leaders in Missouri that in 1831 the Lord had previously warned Church members "that after much tribulation cometh the blessing." Although the Lord had not yet revealed why the "great calamity" had "come upon Zion" or "by what means he [the Lord] will return her back to her inheritance," Joseph remained confident that Zion would be redeemed in God's "own due time." The Prophet advised the Saints not to sell their lands in Zion and encouraged them to seek legal redress from state and federal officials. If the government failed the Saints, they were to plead with the Lord "day and night" for divine justice. Joseph concluded with a prayer that God would remember His promises regarding Zion and deliver the Saints.[16]

On December 16 and 17, Joseph dictated an extended revelation, now Doctrine and Covenants 101, that provided answers to the questions that he, Phelps, and other Saints had been asking. The Lord had allowed the calamity to occur "in consequence of their [the Saints'] transgressions." Nevertheless, the Lord stated, "Notwithstanding their sins my bowels are filled with compassion towards them." Although the Saints were scattered, Zion would "not be moved out of her place." Concerning Zion's redemption, the revelation related a parable of "a certain noble[man]" who had commissioned his servants to protect his vineyard. While the servants disputed among themselves, "the enemy came by night" and "distroyed their works and broke down the Olive trees." The Lord commanded his servant to "take all the strength of mine house" and "redeem my vineyard." Reiterating the affirmation of the U.S. Constitution from Doctrine and Covenants 98, the revelation repeated Joseph Smith's earlier counsel that the Missouri Saints seek redress from civil authorities, with a promise that if government officials rejected Church members' pleas, the Lord would "come forth out of his hiding place & in his fury vex the nation."[17] Doctrine and Covenants 101 provided the Prophet a divinely inspired plan for Zion's redemption—a project that would occupy his attention for the remainder of his life.[18]

By early 1834, a copy of the revelation that would become Doctrine and Covenants 101 had arrived in Missouri, providing William W. Phelps the "word of the Lord"[19] that he had been waiting for. On February 27, he wrote to Joseph Smith, updating him on the Saints' efforts to receive justice in the Missouri court system. As Phelps closed his letter, he alluded to the revelation. Phelps wondered if "the servants of the Lord of the vineyard, who are called and chosen to *prune* it for the last time" would "fear to do as much for Jesus as he did for us"? "No," he answered, "we will obey the voice of the Spirit, that good may overcome the world."[20]

1. See William W. Phelps, "Free People of Color," *Evening and Morning Star,* vol. 2, no. 14 (July 1833), 218–19.

2. See "To His Excellency, Daniel Dunklin, Governor of the State of Missouri," *Evening and the Morning Star,* vol. 2, no. 15 (Dec. 1833), 226–31.

3. "Revelation, 20 July 1831 [D&C 57]," in Revelation Book 1, 93–94, josephsmithpapers.org; see also Doctrine and Covenants 57:2, 11.

4. See "A History, of the Persecution, of The Church of Jesus Christ, of Latter Day Saints in Missouri," *Times and Seasons,* vol. 1, no. 2 (Dec. 1839), 17–20.

5. See "Mary Elizabeth Rollins Lightner," *Utah Genealogical and Historical Magazine,* vol. 17 (July 1926), 196.

6. See "Letter from John Whitmer, 29 July 1833," in Joseph Smith Letterbook 2, page 54, josephsmithpapers.org.

7. Phelps's postscript to "Letter from John Whitmer, 29 July 1833," 55–56.

8. Historical Introduction to "Letter to Church Leaders in Jackson County, Missouri, 10 August 1833," josephsmithpapers.org.

9. See Historical Introduction to "Letter to Church Leaders in Jackson County, Missouri, 18 August 1833," josephsmithpapers.org.

10. "Revelation, 2 August 1833–A [D&C 97]," in Sidney Rigdon, Frederick G. Williams, and Joseph Smith letter to "Beloved Brethren," Aug. 6, 1833, josephsmithpapers.org; see also Doctrine and Covenants 97:10, 18, 21–22, 25–26; "Revelation, 20 July 1831 [D&C 57]," in Revelation Book 1, 93–94, josephsmithpapers.org.

11. "Revelation, 6 August 1833 [D&C 98]," in Sidney Rigdon, Frederick G. Williams, and Joseph Smith letter to "Beloved Brethren," Aug. 6, 1833, 3, josephsmithpapers.org; see also Doctrine and Covenants 98:5–6, 10, 16, 26. However, the revelation also stated that "if that enemy shall escape my vengence . . . thine enemy is in thine hands and if thou reward him according to his works thou art justified if he has saught [sought] thy life" ("Revelation, 6 August 1833 [D&C 98]," 3; see also Doctrine and Covenants 98:28, 31).

12. Historical Introduction to "Letter to Church Leaders in Jackson County, Missouri, 6 August 1833," josephsmithpapers.org; Historical Introduction to "Letter to Church Leaders in Jackson County, Missouri, 10 August 1833," josephsmithpapers.org.

13. Historical Introduction to "Letter, 30 October 1833," in Gerrit J. Dirkmaat, Brent M. Rogers, Grant Underwood, Robert J. Woodford, and William G. Hartley, eds., *Documents, Volume 3: February 1833–March 1834,* vol. 3 of the Documents series of *The Joseph Smith Papers,* ed. Ronald K. Esplin and Matthew J. Grow (Salt Lake City: Church Historian's Press, 2014), 331–35.

14. "Letter from William W. Phelps, 6–7 November 1833," in *Evening and the Morning Star,* Dec. 1833, 119; josephsmithpapers.org.

15. "Letter from William W. Phelps, 14 November 1833," 119; see also Matthew 10:22.

16. Joseph Smith, "Letter to Edward Partridge and Others, 10 December 1833," in Joseph Smith Letterbook 1, 71, 73, josephsmithpapers.org; see also "Revelation, 1 August 1831 [D&C 58]," in Revelation Book 1, 94, josephsmithpapers.org.

17. "Revelation, 16–17 December 1833 [D&C 101]," in Revelation Book 2, 73–83, josephsmithpapers.org; see also Doctrine and Covenants 101:2, 9, 17, 44, 51, 55–56, 89.

18. See Mark Ashurst-McGee, "Zion Rising: Joseph Smith's Early Social and Political Thought," PhD diss., Arizona State University, 2008; see also Matthew C. Godfrey, "'The Redemption of Zion Must Needs Come by Power': Insights into the Camp of Israel Expedition," *BYU Studies Quarterly,* vol. 53, no. 4 (2014), 125–46; Warren A. Jennings, "Importuning for Redress," *Bulletin of the Missouri Historical Society,* vol. 27 (1970), 15–29.

19. Phelps's postscript to "Letter from John Whitmer, 29 July 1833," 55.

20. "Letter from William W. Phelps, 27 February 1834," in *Evening and the Morning Star,* Mar. 1843, 139; josephsmithpapers.org.

A Mission to Canada

D&C 100

Eric Smith

In the fall of 1833, a 54-year-old Church member named Freeman Nickerson rode into Kirtland, Ohio, with a wagon and sought out Joseph Smith. Nickerson and his wife, Huldah, of Perrysburg, New York, had been baptized a few months earlier. Nickerson asked the Prophet to travel with him to Mount Pleasant, Upper Canada, to preach the gospel to two of his sons, Moses and Eleazer Freeman. Mount Pleasant was a small village about 100 miles west of Buffalo, New York, in the area between Lake Erie and Lake Ontario.[1]

Moses Nickerson later recalled that he had provided the impetus for his father's request: "In the month of June [1833], while on a visit to my parents' home [I] heard for the first time what was then known as Mormonism; was favorably inclined towards the doctrine preached, and requested my parents to have some of the elders visit us in Canada. . . . In the month of September of this year 1833, my father and mother visited Kirtland, Ohio, the head quarters of these people, and induced Joseph Smith and Sidney Rigdon to accompany them to Canada."[2]

Joseph's Pressing Concerns

In September 1833, Joseph Smith was living in Kirtland with his wife, Emma, and two young children—Julia, age 2; and Joseph III, just shy of his first birthday. They had previously lost four young children to death.[3] The Prophet, 27 years of age, had preached the gospel message on many earlier journeys but had not until this time served a more formal proselytizing mission.

At least two concerns were occupying the Prophet's attentions at this time that could have made it difficult for him to leave his home and family for an extended period. On August 9, 1833, he learned that the Church's efforts to build the city of Zion in Independence, Jackson County, Missouri, had been dealt a severe blow. A mob had compelled Church members to agree to leave Jackson County by spring

1834. Joseph corresponded directly with the suffering Missouri Saints: "Brethren if I were with you I should take an active part in your sufferings & although nature shrinks yet my spirit would not let me forsake you unto death God helping me Oh be of good cheer for our redemption draweth near Oh God save my Brethren in Zion."[4]

Meanwhile, Joseph was also dealing with a threat closer to home. A former Church member named Doctor Philastus Hurlbut, after being excommunicated in June 1833 for immoral conduct, began an aggressive campaign to discredit Joseph and the Church. His approach included stirring up persecution locally, traveling broadly to gather statements critical of Joseph, and threatening Joseph's life.[5] The Prophet's surviving papers from this period reflect severe anxiety about Hurlbut's activities. In an August 1833 letter to members in Missouri, he reported that Hurlbut was "lieing in a wonderful manner and the peapl are running after him and giveing him mony to brake down mormanism which much endangers our lives."[6] In a journal entry a few months later, the Prophet stated that Hurlbut had "saught the distruction of the sainst in this place and more particularly myself and family."[7] The situation was menacing and the outcome uncertain.

A Prayer for Comfort

Notwithstanding these concerns, Joseph accepted Nickerson's invitation to preach the gospel to his relatives in Canada, and Sidney Rigdon agreed to accompany them. Joseph's journal noted matter-of-factly on October 4: "Makeing preperation to go East with Freeman Nickerson." And on October 5: "This day started on a Journy to the East."[8] The one-month mission through northwestern Pennsylvania and southwestern New York and into what is known today as lower Ontario, Canada, would cover some 500 miles round-trip and include stops in at least 10 towns, with preaching engagements in many of them. The Prophet brought his pocket-size journal with him, and he and Sidney took turns making brief entries in it to chronicle their travels and their preaching.[9]

By October 12, the small party had crossed the northwestern tip of Pennsylvania into New York and reached the Freeman and

Huldah Nickerson home in Perrysburg. Joseph Smith wrote that he felt "very well" in his mind but that he had "much anxiety" about his family,[10] probably in part because of the opposition Hurlbut had stirred up in Kirtland. That anxiety may have led Joseph and Sidney to pray for comfort. A revelation that day (now Doctrine and Covenants 100) declared, "Verily thus saith the Lord unto you my friends Sidney & Joseph your families are well; they are in mine hands, and I will do with them as seemeth me good; for in me there is all power."[11] The Prophet's concern apparently did not completely abate—the next day he asked the Lord to "bless [his] family and preserve them"[12]—but he clearly found comfort in these words, as evidenced by the journal entry he recorded when he arrived back home in Kirtland on November 4 at the conclusion of the mission: "Found my family all well according to the promise of the Lord. for which blessings I feel to thank his holy name; Amen."[13]

The October 12 revelation addressed two other matters. Noting that "I the Lord have suffered you to come unto this place for thus it was expedient in me for the salvation of souls," the Lord promised Joseph and Sidney that "an effectual door shall be opened in the regeons round about in this eastern land." If the missionaries would "lift up" their voices with "solemnity of heart in the spirit of meekness" and declare the words God put into their hearts, the "holy Ghost [would] be shed forth in bearing record unto all things whatsoever" they said. The revelation also gave Joseph and Sidney assurance that Zion would "be redeemed altho she is chasened for a little season."[14]

Arrival at Mount Pleasant

On October 18, the group arrived at their destination in the tiny village of Mount Pleasant, Upper Canada. Sidney Rigdon provided details in Joseph Smith's journal: "Arived at [Eleazer] Freeman Nickerson's in upper Canada having after we came into Canada passed through a very fine country and well cultivated and had many peculiar feelings in relation to both the country and people we were kindly received."[15]

Joseph and Sidney spent the following week and a half preaching in Mount Pleasant and several surrounding villages to large and attentive congregations. The Prophet's journal seems to reflect the urgency and enthusiasm associated with their busy itinerary. On October 24, after Joseph and Sidney held a meeting in Mount Pleasant, Eleazer Freeman Nickerson "declared his full beleif in the truth of the work." He was, the journal records, "with his wife who is also convinced to be baptised on Sunday great excitement prevailes in every place where we have been." On that Sunday, October 27, twelve individuals were baptized. Two more were baptized the following day. Among those baptized were Eleazer Freeman Nickerson, his wife Eliza, and Moses Nickerson.

On the evening of October 28, the missionaries held their last meeting with their little flock in Mount Pleasant. In the Prophet's journal the next morning, Sidney Rigdon recorded: "Held meeting last evening Ordained br E[leazer] F[reeman] Nickerson to the office of Elder had a good meeting one of the sisters got the gift of toungues which made the saints rejoice may God increse the gifts among them for his sons sake this morning we bend our course for home may the Lord prosper our journey Amen."[16] Joseph and Sidney returned by crossing Lake Erie and arrived in Kirtland on November 4.[17]

Two weeks later, Joseph Smith sent a letter to Moses Nickerson to inform him of his safe return and to convey his feelings for the fledgling branch in Mount Pleasant. "I shall expect a communication from you on the reception of this, and hope you will give me information concerning the brethren, their health, faith, &c.," Joseph wrote. He continued: "I can truely say, that with much fervency I have called upon the Lord in behalf of our brethren in Canada. And when I call to mind with what rediness they received the word of truth by the ministry of bro. Sidney and myself, I am truely under great obligation to humble myself in thankfulness before him."

Joseph then pleaded with Nickerson to remain faithful to his new convictions: "You remember the testimony which I bore in the name of the Lord Jesus, concerning the great work which he has brought forth in the last days. You know my manner of communication, how that in weakness and simpleness I declared to you what the Lord had brought forth by the ministering of his holy angels to me, for this generation. I pray that the Lord may enable you to treasure these things up in your mind; for I know that his Spirit will bear testimony to all who seek diligently after knowledge from him. I hope you will search the scriptures, to see whether these things are not also consistant with those things that the ancient prophets and apostles have written."[18]

The Mount Pleasant congregation continued to grow after Joseph and Sidney's departure. By December 1833, there were reportedly 34 members there.[19] The congregation may have reached as many as 50 within the next few years.[20] Eventually, most of the believers there either emigrated to join the Saints in the United States or drifted away from the Church.[21]

Freeman Nickerson, the man who had traveled to Kirtland to ask the Prophet to preach to his sons, participated in the Zion's Camp expedition in 1834 (two sons, Uriel and Levi, accompanied him), gathered with the Saints in Nauvoo, and died in early 1847 in Iowa Territory on the westward migration.[22]

Moses Nickerson and Eleazer Freeman Nickerson joined with the Saints in the western United States for a time in the late 1830s, but both returned to Canada in the early 1840s. Eleazer, who died in 1862, appears to have continued to consider himself a Latter-day Saint.[23] Moses affiliated with two other denominations prior to his death in 1871.[24] In a poignant memoir written late in his life, he expressed admiration for Joseph Smith, whom he had encountered when visiting Nauvoo in the early 1840s: "I here found Joseph Smith living in a tent, having given up his house as a hospital for the sick! He was doing all he could to alleviate their sufferings."[25]

Joseph Smith's mission to Canada opened "an effectual door" for the preaching of the gospel and the saving of souls in more ways than one. In 1836, Apostle Parley P. Pratt traveled to Upper Canada to preach the gospel there. On his journey, Pratt was accompanied by his brother Orson and by Eleazer Freeman Nickerson. In Hamilton, Upper Canada, Parley P. Pratt became acquainted with Moses Nickerson. Moses provided Pratt a letter of introduction to a religious seeker from Toronto named John Taylor.[26]

1. See Joseph Smith, "Journal, 1832–1834," 5–18, josephsmithpapers.org; see also "Nickerson, Freeman," josephsmithpapers.org; Richard E. Bennett, "A Study of the Church of Jesus Christ of Latter-day Saints in Upper Canada, 1830–1850" (master's thesis, Brigham Young University, 1975), 42;

"Mount Pleasant, Upper Canada," josephsmithpapers.org. The author expresses his thanks to Melissa Rehon Kotter and Shannon Kelly for assistance in researching this article.

2. Moses Nickerson, "Autobiography of Moses C. Nickerson," *True Latter Day Saints' Herald,* vol. 17, no. 14 (July 15, 1870), 425; it is not clear from earlier sources whether Huldah went to Kirtland and then accompanied the group on the mission into Canada.

3. See "Joseph Smith Pedigree Chart," josephsmithpapers.org.

4. See Joseph Smith postscript, "Letter to Church Leaders in Jackson County, Missouri, 10 August 1833," 2, josephsmithpapers.org.

5. See Joseph Smith, "Journal, 1832–1834," 45.

6. "Letter to Church Leaders in Jackson County, Missouri, 18 August 1833," 3, josephsmithpapers.org.

7. Joseph Smith, "Journal, 1832–1834," 50.

8. Joseph Smith, "Journal, 1832–1834," 5.

9. See Richard Lloyd Anderson, "Joseph Smith's Journeys," in *2006 Church Almanac* (Salt Lake City: Deseret News, 2005), 141–42.

10. Joseph Smith, "Journal, 1832–1834," 7.

11. "Revelation, 12 October 1833 [D&C 100]," 1, josephsmithpapers.org; punctuation standardized; see also Doctrine and Covenants 100:1.

12. Joseph Smith, "Journal, 1832–1834," 8.

13. Joseph Smith, "Journal, 1832–1834," 18.

14. "Revelation, 12 October 1833 [D&C 100]," 1–2, josephsmithpapers.org; see also Doctrine and Covenants 100:3–5, 7–8, 13.

15. Joseph Smith, "Journal, 1832–1834," 9; spelling standardized.

16. Joseph Smith, "Journal, 1832–1834," 13–14, 16–17; see also Craig James Ostler and William Goddard, "A Brief Descriptive History of the Mormons in Mount Pleasant," in *Regional Studies in Latter-day Saint Church History: Ohio and Upper Canada,* ed. Guy L. Dorius, Craig K. Manscill, and Craig James Ostler (Provo, Utah: Religious Studies Center, Brigham Young University, 2006), 125–57.

17. See Susa Young Gates [Homespun, pseudonym], *Lydia Knight's History: The First Book of the Noble Women's Lives Series* (Salt Lake City: Juvenile Instructor Office, 1883), 22; see also Joseph Smith, "Journal, 1832–1834," 18.

18. "Letter to Moses Nickerson, 19 November 1833," in Letterbook 1, 64–65, josephsmithpapers.org.

19. M. C. Nickerson letter to the editor, *Evening and the Morning Star,* vol. 2, no. 17 (Feb. 1834), 134.

20. See Bennett, "Study of the Church," 75.

21. See Ostler and Goddard, "A Brief History."

22. "Nickerson, Freeman," josephsmithpapers.org.

23. "Nickerson, Eleazer Freeman," josephsmithpapers.org.

24. "Nickerson, Moses Chapman," josephsmithpapers.org.

25. Moses Nickerson, "Autobiography of Moses C. Nickerson," 426; italics in original.

26. See Parley P. Pratt, *The Autobiography of Parley Parker Pratt; One of the Twelve Apostles of The Church of Jesus Christ of Latter-Day Saints* (Chicago: Law, King, and Law, 1888), 142, 145–46; Pratt identified that a "Brother Nickerson" was a traveling companion, that Nickerson had a home in Canada, and that a separate person gave him some money and a letter of introduction to John Taylor. See also Parley P. Pratt letter to the editor, *Latter Day Saints' Messenger and Advocate,* vol. 2, no. 8 (May 1836), 319, where Pratt identified his traveling companions as "O. Pratt and F. Nickerson." As Eleazer Freeman Nickerson was living in Canada at this time (and sometimes went by his middle name), and as Freeman Nickerson (the father) was living in the United States, Eleazer Freeman was presumably the "F. Nickerson" Pratt referred to (see "Nickerson, Freeman" and "Nickerson, Eleazer Freeman," josephsmithpapers.org). John Taylor indicated that the man who provided the letter of introduction was Moses Nickerson (see "John Taylor, autobiography, 1858," in "Historian's Office histories of the Twelve, 1856–1858, 1861," Church History Library, Salt Lake City).

Restoring the Ancient Order

D&C 102, 107

Joseph F. Darowski and James Goldberg

In May of 1829, Joseph Smith and Oliver Cowdery knelt near the Susquehanna River. They had just read about baptism in 3 Nephi and wanted to know where they could find the authority that Jesus had given His ancient disciples. In answer to their prayers, John the Baptist appeared and laid hands on their heads to confer the authority they needed to baptize each other. "Think for a moment," Cowdery later urged his friend W. W. Phelps, "what joy filled our hearts and with what surprise we must have bowed . . . when we received under his hand the holy priesthood."[1]

But the restoration of priesthood authority was not immediately accompanied by a restoration of priesthood organization. Individual priesthood holders could perform ordinances, but how were they to work together to do the work of the Lord?

Conference Governance

Many of the churches active in upstate New York in the 1830s handled business through quarterly conferences of elders, and in its first year the restored Church followed that familiar pattern. After organizing in April, Church leaders held conferences in June and September to report on the Church's progress and to conduct business. This system of quarterly conferences was included in the Church Articles and Covenants (now Doctrine and Covenants 20) when they were recorded in the Church's handwritten book of revelations.[2]

But in 1831, it became increasingly clear that Church conferences would be more than routine meetings. During the year's first conference, a revelation (now Doctrine and Covenants 38) was received that laid out specific projects and goals for the Church to work toward. Soon the number of conferences held to keep up with the Lord's work drastically increased: from August to December of 1831, minutes were recorded for 26 conferences—an average of more than one conference per week.

In one of these conferences, the Prophet emphasized the need to move beyond familiar patterns and to "understand the ancient manner of conducting meetings as they were led by the Holy Ghost."[3] The diverse planning and disciplinary issues facing the young Church required shared effort and inspiration. But if there was too much business to be handled by conferences of all elders, who should be responsible for any given issue?

The Council System

A revelation received on November 11, 1831 (now Doctrine and Covenants 107:60–100), helped the Saints understand how to harness the power of shared inspiration while dividing the complex demands of Church administration. Certain types of cases were assigned to the bishop, who in turn could call counselors to assist him in his duties. A president of the high priesthood would consider more difficult issues, assisted by 12 high priests as counselors. Presidents of the elders, priests, teachers, and deacons would also be called to sit in council with their groups.

But supplementing the familiar conference system with an unfamiliar council system proved to be a gradual process. Presidents for each group were not immediately chosen, and clerks were inconsistent in distinguishing between a conference and a council. In July of 1832, Missouri members "resolved that the mode and manner of regulating the Church of Christ," as shown in the November revelation, "take effect from this time,"[4] but they didn't choose a president of the elders until September.[5] And though he had been sustained as president of the high priesthood and chosen two counselors, Joseph Smith had to gather available high priests to serve on a full president's council each time a need arose.[6]

There were also problems with the behavior of participants in the meetings. Apparently, some would whisper to each other, grow visibly restless, or even leave during the middle of a council session. Personal prejudices and weaknesses also made it difficult to seek the will of the Lord.[7]

Joseph Smith took responsibility for these shared shortcomings. "I have never set before any council in all the order in which a council ought to be conducted," he said during a February 1834 council meeting, "which, perhaps, has deprived the Council of some, or many blessings." He then attempted to "show the order of councils in ancient days as shown to him by vision."[8] The Prophet's vision of a Jerusalem council presided over by the Apostle Peter and two counselors became a model for the organization of the first regular high council,[9] which in turn was to serve as a model for other councils throughout the Church. Minutes showing some of the important features of the council—such as the right of an accused person to have half the council as advocates—were later canonized in Doctrine and Covenants 102.[10]

Before the high council tried its first case, Joseph Smith blessed his two counselors. Next, two fathers—Joseph Smith Sr. and John Johnson—blessed their sons.[11] Just as conferences coexisted with the developing system of councils, the administrative organization of priesthood in the Church would coexist with family-centered priesthood.

Quorums

A week after the Kirtland high council was organized, Parley P. Pratt and Lyman Wight arrived from Missouri to ask for guidance on behalf of the Saints who had been driven from their homes.[12] In response to their visit, Joseph Smith and the high council planned an expedition to assist them.

Both while gathering men and funds in eastern Church branches for what came to be known as Zion's Camp and while traveling from Ohio to Missouri, Joseph Smith spent a significant amount of time in the Church's smaller branches. The council system had helped divide the demands of Church business on priesthood holders' time in Church centers, but less had been done to organize priesthood across physical space, provide uniformity between the two main Church centers, or address the needs of the more remote branches. Further revelation was needed.

In Missouri, where many Church members were gathered near the planned site of Zion, another high council was organized following the model of the first. Again, Joseph Smith blessed the council's president and his two counselors, and again two fathers—this time Peter Whitmer Sr. and Joseph Knight Sr.—blessed their sons.[13] But what should be done for the Church's smaller branches? After returning from Missouri at the end of Zion's Camp, two new priesthood groups were created: the Quorum of the Twelve Apostles, whose duty would include serving as a "travelling, presiding high council" for the branches of the Church, and the Seventies, who would assist the Twelve.[14] In addition to serving existing Church branches, the Twelve and the Seventies were to preach the gospel throughout the world and organize new branches.

In the spring of 1835, the newly called Twelve Apostles were sent on a mission to "regulate" the eastern branches of the Church.[15] Before they left, Joseph Smith provided them with detailed instruction on priesthood organization, now contained in Doctrine and Covenants 107. These instructions to the Twelve clarified relationships within the priesthood. They shed light on the history and roles of the Melchizedek and Aaronic orders of priesthood. They introduced the concept of a "quorum" to explain the unique functions and overlapping authorities of the First Presidency, Twelve Apostles, Seventies, and high councils. They also called for the appointment of patriarchs[16] to perpetuate the familial order of priesthood alongside the administrative order.

Sustaining the New Organization

In the spring and summer of 1835, four sections on priesthood organization were collected at the beginning of the new Doctrine and Covenants, just after the revealed preface. The first was the Church Articles and Covenants (now Doctrine and Covenants 20). Next came the new material from the instruction to the Twelve, which had been combined with an updated version of the November 1831 revelation on priesthood councils into a single section (now Doctrine and Covenants 107). A revelation containing the oath and covenant of the priesthood (now Doctrine and Covenants 84) appeared third. Then came the minutes of the first high council organization, updated with a clarifying reference to the role of the Quorum of the Twelve Apostles. Together, these sections served as a sort of handbook for administering the Church.

On August 17, 1835, Church members formally approved the Doctrine and Covenants, accepting this revealed organization of the priesthood.[17] Over the next seven months, Church leaders took steps to fill offices so that priesthood quorums could be fully organized for sustaining at the dedication of the Kirtland Temple.

1. Oliver Cowdery, "Dear Brother," *Latter Day Saints' Messenger and Advocate,* vol. 1, no. 1 (Oct. 1834), 15–16.

2. "Revelation Book 1," 83, josephsmithpapers.org.

3. "Minute Book 2," 8, josephsmithpapers.org.

4. "Minute Book 2," 28, josephsmithpapers.org.

5. "Minute Book 2," 30, josephsmithpapers.org.

6. See "Minute Book 1," 21, josephsmithpapers.org.

7. See "Minute Book 1," 27, josephsmithpapers.org.

8. "Minute Book 1," 29–30, josephsmithpapers.org.

9. See "Minute Book 1," 30, josephsmithpapers.org.

10. See "Minute Book 1," 30, josephsmithpapers.org; these minutes were revised by Joseph Smith and the high council before their canonization.

11. See "Minute Book 1," 36–37, josephsmithpapers.org.

12. See "Minute Book 1," 41, josephsmithpapers.org.

13. See "Minute Book 2," 44, josephsmithpapers.org.

14. "Doctrine and Covenants, 1835," 84, josephsmithpapers.org.

15. "Record of the Twelve, 14 February–28 August 1835," 4, josephsmithpapers.org.

16. Then referred to as "evangelical ministers"; see "Doctrine and Covenants, 1835," 85, josephsmithpapers.org.

17. See "Minutes, 17 August 1835," in Minute Book 1, 98–106, josephsmithpapers.org.

The Acceptable Offering of Zion's Camp

D&C 103, 105

Matthew C. Godfrey

Twenty-two-year-old Nathan Baldwin was startled when, in the midst of preaching the gospel in Connecticut in February 1834, he felt a prompting to "go west."[1] Nathan, who was born in 1812 in Augusta Township in Upper Canada's Grenville County, had been baptized on April 28, 1833, and had spent time since then preaching in the eastern United States. He quickly obeyed the prompting to go west. "I immediately turned my face to the west," he wrote, "and began to retrace my steps, asking the question at the same time, what shall I go west for?" When he arrived in Oswegatchie, New York, a young man named Reuben Foote told him that the Saints had been ejected from Jackson County, Missouri, in the fall of 1833 and that the Prophet Joseph Smith was planning to lead an expedition to help those displaced Church members. Nathan felt he now understood why the Lord had sent him west—so that he could join the expedition.[2]

The information that he received in Oswegatchie was correct. At about the same time that Nathan felt prompted to travel west, Parley P. Pratt and Lyman Wight had arrived in Kirtland, Ohio, from Missouri to explain to Joseph Smith and the Kirtland high council the plight of the Saints who were now living mainly in Clay County, Missouri. Pratt and Wight wondered how and when Zion would be redeemed, meaning how and when the Saints would regain their Jackson County land. After listening to Pratt and Wight, Joseph Smith declared "that he was going to Zion to assist in redeeming it" and asked for volunteers to go with him.[3]

That same day, Joseph received a revelation, now Doctrine and Covenants 103, which instructed him to recruit as many as 500 "of the strength of [the Lord's] house"—young and middle-aged members of the Church—to go to Zion, where they would reclaim the Lord's vineyard.[4] A few months earlier, in December 1833, the Lord had hinted at this effort to redeem Zion in the revelation that is now Doctrine and Covenants 101. The revelation contained a parable of a nobleman whose vineyard was overrun by his enemies and who instructed his servant to raise an army to retake his land.[5] In the February 1834 revelation, the Lord designated Joseph Smith as the servant in the parable and appointed him to lead an expedition to Zion.[6]

Nathan Baldwin responded to the call for volunteers. On May 3, 1834, he arrived in Kirtland, just two days before Joseph departed with a contingent of men for Missouri.[7] About 20 other individuals left Michigan Territory on May 5 as well, under the leadership of Lyman Wight and Hyrum Smith.[8] With recruits gathered along the way, the expedition—known at the time as the Camp of Israel and later called Zion's Camp—eventually numbered about 205 men and approximately 25 women and children.[9]

Sidney Rigdon and Oliver Cowdery explained the goals of the expedition in a letter sent to Saints throughout the United States, pleading for support. That letter explained that the group would march to Clay County, Missouri, where Church leaders would petition Missouri governor Daniel Dunklin to call out the state militia, something that Joseph Smith and others believed he was willing to do. The militia would escort the Saints back to their lands in Jackson County and would then be discharged. The members of Zion's Camp would remain, serving as a protective force to ensure that Church members were not driven out again.[10]

No one knew, however, just what the reaction of those in Missouri would be when the camp entered the state. Nathan Baldwin fully expected to fight as a member of the camp, and as someone more inclined to peace, that worried him. "Hardly anything could be more repugnant to my feelings than the display of the instruments of death," Baldwin recalled, "but I procured a rifle, equipage and ammunition, and tried to school myself to their practice."[11]

The participants largely paid camp expenses themselves. Church members contributed about $300 to the expedition, but that was not enough. Not long after leaving Kirtland, the members of the camp consecrated their money and created a general fund for expenses. Some members had nothing to consecrate; others, such as John Tanner, contributed as much as $170. Nathan Baldwin felt it an honor to consecrate $14 of his own. The camp was also organized into companies of 12 men each, with each man having a certain responsibility within the company. Nathan was given the assignment of supplying water.[12]

For the next month and a half, Nathan and the rest of Zion's Camp marched through Ohio, Indiana, and Illinois on the way to Missouri. The pace was brisk, as the camp covered as many as 40 miles a day. "As the wagons were mostly filled with baggage, we had to travel on foot," Nathan later remembered. This resulted in sore feet, blisters, and even "toes so gaulded that our stockings were wet with blood."[13] Although some in the camp, such as Sylvester Smith, complained throughout the journey, disgusted with the food the camp had to eat and the lack of water, Nathan (along with the majority of the camp) stoically soldiered on without complaining—even when the only thing he had to drink was dew gathered "by scooping a dish suddenly through the grass."[14]

In early June 1834, the camp crossed the Mississippi River into Missouri.[15] On June 7, they reached the Salt River, where a branch of the Church was located. On June 8, the Kirtland contingent was joined by the Michigan Territory group, and, after reorganizing, on June 12 the camp continued the journey toward Clay County.[16]

On June 19, Nathan remembered, the group "encamped on an eminence between two forks of Fishing River, near a Baptist meeting house, built of hewn logs."[17] As the party prepared the camp for the evening, "several armed men" approached and told the group they would "see hell before morning." A large group of men—Nathan remembered it as 1,600, but others placed it around 500—waited to attack the camp when the sun had set.[18] No sooner had this threat been made, Nathan recalled, than "a small black cloud appeared in the west and increased in size until shortly the whole blue arch was draped in black, presenting a vengeful appearance, while the rain descended in torrents, the winds bellowed and such vivid flashes of lightning and such peals of thunder are seldom seen and heard."[19] Hail fell as well, some "as big as tumblers," breaking off tree limbs and splintering fence rails. The great storm caused the river to become "wonderfully swollen, so that [they] could not advance, neither could [their] enemies reach [them] if they had a mind so to do."

Nathan and other members of the camp perceived the storm as evidence of God's protection, as it prevented the group of men from attacking the camp. "The Lord had previously said He would fight the battles of His saints," Nathan stated, "and it seemed as though the mandate had gone forth from His presence, to ply the artillery of Heaven in defense of His servants."[20]

Two days after the storm, a group of men representing Ray and Clay Counties entered the camp and told Joseph Smith that the camp's approach had enraged the majority of western Missourians. Indeed, some newspapers reported that a large contingent of men had gathered in Jackson County, ready to shed blood, in case the camp crossed the Missouri River. The representatives from Ray and Clay Counties told the camp "what course would be policy for [the camp] to pursue in order to secure" the "favor and protection" of western Missourians.[21] Joseph Smith also learned that Missouri governor Daniel Dunklin did not wish to call out the state militia at that time, meaning that there would be no militia guard to accompany the Saints back to their Jackson County lands.[22]

On June 22, Joseph held a council "to determine what steps" the camp should take.[23] During the council, he dictated what is now Doctrine and Covenants 105—a revelation that, according to camp participant Joseph Holbrook, "show[ed] the mind of God concerning the redemption of Zion."[24] The revelation instructed the camp that the participants were no longer required to redeem Zion at that time, emphasizing that God would fight Zion's battles and that the elders of the Church needed to be endowed with power before Zion's redemption could occur. The revelation also reassured participants that the Lord accepted their offering of time and money to Zion's cause.[25] For Nathan Baldwin, this revelation "was the most acceptable to [him] of anything [he] had ever heard before, the gospel being the exception." Other members of the camp did not share his view. Nathan recalled that some apostatized from the faith because they were upset at not being allowed to fight.[26]

With the camp no longer required to redeem Zion, it began to disband. The discharge was hastened when an outbreak of cholera hit the camp at the end of June. Thirteen camp members died, as well as two members of the Church who were living in Missouri. "Some of the best men in camp" were killed in the epidemic, Nathan recalled. Nathan and those other participants who did not suffer from the disease were pressed into service to take care of those who did.[27]

On July 1, 1834, Nathan received his official discharge from the camp, as well as his portion of the consecrated money that had not been spent. He was due $1.16 but received only one dollar because they did not have exact change. He traveled back to Kirtland over the next several weeks with only that single dollar to sustain him.[28]

Though he experienced privations and difficulties on the trip, Nathan Baldwin's time with Zion's Camp laid a foundation for the rest of his life. He soon had the privilege of participating in the School of the Elders in Kirtland with Joseph Smith and other pupils. He was also among those camp members called to serve in the first Quorum of the Seventy. He would always remember what the Lord had declared in section 105 about the camp's participants: "I have heard their prayers, and will accept their offering."[29]

1. Nathan B. Baldwin, Account of Zion's Camp, 6–7, Church History Library, Salt Lake City.

2. Baldwin, Account of Zion's Camp, 7–8.

3. "Minutes, 24 February 1834," 41–42, josephsmithpapers.org.

4. "Revelation, 24 February 1834 [D&C 103]," 7–18, josephsmithpapers.org.

5. "Revelation, 16–17 December 1833 [D&C 101]," 73–83, josephsmithpapers.org.

6. "Revelation, 24 February 1834 [D&C 103]," 12–13, josephsmithpapers.org.

7. Baldwin, Account of Zion's Camp, 8.

8. Journal of the Branch of the Church of Christ in Pontiac, 1, Church History Library, Salt Lake City.

9. "History, 1838–1856, volume A-1 [23 December 1805–30 August 1834]," 477–78, josephsmithpapers.org; Heber C. Kimball, Autobiography, circa 1842–1858, 11, Church History Library, Salt Lake City; Andrea G. Radke, "We Also Marched: The Women and Children of Zion's Camp, 1834," *BYU Studies,* vol. 39, no. 1 (2000), 149–59.

10. Sidney Rigdon and Oliver Cowdery letter, May 10, 1834, Church History Library, Salt Lake City.

11. Baldwin, Account of Zion's Camp, 8.

12. "Account with the Church of Christ, circa 11–29 August 1834," 1, josephsmithpapers.org; Baldwin, Account of Zion's Camp, 9, 15.

13. Baldwin, Account of Zion's Camp, 9.

14. Baldwin, Account of Zion's Camp, 11–12; "Minute Book 1," 58–59, josephsmithpapers.org.

15. Joseph Smith, "Letter to Emma Smith, 4 June 1834," 56, josephsmithpapers.org.

16. Baldwin, Account of Zion's Camp, 11.

17. Baldwin, Account of Zion's Camp, 12; capitalization standardized.

18. See, for example, George A. Smith, Autobiography, 42–43, Church History Library, Salt Lake City.

19. Baldwin, Account of Zion's Camp, 12.

20. Baldwin, Account of Zion's Camp, 12; capitalization standardized.

21. Baldwin, Account of Zion's Camp, 13; Joseph Smith and others, "Declaration, 21 June 1834," 1–2, josephsmithpapers.org.

22. Joseph Smith and others, "Declaration, 21 June 1834," 1–2, josephsmithpapers.org; "The Mormon Controversy," *Washington D.C. Daily National Intelligencer,* July 23, 1834, 3.

23. William F. Cahoon, Autobiography, 43, Church History Library, Salt Lake City.

24. Joseph Holbrook, Autobiography and journal, 38, Church History Library, Salt Lake City.

25. "Revelation, 22 June 1834 [D&C 105]," 97–100, josephsmithpapers.org.

26. Baldwin, Account of Zion's Camp, 14.

27. Baldwin, Account of Zion's Camp, 14; Max H. Parkin, "Zion's Camp Cholera Victims Monument Dedication," *Missouri Mormon Frontier Foundation Newsletter,* vol. 15 (Fall 1997), 4–5.

28. Baldwin, Account of Zion's Camp, 15.

29. "Revelation, 22 June 1834 [D&C 105]," 98, josephsmithpapers.org.

Warren Cowdery

D&C 106

Lisa Olsen Tait

When his younger brother Oliver, then in his early twenties, became the "second elder" of the restored Church in 1830, Warren Cowdery (who was sometimes known as Dr. Cowdery) owned an apothecary, served as postmaster, and had constructed the first brick house in Freedom, New York.[1] At the time, he and his wife, Patience, were the parents of eight children. Though he apparently learned about the Book of Mormon around the time it was published in 1830, Warren did not join the Church until four years later.[2] He followed the unfolding drama of his brother's faith from a distance. In a January 1834 letter to Oliver, Warren expressed sympathy for the plight of the Saints in Missouri after their recent expulsion from Jackson County, but he still wrote of the members of the Church as "your people" and "your friends."[3]

The likely turning point for Warren Cowdery was a visit from Joseph Smith and Parley P. Pratt in March 1834. Obeying a command to recruit participants and collect donations from Church members in the "eastern countries" for Zion's Camp, Joseph and Parley passed through Freedom and stayed overnight in the home of Warren and Patience Cowdery, where they were treated hospitably "in the full Enjoyment of all the Blessings Both temporal and spiritual of which we stand in need or are found worthy to receive." During the visit, they preached more than once "to a hous crowded full to overflowing," and several people were baptized, including the Cowderys' neighbor Heman Hyde. Pratt later recalled that "thirty or forty" people were baptized and organized into a branch, which became the nucleus for the growth of the Church in that region.[4]

Although there are no surviving records of these first members in the Freedom Branch, it is likely that Warren Cowdery was among them. In the fall of 1834, six months after the visit from Joseph Smith, Warren wrote another letter to Oliver, in which he spoke of the religion "we have both embraced" and referred to the Saints as "our brethren and sisters." Warren's letter suggests his conversion was hard won. He seems to have been keenly aware of the criticism and disapproval of "thousands of respectable people [who] say . . . we are deluded and deceived," feeling the sting of that opposition all the more because of his respectable position in local society. And though he had felt "some manifestations of divine approbation" in his worship in the Freedom Branch, Warren still longed for experiences like his brother's. "I have a thousand times wished I could have that evidence that you have had," he wrote.[5] Warren also expressed a desire for "a preacher of our order" to come into the Freedom area, someone who would "do us good, by strengthening and building us up in the most holy faith."[6]

It must have been unexpected when, two months later, Joseph Smith received a revelation appointing Warren to be a "presiding high priest over my church, in the land of Freedom and the regions round about."[7] As is so often the case, Warren was to be the answer to his own request. And like many of those called to serve since, the words of blessing and the counsel he was given showed that the Lord knew him and would help him succeed in his calling.

In affirming Warren's choice to join the Church, the revelation also implicitly acknowledged the struggle he had experienced. "There was joy in heaven when my servant Warren bowed to my scepter, and separated himself from the crafts of men,"[8] it said. That separation was to become all the more acute, since the revelation instructed that Cowdery was to "preach my everlasting gospel, and lift up his voice and warn the people, not only in his own place, but in the adjoining counties," and he was to "devote his whole time to this high and holy calling."[9] As he did so, the Lord would "give him grace and assurance wherewith he may stand."[10] Ultimately, the revelation said, Warren's success would depend less on his ability than on his humility: "Blessed is my servant Warren, for I will have mercy on him; and, notwithstanding the vanity of his heart, I will lift him up inasmuch as he will humble himself before me."[11]

While records are scanty, we do know that Warren Cowdery filled the position of presiding elder in the Freedom region for the next year—an eventful year in that area. In early April, a conference was held at which Sidney Rigdon of the First Presidency presided.

Commenting on this conference in the newspaper report, Oliver Cowdery observed that the "vast" Freedom region was "anxious to receive instruction concerning the faith and belief of this church, being excited to enquiry by the few elders who have providentially preached in that country."[12] Several weeks later, the Twelve—on their first mission as a quorum—came through the area. They held a conference on May 22–23, at which they defined the geographical limits of the Freedom Conference, which included 12 branches and covered a large portion of western New York.[13] The Freedom Branch was the largest, with 65 reported members.

Topics of discussion at the conference included "the 'Word of Wisdom,' the gift of tongues, prophesying, etc.," and "the redemption of Zion." Five members of the Twelve spoke, after which "the church expressed their determination to put into practice the teachings" given. Later in the year, Orson Pratt visited the area on a mission. He reported baptizing a few people, selling copies of the Book of Mormon and Doctrine and Covenants, and securing several subscriptions to the Church's newspaper, the *Messenger and Advocate.* "There is a prospect of many embracing the gospel in these parts," he wrote.[14]

These and other reports show that Warren Cowdery was part of a dynamic, two-way relationship between the center places and outlying branches of the early Church. As a local Church leader, he would have helped minister to many new converts as they came into the Church, while also helping host and arrange meetings for missionaries and leaders from Kirtland.

Missionary successes could mean quick growth of new branches; some, such as the Freedom Branch, became quite large. But the call to gather with the Saints meant that local leaders often helped oversee rapid decreases in their region's membership. Warren Cowdery's experience again was typical. His report published in February 1835 in the *Messenger and Advocate* gives a vivid glimpse of how fluid the early branches were. The church at Westfield reported 72 members, a substantial number, while the branches in Mendon and Lima reported a total of eight. "From this last mentioned church, the greater part have moved away; some to Kirtland, and some to Missouri, and the eight here mentioned, is the remnant which is left," Cowdery explained. "The church was once large."

Likewise, the 18 members in Java and Weathersfield represented "the remainder of a church," of which "many have moved to the places of gathering."[15] Cowdery himself ultimately joined that gathering. Having served faithfully in Freedom, he and his family sold their property in the fall of 1835 and prepared to move to Kirtland.[16] They arrived early in 1836, just in time to participate in the events surrounding the dedication of the house of the Lord.

Like so many other early Saints who are little known today, Warren Cowdery made important contributions to the Lord's work. He worked in the publishing office in Kirtland and edited the Church's newspaper. As a clerk for Joseph Smith, he helped write down the dedicatory prayer for the Kirtland Temple and kept records of daily events. His most lasting contribution can now be found just a few pages from the revelation directed to him—in 1836, he recorded the entry in Joseph Smith's journal describing the visit of the Savior and other heavenly messengers to Joseph and Oliver in the Kirtland Temple on April 3, 1836.

1. "Cowdery, Warren A.," josephsmithpapers.org.

2. One of Cowdery's neighbors in Freedom, New York, recalled reading some proof sheets of the Book of Mormon that Warren had obtained from Oliver. See William Hyde journal, folder 2, page 5, Church History Library, Salt Lake City.

3. Warren Cowdery letter to Oliver Cowdery, Jan. 14, 1834, in *The Evening and the Morning Star,* Jan. 1834, 127.

4. Mar. 9–12, 1834, Joseph Smith, in "Journal, 1832–1834," josephsmithpapers.org. Parley P. Pratt wrote this entry in Joseph Smith's journal.

5. Parley P. Pratt, *The Autobiography of Parley Parker Pratt; One of the Twelve Apostles of the Church of Jesus Christ of Latter-Day Saints,* ed. Parley P. Pratt Jr. (1874), 117.

6. Warren Cowdery letter to Oliver Cowdery, Sept. 1, 1834, in *Evening and Morning Star,* Sept. 1834, 189.

7. Warren Cowdery letter to Oliver Cowdery, Sept. 1, 1834, in *Evening and Morning Star,* Sept. 1834, 189.

8. Doctrine and Covenants 106:1.

9. Doctrine and Covenants 106:6.

10. Doctrine and Covenants 106:2–3.

11. Doctrine and Covenants 106:8.

12. Doctrine and Covenants 106:7.

13. *Messenger and Advocate,* vol. 1 (Apr. 1835), 108.

14. At this time the term "conference" referred not only to meetings at which Church business was conducted but also to "geographical areas defined for administrative purposes" (see "Conferences" in the Joseph Smith Papers glossary: josephsmithpapers.org). In the meeting held by the Twelve in Freedom, New York, in May 1835, it was determined that "the limits of this conference extend from Lodi in the west, so far East as to include Avon, South to Pennsylvania, and North to Lake Ontario" (Record of the Twelve, 14 February–28 August 1835, 22–23 May 1835, josephsmithpapers.org).

15. *Messenger and Advocate,* vol. 2 (Nov. 1835), 224.

16. *Messenger and Advocate,* vol. 1 (Feb. 1835), 75.

17. Caroline Barnes Crosby and her husband, Jonathan, passed through Freedom on their way to Kirtland in November 1835 and spent a night with Warren Cowdery's family. Caroline reported that the Cowderys had "sold their inheritance in that place and were intending to emigrate west in the spring themselves" (*No Place to Call Home: The 1807–1857 Life Writings of Caroline Barnes Crosby, Chronicler of Outlying Mormon Communities,* ed. Edward Leo Lyman, Susan Ward Payne, and S. George Ellsworth [2005], 38).

"Wrought Upon"
to Seek a Revelation
D&C 108

Lisa Olsen Tait

"At home all this day and enjoyed myself with my family it being Christmas day the only time I have had this privelige so satisfactorily for a long time," Joseph Smith's journal records for December 25, 1835.[1] The next day, a Saturday, Joseph sat down with a few companions and "commenced studeing the Hebrew Language" when a knock came at his door. Standing there was his friend Lyman Sherman. "I have been wrought upon to make known to you my feelings and desires," Sherman told Joseph, "and was promised that I should have a revelation which should make known my duty."[2] The result of this request was the revelation now known as Doctrine and Covenants 108—a brief but powerful statement of personal spiritual assurance that also places Lyman Sherman at the center of larger events.

"Let Your Soul Be at Rest"

On that winter day in 1835, Lyman Sherman was 31 years old, and the fourth anniversary of his baptism was approaching. Early in the fall of 1831, two brothers of his wife, Delcena, who had left home to work, wrote back to the family that they had been baptized into

224

the new "Mormonite" church. "This news came upon us almost as a horror and a disgrace," Delcena's brother Benjamin recalled. Shortly after the first letter arrived, the absent Johnson brothers had sent a package containing the Book of Mormon and "a lengthy explanation" of their new beliefs. After receiving these materials, Benjamin wrote, "My mother, brother Seth, sister Nancy, and Lyman R. Sherman, with some of the neighbors, all devoted to religion, would meet together secretly to read the Book of Mormon and accompanying letter, or perhaps to deplore the delusion into which my brothers had fallen."

This initial skepticism gave way as "their reading soon led to marveling at the simplicity and purity of what they read, and at the spirit which accompanied it, bearing witness to its truth."[3] Lyman and Delcena Sherman and several members of the Johnson family were baptized in January 1832. Members of the Sherman family were also converted.[4] The Shermans moved to Kirtland by mid-1833, where they became acquainted with Joseph Smith and many of the Saints. Their son Albey was about the same age as Joseph Smith III, and the boys were friends.[5]

But though Sherman loved the Saints and had an unwavering faith in the restored gospel, he apparently had doubts about the quality of his own discipleship. The revelation gives us a glimpse of the process Sherman called having been "wrought upon" to seek out the Prophet. The Lord said that Sherman had "obeyed my voice in coming up hither," confirming that he had received promptings from the Spirit to seek out this opportunity. The Lord's counsel to "resist no more my voice" suggests that Sherman had received those impressions on multiple occasions but had hesitated to act on them as he experienced a deep and poignant spiritual search to know of his standing before God. In response to that quest, the revelation assured him that his sins were forgiven and kindly told him, "Let your soul be at rest concerning your spiritual standing."[6]

"You Shall Be Remembered"

The revelation also answered Sherman's request that the Lord would "make known [his] duty." He was already a leader in the emerging priesthood organization of the Church. Earlier in 1835, he had participated in a meeting "of those who journeyed to Zion" with Zion's Camp the previous summer. At this meeting, Joseph Smith announced that "it was the Will of God" that those who had gone to Zion "should be ordained to the ministry and go forth to prune the vineyard for the last time," and the first twelve Apostles of this dispensation were called.[7] Two weeks later, the first quorum of Seventies was organized "to go into all the earth, whither-soever the twelve Apostles should call them."[8] Lyman Sherman was ordained as one of the seven presidents of the Seventy.[9] In his ordination blessing, Sherman was promised, "Your faith shall be unshaken and you shall be delivered from great afflictions. . . . You are a chosen vessel of the Lord."[10]

But before they went out "into all the earth," the Seventies, including Lyman Sherman, were to be central participants in the events surrounding the dedication of the temple in the spring of 1836. The revelation to Lyman Sherman counseled him, "Wait patiently until the solemn assembly shall be called of my servants, then you shall be remembered with the first of mine elders and receive right by ordination with the rest of mine elders whom I have chosen."[11] These promises were fulfilled as Sherman took part in the various meetings and ordinances leading up to the solemn assembly at the dedication of the Kirtland Temple and the spiritual outpouring and "endowment of power" bestowed upon the Saints at that time.

"Strengthen Your Brethren"

Lyman Sherman's service to the Saints in Kirtland shows that he took the revelation's counsel to "strengthen [his] brethren" to heart. Wilford Woodruff, then a young Seventy who had missed the Kirtland Temple dedication and the accompanying spiritual outpouring, noted Sherman's spiritual leadership. At one notable sacrament meeting in the temple, Woodruff wrote, "Elder Sherman sung in the gift of tongues & proclaimed great & marvelous things while clothed upon by the power & spirit of God."[12] During the winter of 1836–37, the Seventies met every Tuesday evening in the west room of the attic story of the temple;[13] on one of these occasions, Sherman ordained a dozen men to the third quorum of Seventies.[14] A highlight of this season was a second solemn assembly held during the first week of April to commemorate the dedication of the temple and to bestow ordinances on those who had not been present the year before.

As internal dissension and external opposition joined forces against the Church, Lyman Sherman and his family remained loyal to Joseph Smith, helping to strengthen the Saints through the trying times. Sherman was appointed to the Kirtland high council in October 1837.[15] He moved to Far West, Missouri, where he was appointed in the fall of 1838 to the Far West High Council.[16] By this time, Joseph Smith and other Church leaders were in jail, and the Saints were in the midst of a desperate flight from the mobs in Missouri. According to Benjamin Johnson, Sherman traveled to visit the Prophet in jail, and it was as a result of this trip that he "took cold" and became very ill.[17] Meanwhile, on January 16, 1839, the First Presidency wrote to Brigham Young and Heber C. Kimball, the senior Apostles, designating Lyman Sherman to fill one of the vacancies in the Quorum of the Twelve.[18] Kimball wrote that he and Young visited Joseph Smith in Liberty Jail on February 8, 1839. He said that when they departed from Far West, "Lyman Sherman was somewhat unwell. In a few days after our return he died. We did not notify him of his appointment."[19]

It was a quiet and sudden end to the mortal ministry of a faithful man. Sherman's death meant hardship for his wife, Delcena, and their six small children, who made their way virtually destitute to Illinois and later to Utah.[20] Like so many early Saints, Lyman Sherman dedicated his life to the cause of establishing Zion and willingly followed the Prophet Joseph Smith in spite of poverty, opposition, and uncertainty. "He was a man of great integrity, a powerful preacher," recalled his brother-in-law Benjamin Johnson.[21] He lived and died fully engaged in fulfilling the Lord's command to "strengthen your brethren in all your conversation, in all your prayers, in all your exhortations, and in all your doings."[22]

1. Joseph Smith, Journal, 1835–1836, 89, josephsmithpapers.org.

2. Joseph Smith, Journal, 1835–1836, 89.

3. Benjamin F. Johnson, *My Life's Review* (Independence: Zion's Printing and Publishing Co., 1947), 11.

4. Elkanah, Almon, Asenath, Cornelia, and Electa Sherman and Julia Hills Johnson (Sherman's mother-in-law) were "baptized by Sylvester Smith & Gideon Carter in Pomfret Chautauqua N. York From May 2nd to May 6 1832" (Gideon H. Carter journal, 1831–32, Church History Library, Salt Lake City).

5. "History of Albey Lyman Sherman," typescript, in private possession.

6. "Revelation, 26 December 1835 [D&C 108]," in Joseph Smith, Journal, September 1835–April 1836, 90, josephsmithpapers.org.

7. Minutes, Feb. 14–15, 1835, in Minute Book 1, 147, josephsmithpapers.org.

8. Joseph Smith, "History, 1838–1856, volume B-1 [1 September 1834–2 November 1838]," 577, josephsmithpapers.org.

9. See "Instruction on Priesthood, between circa 1 March and circa 4 May 1835 [D&C 107]," in Doctrine and Covenants, 1835 ed., 88, josephsmithpapers.org.

10. Minutes, Feb. 28–Mar. 1, 1835, in Minute Book 1, 167, josephsmithpapers.org. Sherman was released as one of the presidents of the Seventies in April 1837, along with five of the other presidents, when it was decided that, since they had previously been ordained high priests, they should take their places in that quorum.

11. "Revelation, 26 December 1835 [D&C 108]," in Joseph Smith, Journal, September 1835–April 1836, 90.

12. Dean C. Jessee, "The Kirtland Diary of Wilford Woodruff," *BYU Studies,*

vol. 12, no. 4 (1972), 382. The meeting was held on January 8, 1837.

13. See Joseph Smith, "History, 1838–1856, volume B-1 [1 September 1834–2 November 1838]," 755.

14. Jessee, "The Kirtland Diary of Wilford Woodruff," 382.

15. Minutes, Oct. 1, 1837, in Minute Book 1, 247, josephsmithpapers.org.

16. Minutes, Dec. 13, 1838, in Minute Book 2, 175, josephsmithpapers.org. Sherman was appointed to fill "the place of Newel Knight untill he returns."

17. Johnson, *My Life's Review,* 52.

18. See Joseph Smith, Sidney Rigdon, and Hyrum Smith letter to Heber C. Kimball and Brigham Young, Jan. 16, 1839, page 1, josephsmithpapers.org.

19. Heber C. Kimball journal quoted in Lyndon W. Cook, "Lyman Sherman—Man of God, Would-Be Apostle," *BYU Studies,* vol. 19, no. 1 (Fall 1978), 124.

20. Johnson, *My Life's Review,* 56; "History of Albey Lyman Sherman," typescript, in private possession.

21. Johnson, *My Life's Review,* 53.

22. "Revelation, 26 December 1835 [D&C 108]," in Joseph Smith, Journal, September 1835–April 1836, 90.

More Treasures Than One
D&C 111
Elizabeth Kuehn

In late July 1836, Joseph Smith Jr., Sidney Rigdon, Oliver Cowdery, and Hyrum Smith started traveling from Kirtland, Ohio, to the eastern United States. In the weeks before their departure, worries about the temporal affairs of the Church weighed heavily on Joseph's mind. In Missouri, the Saints held on to the titles to lands they had been driven from in Jackson County as a sign of their commitment to building Zion, but they had no foreseeable way to return. At the same time, the Church was weighed down with debts after the construction of the Kirtland Temple. What could be done?

These concerns likely continued to occupy Joseph Smith's thoughts as his small group traveled to New York City and Boston.[1] According to a later account, Joseph and other leaders had been told about a hidden treasure in Salem, Massachusetts, and hoped to find it.[2] Both the hope for financial relief and worry over Zion were key parts of the context for a revelation the Prophet received in Salem on August 6, 1836.

"Concern Not Yourselves"

In the revelation, the Lord comforted Joseph and his companions: "Concern not yourselves about your debts, for I will give you power to pay them. Concern not yourselves about Zion, for I will deal merciful[ly] with her."[3] The revelation indicated that there were many treasures to be found in the city "for the benefit of Zion."[4] These would include both financial resources and the spiritual blessing of converts, "whom I will gather out in due time."[5] The treasures might also include important knowledge connected with "the more ancient inhabitants and founders of this city."[6]

Joseph and his three companions followed the direction in the revelation to "tarry in this place"[7] and spent several weeks in Salem, preaching and visiting historic places while hoping to obtain money to help pay Church debts and redeem Zion. But no documents exist indicating that they saw this revelation fulfilled in any way by the time they returned to Kirtland.

What the Lord accomplished through their trip to Salem remains unknown. Some people have assumed that the trip was simply not a success. Others have speculated that perhaps the revelation's instruction to "inquire diligently concerning the more ancient inhabitants of the city,"[8] which included some of Joseph's ancestors, might have helped prepare him to receive vital revelations on proxy work for the dead. But the historical record reveals nothing about what Joseph, Oliver, Sidney, and Hyrum felt about the revelation when they left Salem.

"The Due Time of the Lord"

And yet the revelation was not forgotten. Five years later, at a Philadelphia Church conference in July 1841, Hyrum Smith and William Law of the First Presidency left instructions for Elders Erastus Snow and Benjamin Winchester about Salem. These instructions included a copy of the August 1836 revelation and expressed the First Presidency's belief that "the due time of the Lord had come" for the revelation to be fulfilled and the people of Salem to be gathered into His kingdom.[9]

Erastus Snow was initially reluctant. He had been serving since April 1840 in Pennsylvania, New Jersey, and other areas on the East Coast with much success and had planned to return to Nauvoo in the fall of 1841. He prayed to know the will of the Lord, and the Spirit "continually whispered to go to Salem."[10] He also had business to attend to in Nauvoo, though, and had hoped to return there. It may have been difficult for him to distinguish between his own practical desires and the Lord's promptings.

Following a biblical practice, Elder Snow decided to draw lots to determine where he should go: Nauvoo or Salem. He drew the ballot for Salem—twice—and resolved to go as soon as possible.[11] He arranged for his wife and daughter, who had been traveling with him, to stay with his brother in Woonsocket, Rhode Island, until he could find somewhere in Salem for them. His brother was not a member of the Church but "seemed to take an interest in the work" as Erastus preached in the area, and he hoped that his brother might embrace the gospel.[12]

"Strangers and Alone"

On August 31, 1841, Erastus Snow left his family in Rhode Island and traveled to Boston, where he waited until September 3 for Benjamin Winchester to arrive. The two men then traveled to Salem. "We arrived, Strangers and alone," he wrote, "but trusted in God to direct our course." That night the two missionaries prayed earnestly "that God would open the hearts of the people that we might obtain a hearing."[13] The next day they went forward in faith.

Day and night they preached in Boston and Salem, but without success. After a week, Benjamin Winchester left for Philadelphia and Erastus continued the work in Salem alone, preaching where invited during the week and in a rented Masonic hall on weekends. Despite his efforts and the large crowds who attended, few seemed truly interested in his message. He wrote, "Though I advertised in the papers and circulated gratis a large quantity of our addresses through the city, yet it was a long time before I could get people to take notice of me more than to come and hear and go away again."[14]

The first sustained attention Erastus Snow received was negative. Reverend A. G. Comings, a Baptist minister and editor of a local paper, published articles opposing the Church and refused to print Elder Snow's responses. Eventually, however, Reverend Comings agreed to a series of debates between himself and Elder Snow to take place in November.[15] Lasting six nights, the debates turned public opinion against Comings, since his arguments were "chiefly epethets and insults."[16] Elder Snow wrote that "the chief good which resulted from that discussion was it caused many to investigate the doctrine who otherwise would have thought it unworthy of notice. My meetings afterwards were much better attended than before."[17]

"The First Fruits"

On November 8, 1841—about five months after Hyrum Smith and William Law wrote to Erastus Snow about Salem—he "reaped the first fruits of [his] labours" as a few individuals made baptismal covenants there. The work progressed rapidly through the winter. By early February there were 36 members in Salem.[18] In a report to Hyrum Smith and William Law, Elder Snow reflected, "Had I not known that Jesus had many sheep in this city, I think I should have been disheartened and not tarried to reap where I had sown, for this is the only place in which I ever preached so long without baptizing."[19]

Erastus Snow organized the Salem branch on March 5, 1842, with 53 members.[20] By June 1842 the branch had increased to about 90 members, some of whom moved to Nauvoo and other areas.[21] The faith of these Saints was great, and miracles of healing were among the spiritual gifts they experienced.[22] At a conference in Boston in February 1843, the Salem branch had 110 members. Erastus Snow had also been instrumental in organizing smaller branches in other areas of Massachusetts, including the Georgetown branch, which had 32 members at the 1843 conference.[23] When Elder Snow and his family left New England in the fall of 1843, 75 members from "Boston and the eastern churches" traveled with them to Nauvoo.[24]

"More Treasures Than One"

In the revelation on Salem given on August 6, 1836, the Lord had said the city had "more treasures than one"[25] to help build up the kingdom. While the full extent of that promise may yet be unrealized, the people who joined the Church through Erastus Snow's mission had a lasting impact. They helped build up the Church in the Salem-Boston area, which served as a vibrant and historically significant Church area in the 1840s. Many of these converts gathered to Nauvoo, made important contributions there, and then moved west to help settle the Rocky Mountain region and raise the next generations of Latter-day Saints.[26] Erastus Snow's mission in Salem— like many missions—has had ripple effects of service and faith that continue to bless the world today.

Like the four Church leaders who traveled to the East in 1836, we don't know exactly what treasures the Lord intended to come from Salem. But for Hyrum Smith and Erastus Snow, it was enough to trust in God's words and become, in His due time, instruments in helping His promises be fulfilled.

1. See Joseph Smith, "History, 1838–1856, volume B-1 [1 September 1834–2 November 1838]," 748–49, josephsmithpapers.org; see also "Letter from the Editor," *Latter-day Saints' Messenger and Advocate,* Sept. 1836, 372–75.

2. Ebenezer Robinson, "Items of Personal History of the Editor," *The Return,* July 1889, 105–6. Although Robinson's account was written a half-century after the fact, parts of it are corroborated by a letter from Joseph Smith to Emma Smith dated Aug. 19, 1836. For information on the early American tradition of searching for treasure buried in the earth or hidden in buildings, see Alan Taylor, "The Early Republic's Supernatural Economy: Treasure Seeking in the American Northeast, 1780–1830," *American Quarterly,* vol. 38, no. 1 (1986), 6–34; Ronald W. Walker, "The Persisting Idea of American Treasure Hunting," *BYU Studies,* vol. 24, no. 4 (1984), 429–59. For information about Joseph Smith's earlier participation in treasure-seeking culture, see Richard Lyman Bushman, *Joseph Smith: Rough Stone Rolling* (New York: Alfred A. Knopf, 2005), 49–52.

3. "Revelation, 6 August 1836 [D&C 111]," 36, josephsmithpapers.org; see also Doctrine and Covenants 111:5–6.

4. "Revelation, 6 August 1836 [D&C 111]," 35, josephsmithpapers.org; see also Doctrine and Covenants 111:2.

5. "Revelation, 6 August 1836 [D&C 111]," 35, josephsmithpapers.org; see also Doctrine and Covenants 111:2.

6. "Revelation, 6 August 1836 [D&C 111]," 37, josephsmithpapers.org; see also Doctrine and Covenants 111:9.

7. "Revelation, 6 August 1836 [D&C 111]," 36, josephsmithpapers.org; see also Doctrine and Covenants 111:7.

8. "Revelation, 6 August 1836 [D&C 111]," 36–37, josephsmithpapers.org; see also Doctrine and Covenants 111:9.

9. Erastus Snow journal, 1841–1847, 4, Church History Library, Salt Lake City.

10. Erastus Snow journal, 4.

11. Erastus Snow letter to Hyrum Smith and William Law, Feb. 4, 1842, Erastus Snow Papers, Church History Library, Salt Lake City.

12. Erastus Snow journal, 10.

13. Erastus Snow journal, 12.

14. Erastus Snow letter to Hyrum Smith and William Law, Feb. 4, 1842; spelling modernized.

15. See Erastus Snow journal, 16–17; Erastus Snow letter to Hyrum Smith and William Law, Feb. 4, 1842.

16. Erastus Snow journal, 17.

17. Erastus Snow journal, 17.

18. Erastus Snow letter to Hyrum Smith and William Law, Feb. 4, 1842.

19. Erastus Snow letter to Hyrum Smith and William Law, Feb. 4, 1842.

20. See Erastus Snow journal, 21.

21. See Erastus Snow journal, 27.

22. Erastus Snow journal, 29–30, 35–37.

23. Journal History, Feb. 9, 1843.

24. Erastus Snow journal, 44. For more detail on Erastus Snow's mission in Salem, see Kenneth W. Godfrey, "More Treasures Than One: Section 111," in *Hearken, O Ye People: Discourses on the Doctrine and Covenants* (Sandy, Utah: Randall Book, 1984),196–204.

25. "Revelation, 6 August 1836 [D&C 111]," 37, josephsmithpapers.org; see also Doctrine and Covenants 111:10.

26. Unfortunately, Erastus Snow's journal often contains numbers of baptisms rather than names, making it difficult to identify and trace the lives of all those who joined the Church through his mission. Among those who credited their conversion to him are the family of George and Mary Alley (see George Alley Family Collection, 19th Century Western and Mormon Americana, L. Tom Perry Special Collections,

Harold B. Lee Library, Brigham Young University, Provo, Utah), the family of Nathaniel and Susan Ashby (see Benjamin Ashby autobiography, Church History Library, Salt Lake City), and the family of Howard and Tamson Egan (see *Pioneering the West 1846 to 1878: Major Howard Egan's Diary,* ed. William M. Egan [Howard R. Egan Estate, Richmond, Utah: 1917]). For the perspective of an Ashby descendant on the legacy of Doctrine and Covenants 111 and Erastus Snow's mission, see Kim R. Burmingham, "The 'Insignificant' Scripture," *Ensign,* Aug. 1990, 47–48.

Far West and Adam-ondi-Ahman

D&C 115, 116, 117

Jacob W. Olmstead

During the final months of 1837, apostasy began to affect the Church in Kirtland, Ohio. Many Latter-day Saints were disillusioned by heavy financial losses as a result of the collapse of the Kirtland Safety Society and began to reject the Prophet's temporal and spiritual leadership. Among the dissenters were several members of the Quorum of the Twelve Apostles and Seventies, as well as the Three Witnesses to the Book of Mormon plates. In January 1838, as a result of this widespread apostasy and threats of violence, Joseph Smith and Sidney Rigdon received divine instruction to abandon their labors in Kirtland and to flee to Far West, Missouri. Although the revelation pronounced Joseph's labors "finished in this place," leaving Kirtland meant parting not only from their homes, but from the Church's largest stake and its first and only temple. Nevertheless, Joseph and Sidney were admonished to "arise and get yourselves on to a land which I shall show unto you even a land flowing with milk and honey." [1]

As they approached Far West after a "long & tedious journey," Joseph and Sidney were met by the Missouri Saints "with open armes and warm hearts welcomed us to the bosom of their sosciety." [2]

But news of internal divisions threatening the Church in Far West quickly put a damper on the joyful reunion. Four days prior to the Prophet's March 14 arrival, the Far West stake high council excommunicated an unrepentant William W. Phelps and John Whitmer, both counselors in the Missouri stake presidency. The two were accused of profiting from the sale of land intended for the gathering of the Saints to Far West and also for their part in the presidency's selling of property in Jackson County contrary to previous revelation. The high council had not taken action against David Whitmer, president of the Missouri stake presidency, or assistant president Oliver Cowdery on additional charges. Instead, they waited until after Joseph's arrival to address this unpleasant item of business. Both Whitmer and Cowdery were excommunicated in early April 1838.

Finding a Place for the Kirtland Saints

Far West grew to become the principal Mormon settlement in Missouri following the Saints' displacement from Clay and Ray Counties beginning in mid-1836. At the time of Joseph's arrival in 1838, Far West had a population of 4,900 with "150 homes, four dry goods stores, three family groceries, several blacksmith shops, two hotels, a printing shop, and a large schoolhouse that doubled as a church and a courthouse."[3] Finding affordable settlement lands for the anticipated arrival of a large influx of impoverished Kirtland Saints to Missouri became an immediate priority. On April 26, 1838, a revelation—now Doctrine and Covenants 115—provided some direction to the First Presidency, bishopric, and high council in Far West. In addition to urging the continued development of Far West and the construction of a temple there, the revelation directed "that other places should be appointed for stakes in the regions round about as they shall be manifested unto my Servant Joseph from time to time."[4]

Availability of inexpensive land guided Church leaders as they looked for these "other places" to create new stakes in the region. Although considerable portions of Caldwell County remained unsettled, the land had been surveyed, making it no longer subject to preemption laws. These laws allowed settlers to secure and improve unsurveyed lands without initial payment. Under preemption, those without sufficient means could work secured lands for profit and then be given the first rights to purchase the land after it was surveyed and went on sale from the federal government. Newly created and unsurveyed Daviess County, situated immediately north of Caldwell County, appealed to Church leaders as a potential gathering place for impoverished Saints in northern Missouri.[5]

On May 18, 1838, Joseph Smith led a group of Church leaders including Sidney Rigdon, Thomas B. Marsh, and David W. Patten (all of the Quorum of the Twelve Apostles), Bishop Edward Partridge, and others to the "north countries for the purpose of Laying off stakes of Zion, making Locations & laying claims for the gathering of the Saints for the benefit of the poor, and for the upbuilding of the Church of God."[6] The company traveled northward into Daviess County for several days to the Grand River region, which Joseph Smith's clerk George W. Robinson described as "large[,] beautifull[,] deep." During their expedition, the party found a land with "plenty" of wild game including "Deer, Turkey, Hens, Elk, &c." and prairies thickly covered with grass.[7] The land was indeed "flowing with milk and honey."[8]

The Place Where Adam Shall Come

While the natural abundance of the land in Daviess County provided for the temporal needs of the gathering Saints, revelation also directed the Saints to a place of great spiritual significance. As Joseph, Sidney, and George W. Robinson searched for a location to establish a settlement community near the Grand River, they came to a prominent knoll called Spring Hill. On this trip, Joseph received the revelation known today as Doctrine and Covenants 116, which identified the region as Adam-ondi-Ahman, "because said he it is the place where Adam shall come to visit his people, or the Ancient of days shall sit, as spoken of by Daniel the Prophet."[9]

The Saints knew of Adam-ondi-Ahman from previous revelations to Joseph Smith, which were published several years earlier in the 1835 edition of the Doctrine and Covenants. In what is now Doctrine and Covenants 107, the Lord explained that during Adam's final years, he called his righteous posterity to "the valley of Adam-ondi-Ahman," where he "bestowed upon them his lasting blessing." The revelation further explained that the Lord "appeared unto them" and "administered comfort unto Adam." Being "full of the Holy Ghost," Adam prophesied concerning his posterity "unto the latest generation." [10] In addition to references in the Doctrine and Covenants, the phrase had become a regular part of Mormon worship services through a hymn composed by William W. Phelps titled "Adam-ondi-Ahman." [11] This hymn was included in the first Latter-day Saint hymnal, compiled by Emma Smith and published in the early months of 1836,[12] and the Saints sang this hymn during the Kirtland Temple dedication. [13]

The new revelation concerning Adam-ondi-Ahman suggested a significant role for Adam in the events preceding the Lord's Second Coming. Elaborating on Daniel's vision of the Ancient of Days (see Daniel 7:9, 13–14), Joseph Smith later explained that "all that have had the Keys must Stand before him [Adam] in this grand Council. . . . The Son of Man [Christ] Stands before him & there is given him glory & dominion.—Adam delivers up his stewardship to Christ, that which was delivered to him as holding the Keys of the Universe, but retains his standing as head of the human family." [14]

Gathering to Adam-ondi-Ahman

By revealing the location of Adam-ondi-Ahman to Joseph Smith, the Lord imbued the land in Daviess County with a spiritual history as well as a spiritual future. At a time when the development of the kingdom of God upon the earth appeared on the brink of collapse as a result of apostasy and displacement, this revelation reminded Joseph and the Saints of their place in an unfolding sacred history. Church leaders were no longer solely working to establish a place for refugee Kirtland Saints and others desiring to gather, but they were also engaged in the gathering of the righteous to the location where Adam would one day turn over his stewardship to the Lord prior to the Second Coming.

Upon Joseph's return to Far West on May 21, 1838, he immediately held a council "to consult the bretheren upon the subject of our journey to know whether it is wisdom to go immediately into the north country . . . to secure the land on grand river." After the brethren expressed their feelings on the subject, "the question was put by Prest Smith and carried unanimously in favour of having the land secured on the river and between this place and Far West."[15] Five weeks later, on June 28, 1838, with Joseph Smith acting as chair, the Adam-ondi-Ahman stake of Zion was organized with John Smith called as president.[16] John Smith's second counselor and one of the first Latter-day Saint settlers in Daviess County, Lyman Wight, wrote: "This beautiful country with its flattering prospects drew in floods of emigrants. I had not less than thirty comers and goers through the day during the three summer months." By October, Wight recorded that "upwards of two hundred houses" had been built in Adam-ondi-Ahman with "forty families living in their wagons."[17]

"The More Weighty Matters"

Despite the establishment of this new stake of Zion and the call to settle in northern Missouri, some found it difficult to abandon their homes in Kirtland. Finally, during the summer months of 1838, most of the loyal Saints remaining in Kirtland began to make their way to Missouri. Notably absent from the parties of incoming Saints were William Marks and Newel K. Whitney, a Kirtland bishop and wealthy businessman. The pair initially neglected to gather with the main body of the Church in Missouri in order to settle their business affairs in Kirtland. The two struggled with abandoning the temporal security their businesses and property provided.

On July 8, 1838, Joseph Smith received a revelation (now Doctrine and Covenants 117) directed to Marks and Whitney commanding them to "come forth, and not tarry." The revelation called Marks to "preside in the midst of my people in the City Far West," presumably as the new president of the Missouri stake presidency. As for Whitney, the revelation directed him to "come up unto the land of Adam-ondi-Ahman, and be a bishop unto my people."[18] Using the imagery of Adam's ancient homeland and the infinite blessings promised to Adam's posterity, the revelation queried: "Is there not room enough upon the mountains of Adam-ondi-Ahman, and upon the plains of Olaha Shinehah, or in the land where Adam dwelt, that you should . . . covet that which is but the drop, and neglect the more weighty matters?"[19] Oliver Granger was designated to settle all the Church's accounts in Kirtland, and he delivered a letter to Marks and Whitney containing the revelation. In the letter, the First Presidency expressed confidence in the pair's willingness to obey the revelation and to "act accordingly."[20] Obedient to the instruction, both Marks and Whitney forsook their possessions in Kirtland. Eventually they joined with the main body of the Saints to attend to the "more weighty matters" of administering to the needs of the Saints.

Epilogue

Throughout the summer of 1838, the Saints continued to gather to Far West, Adam-ondi-Ahman, and other Mormon settlements in northern Missouri. In accordance with the command to build up Far West, on July 4, 1838, cornerstones were laid for a temple in that community. Soon a site had also been selected for a temple in Adam-ondi-Ahman. However, the peace and abundance the Saints enjoyed in northern Missouri was short-lived. Simmering mistrust and suspicion between Missourians and Latter-day Saints erupted violently in August 1838. A series of armed conflicts known as the Missouri-Mormon War culminated with the imprisonment of Joseph Smith and the expulsion of the Latter-day Saints from Missouri. After the expulsion of the Saints from their state, Missourians immediately swooped in to lay claim to the Mormon lands and improvements. Although they would go on to establish another covenant community and build a beautiful temple in Nauvoo, the Saints maintained a hope that they would one day return to reclaim these sacred lands in Missouri prior to the Second Coming.

1. "Revelation, 12 January 1838–C," 1, josephsmithpapers.org.

2. "Letter to the Presidency in Kirtland, 29 March 1838," in Joseph Smith, "Journal, March–September 1838," 23–24, josephsmithpapers.org.

3. James B. Allen and Glen M. Leonard, *The Story of the Latter-day Saints* (Salt Lake City: Deseret Book, 1976, reprint 1992), 116–17.

4. "Revelation, 26 April 1838 [D&C 115]," in Joseph Smith, "Journal, March–September 1838," 34, josephsmithpapers.org.

5. For an in-depth discussion of preemption laws and their impact on the Mormon settlement, see Jeffrey N. Walker, "Mormon Land Rights in Caldwell and Daviess Counties and the Mormon Conflict of 1838," *BYU Studies,* vol. 47, no. 1 (2008), 5–55.

6. Joseph Smith, "Journal, March–September 1838," 42, josephsmithpapers.org.

7. Joseph Smith, "Journal, March–September 1838," 43.

8. "Revelation, 12 January 1838–C," 1.

9. Joseph Smith, "Journal, March–September 1838," 43–44.

10. "Doctrine and Covenants, 1835," 86, josephsmithpapers.org; capitalization standardized; see also Doctrine and Covenants 107:53–56.

11. See "Minutes, 28 June 1838," in *Elders' Journal* (Aug. 1838), 61, josephsmithpapers.org. During the organization of the Adam-ondi-Ahman Stake, "Adam-ondi-Ahman" is referred to as "the well known hymn."

12. Although the date of publication is listed as 1835, this first hymnal likely did not actually become available until February or March 1836; see Peter Crawley, *A Descriptive Bibliography of the Mormon Church: Volume One, 1830–1847* (Provo, Utah: BYU Religious Studies Center, 1997), 59.

13. "Kirtland, Ohio, March 27th, 1836," *Latter Day Saints' Messenger and Advocate,* vol. 2, no. 6 (Mar. 1836), 276.

14. "Report of Instructions, between 26 June and 4 August 1839–A, as Reported by Willard Richards," in Willard Richards Pocket Companion, 64, josephsmithpapers.org.

15. Joseph Smith, "Journal, March–September 1838," 44.

16. "Minutes, 28 June 1838," in *Elders' Journal* (Aug. 1838), 60–61.

17. Rollin J. Britton, *Early Days on Grand River and the Mormon War* (Columbia: The State Historical Society of Missouri, 1920), 6–7.

18. Joseph Smith, "Journal, March–September 1838," 57–58; spelling standardized.

19. Joseph Smith, "Journal, March–September 1838," 58; spelling and punctuation standardized.

20. "Letter to William Marks and Newel K. Whitney, 8 July 1838," 2, josephsmithpapers.org.

"Take Special Care of Your Family"

D&C 118, 126

Lisa Olsen Tait and Chad M. Orton

Mary Ann Angell met Brigham Young in Kirtland in 1833. Baptized in 1832, Mary Ann was an early convert to the Book of Mormon. She testified that "the Spirit bore witness to her . . . of the truth of its origin, so strongly that she could never afterwards doubt it."[1] She soon set out for Kirtland, arriving in the spring of 1833.[2]

Brigham Young had lost his first wife, Miriam Works, to consumption a year earlier, so Vilate Kimball, wife of his close friend Heber C. Kimball, had taken in Brigham's two young motherless daughters while Brigham and Heber went out to proclaim their new faith. Now in 1833, Brigham had come to Kirtland to stay.

Within a few months, Brigham and Mary Ann became acquainted. She "felt drawn towards him" when she heard him preach; he was impressed when he heard her bear testimony.[3] They were married early in 1834. Brigham later wrote that Mary Ann "took charge of my children, kept my house, and labored faithfully for the interest of my family and the kingdom."[4]

"Go and Leave Your Family"

Brigham had been transformed by the restored gospel, and his desire to proclaim it could not be contained. "I wanted to thunder, and roar out the gospel to the nations," he later recalled. "It burned in my bones like fire pent up."[5] Although this required arduous travel, often in the face of poverty, sickness, and harsh weather, Brigham went willingly. "It has never entered into my heart," he later declared, "from the first day I was called to preach the Gospel to this day, when the Lord said, 'Go and leave your family,' to offer the least objection."[6]

Mary Ann did not offer any objection either, even when missions and Church service took Brigham from home about half the time during their first five years together. Shortly after their marriage, he was gone four months with Zion's Camp, returning in time for the birth of their first child in October. Early in 1835 he spent five months on a mission as a newly called Apostle. In 1836, he was home during the early months of the year, but his time was consumed with overseeing painting and window glazing for the house of the Lord in Kirtland. Shortly after the dedication of the temple, he departed on another mission that extended from April to September. In 1837, he went on two missions, one in the spring and one in the summer. These separations meant heavy work for Mary Ann, likely out in the fields as well as in the house, in addition to caring for their growing family: Brigham's daughters Elizabeth and Vilate from his first marriage; a son, Joseph, born in 1834; and twins, Mary Ann and Brigham Jr., born in 1836.

Brigham's letters to his family expressed his love and his awareness of their struggles. "Mary I remember you allways in my prayrs," he wrote from Massachusetts in March 1837. "I can vue my famely with the eye of the mind and desire to be with them as so[o]n as duty will permit."[7] In July he expressed his hope that when he returned in the fall he would finally be able to "pay for [his] house" and make some improvements on it "so that I can feele contented about my famely when I leve them." He asked Mary Ann to "get som lumber or timber or ston and if you have a chance to b[u]y enny thing for bilding."[8]

When Brigham returned that fall, however, he found Kirtland in turmoil, rent with dissension and conflict. His loyalty to Joseph Smith made him a target for the Church's opponents, and in December he fled for his life, forced to leave his family behind. Mary Ann and the children were terrorized by apostate mobbers, who frequently came to search her property and bombarded her with "threats and vile language," frightening her to the point of damaging her health. When Mary Ann finally joined Brigham in Far West, Missouri, in the spring of 1838, he was shocked at her condition. "You look as if you were almost in your grave," he told her.[9]

Two Revelations

Shortly after the Young family's arrival, Joseph Smith received an unpublished revelation instructing Brigham that he was not to leave his family again "until they are amply provided for."[10] But a revelation to the Quorum of the Twelve in July 1838—now in Doctrine and Covenants 118—indicated how short that respite would be. In nine months, the Twelve were to depart on a mission to Great Britain, taking leave from Far West on April 26, 1839.[11]

Those nine months proved to be anything but restful. The Saints in Missouri were driven from their homes, and once again Brigham Young was in danger as one of the most wanted Church leaders. The Young family fled together, but they traveled short distances and then waited while Brigham went back to assist other destitute Saints. Mary Ann recalled that by the time they reached safety on the other side of the Mississippi River in Illinois, she had kept house in 11 different places within three months.[12] She was also pregnant.

A Mission across the Waters

As the Saints began gathering again in the area of Commerce, soon to be renamed Nauvoo, Illinois, the Young family found living quarters across the Mississippi River in Montrose, Iowa, where many Saints had taken shelter in abandoned military barracks. In spite of their forced relocation and the press of building a new community, the Twelve were still determined to fulfill the commanded mission to Great Britain.

On July 2, 1839, the Twelve met with the First Presidency at the home of Brigham Young. The Presidency "lade their hands" upon the heads of several present, including Mary Ann Young, "to bless them & their families before they left for other Nations." The Brethren were promised that they would return "to the bosom of [their] families" and that they would convert "many Souls as seals of [their] ministry." [13]

Two months later, on September 14, 1839, Brigham Young bade farewell to Mary Ann again and set out on his mission to England. It would be hard to imagine less favorable circumstances for his departure. "We were in the depths of poverty, caused by being driven from Missouri, where we had left all," he recalled. [14] His wardrobe "had not much of a ministerial appearance," as his cap was made out of "a pair of old pantaloons" and a small "quilt with a comforter run through it" served as his overcoat. [15]

Like many of the Saints at that time, he was suffering from malaria and shaking with fever. His health was so bad that, as he recalled, "I was unable to walk twenty rods without assistance. I was helped to the edge of the river Mississippi and carried across." Nevertheless, he "was determined to go to England or to die trying." [16]

Brigham was not the only one suffering. Mary Ann had given birth only 10 days earlier. The family now consisted of seven children, and they were all "sick and unable to wait upon each other." Nevertheless, Mary Ann crossed the river from Iowa to Illinois so she could bid her husband a final farewell. [17] As Brigham and an equally sick Heber C. Kimball pulled away from Heber's Nauvoo home, Brigham joined his friend in feebly standing up in the wagon in which they were riding to shout, "Hurrah for Israel," in an attempt to cheer those they were leaving behind. [18]

Making Ends Meet at Home

Two months after Brigham's departure, the family ran out of food. Still suffering the effects of malaria, Mary Ann was forced to take action to relieve their hunger. On a "cold, stormy November day," she wrapped herself and her baby Alice in tattered blankets and set off in a small rowboat across the Mississippi River. During the journey, the wind-whipped waves soaked both her and her baby. Upon reaching Nauvoo, she went to the home of a friend, who later recounted, "Sister Young came into my house . . . with her baby Alice in her arms, almost fainting with cold and hunger, and dripping wet." Mary Ann refused her friend's offer to let her stay. "The children at home are hungry, too," she insisted. Procuring "a few potatoes and a little flour," Mary Ann "wended her way to the river bank" to row home. Many times she crossed the river "to obtain the barest necessaries of life," sometimes "in storms that would have frightened women of ordinary courage."[19]

Around this time, Mary Ann was forced out of her room in the old military barracks. She took up residence in a horse stable in Montrose[20] and spent the winter eking out a meager living "sowing [sewing] & washing" for others.[21] The following spring she was given a lot in Nauvoo, on which she planted a garden. Throughout that summer, Mary Ann paddled across the Mississippi River to care for her garden and then paddled "back again at night after her days work was done."[22]

In addition to working in her garden, Mary Ann undertook to build a log cabin on the lot. In September 1840, a year after Brigham left on his mission, she moved her family into their new home in Nauvoo. Vilate Kimball noted that the house "could hardly be called a shelter," but at least it saved her constant trips across the river.[23] Her nephew later recalled that it was simply the "body of a house," with blankets hung over the doors and windows to keep out the elements.[24]

Although Mary Ann had reason to complain, she kept her challenges from Brigham. After learning from others about some of her trials, he wrote her in November 1840: "You may well think that my hart feeles tender toards you, when I relise your patiants and willingness to suffer in poverty and doe everything you can for my children and for me to goe and due the thing the Lord requires of me."[25]

In April 1841, anticipating his return from England, Mary Ann informed Brigham that while she wished to have "a better house to recieve [him] into," she was "thankful for a comfortable shelter from the Storm." She explained that it had "been so difficult to obtain work that what I had done is not done as I wanted itt." Having "done the best [she] could," she thanked her "hevenly Father for all the blessings I recieve and pray the Lord to continue his mercys with us."[26]

Upon returning to Nauvoo on July 1, 1841, after a 22-month absence, Brigham learned just how impoverished Mary Ann and the children had been. He set to work immediately to improve their situation. When not "at the call of bro. Joseph, in the service of the church," Brigham said, "I spent [my time] in draining, fencing and cultivating my lot, building a temporary shed for my cow, chinking and otherwise finishing my house."[27] At the same time, he began work on the red brick home that still stands in Nauvoo, although he was not able to move his family into it until May 1843.[28]

"Your Offering Is Acceptable"

A week after Brigham's return, on July 9, 1841, Joseph Smith visited him at his home. Mary Ann was likely there. No account survives of the conversation or circumstances of the day, but no doubt Joseph saw firsthand the evidence of the Young family's sacrifice and continuing need. He dictated a revelation on the spot, now found in Doctrine and Covenants 126.[29] "Dear & well beloved Brother, Brigham Young," it read, "it is no more required at your hand to leave your family as in times past, for your offering is acceptable to me." He was instructed to "take special care of your family from this time henceforth and forever." Though the revelation was addressed to Brigham, it was an unmistakable affirmation of Mary Ann's sacrifice and faithful support. "This evening I am with my wife a lone by my fire Side for the first time for years," Brigham recorded in his journal six months after returning from England, reflecting the welcome relief his presence at home brought to them both. "We injoi [enjoy] it and feele to pra[i]se the Lord."[30]

The revelation changed where Brigham Young served, but not how much. He was absent from home for only three short missions in the ensuing years, but his time was still dedicated to serving the Lord. Mary Ann continued to support him and to make sacrifices for her faith, including accepting the principle of plural marriage and welcoming new wives into the family. And there were more hardships to come. In the midst of the Saints' forced exodus from

Nauvoo, Mary Ann was said to be "benevolent and hospitable in the extreme," administering generous "advice and assistance" to those in need.[31] Throughout her life, she served family, friends, and fellow Saints and helped build up the kingdom of God.

1. E. B. Wells, "Heroines of the Church: Biography of Mary Ann Angell Young," *Juvenile Instructor,* vol. 26, no. 1 (Jan. 1, 1891), 17.

2. Leonard J. Arrington, *Brigham Young: American Moses* (New York: Alfred A. Knopf, 1985), 37.

3. Wells, "Heroines of the Church," 17; Arrington, *Brigham Young,* 37.

4. "History of Brigham Young," *Latter-day Saints' Millennial Star,* vol. 25, no. 29 (July 18, 1863), 454.

5. Brigham Young, "Discourse," *Deseret News,* Aug. 24, 1854, 1.

6. Arrington, *Brigham Young,* 54.

7. Brigham Young letter to Mary Ann Angell Young, Mar. 24, 1837, quoted in Dean C. Jessee, "Brigham Young's Family: Part I, 1824–1845," *BYU Studies,* vol. 18, no. 3 (1978), 316.

8. Brigham Young letter to Mary Ann Angell Young, July 21, 1836, quoted in Jessee, "Brigham Young's Family," 315.

9. Wells, "Heroines of the Church," 19. Wells mistakenly dates these events to 1836–37, a year earlier than they actually took place.

10. Revelation to Brigham Young, Apr. 17, 1838, in Joseph Smith, "History, 1838–1856, vol. B-1 [1 September 1834–2 November 1838]," 790, josephsmithpapers.org.

11. "Revelation, 8 July 1838–A [D&C 118]," in Joseph Smith, Journal, March–September 1838, 54–55, josephsmithpapers.org; see also Doctrine and Covenants 118:4–5. The revelation stating that the Twelve were to begin their mission for England at the temple site in Far West on April 26, 1839 (see D&C 118), was given during a time of peace. When the date arrived, the Saints had been driven from Missouri by armed mobs. Nonetheless, Brigham and other members of the Twelve felt that they needed to return to the state to fulfill the revelation. Enemies of the Church, knowing that the revelation mentioned a specific day and date, had vowed that they would not allow it to be fulfilled, hoping to thus prove that Joseph Smith was not a prophet. While some argued that under the circumstances the Lord would take the "will for the deed," Brigham and others felt that they needed to have "faith to go forward and accomplish it" (Wilford Woodruff, "Discourse," *Deseret News,* Dec. 22, 1869, 543). Although facing the threat of death or imprisonment, Church leaders gathered at the temple site during the predawn hours and fulfilled the revelation. Because of their threats, mob leaders had convinced themselves that no effort would be made to carry out the stipulated meeting and had left no guard at the site.

12. Wells, "Heroines of the Church," 19.

13. Wilford Woodruff journal, July 2, 1839, in *Wilford Woodruff's Journal: 1833–1898, Typescript,* ed. Scott G. Kenney, 9 vols. (Midvale, Utah: Signature Books, 1983–85), 1:342.

14. Brigham Young, "Discourse," *Deseret News,* Aug. 3, 1870, 307.

15. "History of Brigham Young," *Latter-day Saints' Millennial Star,* vol. 25, no. 43 (Oct. 24, 1863), 679; Brigham Young, "Sermon," *Deseret News,* Sept. 17, 1856, 219.

16. Brigham Young, "Discourse," *Deseret News,* Aug. 3, 1870, 307.

17. "History of Brigham Young," *Latter-day Saints' Millennial Star,* vol. 25, no. 41 (Oct. 10, 1863), 646.

18. *President Heber C. Kimball's Journal: The Faith-Promoting Series,* no. 7 (Salt Lake City: Juvenile Instructor Office, 1882), 100.

19. E. B. Wells, "Heroines of the Church: Biography of Mary Ann Angell Young," *Juvenile Instructor,* vol. 26, no. 2 (Jan. 15, 1891), 56–57. Wells identifies Mary Ann's friend in the story only as "an intimate friend of Sister Young from the days of Kirtland."

20. Historian's Office journal, Sept. 4, 1859, image 211, Church History Library, Salt Lake City.

21. Joseph Watson Young autobiography [n.d.], 23, Church History Library, Salt Lake City.

22. Joseph Watson Young autobiography, 23.

23. Vilate Kimball letter to Heber C. Kimball, Sept. 6, 1840, Church History Library, Salt Lake City.

24. Joseph Watson Young autobiography, 23.

25. Brigham Young letter to Mary Ann Angell Young, Nov. 12, 1840, quoted in Jessee, "Brigham Young's Family," 319.

26. Mary Ann Angell Young letter to Brigham Young, Apr. 15, 17, and 30, 1841, quoted in Jessee, "Brigham Young's Family," 322.

27. "History of Brigham Young," *Deseret News,* Mar. 10, 1858, 3.

28. See "History of Brigham Young," *Deseret News,* Mar. 17, 1858, in Jessee, "Brigham Young's Family," 324.

29. "History of Brigham Young," *Latter-day Saints' Millennial Star,* vol. 26, no. 5 (Jan. 30, 1864), 71.

30. "Revelation, 9 July 1841 [D&C 126]," in Book of the Law of the Lord, 26, josephsmithpapers.org; punctuation modernized; see also Doctrine and Covenants 126:1–3.

31. Brigham Young journal, Jan. 18, 1842, image 37, Brigham Young Collection, Church History Library, Salt Lake City.

32. Wells, "Heroines," 58.

"The Tithing of My People"
D&C 119, 120

Steven C. Harper

After a challenging year in Kirtland, Ohio, Joseph Smith arrived in Far West, Missouri, in early 1838, ready to make a new start. Shortly after his arrival, he received a revelation calling for Far West to be built up as a holy city with a temple at its center.[1] In the same revelation, the Lord forbade the First Presidency from borrowing money to accomplish these aims. They had borrowed to finance the house of the Lord in Kirtland, Ohio, and though the blessings were worth every penny, they were still struggling to pay off those debts.[2] How would the Saints raise the necessary means to build yet another temple city?

This was not a new question for the young Church. The Lord gave the law of consecration in 1831 in Kirtland to address some of the same concerns.[3] In it the Lord commanded the Saints to freely offer what He had blessed them with to the bishop, who would then consecrate a stewardship to them on the Lord's behalf. As stewards, the Saints would be "amply supplied" with what they needed and expected to return any surplus to the bishop of the Church to "administer to the poor and needy," purchase land for the Saints, and build Zion.[4]

The Lord's revelations on consecration emphasized the doctrines of individual agency, stewardship, and accountability. Joseph taught these principles to the bishops, and they in turn emphasized the voluntary nature of the offerings and the conditional blessings associated with them.[5]

Throughout most of the 1830s, there were two bishops: Edward Partridge served the Saints in Missouri—or Zion, the center of the Church—while Newel K. Whitney served the Saints in the Church's only stake at that time, in Kirtland, Ohio. Joseph and the bishops tried to help the Saints obey the law, but reluctant Saints and hostile neighbors hindered these efforts. Their ministry was doubly challenging in 1837 because the Church owed large debts, and the United States slumped into a long economic depression.

Saints at the time understood *tithing* to refer to any amount of freely consecrated goods or money. In September 1837, Bishop Whitney and his counselors in the Kirtland bishopric declared that "it is the fixed purpose of our God . . . that the great work of the last days was to be accomplished by the tithing of his saints." Referring to the promise in Malachi 3:10, they urged the Saints to "bring their tithes into the store house, and after that, not before, they were to look for a blessing that there should not be room enough to receive it."[6]

A few months later, the bishopric in Missouri proposed a similar but more specific policy: each household should offer a tithe of 2 percent of its annual worth after paying the household's debts. This, the bishopric in Zion wrote, "will be in some degree fullfilling the law of consecration."[7]

In early 1838, as Joseph Smith was preparing to move his family from Kirtland to Far West, Thomas Marsh wrote him a letter from Missouri, conveying his feeling that "The church will rejoice to come up to the law of consecration, as soon as their leaders shall say the word, or show them how to do it."[8]

At the time Joseph Smith arrived in Far West, the Saints were flocking to this new headquarters from branches of the Church in the United States and Canada. They settled throughout the region, necessitating the formation of a new stake. By July of 1838, the prospects of establishing an enduring stronghold in northern Missouri appeared promising. But the daunting task of building a temple loomed. The Church needed to raise the means to build the Lord's house in spite of other pressing needs.

251

With this challenge in mind, Joseph gathered several leaders on Sunday morning, July 8, 1838. It was apparently in this meeting that he received both the revelation on tithing (now canonized as Doctrine and Covenants 119) and the revelation on the disposition of tithes (now Doctrine and Covenants 120).[9]

Joseph prayed, "O! Lord, show unto thy servents how much thou requirest of the properties of thy people for a Tithing?"[10] The prayer is recorded in the Prophet's journal, followed by the word "Answer" and then the revelation that is now Doctrine and Covenants 119. "I require all their surpluss, property to be put into the hands of the Bishop of my Church," the Lord said.[11] Then, in what is now Doctrine and Covenants 119:2, the Lord stated the reasons the Saints should tithe.[12] They are the same reasons noted previously for obeying the law of consecration recorded in what is now Doctrine and Covenants 42: to relieve poverty, purchase land for the Saints, and build a temple and build up Zion so that those who make and keep covenants can gather to a temple and be saved.[13]

"This," the revelation says, "shall be the beginning of the tithing of my people." That instance of the word *tithing* is the first of three (*tithing* or *tithed*) in section 119. All of them refer to the Saints' voluntary offering of surplus property. "And after that," the revelation says, "those who have thus been tithed shall pay one-tenth of all their interest annually." The revelation does not call it a lesser law to be replaced someday, but "a standing Law unto them forever" and applicable to all Saints everywhere.[14]

The revelation ends with this ominous warning: "If my people observe not this Law, to keep it holy, and by this law sanctify the Land of Zion unto me, that my Statutes and Judgements, may be kept thereon that it may be most holy, behold verrily I say unto you, it shall not be a land of Zion unto you."[15]

Saints in Far West heard the revelation read in the Sunday meeting held that day. Those in outlying areas heard it in the weeks that followed.[16] Bishop Partridge, who was present at the meeting in which the revelation was apparently received, wrote from Missouri to Bishop Whitney in Ohio and explained how it was to be followed: "The saints are required to give all their surplus property into the hands of the bishop of Zion, and after this first tithing they are to

pay annually one tenth of all their interest." Bishop Partridge understood "one tenth of all their interest" annually to mean 10 percent of
what Saints would earn in interest if they invested their net worth
for a year.[17]

Shortly after Joseph received the revelation in section 119, he assigned
Brigham Young to go among the Saints "and find out what surplus
property the people had, with which to forward the building of the
Temple we were commencing at Far West." Before setting out, Brigham
asked Joseph, "'Who shall be the judge of what is surplus property?'
Said he, 'Let them be the judges themselves.'"[18]

As they were taught the will of the Lord, the Saints became
accountable stewards who could choose whether or not to pay their
tithes of their own free will. "Saints have come up day after day to
consecrate," the Prophet's journal says, "and to bring their offerings
into the store house of the lord."[19] But not all Saints exercised their
agency to be wise stewards. Brigham Young later lamented that
some Saints were stingy with their offerings.[20]

At this time, the Lord also gave Joseph the revelation now found
in Doctrine and Covenants 120, "making known the disposition of
the properties tithed, as named in the preceeding [preceding] revelation."[21] It assigned the First Presidency, the bishopric in Zion, and
the high council in Zion to decide how to use the tithes, making
their decisions, the Lord said, "by mine own voice unto them."[22]

Joseph Smith's journal notes that the newly revealed council
soon met in Far West to "take into concideration, the disposing of
the publick properties in the hands of the Bishop, in Zion, for the
people of Zion have commenced liberally to consecrate agreeably
to the revelations, and commandments." The council agreed that the
members of the First Presidency should use the funds they needed
"and the remainder be put into the hands of the Bishop or Bishops,
agreeably to the commandments, and revelations."[23]

When what is now Doctrine and Covenants 120 was revealed in
1838, Far West served as Church headquarters, and the bishop and
high council there served on the council with the First Presidency.
Later, the Church's traveling high council, the Quorum of the Twelve
Apostles, became the Church's general high council and a Presiding

Bishopric was appointed; thus, today the council is composed of the First Presidency, the Quorum of the Twelve Apostles, and the Presiding Bishopric.[24]

Sadly, during the autumn of 1838, the Saints were driven from Missouri, their Zion-building project apparently on temporary hold and the temple marked out by only a few stones. Exiled from Missouri, the Saints regrouped in Illinois, joined by thousands of converts from the British Isles, the eastern states, and Canada. There Joseph led them as he always had—revealing the way forward line upon line—until they understood and paid, as tithing, a tenth of their overall increase, together with other freewill offerings of time, talent, and surplus property.[25] When the Apostles invited the Saints to offer all they could toward the construction of a temple in Nauvoo, many responded, offering tools, land, furniture, and money.[26] John and Sally Canfield consecrated all they had, including themselves and their two children, "to the God of He[a]ven and for the Good of his Cause." In a note to Brigham Young, Brother Canfield wrote, "All I possess I freely give to the Lord and into thy hands."[27]

There in Nauvoo, then in Utah, and then throughout the world, the Latter-day Saints learned that if they obeyed even just the instruction to offer a tenth of their annual increase, the Church could pay its debts and begin to carry out the Lord's instructions to build temples, relieve poverty, and build Zion. The money offered is calculable. The blessings are not.

1. See "Revelation, 26 April 1838 [D&C 115]," in Joseph Smith, Journal, Mar.–Sept. 1838, 33, josephsmithpapers.org; see also Doctrine and Covenants 115:7–8.

2. See "Revelation, 26 April 1838 [D&C 115]," in Joseph Smith, Journal, 33; see also Doctrine and Covenants 115:13; Joseph Smith, "Discourse, 6 April 1837, josephsmithpapers.org."

3. See Steven C. Harper, "The Law: D&C 42," history.lds.org.

4. "Revelation, 9 February 1831 [D&C 42:1–72]," josephsmithpapers.org; see also Doctrine and Covenants 42:30–36.

5. Newel K. Whitney and others, "To the Saints scattered abroad," Sept. 18, 1837, in *Latter-day Saints' Messenger and Advocate,* vol. 3, no. 12, Sept. 1837, 561–64; see also Joseph Smith letter to Edward Partridge, May 2, 1833, josephsmithpapers.org; Joseph Smith, "Letter to Church Leaders in Jackson County, Missouri, 25 June 1833"; Joseph Smith, "Letter to Edward Partridge and Others, 30 March 1834," josephsmithpapers.org.

6. Newel K. Whitney and others, "To the Saints scattered abroad," 562.

7. Minute Book 2, Dec. 6–7 1837, 89–90, josephsmithpapers.org.

8. "Letter from Thomas B. Marsh, 15 February 1838," 45, josephsmithpapers.org.

9. There are five revelations dated July 8, 1838, in Joseph Smith's journal. The

journal is explicit that the first revelation, directed to Thomas B. Marsh, was received in the leadership meeting. The journal is not explicit as to whether the next four revelations were received in the same setting. The fifth revelation—directed to William Marks, Newel K. Whitney, and Oliver Granger—was copied in a letter written later in the day from the First Presidency to Marks and Whitney. The letter states that the revelation had been "recd. this morning." There is some indication that the revelations were recorded in Joseph Smith's journal in chronological order, which would imply that all five revelations were received on the morning of July 8, 1838, apparently in the leadership meeting that was mentioned in the introduction to the first revelation.

10. "Revelation, 8 July 1838–C [D&C 119]," in Joseph Smith, "Journal, March–September 1838," July 8, 1838, 56, josephsmithpapers.org.

11. "Revelation, 8 July 1838–C [D&C 119]," 56.

12. "Revelation, 8 July 1838–C [D&C 119]," 56.

13. See "Revelation, 9 February 1831 [D&C 42:1–72]," 3, josephsmithpapers.org; see also Doctrine and Covenants 42:30–36.

14. "Revelation, 8 July 1838–C [D&C 119]," 56; punctuation modernized; see also Doctrine and Covenants 119:4, 7.

15. "Revelation, 8 July 1838–C [D&C 119]," 56; see also Doctrine and Covenants 119:6.

16. See Joseph Smith journal, July 8, 1838, in Dean C. Jessee, Mark Ashurst-McGee, and Richard L. Jensen, eds., *Journals, Volume 1: 1832–1839,* vol. 1 of the Journals series of *The Joseph Smith Papers,* ed. Dean C. Jessee, Ronald K. Esplin, and Richard Lyman Bushman (Salt Lake City: Church Historian's Press, 2013), 281, 288. Joseph and his counselors in the Presidency and their scribe George W. Robinson visited Adam-ondi-Ahman about two days after the July 8, 1838, meeting held in Far West (see Joseph Smith, "History, 1838–1856, volume B-1 [1 September 1834–2 November 1838]," 804, josephsmithpapers.org;

see also Joseph Smith journal, July 26, 1838, in Jessee, Ashurst-McGee, and Jensen, eds., *Journals, Volume 1: 1832–1839,* 291).

17. Bishop Partridge explained, saying, "If a man is worth a $1000, the interest on that would be $60, and one/10. of the interest will be of course $6" (Edward Partridge letter to Newel K. Whitney, July 24, 1838, in Reynolds Cahoon letter to Newel K. Whitney, July 24, 1838, Church History Library, Salt Lake City). Six percent was a common interest rate at the time (see the forthcoming publication of *The Joseph Smith Papers, Documents, Volume 6: February 1838– August 1839*).

18. "Discourse," *Deseret News,* June 20, 1855, 117; punctuation modernized.

19. Joseph Smith journal, July 27, 1838, in "Journal, March–September 1838," 60, josephsmithpapers.org. Some members may have been pressured to consecrate. Dissenters later claimed that members of a Mormon paramilitary group in Missouri called the Danites "put to rights physically" that which could not be "put to rights by teachings & persuaysons" (Joseph Smith journal, July 27, 1838, in "Journal, March–September 1838," 61).

20. "Discourse," *Deseret News,* June 20, 1855, 117.

21. "Revelation, 8 July 1838–D [D&C 120]," in Joseph Smith, "Journal, March–September 1838," July 8, 1838, 57.

22. "Revelation, 8 July 1838–D [D&C 120]," 57.

23. Joseph Smith journal, July 26, 1838, in "Journal, March–September 1838," 59, josephsmithpapers.org.

24. See Robert D. Hales, "Tithing: A Test of Faith with Eternal Blessings," *Ensign,* Nov. 2002, 28.

25. Mitchell K. Schaefer and Sherilyn Farnes, "'Myself . . . I Consecrate to the God of Heaven': Twenty Affidavits of Consecration in Nauvoo, June–July 1842," *BYU Studies,* vol. 50, no. 3 (2011), 101–32.

26. Brigham Young and others, "Baptism for the Dead," *Times and Seasons,* vol. 3, no. 4 (Dec. 15, 1841), 625–27.

27. Schaefer and Farnes, "'Myself . . . I Consecrate,'" 112–13.

Within the Walls of Liberty Jail

D&C 121, 122, 123

Justin R. Bray

On December 1, 1838, a Latter-day Saint named Caleb Baldwin was incarcerated in the lower level of Liberty Jail in Clay County, Missouri, on charges of "crimes of High Treason."[1] His prison companions included members of the First Presidency of The Church of Jesus Christ of Latter-day Saints: Joseph Smith, Hyrum Smith, and Sidney Rigdon, as well as Lyman Wight and Alexander McRae. The six detainees' nearly four-month confinement became the final episode of an eventful and often troubled history of the Latter-day Saints in Missouri.

Within the walls of Liberty Jail, Baldwin scribed some of Joseph Smith's most profound reflections in letters to the scattered and destitute Latter-day Saints—portions of which were later canonized as Doctrine and Covenants sections 121, 122, and 123. Some of these passages have become scriptural gems, often cited in Latter-day Saint discourse over the years.

While the story of Liberty Jail has been told and retold from the perspective of Joseph Smith, the experience of the other incarcerated men provides additional insight. Baldwin, who was the most senior of the group, struggled physically and emotionally in the dungeon level of Liberty Jail. The inspiring words that came to Joseph as he dictated his letter provided comfort and counsel to Baldwin, the 47-year-old father of 10 who longed to be with his family during his four-month confinement.

Early Conflict in Missouri

The Latter-day Saints' eventful history in Missouri began in 1831, when a revelation to Joseph Smith identified Jackson County as the site of Zion, the New Jerusalem (see D&C 57:1–3). By 1833, the Latter-day Saints in Jackson County numbered more than a thousand—about a third of the county's population—and religious, political, and cultural differences created inevitable tension between the new and old settlers. After peaceful requests that the Latter-day Saints relocate their faith and families went unheeded, a large group of organized Missourians raided the home of William W. Phelps, destroyed the printing press of the *Evening and Morning Star,* and tarred and feathered Edward Partridge and Charles Allen.[2]

While the Latter-day Saints sought redress through written petitions, they also organized themselves militarily to protect their families in case of armed conflict. Even after the Latter-day Saints moved to Caldwell County in northwestern Missouri, which had been created by the state legislature exclusively for them, "battles" were fought at Gallatin, DeWitt, Blue River, Crooked River, and Hawn's Mill in what became known as the Missouri-Mormon War.[3]

In October and November 1838, General Samuel D. Lucas, a leader in the Missouri Militia, imprisoned several prominent Latter-day Saints, including Joseph Smith, Hyrum Smith, Sidney Rigdon, Parley P. Pratt, George W. Robinson, and Amasa Lyman. Caleb Baldwin, Lyman Wight, and other indicted Latter-day Saints joined Joseph and his cohorts at a preliminary hearing in Richmond, Missouri, bringing the total number of arraigned Latter-day Saints to 64. During the hearing, Judge Austin A. King singled out Baldwin and offered him his freedom if he would renounce his religion and forsake the Prophet Joseph—an offer Baldwin rejected. The same deal was then made to the other detainees, all of whom "returned an answer similar to that of Mr. Baldwin."[4]

Judge King ultimately found sufficient probable cause to lock away a number of the Latter-day Saint leaders. Joseph Smith, Hyrum Smith,

Sidney Rigdon, Lyman Wight, Alexander McRae, and Caleb Baldwin were to be taken to Liberty Jail in Clay County, as the jails in the counties where the alleged crimes occurred were not large enough for so many prisoners. On December 1, 1838, Joseph Smith entered the jail and "lifting his hat, he said, in a distinct voice, 'Good afternoon, gentlemen.' The next moment he had passed out of sight. The heavy door swung upon its strong hinges and the Prophet was hid from the gaze of the curious populace who had so eagerly watched."[5]

Liberty Jail

Spending more than four months in the snug jail proved a daunting experience. Four-foot-thick stone walls, a six-foot ceiling, and constant harassment by guards caused Joseph and his companions to describe the structure as "hell surrounded with demons."[6] The detainees were placed in the lower-level dungeon, where temperatures dropped, light dimmed, odors reeked, and time seemed to slow. Only "dirty straw couches" prevented the prisoners from sleeping on the stone floor, but even those wore out after a while.[7]

As was the case in other 19th-century county jails, the food sickened the prisoners. Joseph and his companions described their daily meals as "very coarse and so filthy that we could not eat it until we were driven to it by hunger." When the prisoners finally ate their servings, the food caused them to vomit "almost to death." Some of the detainees suspected the guards of poisoning their food and water or even feeding them human flesh.[8]

Word spread of the Latter-day Saint prisoners at Liberty Jail, and "the place took on some aspects of a zoo." Locals visited the jail in droves to gape at the prisoners, and their taunts and jeers echoed through the stone walls. Hyrum Smith complained, "We are often inspected by fools who act as though we were elephants or dromedarys or sea hogs or some monstrous whale or sea serpents."[9]

Day after day the men languished in jail, and the emotional sting slowly and continuously tested their faith. "Our souls have been bowed down and we have suffered much distress . . . and truly we have had to wade through an ocean of trouble," Joseph wrote.[10]

The four-month confinement in Liberty Jail also took a heavy physical toll on the prisoners. Sunlight barely crept through two small, iron-barred windows that were too high to see through, and long hours in the darkness caused the men's eyes to strain, as one of the jailers later remembered. While a small fire was allowed, without a chimney to channel the smoke, the prisoners' eyes became even more irritated. Their ears ached, their nerves trembled, and Hyrum Smith even went into shock at one point. Sidney Rigdon, the second-oldest member of the company next to Baldwin, was in such poor health that, lying in an inclined bed, he petitioned for an early release. His eloquent speech and severe infirmity caused the judge to discharge Rigdon ahead of schedule.[11]

Perhaps most disheartening to the remaining prisoners was the idea of Latter-day Saint families, including their own, scattered, destitute, and driven throughout the state of Missouri. Baldwin and his fellow prisoners felt loneliness and separation in Liberty Jail, but while the other inmates were regularly reassured of their friends' and families' well-being through visits and letters, Baldwin received only one brief visit from his wife, Nancy, just before Christmas in 1838, and there is no record of further communication with her or their 10 children during the three months that followed.[12]

Seemingly helpless, the prisoners twice attempted to flee the jail, on February 6 and March 3, 1839, but watchful guards put a stop to their daring getaways. Two weeks later, on March 15, the five men petitioned to be released for unlawful detention. Baldwin's two-page appeal evidenced his desperate desire to be reunited with his family, who had "been driven out of the State since his confinement without any means for their support."[13] In addition, Baldwin had learned that his son, also named Caleb, had been "beaten nearly to death by Missourians with hickory sticks."[14] Thus, having been detained "without the least shadow of testimony against him," Baldwin asked that the "high hand of oppression" cease and he be acquitted of all charges.[15] Despite the prisoners' petitions, sufficient evidence apparently existed to keep them detained.[16]

Two days later, on March 17, Samuel Tillery, one of the jailers, inspected the lower-level dungeon and found an auger handle, which he believed was being used by the prisoners to chisel their way through the thick walls. Tillery ordered 25 men downstairs to finish the search, then ordered his contingent to chain Joseph Smith and the prisoners to the floor. Having already bottled up three and a half months of stress, anguish, and frustration, Baldwin furiously rose to his feet, looked the jailer in the eye, and affirmed, "Tillery, if you put those chains on me I will kill you, so help me God!"[17] In the words of Hyrum Smith, Tillery "soon calmed down and agreed to call again and settle the matter."[18] While Baldwin's fiery threat temporarily settled the dispute, the prisoners were put under even heavier guard.

Just three days after the scuffle with Samuel Tillery, Baldwin was still on edge and wondered if he would ever see or hear from his family again. Joseph Smith began dictating a letter that undoubtedly lifted Baldwin's spirit—a letter that has since brought comfort and counsel to millions of Latter-day Saints.

Letter to the Saints

Alexander McRae scribed most of the letter addressed to "the church of Latterday saints at Quincy Illinois and scattered abroad and to Bishop Partridge in particular," although Baldwin helped pen 2 of the letter's 29 pages. Historians Dean Jessee and John Welch noted that Joseph Smith's lengthy missive is a Pauline-like epistle. For example, Joseph called himself "a prisoner for the Lord Jesus Christ's sake" and wrote that "nothing therefore can seperate us from the love of God," language similar to the Apostle Paul's writings to the Ephesians and Romans.[19] Joseph then detailed the sufferings of the "poor and much injured saints," including the families wandering helplessly and hopelessly between Missouri and Illinois, as well as the dismal experience he and his companions were having in Liberty Jail.[20]

After rendering a soul-wrenching account of the callous and merciless acts of some of their Missouri neighbors, Joseph uttered the first words of what is now section 121 of the Doctrine and Covenants: "O God where art thou and where is the pavilion that covereth thy hiding place how long shall thy hand be stayed and thine eye yea thy pure eye behold from the etearnal heavens the rongs of thy people and of thy servants and thine ear be penetrated with their c[ri]es yea o Lord how long shall they suffer these rongs and unlawfull oppressions before thine hart shall be softened towards them and thy bowels be moved with compassion to-words them."[21]

Joseph's heavenly plea was not immediately answered. He continued to reflect on the violent acts against the Latter-day Saints and wondered when justice would come upon his oppressors. Finally, after narrating seven pages of misery and angst, a consoling reassurance came to the Prophet Joseph: "My son pease be unto thy soul thine advirsity and thy afflictions shall be but a small moment and then if thou indure it well God shall exalt the[e] on high thou shalt tryumph over all [thy] foes." The Lord also assured Joseph that "if the verry jaws of hell shall gap[e] open her mouth wide after thee know thou my son that all these things shall give thee experiance and shall be for thy good. The son of man hath desended below them all art thou greater than he?"[22]

These comforting words triggered a sense of confidence in Joseph. He said that God "would have a tried people" and that the Latter-day Saints' experience in Missouri was "a tryal of our faith equal to that of Abraham." Inasmuch as Abraham was saved from sacrificing his son Isaac, so would the Latter-day Saints be delivered from their trials if they remained faithful.[23]

Joseph then provided instructions on a number of additional matters. First, he directed how to conduct upcoming conferences and council meetings, giving his prison companions hope that they would soon convene again with the Saints. Another item of business was the purchase of property in Iowa Territory. Joseph believed the land would "be of grate benefeit to the church" and counseled Edward Partridge and others on how to properly negotiate the transaction, emphasizing the importance of doing so without greed or self-indulgence. He also advised Church leaders to remember those in need and "bare the infermities of the weak."[24]

The letter then turned to why many are called but few chosen, words Jesus used in the New Testament (see Matthew 22:14). Joseph lamented that he and the Latter-day Saints had learned "by sad experience" of the destructive power of pride. Joseph may have been reflecting on some of his close friends, such as William W. Phelps and Frederick G. Williams, who had recently apostatized and aided in his imprisonment. (Both would eventually return to full fellowship in the Church.) Joseph laid out attributes that holders of the priesthood and all Latter-day Saints should seek to attain if they hope to have influence with others: gentleness, meekness, persuasion, long-suffering, kindness, charity, virtue, and love.[25]

Near the end of the letter, Joseph returned to the persecution the Latter-day Saints had suffered in Missouri. Joseph believed the Constitution of the United States to be "a glorious standard" that ensured freedom of worship, and he asked the Saints to sign affidavits detailing their grievances and maltreatment. Without a guarantee of receiving anything in return, Joseph and the Saints were determined nonetheless to "present [their affidavits] to the heads of government," fulfilling a commandment given by the Lord.[26]

Joseph Smith's lengthy letter has had a lasting impact. It not only counseled poor Baldwin in prison and the Saints suffering mayhem in Missouri but was continually republished for many years in the *Times and Seasons, Millennial Star,* and *Deseret News.*[27] Eventually, extracts were canonized as Doctrine and Covenants sections 121, 122, and 123, and those passages continue to provide comfort and direction to anyone mining the scriptures for meaning.

The prison companions eventually managed to "escape" legal authorities while being escorted to a hearing in Boone County, Missouri, in April 1839. Their guards turned a blind eye and allowed the prisoners to flee from custody after leading them away from enemies of the Latter-day Saints in Clay County. Baldwin became separated from Joseph and the others on several occasions after their getaway, but all the prisoners ultimately crossed into Illinois, finally reuniting with family, friends, and the rest of the Latter-day Saint refugees.[28]

1. Joseph Smith, "History, 1838–1856, volume C-1 [2 November 1838–31 July 1842]," 858, josephsmithpapers.org.

2. Orson F. Whitney, "An Ensign for the Nations: Sketch of the Rise and Progress of Mormonism," *Latter-day Saints' Millennial Star,* vol. 61, no. 28 (July 13, 1899), 434–35.

3. See Alexander L. Baugh, "The Final Episode of Mormonism in Missouri in the 1830s: The Incarceration of the Mormon Prisoners at Richmond and Columbia Jails, 1838–1839," *John Whitmer Historical Association Journal,* vol. 28 (2008), 1–34.

4. Clark V. Johnson, ed., "Mormon Redress Petitions: Documents of the 1833–1838 Missouri Conflict" (Provo, Utah: Religious Studies Center, Brigham Young University, 1992), 685–86.

5. Lyman Omer Littlefield, *Reminiscences of Latter-day Saints: Giving an Account of Much Individual Suffering Endured for Religious Conscience* (Logan: Utah Journal Company Printers, 1888), 79–80.

6. Dean C. Jessee, "'Walls, Gates and Screeking Iron Doors': The Prison Experience of Mormon Leaders in Missouri, 1838–1839," in Davis Bitton and Maureen Ursenbach Beecher, *New Views of Mormon History: A Collection of Essays in Honor of Leonard J. Arrington* (Salt Lake City: University of Utah Press, 1987), 25.

7. Jessee, "Walls, Gates, and Screeking Iron Doors," 25.

8. Jessee, "Walls, Gates, and Screeking Iron Doors," 27.

9. Jessee, "Walls, Gates, and Screeking Iron Doors," 27.

10. Joseph Smith Jr., "Communications," *Times and Seasons,* vol. 1, no. 6 (Apr. 1840), 85.

11. Richard S. Van Wagoner, *Sidney Rigdon: A Portrait of Religious Excess* (Salt Lake City: Signature Books, 1994), 254–55.

12. See Mary Audentia Smith Anderson, ed., *Joseph Smith III and the Restoration* (Independence, Missouri: Herald House, 1952), 13–14.

13. Caleb Baldwin petition, Liberty, Missouri, Mar. 15, 1839, Church History Library, Salt Lake City.

14. "John Gribble, Paragoonah, 1864 July 7," Church History Library, Salt Lake City.

15. Caleb Baldwin petition.

16. See Jeffrey N. Walker, "Habeas Corpus in Early Nineteenth-Century Mormonism: Joseph Smith's Legal Bulwark for Personal Freedom," *BYU Studies,* vol. 52, no. 1 (2013), 27.

17. Obituary of Caleb Baldwin, in *Journal History of The Church of Jesus Christ of Latter-day Saints,* June 11, 1849, Church History Library, Salt Lake City; see also Elden J. Watson, ed., *Manuscript History of Brigham Young, 1847–1850* (Salt Lake City: J. Watson, 1971), 211.

18. Jessee, "Walls, Gates, and Screeking Iron Doors," 31.

19. "Letter to the Church and Edward Partridge, 20 March 1839-A," 1–2, josephsmithpapers.org; see also Dean C. Jessee and John W. Welch, "Revelations in Context: Joseph Smith's Letter from Liberty Jail, March 20, 1839," *BYU Studies,* vol. 39, no. 3 (2000), 126; Ephesians 3:1 and Romans 8:35.

20. "Letter to the Church and Edward Partridge," 7; see also Jessee and Welch, "Revelations in Context," 135.

21. "Letter to the Church and Edward Partridge," 3–4, josephsmithpapers.org; see also Doctrine and Covenants 121:1–3.

22. "Letter to the Church and Edward Partridge," 4, 8; see also Doctrine and Covenants 121:7–8.

23. "Letter to the Church and Edward Partridge," 10; see also Jessee and Welch, "Revelations in Context," 136.

24. "Letter to the Church and Edward Partridge," 1, 2; see also Jessee and Welch, "Revelations in Context," 140.

25. Doctrine and Covenants 121:39, 41–46.

26. "Letter to the Church and Edward Partridge, 20 March 1839-B," 8, josephsmithpapers.org; see also Doctrine and Covenants 123:1–6; Jessee and Welch, "Revelations in Context," 130.

27. Jessee and Welch, "Revelations in Context," 144.

28. For additional information regarding the escape from Liberty Jail, see Alexander L. Baugh, "'We Took Our Change of Venue to the State of Illinois': The Gallatin Hearing and the Escape of Joseph Smith and the Mormon Prisoners from Missouri, April 1839," *Mormon Historical Studies,* vol. 2, no. 1 (Spring 2001), 59–82.

Organizing the Church in Nauvoo

D&C 124, 125

Alex D. Smith

A New Gathering Place

After being driven from their homes in northern Missouri, the Saints fled east to the Mississippi, taking refuge for the winter of 1838–39 in various settlements along the river in Iowa Territory and Illinois, with the largest number of Saints congregating in and around Quincy, Illinois. Forced to abandon any immediate hopes of having their land of Zion in Jackson County, Missouri, restored to them, Church leaders looked for a new central gathering place for the Saints. By summer 1839 they had purchased the area of Commerce in Hancock County, Illinois, and extensive tracts of land across the river in Iowa Territory. Commerce was selected as the new gathering place, and the Saints quickly renamed their new city Nauvoo.

Having learned from the experiences of being driven from their homes first in Jackson County, Missouri, and later from Caldwell, Daviess, and Ray Counties in northern Missouri, the Saints were determined to take advantage of the powers of government. They set about trying to establish a city in their new Illinois home where they would be free to exercise their religious rights with the protection of legal authority.

On December 16, 1840, Illinois Governor Thomas Carlin and the legislature of Illinois, initially eager to court the votes of the large number of Mormon refugees from Missouri and outraged at the atrocities the Saints had suffered at the hands of their Missouri neighbors, passed "An Act to Incorporate the City of Nauvoo." This charter granted extensive legal powers to the citizens of Nauvoo, including, among other powers, the ability to organize a legislative body of their own to create laws within the city, the power to create the Nauvoo Legion as a subset of the state militia, and the authority to establish a university within the city.[1] Around the same time the Saints were trying to secure their city's charter they also sought to incorporate the Church in the state of Illinois, with Joseph Smith as trustee.[2] In the context of these efforts to establish a new city for the Saints on the banks of the Mississippi, Joseph Smith received a revelation on January 19, 1841, identifying Nauvoo as a temple city and a new gathering place, giving instructions to Church leaders, and establishing the organization of the Church in Nauvoo. This revelation is now found in Doctrine and Covenants 124.

The Nauvoo Sections of the Doctrine and Covenants

While the vast majority of the existing accounts of Joseph Smith's public sermons date from the Illinois period of Church history, the opposite is true of records of his revelations. In the current edition of the Doctrine and Covenants, 135 sections were written during Joseph Smith's lifetime, and only nine of those date from the five years that the Prophet lived in Nauvoo. Of the 110 sections canonized during Joseph Smith's lifetime (those that were included in the 1844 edition of the Doctrine and Covenants), only three date from the Illinois period.[3]

Comparing the nine currently canonized sections of the Doctrine and Covenants recorded during Joseph Smith's years in Illinois highlights the importance of the revelation received on January 19, 1841. Doctrine and Covenants 125, a brief revelation received in March 1841, concerns the establishing of the Zarahemla stake across the Mississippi River, in Iowa Territory. The next recorded revelation (now Doctrine and Covenants 126) was received in July

1841 and includes personal instruction to Brigham Young regarding his missionary service. Doctrine and Covenants 127 and 128 are September 1842 letters of instruction from Joseph Smith to the Saints in Nauvoo, describing, among other things, the principle of baptism for the dead. These two letters, written while Joseph Smith was in hiding and cherished by the Saints as inspired communications from their absent prophet were, along with Doctrine and Covenants 124, the only Illinois-era revelations or instructions canonized during the Prophet's lifetime.

The next three sections of the current Doctrine and Covenants—sections 129, 130, and 131—contain excerpts from instructions Joseph Smith gave in 1843 in Nauvoo (section 129) and the small town of Ramus, Illinois (sections 130 and 131). Section 132 deals with plural and celestial marriage, and, while recorded in 1843, portions of it were known to Joseph Smith prior to his arrival in Nauvoo. Furthermore, its circulation was limited during the Prophet's life to only his closest and most loyal friends. Thus, though relatively few organizational or instructional revelations were recorded during the final years of Joseph Smith's life, the lengthy and complex revelation received on January 19, 1841, was an exception. For Church members at the time, it was, in many ways, *the* Nauvoo revelation.

It was widely known among Church members almost immediately upon its reception. It was the first text inscribed by general Church clerk Robert Thompson in the Book of the Law of the Lord, a record designed to contain Joseph Smith's revelations and which also became the first tithing book of the Church.[4] It was read before the Saints at the April 1841 general conference of the Church in Nauvoo—the first conference following the receipt of the revelation.[5] Joseph Smith, Brigham Young, and other Church leaders made frequent reference to the revelation's injunctions to build the temple and the Nauvoo House.[6] In addition to organizing the leadership of the Church in Nauvoo by divine mandate, the revelation quickly became a source of direction and purpose for the Saints living there.

Contents of Doctrine and Covenants 124

Doctrine and Covenants 124 could almost be considered an ecclesiastical charter for the Church in Nauvoo, in much the same way that the act to incorporate the city served the civic needs of the community. The revelation's opening lines dictated that the stake of Nauvoo was to be a new central gathering place for the Saints, a "corner stone of Zion."[7] The commandment to build a temple in Nauvoo demonstrated that the new city was not simply to be a temporary refuge but a more permanent home.[8]

The expulsion of the Saints from Missouri and the establishing of new stakes on the western border of Illinois and across the river in Iowa Territory, together with the creation of a new city and home for the Saints, effectively provided a new beginning for the Church. This period of transition and the subsequent need for a new organization was reflected in much of the revelation's content. Early in the revelation, several personal assignments are given to Church members, and the revelation concludes with a list of the appointments of the Church's governing officers, including the First Presidency, Quorum of the Twelve Apostles (identified in the revelation as the "Twelve traveling council"), and a new stake high council for Nauvoo, along with other quorums.

A proclamation to "all the kings of the world" was called for by the revelation, which further reflected the expansive vision of what Nauvoo was to become. After repeated experiences of being driven from their homes, the words of the revelation describing the purpose of the proclamation would have given new hope: "For behold I am about to call upon them [the 'kings and authorities' of the world] to give heed to the light and glory of Zion, for the set time has come, to favor her."[9]

Wording of the proclamation was to include an invitation to "come ye with your gold and your silver, to the help of my people, to the house of the daughter of Zion."[10] This concept of inviting visitors to come to Nauvoo and learn of the gospel and assist the Saints was inseparably connected with another prominent subject of the revelation—the construction and purpose of the Nauvoo House.

The revelation commanded that two buildings be built: a temple and a hotel, or "boarding house," called the Nauvoo House. Both were referred to as "a house unto my name," both were to be holy places, worthy of the Lord's acceptance, and both were to become the central building projects of the Saints for the next six years.[11] The plans for the temple embodied important new developments in Joseph Smith's understanding and teachings regarding temples, notably the inclusion of a font in which the Saints could perform baptisms on behalf of their deceased family members and friends. This font was first called for in the January 19, 1841, revelation.

While the temple occupies the place of greatest significance spiritually and historically, more of the revelation is devoted to the Nauvoo House than to any other subject. It was to be a residence for Joseph Smith, his family, and their posterity.[12] It was to be a "house for boarding; a house that strangers may come from afar to lodge therein," where a traveler would "find health and safety, while he shall contemplate the word of the Lord, and the corner stone I have appointed for Zion." Those who managed it would "not suffe[r] any pollution to come upon it—It shall be holy, or the Lord your God will not dwell therein."[13]

Joseph Smith repeatedly emphasized the importance of the Nauvoo House. At a meeting at the site of the uncompleted temple on February 21, 1843, the Prophet stated, "The building of N[auvoo] House is just as sacred in my view as the Temple. I want the Nauvo[o] House bui[l]t it must be built, our salvation depends upon it. When men have done what they can or will for the temple. let them do what they can for the Nauvoo House."[14] A month and a half later at a conference of the Church in Nauvoo, he said, "It is important that this confernce gives importance to the N[auvoo] House. as a prejudice exists against the Nauvoo. House in favor of the Lords House."[15]

For the duration of the Saints' time in Nauvoo, the fulfillment of the various commandments and responsibilities outlined in this revelation remained the highest priority. The length of their stay in Illinois, however, would not be as long as anticipated, and some of what they hoped to accomplish would never be completed.

Legacy of the Revelation

The Nauvoo experience can be understood more accurately in the context of this revelation and the attempts of the Saints to be obedient to its commandments. William Clayton, temple recorder and frequent scribe for Joseph Smith, expressed his motivations and those of his fellow Church members in his journal on May 31, 1845: "Our anxiety is to finish the Temple and the Nauvoo House . . . that we may be permitted to fulfil the commands of the Almighty in relation to this place." [16] Unfortunately, one after another, their assignments, promised blessings, and aspirations were met with challenges and frustration.

John C. Bennett, Nauvoo's first mayor and later a member of the First Presidency, was promised that his "reward shall not fail if he receive counsel." But he apostatized only a year and a half later and became a bitter opponent of the Church. [17]

General Church clerk Robert B. Thompson, appointed by the revelation as one of those who should author the proclamation, died only seven months later. It was not until years later, following the Prophet's death, that the proclamation was written. It was finally composed by Parley P. Pratt in 1845, and published as *Proclamation of the Twelve Apostles of the Church of Jesus Christ, of Latter-Day Saints.* [18]

Due to the Saints' impoverished condition and the press of building a new city, both the temple and the Nauvoo House progressed slowly. The two buildings competed for the same labor and material resources, and both projects lagged. Ultimately, in the fall of 1845, when it was clear that the Saints' time in Nauvoo was limited, it became necessary to favor the completion of the temple, and in a meeting on the evening of Sunday, September 14, it was reluctantly "agreed to turn more force of hands to the Temple even if it have to hinder the Nauvoo House." [19] Construction on the temple progressed sufficiently that it could be used during the winter of 1845–46 for meetings and the performance of ordinances.

The January 19, 1841, revelation could almost be considered a vision of what might have been. The Prophet and the patriarch of the Church were killed, the Nauvoo House was never completed as designed, the majority of the Saints left their homes on the banks of the Mississippi to head west to the Great Basin, and their beloved temple, only just completed after years of diligent labor, had to be offered up for sale to meet financial needs.[20]

But Nauvoo's history is also a testament to the faith of the Saints, their understanding of the importance of the divine directions contained in this revelation, and their continued efforts to fulfill them. Indeed, it would be a disservice to consider the sum total of their efforts to live this revelation a failure or to view these years only through the lens of the tragic conclusion of their habitation in Illinois.

For years Nauvoo was a refuge, a place of healthy industry, and a home for the Saints. It was a place where the "light and glory of Zion" were visible to numerous visitors who came and, in some cases, "contemplate[d] the word of the Lord." Its "favor," demonstrated in the lives of the Church members who lived there, did not fail to attract the attention of the world.[21]

1. "An Act to Incorporate the City of Nauvoo," Dec. 16, 1840, *Laws of the State of Illinois* (1840–41), 52–57; "Miscellaneous," *Times and Seasons*, vol. 2, no. 6 (Jan. 15, 1841), 281–86.

2. An act to incorporate the Church at Nauvoo, Senate Bill no. 43, Bills, Resolutions, and Related General Assembly Records, 1st–88th bienniums, 1819–1994, Illinois State Archives, Springfield, Illinois; Appointment, Feb. 2, 1841, Hancock County, Illinois, Bonds and Mortgages, vol. 1, page 97, U.S. and Canada Record Collection, Family History Library, Salt Lake City.

3. While the 1844 edition of the Doctrine and Covenants was not printed until after the martyrdom, selection of content and most of the work on the edition was completed prior to Joseph Smith's death (see Doctrine and Covenants, 1844 ed., josephsmithpapers.org; see also Peter Crawley, *A Descriptive Bibliography of the Mormon Church: Volume One, 1830–1747* [Provo, Utah: Religious Studies Center, Brigham Young University, 1997], 277–80).

4. See "Revelation, 19 February 1841 [D&C 124]," in The Book of the Law of the Lord, 3–15, josephsmithpapers.org.

5. On April 7, 1841, Nauvoo Mayor John C. Bennett "read the revelations from 'The Book of the Law of the Lord,' which had been received since the last general Conference, in relation to writing a proclamation to the kings of the earth, building a Temple in Nauvoo, the organization of the church &c" ("Minutes of the general conference," *Times and Seasons*, vol. 2, no. 12 [Apr. 15, 1841], 386).

6. See, for instance, Joseph Smith's journal entry for February 21, 1843, in Joseph Smith, "Journal, December 1842–June 1844; Book 1, 21 December 1842–10 March 1843," 200, josephsmithpapers.org; see also Joseph Smith's journal entry for December 22, 1841, in Joseph Smith, "Journal, December 1841–December 1842," 36, josephsmithpapers.org.

7. "Revelation, 19 February 1841 [D&C 124]," in The Book of the Law of the Lord, 3; see also Doctrine and Covenants 124:2. While the manuscript version of the January 19, 1841, revelation that was placed in the cornerstone of the Nauvoo House is likely the original and predates the version copied into the first pages of the Book of the Law of the Lord, the former received significant water

damage prior to being removed from the cornerstone, and the text is too faint to read in places. For this reason, all quotes herein from the revelation are taken from the version copied into the Book of the Law of the Lord.

8. The decision to build a temple in Nauvoo predated the January 19, 1841, revelation by some time. The temple's construction was discussed, and an initial committee was assigned to oversee the project at the October 1840 Church conference in Nauvoo (see "Minutes of the general conference of the church of Jesus Christ of Latter Day Saints," *Times and Seasons,* vol. 1, no. 12 [Oct. 1840], 186).

9. "Revelation, 19 February 1841 [D&C 124]," in The Book of the Law of the Lord, 3; see also Doctrine and Covenants 124:5–6.

10. "Revelation, 19 February 1841 [D&C 124]," in The Book of the Law of the Lord, 4; see also Doctrine and Covenants 124:11.

11. "Revelation, 19 February 1841 [D&C 124]," in The Book of the Law of the Lord, 4–5; see also Doctrine and Covenants 124:22, 24, 27.

12. "Revelation, 19 February 1841 [D&C 124]," in The Book of the Law of the Lord, 7; see also Doctrine and Covenants 124:56.

13. "Revelation, 19 February 1841 [D&C 124]," in The Book of the Law of the Lord, 5; see also Doctrine and Covenants 124:23–24.

14. Joseph Smith, "Journal, December 1842–June 1844; Book 1, 21 December 1842–10 March 1843," 200. An early indication that Joseph Smith considered the Nauvoo House to be important deals with the 1841 cornerstone deposit ceremonies of the Nauvoo Temple and Nauvoo House. Items of historical significance were deposited in the cornerstone of the Nauvoo Temple on September 25, 1841, but it

was in the cornerstone of the Nauvoo House a week later (October 2, 1841) that the original manuscript of the Book of Mormon was placed, along with a draft version of the January 19, 1841, revelation and other items (see Joseph Smith, "Journal, December 1841–December 1842," 43).

15. Joseph Smith, "Journal, December 1842–June 1844; Book 2, 10 March 1843–14 July 1843," 50–51, josephsmithpapers.org. Joseph gave the following instruction to the Twelve when instructing them on April 19 about their mission: "Dont be scart about the temple. dont say any thing against it. but make all men know your mission is to build the Nauvoo House."

16. William Clayton journal, May 31, 1845, Church History Library, Salt Lake City.

17. "Revelation, 19 February 1841 [D&C 124]," in The Book of the Law of the Lord, 4; see also Doctrine and Covenants 124:16–17; "Bennett, John Cook," josephsmithpapers.org.

18. "Death of Col. Robert B. Thompson," *Times and Seasons,* vol. 2, no. 21 (Sept. 1, 1841), 519–20; [Parley P. Pratt], *Proclamation of the Twelve Apostles of the Church of Jesus Christ, of Latter-Day Saints* (New York: Samuel Brannan and Parley P. Pratt, 1845); see also Crawley, *A Descriptive Bibliography,* 294–96.

19. William Clayton journal, Sept. 14, 1845.

20. The following advertisement ran from May 15 to December 23, 1846, in the *New Citizen* [Nauvoo, Illinois]: "Temple for Sale. The undersigned Trustees of the Latter Day Saints propose to sell the Temple on very low terms, if an early application is made. The Temple is admirably designed for Literary or Religious purposes."

21. "Revelation, 19 February 1841 [D&C 124]," in The Book of the Law of the Lord, 3, 5; see also Doctrine and Covenants 124:6, 23.

Letters on Baptism for the Dead
D&C 127, 128
Matthew McBride

When the Lord restored through Joseph Smith the doctrine of the redemption of the dead through the performance of proxy baptisms, He answered age-old questions and satisfied deep longings. For centuries, Christians had debated what would happen after this life to the untold millions who lived without knowledge of the gospel of Jesus Christ. Joseph Smith himself had agonized over the fate of his beloved brother Alvin, an honest but unbaptized Christian.

In January 1836, Joseph Smith saw a vision of the celestial kingdom in which he learned that those who did not receive the fulness of the gospel in this life but would have if given the chance, such as his brother Alvin, would not be denied the highest rewards in the life to come. With this vision, the Lord began to gradually reveal the doctrines and practices surrounding baptism for the dead to Joseph Smith and his successors over the course of several years.

Joseph's vision affirmed God's mercy, but it was not entirely clear whether the scriptural requirement of baptism would be waived for Alvin and others like him or whether it would be fulfilled in some other way. Some Latter-day Saints recognized this gap in their knowledge. Joseph Fielding, for example, "thought much on the subject of the redemption of those who died under the broken covenant" and speculated that "perhaps those who receive the priesthood in these last days would baptize them at the coming of the Savior."[1]

But at the funeral of Seymour Brunson on August 15, 1840, Joseph Smith taught the principle that men and women on earth could act for their deceased kin and fulfill the requirement of baptism on their behalf. The Saints joyfully embraced this opportunity and began almost immediately to be baptized for departed loved ones in rivers and streams near Nauvoo.

Then, in January 1841, Joseph Smith received an important revelation that not only called for the construction of a temple in Nauvoo but forever linked the ordinance of baptism for the dead with temples: "For a baptismal font there is not upon the earth; that they, my saints may be baptized for those who are dead, for this ordinance belongeth to my house."[2] The Nauvoo Saints rapidly pushed forward construction on the temple, and by November 1841, the basement was enclosed, and a suitable font had been carved out of wood.

Baptism for the Dead Letters

Further instructions and clarification on this new practice were to come. In August 1842, Joseph Smith was accused as an accessory in the attempted murder of Lilburn W. Boggs, the former governor of Missouri. To avoid arrest, Joseph remained more or less in hiding for about three months in the homes of trusted friends. Wilford Woodruff wrote in his journal that though "Joseph has been deprived of the privilege of appearing openly," yet "the Lord is with him as he was upon the Isle of Patmos with John," intimating that Joseph had experienced spiritual manifestations during his absence from public life.[3]

On August 31, Joseph appeared briefly to speak to a small gathering of Female Relief Society members and communicated for the first time on record what he had learned in the previous weeks: "All persons baptized for the dead must have a recorder present, that he may be an eyewitness to record and testify of the truth and validity of his record. It will be necessary, in the Grand Council, that these things be testified."[4]

The following day, he began writing a letter to the Church that would later become Doctrine and Covenants 127. In this letter, Joseph explained his absence due to the charges against him and reassured the Saints that when "the storm is fully blown over, then I will return to you again." He said the Lord had revealed to him the necessity of a recorder for baptisms for the dead and explained the reason why: "That in all your recordings, it may be recorded in heaven. . . . And again, let all the records be had in order, that they may be put in the archives of my Holy Temple, to be held in remembrance from generation to generation, saith the Lord of Hosts."[5]

He concluded his letter by saying that he desired to speak "from the Stand, on the subject" but would have to be content to "send it you by Mail." He accordingly had Erastus Derby deliver the letter to William Clayton that Sunday, September 4, "to be read before the saints when assembled at the Grove." Joseph's journal reports with satisfaction, "When this letter was read before the brethren it cheered their hearts and evidently had the effect of stimulating them and inspiring them with courage, and faithfulness."[6]

On September 7, Joseph Smith dictated a second letter on the same subject, "which he ordered to be read next Sabbath," September 11. This second letter is now found in Doctrine and Covenants 128. In it, the Prophet gave a more detailed record-keeping proposal, calling for witnesses, a recorder in each of Nauvoo's 10 wards, and a general recorder who would compile all the ward records into a "general Church Book."[7]

Joseph then offered a lengthy scriptural justification for the practice of baptisms for the dead and the necessity of a recorder. He taught that ordinances for the dead created necessary and eternal bonds between generations: "The earth will be smitten with a curse, unless there is a welding link of some kind or other, between the fathers and the children, upon some subject or other. And behold! what is that subject? It is the baptism for the dead. For we without them, cannot be made perfect. Neither can they, without us, be made perfect."[8]

He concluded with this rousing and well-known call to action: "Brethren, shall we not go on in so great a cause? Go forward and not . . . backward. Courage, brethren! and on to the victory. Let your hearts rejoice and be exceeding glad. Let the earth break forth into singing. Let the dead speak forth anthems of eternal praise to the king Immanuel, who hath ordain'd, before the world was, that which would enable us to redeem them out of their prisons; for the prisoner shall go free. . . . Let us present in his holy Temple, when it is finished, a Book, containing the Records of our dead, which shall be worthy of all acceptation."[9]

These two letters from Joseph Smith were canonized in 1844 and have been a part of the Doctrine and Covenants ever since. The Saints minutely followed the directions given in these letters, and recorders for each ward were called. The recorders used a common certificate or form to record baptisms: "I certify that upon the day of the date hereof, I saw and heard the following Baptisms take place in the Font in the Lord's House in the City of Nauvoo, Illinois; to wit [blank] and that [blank] and [blank] were present as Witnesses to said Baptisms, and also that said Record has been made by me and is true."[10]

"Line upon Line"

After Joseph Smith's death in June 1844, Brigham Young assumed leadership of the Church as President of the Quorum of the Twelve Apostles. During the winter of 1844–45, he introduced an additional refinement to the practice of baptisms for the dead and explained this development at the April 1845 conference.

In their hurry to administer this ordinance for their loved ones, the Saints had performed the baptisms without regard to gender, men being baptized for women and women for men. Henceforth, Young taught that the Saints "never will see a man go forth to be baptized for a woman, nor a woman for a man." Why, then, had this practice been allowed to persist? "When an infinite being gives a law to his finite creatures, he has to descend to the capacity of those who receive his law, when the doctrine of baptism for the dead was first given, this church was in its infancy. . . . The Lord has led this people all the while in this way, by giving them here a little and there a little, thus he increases their wisdom, and he that receives a little and is thankful for that shall receive more."

Alluding to Joseph Smith's letters, Young explained, "When it was first revealed all the order of it was not made known, afterwards it was made known, that records, clerks, and one or two witnesses were necessary or else it will be of no value to the saints." He concluded, "Joseph in his life time did not receive every thing connected with the doctrine of redemption, but he has left the key with those who understand how to obtain and teach to this great people all that is necessary for their salvation and exaltation in the celestial kingdom of our God."[11]

1. Joseph Fielding, letter to the editor, Dec. 28, 1841, in *Times and Seasons,* vol. 3, no. 5 (Jan. 1 1842), 649.

2. "Revelation, 19 January 1841 [D&C 124]," in Book of the Law of the Lord, 5, josephsmithpapers.org.

3. Wilford Woodruff journal, Sept. 19, 1842, in *Wilford Woodruff's Journal: 1833–1898, Typescript,* ed. Scott G. Kenney, 9 vols. (Midvale, Utah: Signature Books, 1983–85), 2:187.

4. Joseph Smith, in *History of the Church,* 5:141.

5. Doctrine and Covenants, 1844 ed., 419–20, josephsmithpapers.org.

6. Joseph Smith, "Journal, December 1841–December 1842," 189–90, josephsmithpapers.org.

7. Joseph Smith, "Journal, December 1841–December 1842," 192, 197; see also Doctrine and Covenants 128:4. While it is evident that some records of baptisms for the dead had been kept prior to this revelation, they were not as complete nor as uniform as they might have been.

8. Joseph Smith, "Journal, December 1841–December 1842," 199.

9. Joseph Smith, "Journal, December 1841–December 1842," 200.

10. Loose certificate inserted inside front cover of Baptisms for the Dead, Book C, September 1842–June 1843, microfilm copy of holograph, Family History Library, Salt Lake City.

11. Brigham Young, "Speech," *Times and Seasons,* vol. 6, no. 12 (July 1, 1845), 954–55.

"Our Hearts Rejoiced to Hear Him Speak"

D&C 129, 130, 131

Matthew McBride

William Clayton walked the last nine miles to Nauvoo. The boat he and his company had taken down the Mississippi toward their new home had stopped short of Nauvoo for the night. But after an 11-week, 5,000-mile journey from his home in Penwortham, England, William could wait no longer. He and a few friends trudged through the wintry early morning and arrived on foot just before noon, November 24, 1840. A convert of three years, William had testified of Joseph Smith's prophetic call in his homeland. Now he was eager to meet the Prophet in person.

He soon met Joseph Smith and shared some of his early impressions in letters to his friends back in England. "Last night many of us were in company with Brother Joseph, [and] our hearts rejoiced to hear him speak of the things of the Kingdom," he wrote. "If I had come from England purposely to converse with him a few days I should have considered myself well paid for my trouble," he wrote on another occasion.[1]

William set about to make a life and a home for himself and his wife Ruth, who was expecting their second child at the time they arrived. The Claytons' first year in their new home proved difficult, however. They purchased land on the west side of the Mississippi River, opposite Nauvoo, where they attempted to make a living as farmers. William had been a factory bookkeeper in an industrial English town and had neither the skill nor the physical makeup of a farmer. His efforts were soon toppled by a crop failure and a long bout with malaria.

Brought low by this turn of events, William took the advice of the missionary who had converted him, Heber C. Kimball, and moved his family back across the river to Nauvoo in December 1841. William's former fellow counselor in the British Mission presidency, Willard Richards, was serving as Joseph Smith's secretary and needed an assistant he could trust. Heber soon came to William asking him to report to Joseph Smith's office. There, on February 9, 1842, William agreed to become a secretary and scribe to the Prophet.

Secretary and Scribe

Over the next two and a half years, William Clayton had a closer view of Joseph Smith's personal and public life than almost anyone. He was with Joseph almost every day and was deeply involved in Joseph's business, political, and religious affairs. Their friendship gave William a unique opportunity to assess Joseph's character up close, including his faults. He knew as well as anyone that Joseph was just a man, but for William, Joseph's shortcomings were unimportant when weighed against the soul-expanding teachings the Lord delivered through His prophet. Through their association in Nauvoo, William became a stubborn lifelong defender of Joseph Smith.

In his work as secretary, William Clayton recorded the most significant revelations, teachings, and sermons given by Joseph Smith during the eventful final two years of the Prophet's life. He recorded Joseph's instructions on baptisms for the dead and the revelation on eternal and plural marriage, both of which later became part of the Latter-day Saint scriptures. He was also one of the scribes who kept an account of Joseph's most well-known sermon, the King Follett discourse. He valued these teachings beyond price and seemed to sense the importance of preserving them.

Joseph Smith felt a growing urgency to communicate spiritual knowledge to the Saints. During his time in Nauvoo he gave one powerful public sermon after another and shared equally powerful teachings and ordinances in private councils with his trusted friends. Joseph Smith did not deliver these teachings as formal revelations the way he often had earlier in his ministry, but William Clayton hung on every word. He recorded the Prophet's sayings in his own diary or in the journal he kept for Joseph, and these entries were later used as the basis for several sections of the Doctrine and Covenants.

Precious Teachings

William was present when Joseph Smith met with Parley P. Pratt on February 9, 1843, and shared with him knowledge about how to discern heavenly messengers from Satan and his angels. These instructions related to temple teachings that Joseph had shared with members of his trusted circle while Parley had been away in England. William recorded the instructions in Joseph's journal, and they were later canonized as Doctrine and Covenants 129.[2]

On April 2, 1843, Joseph visited a stake conference in Ramus, Illinois, 20 miles east of Nauvoo. An American religious leader named William Miller had predicted that the Second Coming of Jesus Christ would occur the following day. Joseph took this occasion to assure the Saints in Ramus that the Lord had not revealed the time of His coming. Joseph also taught that God was an embodied personage; that all things past, present, and future are present before Him; and that our social relationships will endure in the eternities. William Clayton's record of these gems in his personal journal became the basis for the text of Doctrine and Covenants 130.[3]

Doctrine and Covenants 131 is composed largely of several short journal entries kept by William during May 1843.[4] Among these were teachings regarding eternal marriage given in Ramus at the home of Benjamin and Melissa Johnson on May 16. The Johnsons had been married since Christmas Day 1841, but Joseph told them he intended to marry them according to the law of the Lord. Benjamin jokingly said he would not marry Melissa again unless she courted him. But Joseph was in earnest. He taught that men and women needed to enter into the new and everlasting covenant of marriage in order to obtain God's highest blessings. He then sealed Benjamin and Melissa for eternity.[5]

For William, recording these prophetic utterances was more than a duty; it was one of the great privileges of his life. He thrilled at the way Joseph Smith collapsed the distance between this world and the next and made the things of eternity feel tangible and real. When the Nauvoo Saints listened to Joseph speak, the many hardships they faced—death, sickness, poverty, and hunger—were swallowed up in anticipation of a millennial future and the promise that ties of family and friendship would outlast this life. William Clayton's delight in recording the words of Joseph Smith has had a lasting influence on Church teachings and continues to bless Latter-day Saints today.

1. William Clayton letters quoted in James B. Allen, *No Toil nor Labor Fear: The Story of William Clayton* (Provo, Utah: Brigham Young University Press, 2002), 61, 63. This book is the best treatment of William Clayton's life generally and of his friendship with Joseph Smith. Allen's analysis of Clayton's views of Joseph Smith forms the basis for this article.

2. See "Journal, December 1842–June 1844; Book 1, 21 December 1842–10 March 1843," 172–76, josephsmithpapers.org.

3. See "William Clayton, Journal Excerpt, 1–4 April 1843," josephsmithpapers.org.

4. Several of these journal entries are reproduced in Allen, *No Toil nor Labor Fear*, 393–96.

5. See Benjamin F. Johnson, *My Life's Review* (Independence, Missouri: Zion's Printing and Publishing, 1947), 96–97. For more on the context of Doctrine and Covenants 131, see Steven C. Harper, *Making Sense of the Doctrine and Covenants: A Guided Tour through Modern Revelations* (Salt Lake City: Deseret Book, 2008), 477–79.

Mercy Thompson and the Revelation on Marriage

D&C 132

Jed Woodworth

Robert Thompson was in the prime of life when he passed away unexpectedly in the fall of 1841, a victim of the malarial fevers that laid low so many Latter-day Saints in the mosquito-ridden swamplands on the banks of the Mississippi River. The private secretary of Joseph Smith and a coeditor of the Church's newspaper, *Times and Seasons,* Thompson appeared to have a bright future. One day he was healthy. Ten days later he was gone, cut down at age thirty, his wife and three-year-old daughter now alone.

Thompson was not a difficult man to love. Friends remembered him as a "fond husband, a tender parent and a true and faithful friend."[1] His wife, Mercy, admired his bravery at the end. "He endured his sufferings with great Patience, not a murmuring word escaped his Lips." He spent his last moments, she said, testifying "that he had not followed cunningly devised Fables, that he had been raised from the Dunghill and made to sit among Princes."[2]

The premature death of a family member has been an all-too-common occurrence throughout human history. Often it was a woman whose death in childbirth left little ones without the gentle caress of their mother's hand. Not until the 20th century could most families in the industrialized world expect not to lose an infant or a young child to accident or disease. From the beginning of time, death has lurked as a reminder of both the fragility of life and our longing for its continuance.

Over and against this culture of death, a revelation received by Joseph Smith promised that our most cherished relationships can persist in the next life. Mothers and fathers, wives and husbands, parents and children can be with one another again, our kinships and friendships enduring into the eternities. The remarkable terms of these promises are found in this revelation, known today as Doctrine and Covenants 132.

Heaven and Earth

Two main conceptions of heaven have predominated during 2,000 years of Christian history. The most common view imagines single and solitary angels worshipping and praising God in perfect union. This view draws a sharp distinction between this world and the next and privileges the role of the intellect in the afterlife. The focus is on the contemplation of God and His greatness, not on human relationships. Earthly connections are temporal and thus destined to end at death.[3]

The other main conception emphasizes the presence of friends and family in the afterlife. The worship of God persists, but the society of loved ones becomes essential to eternal bliss. The material and the eternal worlds overlap, and ordinary life becomes part of God's holy work. The idea of a social heaven grew in popularity during the 19th century. American novelist Elizabeth Stuart Phelps captured the great appeal of this view for a generation that had lost relatives prematurely in the U.S. Civil War. "Would it be like Him," Phelps's novel *The Gates Ajar* asks, "to suffer two souls to grow together here, so that the separation of a day is pain, and then wrench them apart for all eternity?"[4]

Joseph Smith's revelation on marriage, recorded in July 1843, made no effort to model the afterlife on sentimental Victorian life as Phelps did. The revelation confirmed that human relationships will persist, but only on condition. All social commitments are destined to end at death unless they are made in view of eternity and performed by one with the priesthood authority to seal on earth as in heaven. Marriages that persist after we die, section 132 says, are entered into "for time and for all eternity," and are "sealed by the Holy Spirit of promise, of him . . . whom I have appointed on the earth to hold this power." Those who do not enter into such covenants, prior to the Resurrection of the dead, become "angels in heaven," appointed to remain "separately and singly."[5]

Mercy and Robert

Mercy Rachel Fielding was born in 1807 to pious Methodists who tenant farmed in a tiny rural village 60 miles north of London. At age twenty-four, she immigrated to York (now Toronto), Canada, along with her older brother Joseph. Soon joined by their sister Mary, the three Fieldings started attending meetings of a group of Methodist seekers who believed that all the churches they knew had lost their way. When missionary Parley P. Pratt arrived in York in the spring of 1836, the Fieldings found the answer to their problem. Mercy, Mary, and Joseph were baptized in a local creek, and they moved to Church headquarters in Kirtland, Ohio, the following spring.[6]

In Canada, Mercy met Robert Blashel Thompson, whose path mirrored her own in many ways. Born in 1811 in Yorkshire, England, he had joined as a young man a group of dissenters called the Primitive Methodist Society, who sought a return of spiritual gifts. He moved to Canada in 1834, heard the message of Parley P. Pratt, and was baptized the same month as the Fieldings. Robert Thompson and Mercy Fielding were kindred spirits, and soon after their arrival in Kirtland, the two married in June 1837.[7]

After the marriage, Mercy's sister Mary began boarding with cousins of Joseph and Hyrum Smith and in this way became better acquainted with these brothers, whom she quickly grew to love. Her heart drew out in sympathy to Hyrum when his wife, Jerusha, died in the fall of 1837 after a difficult childbirth that left their five children under 10 years old without a mother. Joseph inquired of the Lord what Hyrum should do. The answer was that he should marry

Mary Fielding right away. Trusting Joseph's inspiration, Mary married Hyrum on Christmas Eve 1837.[8]

Thereafter, Mercy and Robert's lives became intertwined with Mary and Hyrum's. Hyrum led the Thompsons on the thousand-mile trek from Ohio to Missouri, where the Saints relocated in 1838. Later, when Hyrum and Joseph were incarcerated in Liberty Jail, Mercy and Mary visited the prisoners on a cold February night, bringing with them Hyrum's new infant son, little Joseph F., the future prophet. Having recently given birth herself, Mercy nursed Joseph F. on that occasion when Mary was too sick to do so. Mercy and Robert kept Mary and Hyrum's children during Hyrum's incarceration, and in Nauvoo, the two families built homes next to one another.[9]

The Smiths and the Thompsons grew even closer after Robert's death. One night in the spring of 1843, Mercy was sleeping at Mary's home, keeping her sister company while Hyrum was away from Nauvoo on business. Mercy dreamed that she was standing in a garden with Robert. She heard someone repeat their marriage vows, though she couldn't make out whose voice it was. As one attuned to the variety of ways God spoke, Mercy understood the dream as a message from God. "I awoke in the Morning deeply impressed by this Dream which I could not interpret."[10]

Later that night, Hyrum returned home and reported having had "a very remarkable Dream" while he was away from home. He had seen his deceased wife Jerusha and two of their children who had died prematurely.[11] Hyrum was no clearer on the meaning of his dream than Mercy's was on hers. But the timing of the dreams was uncanny. Upon his arrival home, Hyrum found a message from his brother Joseph asking him to come to his house. "To his amazement," Mercy reported, Hyrum found that Joseph had received a revelation stating that "marriages contracted for time only lasted for time and were no more one until a new contract was made, for All Eternity."[12] This revelation would later be recorded and canonized as Doctrine and Covenants 132.[13]

Robert Thompson was dead, and so was Jerusha Smith. How could a new marriage contract be made when only one spouse was living? Joseph Smith's answer was that a living person could stand in as a proxy for the dead person. Since the fall of 1840, the Saints had performed vicarious baptisms for deceased ancestors who had died before hearing about the restored gospel. Now the same principle was to be extended to marriage. Husband and wife could be "sealed" to one another, bound in heaven as they had been bound on earth.[14] A marriage that once ended in time—"till death do you part"—could be performed again "for time and for all eternity," sealed by priesthood authority. In this way, the marriage could last into the eternities.[15]

The prospect thrilled Mercy. There was no question that, if given the chance, she would choose to spend eternity with Robert. She missed him and wanted to be near him. He was the sort of man who inspired her to become the person she most wanted to be, a disciple of the Lord Jesus Christ. "In meekness, humility, and integrity he could not be easily exceled if equald," she said of Robert.[16]

On a Monday morning in late May 1843, Mercy Thompson and her sister Mary, along with Hyrum and Joseph Smith, met in a room on the second floor of Joseph's house. Joseph married Mercy and Robert for time and eternity, with Hyrum standing in for Robert.[17] Following this ceremony, Joseph married Hyrum and Mary for time and eternity. Mercy's exuberance knew no bounds. "Some may think I could envy Queen Victoria in some of her glory," she said. "Not while my name stands first on the list in this Dispensation of women sealed to a Dead Husband through divine Revelation."[18]

Plurality

Mercy Thompson's sealing to her deceased husband offered profound comfort in the midst of loneliness and uncertainty. But the promises applied to the distant scene, to some undetermined time when the Thompsons would be reunited. Until then, Mercy had a life to lead and a child to care for. Who would provide? In Mercy's place and time, few occupations were open to women. After Robert's death, she did what widows for centuries had done: she took in boarders. "With diligence and the blessing of the Lord," she recounted, "our wants were supplied."[19]

Still, "it was a lonesome life," and "being deprived of the Sosiety of such a Husband caused me to mourn so deeply that my Health was much impaired." In Latter-day Saint belief, the earth is alive with heavenly communication, the angels invested in comforting the burdens of the bereaved. During that summer, an angel visited Joseph Smith. It was Robert Thompson, his former clerk. He "appeared to [Joseph] several times telling him that he did not wish me to live such a lonely life," Mercy recounted. The angel proposed a shocking solution: Hyrum was to "have me seal'd to him for time," Mercy recalled.[20] In other words, Robert Thompson requested that Hyrum marry Mercy as a plural wife for this life, "for time." Mercy and Robert, meanwhile, would remain sealed in the eternities.

Around the same time as Robert Thompson's appearance, Joseph Smith committed section 132 to writing, dictating the revelation to his secretary William Clayton in the small office at the back of Joseph's red brick store.[21] Parts of the revelation had been known to Joseph long before, probably as early as 1831 while he worked on his inspired revision of the Old Testament.[22] Why, Joseph had asked God in prayer, did He justify Abraham, Isaac, Jacob, and others in "having many wives and concubines"? The answer was not immediately apparent because Joseph's own culture and upbringing shunned plural marriage. The revelation answered simply and directly: God had "commanded" plural marriage, and because the biblical patriarchs "did none other things than that which they were commanded, they have entered into their exaltation."[23]

Section 132 thus answered a question long debated within Western culture. On the one side were those who argued that God approved plural marriage among the ancients. St. Augustine thought Old Testament plural marriage was a "sacrament" that symbolized the day when churches in every nation would be subject to Christ.[24] Martin Luther agreed: Abraham was a chaste man whose marriage to Hagar fulfilled God's sacred promises to the patriarch.[25] Luther hypothesized that God might sanction plural marriage in modern times under limited circumstances. It "is no longer commanded," he observed, "but neither is it forbidden."[26]

On the other side of the debate were those who argued that the Old Testament patriarchs had gone astray in practicing plural marriage. John Calvin, Luther's 16th-century contemporary, believed that plural marriage perverted the "order of creation" established with the monogamous marriage of Adam and Eve in the Garden of Eden.[27] Calvin had a profound influence on early American religious attitudes. Not all Americans agreed that the biblical patriarchs had erred, but Joseph Smith's contemporaries overwhelmingly followed Calvin in the belief that plural marriage in modern times was wrong under any circumstance.[28]

Section 132 stood above this debate, approving of the patriarchs' actions in God's own voice. Plural marriage, the revelation said, had helped fulfill the promise God had made to Abraham that his seed would "continue as innumerable as the stars."[29] Nevertheless, the revelation went on to take a much bolder step than vindicating the patriarchs. As the seed of Abraham, Latter-day Saints were commanded for a time to practice plural marriage. "Go ye, therefore, and do the works of Abraham."[30]

Joseph Smith had been reluctant to enter plural marriage at first, fully realizing the persecution it would bring to the Church. Monogamy was then the only form of marriage legally accepted in the United States, and opposition was sure to be fierce. Joseph himself had to be convinced of the propriety of plural marriage. Three times an angel appeared to him, urging him to move forward as directed.[31] He eventually entered plural marriage and introduced the principle to other followers in Nauvoo as early as 1841. Committing the revelation to writing allowed him to more easily spread the message of this new commandment, which was introduced cautiously and incrementally.[32]

Mercy and Hyrum

Eternal marriage struck Mercy Thompson far more favorably than plural marriage did. By training and disposition, she opposed marrying an already married man. The prospect of living in the same home with her sister and closest friend, Mary, did nothing to diminish her unease. Joseph sent Mary to open up the subject with Mercy, thinking it would be better received. The choice of emissary had no effect. "This subject when first communicated to me," Mercy recounted, "tried me to the very core all my former traditions and every natural feeling of my Heart rose in opposition."[33]

Hyrum spoke to her next. He was sympathetic to Mercy's feelings, having once opposed plural marriage himself. Joseph had sought to gauge his brother's feelings, holding back this most difficult and controversial of teachings until Hyrum was open to persuasion. Hyrum was ultimately converted to the principle when he realized that he had married two women on earth whom he could not bear to part with in eternity. On the same day he was sealed to Mary for time and eternity, Mary stood as proxy while he was sealed to Jerusha, thus sealing Hyrum to both his wives for eternity.[34]

Mercy was not being asked to become the wife of Hyrum Smith for eternity. The message from Robert Thompson was that Hyrum should marry Mercy for time; or, in Mercy's words, until such time as Hyrum "would deliver me up on the morning of the day of the resurrection to my husband Robert Blashel Thompson."[35] The marriage with Hyrum was like the levirate marriages of the Old Testament in which the man was commanded to marry the wife of his deceased brother.[36] This combination of patriarchal practice and angelic appearance made sense to biblical restorationists like Hyrum Smith. He told Mercy that when he first learned of Robert Thompson's request, "the Holy Spirit rested upon him [Hyrum] from the Crown of his Head to the Soles of his Feet."[37]

Latter-day Saint women who were converted to the principle of plural marriage in Nauvoo often reported spiritual experiences confirming their decision. They saw a light, felt peace, or, in one case, saw an angel. Mercy Thompson left no record of such experiences. She later said she believed the principle "because I could read it for myself in the bible and see that that it was practiced in those days, and the Lord approved of it and sanctioned it."[38]

But biblical logic alone was not enough for Mercy. Joseph himself eventually spoke with her, and it was his testimony that won her over. Robert Thompson appeared to him more than once, he explained, the last time "with such power that it made him tremble." Joseph was not inclined to act on the request at first. Only after he prayed to the Lord and learned that he was to "do as my servant hath required" did he tell Hyrum about the vision.[39]

As a believer in spiritual gifts, Mercy Thompson trusted that her deceased husband had made a communication.[40] And, after half a dozen years of closely observing Joseph Smith, she believed that he was "too wise to err and too good to be unkind."[41] The request to marry Hyrum, she concluded, was "the voice of the Lord speaking through the mouth of the prophet Joseph Smith."[42]

Joseph Smith took the protestations of women like Mercy Thompson seriously. No one, woman or man, found plural marriage easy to accept on first hearing.[43] Joseph did not compel women to accept plural marriage by the force of his own command any more than he did men.[44] Women and men were encouraged to reflect and pray and arrive at their own decision. Mercy called for the manuscript copy of the revelation written on foolscap paper and kept it in her home for four or five days, studying over the contents in her mind.[45] Only after much prayer and pondering did she give her consent. On August 11, 1843, Joseph Smith married Hyrum and Mercy at Mary and Hyrum's house on the corner of Water and Bain Streets in Nauvoo. On Joseph's recommendation, Hyrum built an additional room to the house, and Mercy moved into it.

Time and Eternity

During their brief life together, Hyrum's projects became Mercy's projects, and vice versa. Mercy helped write out the inspired words that flowed from Hyrum's mouth as he blessed Church members in his role as Patriarch to the Church. The great project that consumed hearts and minds was the Nauvoo Temple. At some point, after seeking the Lord earnestly to know what she could do to accelerate the completion of the temple, Mercy heard these words enter into her mind: "Try to get the Sisters to subscribe one Cent per Week for the purpose of buying glass and nails." She said Hyrum was "much pleased" with the revelation and did everything he could to push it forward by urging public audiences to subscribe as Mercy had requested.[46] With Hyrum's help, she and Mary raised over $1,000— no small sum in those days—for the cause.[47]

Mercy and Hyrum had been married just 10 months when a mobber's bullet took Hyrum's life at Carthage. Mercy had lost another husband in the prime of life. She grieved the loss of Hyrum, whom she described as being "an affectionate Husband, a loving

Father, a faithful Friend, and a warm hearted Benefactor."[48] But her connection to Mary would always be a source of strength. Mercy and her daughter, Mary Jane, now six, were left to tend the house with Mary and her two children with Hyrum, along with the five children of Hyrum and Jerusha, for whom Mary had become stepmother.

In 1846, Mercy and Mary, along with their brother Joseph, set out on a new journey together. They joined thousands of their fellow sufferers on a 1,400-mile trek to a new Zion that was beyond the boundaries of the United States at the time. They arrived in the Salt Lake Valley the following year. Mary died of pneumonia in 1852. Mercy lived the next four decades in Salt Lake City, faithful to the end, serving in the Church wherever she could and helping to mother the children Mary and Hyrum had left behind.

Mercy's connection to Hyrum would always be a source of deep gratitude. But she lived for a reunion with Robert, her "beloved" husband and the choice of her youth. Through her death in 1893, she retained the name Mercy R. Thompson, the name she had taken upon her marriage to Robert. Doctrine and Covenants 132 had promised her that she and Robert would one day, if faithful, "inherit thrones, kingdoms, principalities, and powers." They would enjoy "a continuation of the seeds forever and ever."[49] She believed in these promises and lived her life so that she might one day realize them.

1. "Death of Col. Robert B. Thompson," *Times and Seasons,* Sept. 1, 1841, 519.

2. Mercy Fielding Thompson, Robert B. Thompson biography by Mercy R. Thompson, 1854 November, Church History Library, Salt Lake City. Thompson's language comes from Psalms 113:7–8.

3. Colleen McDannell and Bernhard Lang, *Heaven: A History* (New Haven, CT: Yale Nota Bene, 2001).

4. Jan Swango Emerson and Hugh Feiss, eds., *Imagining Heaven in the Middle Ages* (New York: Garland, 2000); Jeffrey Burton Russell, *A History of Heaven: The Singing of Silence* (Princeton, NJ: Princeton University Press, 1997). Shakespeare compared marriage to food—something to be savored and enjoyed while it lasted, until eventually it rotted away. See Lisa Hopkins, *The Shakespearean Marriage:* *Merry Wives and Heavy Husbands* (London: Macmillan, 1998), 70–71.

5. Elizabeth Stuart Phelps, *The Gates Ajar,* 4th ed. (London: Sampson, Low, Son, & Marston, 1870), 54. On Phelps's immense popularity, see McDannell and Lang, *Heaven,* 265–66. Similar arguments are found in the poems of Emily Dickinson. See Barton Levi St. Armand, "Paradise Deferred: The Image of Heaven in the Work of Emily Dickinson and Elizabeth Stuart Phelps," *American Quarterly,* vol. 29 (Spring 1977), 55–78.

6. Doctrine and Covenants 132:7, 15–18. Moreover, the revelation went well beyond standard social conceptions of the afterlife by making procreation—"a continuation of the seeds" (D&C 132:19)—part of God's plan for human beings in the life to come.

7. Leonard J. Arrington, Susan Arrington Madsen, and Emily Madsen Jones, *Mothers of the Prophets*, rev. ed. (Salt Lake City: Deseret Book, 2009), 88–95; Parley P. Pratt, *The Autobiography of Parley Parker Pratt* (New York: Russell Brothers, 1874), 146–54.

8. Thompson, Robert B. Thompson biography by Mercy R. Thompson

9. Arrington, Madsen, and Jones, *Mothers of the Prophets*, 96–98; Jeffrey S. O'Driscoll, *Hyrum Smith: A Life of Integrity* (Salt Lake City: Deseret Book, 2003), 163–64.

10. Jennifer Reeder, "'The Blessing of the Lord Has Attended Me': Mercy Rachel Fielding Thompson (1807–1893)," in Richard E. Turley Jr. and Brittany A. Chapman, eds., *Women of Faith in the Latter Days: Volume One, 1775–1820* (Salt Lake City: Deseret Book, 2013), 424–25. The Smiths occupied lot 3 of block 149, the Thompsons lot 1 of the same block, the backyards of the properties touching one another.

11. Mercy Rachel Fielding Thompson, Reminiscence, in Carol Cornwall Madsen, ed., *In Their Own Words: Women and the Story of Nauvoo* (Salt Lake City: Deseret Book, 1994), 194–95.

12. These children were Mary Smith (1829–32) and Hyrum Smith (1834–41).

13. Thompson, Reminiscence, 195; spelling modernized.

14. The revelation on marriage was first published as an extra to the September 14, 1852, issue of the *Deseret News*. It became section 132 of the 1876 edition of the Doctrine and Covenants.

15. Doctrine and Covenants 132:46.

16. Doctrine and Covenants 132:7. Christians had long understood Matthew 22:23–30 to justify the end of marriages in the afterlife. Doctrine and Covenants 132:15–17 reinterpreted the passage to mean that some marriages would end while others would endure.

17. Mercy Fielding Thompson, Autobiographical sketch, Church History Library, Salt Lake City; punctuation added.

18. Thompson, Reminiscence, 195. Several other couples were married for eternity on this same occasion: Brigham Young and his wife Mary Ann Angell; Brigham Young and his deceased wife, Miriam Works (with Mary Ann Angell acting as proxy); and Willard Richards and his wife, Jennetta Richards. Joseph Smith journal, May 29, 1843, Joseph Smith Collection, Church History Library, Salt Lake City; Lyndon W. Cook, *Nauvoo Marriages, Proxy Sealings, 1843–1846* (Provo, UT: Grandin Book, 2004), 5.

19. Thompson, Reminiscence, 195; spelling modernized.

20. Thompson, Autobiographical sketch. The Thompsons took boarders even before Robert died. Mercy continued on with the practice.

21. Mercy Fielding Thompson letter to Joseph Smith III, Sept. 5, 1883, Joseph F. Smith Papers 1854–1918, Church History Library, Salt Lake City.

22. Brian C. Hales, *Joseph Smith's Polygamy*, 3 vols. (Salt Lake City: Greg Kofford Books, 2013), 2:64–65. Clayton later reported that Joseph Smith committed the revelation to writing, at Hyrum Smith's suggestion, in order to persuade Joseph's wife Emma Smith that she should cease her opposition to plural marriage. Emma had accepted plural marriage for a time but was opposed to the principle by July 12, 1843, when the revelation was written down. William Clayton statement, Feb. 16, 1874, in Andrew Jenson, "Plural Marriage," *Historical Record*, May 1887, 225–26.

23. Danel W. Bachman, "New Light on an Old Hypothesis: The Ohio Origins of the Revelation on Eternal Marriage," *Journal of Mormon History*, vol. 5 (1978), 19–32.

24. Doctrine and Covenants 132:1, 37.

25. Augustine, "The Excellence of Marriage" [ca. 401], trans. Ray Kearney, in *The Works of Saint Augustine: Marriage and Virginity*, ed. John E. Rotelle, vol. 9 (Hyde Park, NY: New City Press, 1999), 49, 51.

26. Martin Luther, "Genesis: Chapter Sixteen," in *Luther's Works*, 54 vols., ed. Jaroslav Pelikan, trans. George Schick (St. Louis: Concordia Publishing House, 1961), 3:45–46.

27. Martin Luther, "The Estate of Marriage" [1522], in *Luther's Works*, ed. and trans. Walther I. Brandt (Philadelphia: Muhlenberg Press, 1962), 45:24. Luther recommended that the English king Henry VIII enter plural marriage before he divorced Catherine of Aragon. Luther to Robert Barnes, Sept. 3,

1531, in *Luther's Works,* ed. and trans. Gottfried G. Krodel (Philadelphia: Fortress Press, 1975), 50:33.

28. John Witte Jr. and Robert M. Kingdon, *Sex, Marriage, and Family in John Calvin's Geneva: Volume 1: Courtship, Engagement, and Marriage* (Grand Rapids, MI: William B. Eerdmans, 2005), 223; John L. Thompson, "The Immoralities of the Patriarchs in the History of Exegesis: A Reappraisal of Calvin's Position," *Calvin Theological Journal,* vol. 26 (1991), 9–46.

29. Calvin's opposition, of course, reflected a much older opposition on the part of the Catholic Church, which prohibited polygamy as early as the fourth century and by the late Middle Ages had written that prohibition into canon law (John Witte, *From Sacrament to Contract: Marriage, Religion, and Law in the Western Tradition* [Louisville, KY: Westminster University Press, 2012], 61, 99–100). Many Americans saw the patriarchs' behavior in both relativistic and progressive terms: appropriate in its own place and time but outmoded for people living in enlightened times. On the association of anti-polygamy with Enlightenment rationalism, see Nancy F. Cott, *Public Vows: A History of Marriage and the Nation* (Cambridge, MA: Harvard University Press, 2000), 18–23.

30. Doctrine and Covenants 132:30, 37. For an expansion on this theme, see Belinda Marden Pratt, *Defense of Polygamy, by a Lady of Utah, in a Letter to Her Sister in New Hampshire* (1854), 7–8.

31. Doctrine and Covenants 132:32.

32. Brian C. Hales, "Encouraging Joseph Smith to Practice Plural Marriage: The Accounts of the Angel with a Drawn Sword," *Mormon Historical Studies,* vol. 11, no. 2 (Fall 2010), 55–71.

33. By the time the Saints entered the Salt Lake Valley, at least 196 men and 521 women had begun practicing plural marriage. See Hales, *Joseph Smith's Polygamy,* 1:3, 2:165.

34. Thompson, Autobiographical sketch.

35. Cook, *Nauvoo Marriages, Proxy Sealings,* 3. The conversion of Hyrum Smith to plural marriage is variously dated to 1842 or 1843. Brigham Young sermon, Oct. 8, 1866, Historian's Office reports of speeches, Church History Library, Salt Lake City; Andrew F. Ehat, *A Holy Order: Joseph Smith,*

the Temple, and the 1844 Mormon Succession Question* (Printed by author, 1990), 28–32; Ruth Vose Sayers, Affidavit, May 1, 1869, Joseph F. Smith Affidavit Books, 5:9, Church History Library, Salt Lake City.

36. Mercy Thompson, Testimony, Church of Christ in Missouri v. Reorganized Church of Jesus Christ of Latter Day Saints, 70 F. 179 (8th Cir. 1895), in United States testimony 1892, typescript, 247, Church History Library, Salt Lake City.

37. Deuteronomy 25:5–10.

38. Thompson to Smith, Sept. 5, 1883.

39. Thompson, Testimony, 239.

40. Thompson to Smith, Sept 5, 1883; see also Thompson, Testimony, 263.

41. One of the spiritual gifts was to "believe on" the testimony of another. Doctrine and Covenants 46:14.

42. Thompson, Autobiographical sketch. For the range of these observations, see Mercy Fielding Thompson, "Recollections of the Prophet Joseph Smith," *Juvenile Instructor,* July 1, 1892, 398–400.

43. Thompson, Testimony, 248.

44. For examples, see "Plural Marriage in Kirtland and Nauvoo," Gospel Topics, topics.lds.org.

45. In private conversation, for example, Joseph Smith often launched plural marriage proposals by speaking in the first person singular ("I have been commanded") and then teaching and reasoning with prospective brides rather than relying exclusively on a claim to authority. See, for example, Lucy Walker Kimball Smith, "A Brief Biographical Sketch of the Life and Labors of Lucy Walker Kimball Smith," Church History Library, Salt Lake City; Emily Dow Partridge Young, Diary and reminiscences, Church History Library, Salt Lake City. For examples of women who rejected Joseph Smith's proposals and nevertheless remained in the Church without any apparent negative repercussions, see Hales, *Joseph Smith's Polygamy,* 1:274–75; 2:31, 120; Patricia H. Stoker, " 'The Lord Has Been My Guide': Cordelia Calista Morley Cox (1823–1915)," in Richard E. Turley Jr. and Brittany A. Chapman, eds., *Women of Faith in the Latter Days: Volume 2, 1821–1845* (Salt Lake City: Deseret Book, 2012), 53–54.

46. Thompson, Testimony, 250–51. On the priestly appeal of plural marriage for women, see Kathleen Flake, "The Emotional and Priestly Logic of Plural Marriage" (2009), *The Arrington Lecture,* no. 15.

47. Thompson, Autobiographical sketch.

48. "Notice," *Times and Seasons,* Mar. 15, 1845, 847. The figure was probably larger by the time the Nauvoo Temple was dedicated in December 1845.

49. Thompson, Autobiographical sketch; punctuation added.

50. Doctrine and Covenants 132:19.

Of Governments and Laws

D&C 134

Spencer W. McBride

Lyman Wight looked with pride upon his father's military service during the American Revolution. To Wight, American victory in that conflict had done more than secure independence for the United States; it had secured rights to life and liberty for the American people. Wight believed those values were the lasting legacy of the American Revolution and enlisted to fight in the War of 1812 to protect them.

However, Wight's optimistic perception of these American ideals was severely challenged by his experiences as a Church member living in Missouri during the 1830s. When he and more than one thousand other Latter-day Saints moved to Jackson County, Missouri, between 1831 and 1832, many residents of the county disliked Mormon beliefs and feared their potential influence on local politics. But rather than honor the rights of Church members to worship and vote according to the dictates of their own consciences, Jackson County residents used extralegal violence to force the Saints to either forsake their faith or leave the county. Acting as vigilantes, these Missouri citizens physically abused Church members living in the county, destroyed their property, and eventually ordered them to leave.[1]

Wight was dismayed that officials in the state and federal governments would condone and even encourage such actions against members of the Church. In a petition to the United States

Senate several years later, he would declare that his "father was a revolutiona[ry] soldier" and that these violations of Church members' citizenship rights "[were] not the liberties he [gave] for me and my posterity."[2] Wight's petition revealed a tension between the loyalty he felt to his country, his disdain for the actions of many of the men elected to govern that country, and his devotion to a faith he believed would outlast all earthly governments.

Redress

Like Lyman Wight, Church leaders had a complicated relationship with both the local and national governments. When members of the Church in Jackson County were driven from their homes in November 1833, Church leaders believed that the governments of Missouri and the United States had each failed to protect the citizenship rights of the Missouri Saints and felt compelled to protest the actions (and inaction) of elected officials that led to the Saints' expulsion. At the same time, they began to make legal and political appeals to these same governments for the restoration of their property and citizenship rights in Jackson County.

A few prominent citizens were sympathetic to the plight of the Saints, but many were suspicious of the Saints' motives. The Church's commitment to the authority of revelation and the rapid gathering of Church members in Ohio and Missouri raised concerns among some Americans that the Church aimed to establish its own society that ignored the laws and authority of the United States. How could Church leaders protest their mistreatment by government while also expressing their support for government and even petitioning the government for assistance?

The Declaration

On August 17, 1835, in the midst of the Saints' attempts to petition the government for help, Oliver Cowdery and Sidney Rigdon presented a document titled "Declaration of Government and Law" to Church members in Kirtland, Ohio. The declaration—now Doctrine and Covenants 134—sought to address all of the Saints' concerns.[3] By stating that "governments were instituted of God for the benefit of man" and that God would hold individuals "accountable for their acts"[4] as government officials, the declaration described civil governments as secular institutions whose actions had spiritual consequences. By explaining that every government official "should be honored in his station" and "that to the laws all men owe respect and deference,"[5] the declaration emphasized the Church's teachings that its members should be law-abiding citizens who contribute to the "peace and harmony"[6] of the societies in which they reside. It insisted that the government should secure the right of its citizens to worship according to the dictates of their own consciences and that religious groups experiencing abuse because of their religious practices were justified in petitioning the government for redress. Indirectly addressing the Saints' recent experiences in Jackson County, the declaration insisted on the right of citizens to defend themselves against religious persecution if the government was unresponsive to their appeals for help.

Church members accepted the declaration and included it in the first edition of the Doctrine and Covenants. Unlike other sections of that book in which God revealed His will to the Saints, this section consisted of the Saints explaining their perspective and beliefs to the general public. It was most likely authored by Oliver Cowdery, as he had written on many of the topics it addressed in recent newspaper editorials.[7] Although Joseph Smith was away in Michigan Territory when the declaration was presented to the Church, he accepted it and referenced it later in his speaking and writing.[8]

How the Declaration Was Used

Especially after 1838, when the Saints were driven out of Missouri by the governor's executive order, Joseph and other Church leaders invoked the declaration's principles as they fought for Church members' citizenship rights. For example, in 1840 while Joseph was in the eastern United States petitioning the federal government for redress after the confiscation of Church members' property in Missouri, he wrote a letter to the editor of a Pennsylvania newspaper in which he answered claims made by some of the Church's detractors in that area. In composing the letter, however, Joseph simply copied the text of the declaration on government, substituting "I believe" in every instance where the declaration contained the phrase "we believe."[9]

A few months later, Joseph, Sidney Rigdon, and Elias Higbee secured a hearing before a committee of United States senators to address the Missouri persecutions. In that hearing, Congressman John Jameson of Missouri tried to justify past violence against Church members by claiming that Joseph had given his followers liberty to ignore the laws of the land. Elias Higbee adamantly denied this claim, arguing that the Church "held to no such doctrine nor believed in any such thing," and directed the committee to the 1835 "Declaration of Government and Law" in the Doctrine and Covenants as proof that they "had published long ago [their] belief on that subject."[10] This 1840 Senate committee declined to grant the Church redress for their persecutions, but Church leaders held to the values described in the declaration.

Two years later, when Church leaders wrote the now-famous "Wentworth Letter" as a brief description of the Church's history and beliefs, the principles set forth in the declaration on government appear to have inspired the content of two different statements. Those statements, now known respectively as the eleventh and twelfth articles of faith, affirm the Church's stance on the freedom of all men and women to worship God according to the dictates of their own conscience and its teachings that Church members are subject to government officials and should be obedient to the laws of the land in which they reside.[11]

Render unto Caesar

Church leaders in the 1830s had to navigate a complicated political landscape, but their situation was hardly unprecedented. Religious groups seeking to establish a kingdom of God on earth have always needed to interact carefully with secular "powers that be."[12] Jesus Christ faced similar challenges during His mortal ministry. When He was accused of trying to usurp political power from Jewish and Roman officials, He declared that His "kingdom is not of this world"[13] and directed His disciples to "render therefore unto Caesar the things which are Caesar's; and unto God the things that are

God's."[14] In this sense, the 1835 "Declaration of Government and Law" echoed Jesus's approach to building up His Church within the borders of sovereign nations.

"I volunteered to defend my [cou]ntry in the last war [the War of 1812]," Lyman Wight wrote in an 1839 petition to the United States Senate, "yet I [cannot live] in the State of Missouri without de[nying my] religion." And so the self-proclaimed patriot lamented that he did not "feel satisfied to live [in s]uch bondage in what is called a free government."[15] Wight's petition epitomized one of the primary principles in the "Declaration of Government and Law"— that Church members owe allegiance to their country but should simultaneously work to build governments that secure the liberty and rights of all citizens.

1. See John Whitmer, "Letter from John Whitmer, 29 July 1833," in Joseph Smith Letterbook 2, 52–56, josephsmithpapers.org.

2. Lyman Wight, Petition to the United States Senate, 1839, page 3, Church History Library, Salt Lake City.

3. "Declaration of Government and Law, 17 August 1835 [D&C 134]," in Doctrine and Covenants (1835 ed.), 252–54, josephsmithpapers.org.

4. "Declaration of Government and Law, 17 August 1835 [D&C 134]," 252.

5. "Declaration of Government and Law, 17 August 1835 [D&C 134]," 252.

6. "Declaration of Government and Law, 17 August 1835 [D&C 134]," 253.

7. Oliver Cowdery, "Prospects of the Church," *Evening and Morning Star*, vol. 1, no. 10 (Mar. 1833), 151–53; Oliver Cowdery, "To the Patrons of the Evening and the Morning Star," *Evening and Morning Star*, vol. 2, no. 15 (Dec. 1833), 125–26.

8. Historical Introduction for "Doctrine and Covenants, 1835," josephsmithpapers.org.

9. Joseph Smith, "Letter to Editor, 22 January 1840," josephsmithpapers.org.

10. Elias Higbee, "Letter from Elias Higbee, 21 February 1840," in Joseph Smith Letterbook 2, 100, josephsmithpapers.org.

11. Joseph Smith, "Church History," *Times and Seasons,* vol. 3, no. 9 (Mar. 1, 1842), 710; josephsmithpapers.org.

12. Romans 13:1.

13. John 18:36.

14. Matthew 22:21.

15. Lyman Wight, Petition to the United States Senate, 4.

Remembering the Martyrdom
D&C 135
Jeffrey Mahas

When Joseph and Hyrum Smith left for a jail in Carthage, Illinois, to wait for a legal hearing, few suspected the two were leaving their homes for the last time. Joseph had faced imprisonment, mob violence, and death threats before, and he had always returned to lead the Saints forward. Hyrum, too, had endured periods of persecution with the Saints and had always emerged ready to rebuild and press forward.

But in the late afternoon of June 27, 1844, a lynch mob stormed Carthage Jail and murdered them both.

News of the violent deaths of the two brothers shocked the Saints in Nauvoo. In one day, they had lost their prophet and their patriarch. For many, Joseph and Hyrum were also friends and role models, men who had helped and blessed them in times of need. In the days, weeks, and months following the martyrdom, the Saints grappled with how to describe their reactions to the deaths.[1] Their letters, journals, and public writings stand alongside printed tributes to Joseph and Hyrum, such as the one now canonized in Doctrine and Covenants 135, as witnesses to the mission of the two men who served so faithfully and then sealed their testimony with their blood.

Letters

Many Latter-day Saints in Nauvoo had friends and family members who were far away from the city at the time of the martyrdom. They were left with the difficult task of breaking the news to their loved ones.

"I shall not attempt to discribe the scene that we have passed through," Vilate Kimball wrote to her husband, Heber, who was in the eastern United States promoting Joseph's presidential campaign. "God forbid that I should ever witness another like unto it. . . . Every heart is filled with sorrow, and the very streets of Nauvoo se[e]m to mo[u]rn." Like many, she also expressed concern about the threat of continuing violence against the Saints. "Where it will end," she warned Heber, "the Lord only knows."[2]

Almira Mack Covey, a cousin to the Smith brothers, wrote to her family about watching the bodies of Joseph and Hyrum return to Nauvoo. "You can judge what were our feelings better than I can tell them," she wrote, "but this much I can say that a dry eye I did not behold that day among that large assembly of people. It was enough to rend the heart of a stone to behold two Prophets of the Lord laid prost[r]ate."[3]

Sarah M. Kimball, who had played a key role in the founding of the Relief Society, was also among those who saw the bodies returned to the city. "The scene of the reception of those corpses in nauvoo can be better imagined than described," she wrote to a friend, "for pen was never made competent to do it justice." Though it would have been impossible to capture the grief of the whole city, Kimball did try to describe the grief of one woman: the day after the murders, she had gone to sit with Lucy Mack Smith. Sarah Kimball remembered holding Lucy Mack Smith's trembling hand and hearing her question between sobs, "How could they kill my poor boys, O how could they kill them when they were so precious?"[4]

Journals

Other writers tried to record details about the martyrdom and their responses to it by writing reflective entries in their journals. Rather than focusing on the moment and on immediate worries, as letters often did, journal entries often tried to sift out valuable details for future generations and to make spiritual sense of the tragedy. In seeking an explanation or precedent for the loss of their leaders, the Saints often turned to the Bible. Many compared the murders to biblical events, from the killing of Abel to the Crucifixion of Jesus Christ. They often identified Joseph and Hyrum as among the many martyrs "that were slain for the word of God, and for the testimony which they held" mentioned in the book of Revelation. Accordingly, they believed that the two brothers were now numbered among those pleading to heaven, "How long, O Lord, holy and true, dost thou not judge and avenge our blood on them that dwell on the earth?"[5]

The events at Carthage led Joseph Fielding to fill several pages of his journal with commentary on the life, mission, and death of Joseph Smith. Fielding wrote that the arrival of the two martyrs' bodies "was the most solemn Sight that my Eyes ever beheld." While he "had often re[a]d of the Martyrs of old," Fielding wrote that he was now himself a witness for "2 of the greatest of Men who sealed the Truth which they had held and taught with their Blood." In the end, he believed, Joseph and Hyrum would be justly "ranked with the Martyrs of Jesus Christ."

In addition to looking to the martyrs of the past for understanding, Fielding had an eye to the future of the Lord's work. "Joseph and Hyram had done all that they could have done," he wrote, "and the Foundation of the great Work of the last Days was laid." Building on that foundation, Fielding was sure, the work Joseph and Hyrum had lived and died for "could be finished by the 12 Appostles who had been instructed in all things pertaining to the Kingdom of God on the Earth."[6]

Zina Huntington Jacobs, who had been sealed to Joseph Smith as a plural wife, recorded her shock upon seeing "the lifeless speechless Bod[i]es of the [two] Marters," noting that "little did my heart ever think that mine eyes should witness this awful seen."[7] In her journal,

Jacobs counted the cost of the martyrdom for the men's families, the community, and humanity as well as for the Church, describing Joseph and Hyrum not only as "the Prophet and Patrarch of the Church of the Later day Saints," but also as "kind husbands," "affectionate Father[s]," "venerable statesman," and "Friends of man kinde."

For Jacobs, the murders of Joseph and Hyrum were evidence of the wickedness of the world. In her journal, she prayed that God would acknowledge "the innosent blood that has be[e]n shed" and asked "how long must widows mourn and orphans cry before thou wilt avenge the Earth and cause wick[ed]ness to seace"?[8] On July 4, about a week after the martyrdom, Jacobs noted that it was Independence Day for the United States, and she contrasted the promise of American freedom and justice with the brutal murder of the two brothers. "The once noble banner of liberty is fallen," she wrote. "The bo[a]sted land of fre[e]dom is now sta[i]ned with innocent blood."[9]

William Clayton, a British immigrant and one of Joseph Smith's clerks, wrote in his journal a meticulous account of how Joseph and Hyrum had been killed, an account pieced together from interviews with Willard Richards, John Taylor, and others who had been present. After reviewing the evidence, Clayton placed much of the blame for the murders with government officials, including Illinois governor Thomas Ford. "He had pledged his faith and the faith of the State that they should be protected from all harm," Clayton noted. And yet the militia that was supposed to protect Joseph and Hyrum had cooperated with the mob. Like Zina Jacobs, Clayton saw a broad contrast between American ideals of religious liberty and the reality the Saints were experiencing. "Liberty is fled," he wrote. He coolly added that there was "no public celebration in Nauvoo" on July 4.[10] With his faith in the nation shattered, Clayton turned to God. "We look to thee for justice,"[11] he wrote.

Poetry

Some Latter-day Saints shared their reactions by publishing poetry in the *Times and Seasons,* a newspaper run by the Church. The authors included accomplished poets such as Eliza R. Snow, William W. Phelps, John Taylor, and Parley P. Pratt as well as anonymous Latter-day

Saints.[12] Different writers focused on different emotions. William W. Phelps's "Praise to the Man" reflected on the legacy Joseph had left and looked forward to his work on the other side of the veil. John Taylor's "O Give Me Back My Prophet Dear" spoke with longing about the loss of two beloved leaders. These and some other poems were published as lyrics with suggested popular melodies. A few were later included in Latter-day Saint hymnals and continue to be sung today.[13]

Many of the poems mixed grief and outrage over the murders with reference to past martyrs, even Jesus Christ. In her poem published in the July 1, 1844, edition of the *Times and Seasons,* which announced the murder, Eliza R. Snow wrote:

> *Now Zion mourns—she mourns an earthly head:*
>
> *The Prophet and the Patriarch are dead!*
>
> *The blackest deed that men or devils know*
>
> *Since Calv'ry's scene, has laid the brothers low!*
>
> *One in their life, and one in death—they prov'd*
>
> *How strong their friendship—how they truly lov'd:*
>
> *True to their mission, until death, they stood,*
>
> *Then seal'd their testimony with their blood.*[14]

Editorials

As many of the Saints crafted and shared their personal responses to the tragedy in letters, journals, and poems, Church leaders and representatives felt an obligation to report and comment on the deaths in editorials, seeking in doing so to provide news and comfort to Latter-day Saints everywhere. On July 1, Apostles Willard Richards and John Taylor, who had been with the brothers in Carthage Jail when the mob attacked, attached their names to a notice in the *Times and Seasons* by newspaper editor William W. Phelps. Their editorial urged Latter-day Saints to "hold fast to the faith that has been delivered to them in the last days" and placed Joseph and Hyrum within a long line of biblical martyrs. The three men reminded the Latter-day Saints that "the murder of Abel; the assassination of hundreds; the righteous blood of all the holy prophets, from Abel to Joseph, sprinkled with the best blood of the Son of God, as the crimson sign of remission, only carries conviction to the business and bosoms of all flesh, that the cause is just and will continue; and blessed are they that hold out faithful to the end." [15]

In the next edition of the *Times and Seasons,* Phelps published a longer editorial about the murders that included a report of Joseph's words as he left for Carthage. "I am going like a lamb to the slaughter," the Prophet had said, "but I am calm as a summer's morning: I have a conscience void of offence toward God, and toward all men: I shall die innocent." Phelps also reported that "Joseph's last exclamation was '*O Lord my God!*'" [16] Around the same time that Phelps published his editorial, Willard Richards wrote his own detailed account of the murders, which included for the first time the report of the last words of Hyrum: "I'm a dead man." Richards's account was published on July 24, 1844, in Nauvoo's local newspaper. [17]

The Doctrine and Covenants

While many outside observers expected the Church to collapse following the murders of Joseph and Hyrum, the work of the Church continued despite their deaths. During the last two years of Joseph's life, Church leaders had been working on a new edition of the Doctrine and Covenants. Just prior to the deaths of Joseph and Hyrum, they had announced an expected publication date for mid-July of 1844. [18]

The publication was only slightly delayed by the unrest preceding and following the events at Carthage Jail. Soon after the martyrdom, the decision was made to go ahead with the printing but to add a final section to "close" the book with a statement regarding the deaths. The statement was likely written in July or August, as the volume was published and in use by September. [19] This statement, titled "Martyrdom of Joseph Smith and Hyrum Smith," has been canonized as Doctrine and Covenants 135.

Since at least the early 20th century, commentators and Church leaders had assumed that the statement was written by John Taylor, an Apostle and the head of the printing office. [20] The section was never attributed to Taylor during his lifetime, however, and it may have been the work of Taylor, Richards, Phelps, or another regular contributor in the Nauvoo printing office. Regardless of authorship, the statement drew heavily on the eyewitness testimonies of Taylor and Richards and quoted from earlier newspaper editorials and notices published by the Church that they had helped write. Like those earlier published accounts, this statement echoed themes of martyrdom, innocence, and divine judgment—themes that likewise appeared in the private writings of Latter-day Saints.

Because the printers had to fit the statement into an already typeset (though not yet printed) volume, the section was printed in significantly smaller font than the rest of the volume and fit into the page and a half of blank space between the previous section and the index. As a result of its placement in the Doctrine and Covenants, this statement was widely read and quoted and has become the official epitaph for Joseph Smith and his brother Hyrum.

1. See Samuel Morris Brown, *In Heaven as It Is on Earth: Joseph Smith and the Early Mormon Conquest of Death* (New York: Oxford University Press, 2012), 287–98.

2. Vilate M. Kimball letter to Heber C. Kimball, June 30, 1844, Church History Library, Salt Lake City.

3. Almira M. Covey letter to Harriet Mack Whittemore, July 18, 1844, Harriet Mack Whittemore Correspondence, Church History Library, Salt Lake City; capitalization modernized.

4. Sarah M. Kimball letter to Sarepta Heywood, circa 1844, Joseph L. Heywood Letters, Church History Library, Salt Lake City; punctuation modernized.

5. Revelation 6:9–10.

6. Joseph Fielding journal, December 1843–March 1859, 47–51, Church History Library, Salt Lake City.

7. Zina D. H. Young diaries, June 28, 1844, Church History Library, Salt Lake City.

8. Zina D. H. Young diaries, June 26, 1844.

9. Zina D. H. Young diaries, July 4, 1844.

10. William Clayton journal, July 4, 1844, quoted in James B. Allen, *No Toil nor Labor Fear: The Story of William Clayton* (Provo, Utah: Brigham Young University Press, 2002), 149.

11. William Clayton journal, June 28, 1844, quoted in Allen, *No Toil nor Labor Fear,* 137.

12. See Davis Bitton, "The Martyrdom of Joseph Smith in Early Mormon Writings," in Roger D. Launius and John E. Hallwas, eds., *Kingdom on the Mississippi Revisited: Nauvoo in Mormon History* (Urbana and Chicago: University of Illinois Press, 1996), 181–97; see also Benjamin E. Park, " 'We Announce the Martyrdom': The Murder of Joseph Smith as Portrayed in *Times and Seasons* Poetry," *Selections from the Religious Education Student Symposium 2008* (Provo, Utah: Brigham Young University Religious Studies Center, 2008), 34–47.

13. "Joseph Smith," *Times and Seasons,* vol. 5, no. 14 (Aug. 1, 1844), 607; John Taylor, "The Seer," *Times and Seasons,* vol. 5, no. 24 (Jan. 1, 1845), 775; "Poetry," *Times and Seasons,* vol. 6, no. 14 (Aug. 1, 1845), 991; *Sacred Hymns and Spiritual Songs for The Church of Jesus Christ of Latter-day Saints,* 19th ed. (Liverpool, England: George Teasdale, 1889), 89, 278, 314.

14. Eliza R. Snow, "The Assassination of Gen'ls Joseph Smith and Hyrum Smith," *Times and Seasons,* vol. 5, no. 12 (July 1, 1844), 575.

15. W. W. Phelps, Willard Richards, and John Taylor, "To The Church of Jesus Christ of Latter Day Saints," *Times and Seasons,* vol. 5, no. 12 (July 1, 1844), 568.

16. "The Murder," *Times and Seasons,* vol. 5, no. 13 (July 15, 1844), 585.

17. Willard Richards, "Two Minutes in Jail," *Nauvoo Neighbor,* July 24, 1844, 3.

18. See "Book of Doctrine and Covenants," *Times and Seasons,* vol. 3, no. 5 (Jan. 1, 1842), 639; see also "Notice," June 11, 1844, in *Nauvoo Neighbor,* vol. 2, no. 9 (June 26, 1844), 4.

19. Peter Crawley, *A Descriptive Bibliography of the Mormon Church: Volume One, 1830–1847* (Provo, Utah: Brigham Young University Religious Studies Center, 1997), 279.

20. See Robert J. Woodford, "The Historical Development of the Doctrine and Covenants, Volume I" (PhD diss., Brigham Young University, 1974), 1794.

"This Shall Be Our Covenant"

D&C 136

Chad M. Orton

In February 1846, Brigham Young led a handpicked vanguard company of 300 men across the ice-filled Mississippi River. At the time, their plan was to reach a place of refuge in the Rocky Mountains that summer and plant crops to feed those who would follow that year. But the ensuing months did not go according to plan. Heavy rains caused streams and rivers to rise well above normal levels, turning Iowa's rolling plains into muddy quagmires. At the same time, over 1,000 Saints, many of them poorly prepared for the journey, insisted on joining the advance company, longing to be close to Church leaders in a time of uncertainty. Progress slowed so much that Brigham Young gave up on reaching his envisioned destination that year and established Winter Quarters on the banks of the Missouri River instead.

Besides this advance group of pioneers, thousands of other Latter-day Saints left Nauvoo, most according to a prearranged schedule. By the fall of 1846, more than 7,000 people were living at Winter Quarters in caves, wagons, makeshift hovels, and hastily built cabins. Another 3,000 wintered at various locations along the trail under similar conditions. Many were sick from malnutrition and exposure, and some were experiencing a crisis of faith. These trying circumstances made the winter of 1846–47 among the most difficult periods of Brigham Young's life. He felt "like a father with a great family of children around [him]" and later recalled that his responsibilities pressed down upon him like a "twenty-five ton weight."[1]

By January 1847, he had lost so much weight that his clothes no longer fit. He had worried about the Saints, counseled about what to do, and prayed for divine guidance. And then, on January 14, 1847, the answer came. Two days later, Brigham Young invited the Saints to accept the "Word and Will of the Lord" (D&C 136).[2] Since the revelation begins by addressing "the Camp of Israel in their journeyings to the West" (D&C 136:1), some have assumed that the revelation is a simple how-to guide for organizing pioneer companies and have underestimated the role it played in refocusing Brigham Young and the Church. By helping the Saints remember that their conduct on the journey was as important as their destination, the revelation helped transform the westward migration from an unfortunate necessity into an important shared spiritual experience.

Heeding the Word

Having received the answers to his prayers, Brigham Young immediately went to work to ensure that the Saints knew with certainty what the Lord expected of them. Joseph Smith had already taught many principles found in the revelation, but they had not always been an important part of the 1846 exodus. While some Saints had willfully ignored counsel during the previous year's journey, even more had not sufficiently been taught. Brigham enlisted the help of the other Apostles to teach the revealed principles as commanded in the revelation.[3] Upon learning of the revelation, Horace Eldredge concluded "that its execution would prove [their] salvation."[4] Hosea Stout observed that following the revelation would bring needed calm and unity in the face of unexpected trials; it would "put to silence the wild bickering" that had complicated the journey across Iowa.[5] As they placed their trust in the revealed word, the people no longer felt the urgency to travel physically with the Twelve. The Twelve, in turn, were free to provide general leadership for the Church rather than having to worry about the day-to-day operations of a specific group.

During Zion's Camp in 1834, Joseph Smith had used an organizational model of a presidency of three with captains of hundreds, fifties, and tens. Brigham Young had attempted to implement this pattern before the Saints left Nauvoo, but it was not given a high priority. Now in 1847, the way that the Saints were organized would become so important that even before Brigham finished writing down the revelation, he proposed "that letters be written to instruct [the] brethren how to organize companies for emigration."[6]

Besides appointing captains, Brigham oversaw two more organizational changes. The size of a company would be limited to no more than 100 wagons. And once individuals became part of a company, they would be expected to travel together throughout the journey. These changes were a marked departure from the loose organization that characterized the Saints' exodus across Iowa. Although the ideal was not always realized, beginning in 1847 the Mormon exodus became "the most carefully orchestrated, deliberately planned, and abundantly organized hegira in all of American history," in contrast to the fluid movement between companies so common among non–Latter-day Saint emigrants who were also heading west.[7]

In addition to ensuring that the Saints were organized according to the word of the Lord, Brigham Young and the Twelve undertook to show the Saints how to live according to the will of the Lord. Brigham came to understand that rather than simply blazing a trail that others would follow, the 1847 vanguard company was establishing a covenant path. Thus, all those who were to make the journey were to travel "with a covenant and promise to keep all the commandments and statutes of the Lord" (D&C 136:2). The revelation further declares, "This shall be our covenant—that we will walk in all the ordinances of the Lord" (D&C 136:4).

During the months leading up to the exodus from Nauvoo, Church leaders had made a concerted effort to ensure that as many Saints as possible could make sacred covenants by participating in temple ordinances. If they were striving to keep their covenants and live the commandments, they could claim the promised "power from on high" to bless and assist them.[8] The Lord further reminded the Saints: "I am he who led the children of Israel out of the land of Egypt; and my arm is stretched out in the last days, to save my people Israel"

(D&C 136:22).[9] Other defining characteristics of the covenant path included the reminder for the Saints to assist those in need by bearing "an equal proportion, according to the dividend of their property." The charge also included the Lord's promise to the Saints if they willingly did so: "You shall be blessed in your flocks, and in your herds, and in your fields, and in your houses, and in your families" (D&C 136:8, 11).[10] The virtues of patience, humility, and gratitude in keeping covenants and attending to temporal stewardships outlined in the revelation would also assist the Latter-day Saint pioneers in settling the wilderness, establishing new homes and communities, and laying the foundation for a church destined to fill the world.[11]

Walking the Covenant Path

With new understanding came renewed energy. As God's people, they had the privilege and the responsibility to undertake the journey differently. Lack of physical preparation and food had been major issues during the Saints' journey across Iowa. Now Brigham came to believe that the success of their endeavor depended less on manpower, maps, wagons, and supplies and more on heeding the word and will of the Lord. The Lord could cause it to rain manna on the plains of America if need be, so long as the Saints put their trust in Him. The Saints had no need to overload their wagons out of fear.[12] To reinforce this point, Brigham Young reduced the vanguard company to just 144 men and instructed them to bring just 100 pounds of food per person on their journey into the wilderness.[13] All "who had not faith to start with that amount" could stay at Winter Quarters, he declared.[14] He "warned all who intended to proceed to the mountains that iniquity would not be tolerated in the Camp of Israel" and further declared, "I did not want any to join my company unless they would obey the word and will of the Lord, live in honesty and assist to build up the kingdom of God."[15]

Within days of receiving the "Word and Will of the Lord," Brigham proposed a social to show "to the world that this people can be made what God designed them." Dancing was often thought of as an immoral form of recreation in 19th-century America, but Brigham taught the vanguard company: "There is no harm [that] will arise from merriment or dancing if brethren, when they have indulged in it, know when to stop" and never "forget the object of this journey."[16] In inviting the Saints to dance, Brigham was heeding revealed counsel: "If thou art merry, praise the Lord with singing, with music, with dancing, and with a prayer of praise and thanksgiving" (D&C 136:28).

With preparations in place, Brigham felt confident that the Lord would help them, even with circumstances beyond their control. When individuals in the advance company expressed concerns that they might not reach their destination in time to plant crops, Brigham declared, "Well, suppose we did not. We [have] done all we could and traveled as fast as our teams were able to go." If the Saints "had done all [they] could," he would feel "just as well satisfied as if [they] had a thousand acres planted with grain. The Lord would do the rest."[17] He went on, "I never felt clearer in my mind than on this journey. My peace is like a river between my God and myself."[18]

A Time of Learning

The journey from Winter Quarters to the Salt Lake Valley became a training ground for Church leaders and members alike. George A. Smith felt that participants would "look back at this journey as one of the greatest Schools they ever were in," while Wilford Woodruff wrote, "We are now in a place where we are proving ourselves."[19] For Brigham Young and the Saints, the journey became both a chance to prove their faith by obeying counsel and an exercise in proving the Lord. The noticeable change among the Saints following the revelation prompted William Clayton to observe, "It truly seemed as though the cloud had burst, and we had emerged into a new element, a new atmosphere, and a new society."[20]

The 1847 journey of the vanguard company was not without its trials, even with the Saints' renewed commitment. The initial plan was to leave "one month before grass grows" but no later than March 15.[21] However, spring was late in coming, and the early grass grew weeks later than normal. As a result of the unseasonably cold weather, the company was not able to leave their rendezvous location until mid-April.[22] The excitement of finally beginning the journey was soon tempered by the realities of bitterly cold nights, windswept prairies, challenging river crossings, the loss of cattle, and days filled with long, monotonous travel.

At times Brigham Young, having become passionately committed to the principles in the revelation, found himself frustrated with the behavior of some company members. In late May, he read "the Word and Will of the Lord" to the company and "expressed his views & feelings . . . that they were forgetting their mission." He further proclaimed that he would "rather travel with 10 righteous men who would keep the commandments of God than the whole camp while in a careless manner & forgetting God." [23] The following day he declared that he wanted the company "to covenant to turn to the Lord with all their hearts." He reminded them to act like a covenant people: "I have said many things to the brethren about the strictness of their walk and conduct when we left the gentiles. . . . If we don't repent and quit our wickedness we will have more hindrances than we have had, and worse storms to encounter." Having reproved with sharpness, he then "very tenderly blessed the brethren and prayed that God would enable them to fulfill their covenants." [24]

The 1847 immigration stands in dramatic contrast to the previous year. While the vanguard company had traveled less than 300 miles in 1846—an average of a little more than two miles a day—the first pioneer company traveled more than 1,000 miles in 111 days, averaging more than four times the distance per day over the previous year.

Many have attributed the success of the Mormon migration to Brigham Young's personal leadership, but he readily acknowledged God's hand in the work. "What I know," he said, "I have received from the heavens. . . . Men talk about what has been accomplished under my direction, and attribute it to my wisdom and ability; but it is all by the power of God, and by intelligence received from him." [25] As a result of the lessons learned in 1847, the anxiety that Brigham Young felt at Winter Quarters faded away. Having proved the word and will of the Lord and having subsequently incorporated its principles into his life, he later found himself "full of peace by day and by night" and sleeping as "soundly as a healthy child in the lap of its mother." [26]

1. Brigham Young letter to Jesse C. Little, Feb. 26, 1847, Brigham Young office files, Church History Library, Salt Lake City; Brigham Young sermon, July 31, 1853, as published in *Journal of Discourses,* 26 vols. (London: Latter-day Saints' Book Depot, 1855–86), 1:166. During this time, Brigham Young was described as follows: "Our President [doesn't] stick [balk] at anything that tends to advance the gathering of Israel, or promote the cause of Zion in these last days; he sleeps with one eye open and one foot out of bed, and when anything is wanted, he is on hand" (Historian's Office, History of the Church, Jan. 7, 1847, Church History Library, Salt Lake City).

2. Historian's Office, History of the Church, Jan. 16, 1847.

3. Historian's Office, History of the Church, Jan. 27, 1847.

4. Historian's Office, History of the Church, Jan. 16, 1847.

5. Hosea Stout diary, Jan. 14, 1847, as published in *On the Mormon Frontier: The Diary of Hosea Stout,* 2 vols., ed. Juanita Brooks (Salt Lake City: University of Utah Press and Utah State Historical Society, 1964), 1:229.

6. Historian's Office, History of the Church, Jan. 14, 1847.

7. Richard E. Bennett, *We'll Find the Place: The Mormon Exodus, 1846–1848* (Salt Lake City: Deseret Book, 1997), 73.

8. Doctrine and Covenants 95:8.

9. While the revelation tied the Latter-day Saints back to ancient Israel, it also provided a link to the journey of Lehi and Nephi, in which the Lord made a similar proclamation: "Inasmuch as ye shall keep my commandments, ye shall prosper, and shall be led to a land of promise; . . . I will prepare the way before you, if it so be that ye shall keep my commandments; wherefore, inasmuch as ye shall keep my commandments ye shall be led towards the promised land; and ye shall know that it is by me that ye are led. Yea, . . . and that I, the Lord, did deliver you" (1 Nephi 2:20; 17:13–14). The reference to covenants and obedience, however, also served as a warning. After the Saints failed to redeem Zion in 1834, the Lord declared: "Were it not for the transgressions of my people, speaking concerning the church and not individuals, they might have been redeemed even now. But behold, they have not learned to be obedient to the things which I required at their hands" (D&C 105:2–3).

10. Throughout the Doctrine and Covenants, the Lord makes clear the Church's responsibility, including "Look to the poor and needy, and administer to their relief that they shall not suffer" (D&C 38:35) and "Thou wilt remember the poor, and consecrate of thy properties for their support" (D&C 42:30). See also D&C 38:16; 42:31, 34, 39; 44:6; 52:40; 83:6; 84:112; 104:18; 105:3. As the Saints were preparing to leave Nauvoo, during the October 1845 general conference Brigham "moved that [they] take all the saints with [them], to the extent of [their] ability, that is, [their] influence and property." Only 214 individuals, however, signed this "Nauvoo Covenant." Beginning with the 1847 exodus, Brigham put a renewed emphasis upon all Church members accepting their responsibility to assist others in need according to their ability. See *History of the Church,* 7 vols. (Salt Lake City: Deseret Book, 1976–80), 7:465.

11. Clarissa Young Spencer concluded, "One of Father's most outstanding qualities as a leader was the manner in which he looked after the temporal and social welfare of his people along with guiding them in their spiritual needs" (Clarissa Young Spencer and Mable Harmer, *Brigham Young at Home* [Salt Lake City: Deseret Book, 1963], 169). Another daughter, Susa Young Gates, felt that her father "manifested even more godly inspiration in his carefully regulated social activities and associated pleasure than in his pulpit exercises. He kept the people busy, gave legitimate amusements full sway and encouraged the cultivation of every power, every gift and emotion of the human soul." She noted that "people would have had in those grinding years of toil, too few holidays and far too little of the spirit of holiday-making which is the spirit of fellowship and socialized spiritual communion, but for Brigham Young's wise policy" (Susa Young Gates and Leah D. Widtsoe, *The Life Story of Brigham Young* [New York: Macmillan, 1930], 266; spelling modernized). As with other aspects of the word and will

of the Lord, while the implementa-
tion and successful oversight were
Brigham's, the inspiration was the
Lord's.

12. Four days after receiving section
136, he publicly proclaimed that he
"had not cattle sufficient to go to
the mountains" but that he "had no
more doubts nor fears of going to the
mountains, and felt as much security
as if [he] possessed the treasures of the
East" (Historian's Office, History of the
Church, Jan. 18, 1847).

13. Although it is widely believed that
Brigham selected only 143 men for
the company (plus 3 women and 2
children), Ellis Eames was originally
appointed as part of the company but
dropped out soon after leaving Winter
Quarters, reportedly because of illness.
He has generally not been counted
as a member of the original company
because of the short period of time he
spent in it. By 1849 Eames had reached
Utah, and in 1851 he became Provo's
first mayor (John Clifton Moffitt,
The Story of Provo, Utah [Provo, UT:
Press Publishing, 1975], 266). Orson F.
Whitney noted that "twelve times
twelve men had been chosen." From
this, a popular belief arose that the
number was to represent twelve men
for each of the twelve tribes of Israel,
another covenant people. Whitney may
have believed this, but he recognized
it was largely a matter of speculation:
"Whether designedly or otherwise
we know not" (Orson F. Whitney,
History of Utah, 4 vols. [Salt Lake City:
George Q. Cannon and Sons, 1892–
1904], 1:301).

14. Historian's Office, History
of the Church, Mar. 3, 1847.

15. Historian's Office, History
of the Church, Jan. 18, 1847.

16. Historian's Office, History of the
Church, Feb. 5, 1847; Norton Jacob
journal, May 28, 1847, as published
in *The Mormon Vanguard Brigade
of 1847: Norton Jacob's Record,* ed.
Ronald O. Barney (Logan: Utah State
University Press, 2005), 150; spelling
and capitalization modernized.

17. *The Record of Norton Jacob,* ed.
C. Edward Jacob and Ruth S. Jacob
(n.p.: Norton Jacob Family Association,
n.d.), 50.

18. Historian's Office general Church
minutes, May 23, 1847, Church
History Library, Salt Lake City;
spelling modernized.

19. Historian's Office general Church
minutes, May 23, 1847; Wilford
Woodruff journal, May 16, 1847,
in *Wilford Woodruff's Journal:
1833–1898, Typescript,* 9 vols., ed.
Scott G. Kenney (Midvale, UT:
Signature Books, 1983–85), 3:177;
spelling modernized.

20. William Clayton diary, May 29, 1847,
in An *Intimate Chronicle: The Journals
of William Clayton,* trade ed., ed.
George D. Smith (Salt Lake City:
Signature Books, 1995), 333.

21. Bennett, *We'll Find the Place,* 69.

22. Members of the vanguard company
had begun gathering to the appointed
rendezvous location on the Elkhorn
River, approximately 20 miles west
of Winter Quarters, by early April.
It wasn't until April 16, however, that
Brigham Young officially organized
the company into hundreds, fifties,
and tens, and they began their journey
together from the Elkhorn as a group.

23. Wilford Woodruff journal, May 28,
1847, in *Wilford Woodruff's Journal,*
3:186; spelling and capitalization
modernized.

24. William Clayton diary, May 29, 1847,
in *An Intimate Chronicle,* 325, 330–31.

25. Brigham Young sermon, May 18, 1873,
as published in *Journal of Discourses,*
16:46.

26. Brigham Young sermon, Jan. 12, 1868,
as published in *Journal of Discourses,*
12:151; Brigham Young sermon,
Oct. 7, 1859, as published in *Journal
of Discourses,* 7:281.

Susa Young Gates
and the Vision of the Redemption of the Dead

D&C 138

Lisa Olsen Tait

On the evening of Friday, November 5, 1918, Susa Young Gates and her husband, Jacob, stopped by the home of some close friends to pick up a box of apples. That home was the Beehive House, on the corner of State Street and South Temple in Salt Lake City, and those friends were Joseph F. Smith, President of The Church of Jesus Christ of Latter-day Saints, and his wife Julina Smith. Susa and Joseph had known each other since Susa's childhood, in the 1860s, when he was a frequent visitor in the home of her father, Brigham Young. The Gateses and the Smiths had served together as missionaries in Hawaii in the 1880s and had remained close friends ever since. Susa and Joseph forged a particularly close friendship. She called him "My Beloved and Honored Friend and Brother"; he called her his "beloved Sister" and expressed "the truest brotherly love" for her.[1] What happened during her visit that evening would become a crowning expression of that friendship and a deeply personal affirmation of Susa's tireless efforts in what she called the "work of redeeming the dead."[2]

"A Greater Work"

Susa Young Gates was one of the most prominent Latter-day Saint women of her time. A woman of indomitable energy and determination, she had worked for decades as a writer, editor, educator, and leader in the Young Ladies' Mutual Improvement Association (YLMIA), the Relief Society, and various national women's organizations. But in 1918 her driving interest was genealogy and temple work, an area in which she had been a leading Latter-day Saint advocate for over a decade.[3]

Susa felt a sacred sense of personal mission in this work. In 1902, returning from a meeting of the International Council of Women in Europe, Susa had become seriously ill. In London she sought a priesthood blessing from Elder Francis M. Lyman, then serving as president of the European Mission, and in that blessing he told her, "You shall live to perform temple work, and you shall do a greater work than you have ever done before." This commission became a driving force in her life. "I had been interested in Temple work before," she said, "but now I felt that I must do something more, something to help all the members of the Church."[4]

Susa could hardly have done any more than she went on to do for the cause of family history and temple work. She wrote countless newspaper and magazine articles, taught class after class, and took the message on the road to many stakes and wards. She visited genealogical libraries in the eastern United States and England and corresponded with genealogists from many other countries, seeking greater knowledge and expertise. She served on the general board of the Relief Society, where she succeeded in having lessons on genealogy (most of which she also wrote) incorporated into the curriculum. She published a 600-page reference book on surnames and contributed frequently to a new magazine devoted to genealogical research.[5] With all this effort, she also found time to serve for decades as a temple ordinance worker. Susa's work was integral to the establishment of family history as a focus for Latter-day Saints.

In these efforts she worked closely with Elder Joseph Fielding Smith—assistant Church historian, son of the Church President, and, after 1910, a member of the Quorum of the Twelve Apostles.

Elder Smith also served as secretary of the Utah Genealogical Society, the Church's official genealogical organization. Susa referred to Elder Smith as "the Apostle to the spirits in prison" and as "the eloquent spokesman" of genealogy and temple work.[6] Susa and Elder Smith spoke together at genealogical meetings—she provided practical instruction in methodology, and he laid out the theological foundations of the work. Thanks to their efforts and those of several like-minded associates, thousands of Latter-day Saints received training and encouragement in performing family history and temple work.

Despite these accomplishments, Susa often felt that she was waging an uphill battle. She believed that too many Latter-day Saints exhibited "a very general indifference" toward genealogy and temple work.[7] "Not even an angel from heaven could induce some of these club women and these successful business men to set aside a portion of their time for temple work," Susa wrote to a friend.[8]

When she visited President Smith that night in November 1918, Susa had recently been reminded of the widespread lack of enthusiasm for family history work. Members of the Relief Society general board had nearly voted to discontinue genealogy lessons. "I have had to take the part of the genealogical work against all others," she wrote in one letter. She had barely succeeded in preserving it as part of the curriculum.[9] At the October 1918 Relief Society conference, stake leaders reported that the genealogy lessons were too difficult. They suggested that the lessons be "simplified" and "emphasis placed on the spiritual rather than on the educational side of this study." Susa assured them that the recently published *Surname Book and Racial History* would help make the lessons more accessible.[10] But she had long insisted that the spiritual and the practical dimensions of genealogy were complementary. "All the desired inspiration in the world will not save our dead," she declared. "We must also have information in order to consummate that noble work."[11] She labored on, making every effort to provide both information and inspiration to her fellow Saints.

"The Hosts of the Dead"

In November 1918 President Smith was ill—elderly, frail, and declining rapidly. He had spent much of the year at home, unable to maintain the demanding pace that characterized most of his life. His age-related ailments were compounded by heavy grief. In January his beloved eldest son, Elder Hyrum M. Smith, had died suddenly of a ruptured appendix. "My soul is rent, my heart is broken! O God, help me!" President Smith exclaimed at the time.[12] But the blows kept coming. In February a young son-in-law died after an accidental fall. And in September, Hyrum's wife, Ida, died just a few days after giving birth, leaving five orphaned children. Meanwhile, the Great War (World War I) was dragging to a close, leaving unimaginable carnage and devastation in its wake, and a worldwide influenza pandemic was claiming millions of victims. For President Smith, it was a time of deeply personal pain amid much global suffering.[13]

These catastrophes formed a visible backdrop at the October general conference. Attendance was noticeably diminished, "owing to so many of the Priesthood being absent in the war."[14] The growing flu epidemic likely kept people home as well. Mustering his failing strength, President Smith made a surprise appearance and presided at four sessions of the conference. "I have been undergoing a siege of very serious illness for the last five months," he said in his opening remarks. "Although somewhat weakened in body," he affirmed, "my mind is clear with reference to my duty." Then President Smith hinted at a message he was still struggling to find words to express. "I will not, I dare not, attempt to enter upon many things that are resting upon my mind this morning," he said, "and I shall postpone until some future time, the Lord being willing, my attempt to tell you some of the things that are in my mind, and that dwell in my heart."[15] He continued: "I have not lived alone these five months. I have dwelt in the spirit of prayer, of supplication, of faith and of determination; and I have had my communication with the Spirit of the Lord continuously."[16]

President Smith's remarks undoubtedly referred in part to the events of the previous day, October 3, 1918, when he had experienced a remarkable vision of the Savior's visit to the spirit world (now recorded in Doctrine and Covenants 138). In this vision,

President Smith saw "the hosts of the dead" awaiting the Savior's arrival. Wondering how Christ could have accomplished His ministry among the dead in "the brief time intervening between the crucifixion and his resurrection," President Smith saw that He "organized his forces and appointed messengers" from among the righteous spirits and "spent his time during his sojourn in the world of spirits, instructing and preparing the faithful spirits of the prophets who had testified of him in the flesh" to carry the message of redemption to the spirits of those who had not heard or had not received the gospel in their mortal lives.[17]

President Smith's desire to speak of these things to the Saints in person was not fulfilled. Ten days after general conference, he dictated the vision to his son Joseph Fielding Smith.[18] Two weeks later, on October 31, Joseph Fielding Smith read the text to the First Presidency and Quorum of the Twelve Apostles at their regular council meeting in the temple. It was "fully endorsed by all the brethren," he recorded, and they made plans to publish it in the December issue of the *Improvement Era*.[19] A week after that notable meeting, Susa and Jacob Gates made their visit to the Smith home.

"An Exquisite Joy and Comfort"

As the Gateses visited with members of the Smith family, President Smith summoned Susa to come into his room. "I comforted him all I could in his severe illness," Susa wrote.[20] He told her, "You are doing a great work, greater than you know anything about." After a few minutes President Smith and Susa were joined by Jacob and Julina and others (presumably Smith family members), and President Smith gave Susa a paper to read. It was a transcript of the account of his vision. "How blest, O how blest I am to have the priviledge!" Susa wrote in her journal that night. "To be permitted to read a revelation before it was made public, to know the heavens are still opened."[21]

Susa's description of the vision highlighted the aspects she found most compelling: "In it he tells of his view of Eternity; the Savior when He visited the spirits in prison—how His servants minister to them; he saw the Prophet and all his associate Brethren laboring in the Prison Houses; Mother Eve & her noble daughters engaged in the same holy cause!" Long an advocate for women's causes, Susa rejoiced at the specific mention of women in the revelation, grateful "to have Eve and her daughters remembered."[22] And she rejoiced in the revelation's affirmation of the work on behalf of the dead. "Above all," she wrote, "to have this given at a time when our Temple work and workers & our genealogy need such encouragement. No words of mine can express my joy and gratitude."[23] "Think of the impetus this revelation will give to temple work throughout the Church!" she later wrote to a friend.[24]

Two weeks later, on November 19, 1918, President Joseph F. Smith died. The announcement and publication of his vision appeared alongside the many tributes published at the time of his passing. In the *Relief Society Magazine,* editor Susa Young Gates published a lengthy tribute to President Smith and his wives, along with eulogies from various leading women in the Church. She then included the full text of the "Vision of the Redemption of the Dead," as it was called, but without disclosing her personal experience with it. Here she expanded on her private comments about the reference to Eve and her daughters in the text: "This is unusual—the mention of women's labors on the Other Side." Susa felt that "the direct view of [women] associated with the ancient and modern prophets and elders confirms the noble standard of equality between the sexes which has always been a feature of this Church."[25]

She continued: "The Vision's principal message to this people is a clarion call for them to awake to the immediate necessity of looking after their dead."[26] In spite of the setbacks and challenges in this effort, President Smith's vision was "an exquisite joy and comfort" to her.[27] Seven decades earlier, Joseph Smith had written to the Saints on the same subject, "Shall we not go on in so great a cause?"[28] Now Susa Young Gates, with renewed vision and commitment, continued the call: "May the people, and especially our sisters, rise to the measure of fulness in response to this heavenly manifestation!"[29]

1. Susa Young Gates letter to Joseph F. Smith, Oct. 14, 1918, Church History Library, Salt Lake City, Utah; Joseph F. Smith Christmas card to Susa Young Gates, Dec. 26, 1914, Church History Library, Salt Lake City, Utah.

2. Susa Young Gates, "A Friend of the Helpless Dead," *Relief Society Magazine,* vol. 4, no. 9 (Sept. 1917), 486.

3. An overview of Susa Young Gates's leadership of genealogical efforts is found in James B. Allen, Jessie L. Embry, and Kahlile B. Mehr, *Hearts Turned to the Fathers: A History of the Genealogical Society of Utah, 1894–1994* (BYU Studies, 1995), 59–90.

4. "Susa Young Gates," *Utah Genealogical and Historical Magazine,* vol. 24 (July 1933), 98–99.

5. See Susa Young Gates, ed. and comp., *Surname Book and Racial History: A Compilation and Arrangement of Genealogical and Historical Data for Use by the Students and Members of the Relief Society of the Church of Jesus Christ of Latter-day Saints* (Salt Lake City: General Board of the Relief Society, 1918). The magazine was the *Utah Genealogical and Historical Magazine,* published quarterly by the Utah Genealogical Society beginning in 1910.

6. Susa Young Gates, remarks at the Relief Society genealogical convention, Oct. 7, 1918, quoted in Amy Brown Lyman, "General Conference of Relief Society," *Relief Society Magazine,* vol. 5, no. 12 (Dec. 1918), 676.

7. Susa Young Gates, "Inspiration versus Information," *Utah Genealogical and Historical Magazine,* vol. 9 (July 1918), 131.

8. Susa Young Gates letter to Elizabeth C. McCune, Nov. 14, 1918, Church History Library, Salt Lake City.

9. Susa Young Gates letter to Elizabeth C. McCune, Oct. 4, 1918, Church History Library, Salt Lake City.

10. Amy Brown Lyman, "General Conference of Relief Society," 661–62.

11. Gates, "Inspiration versus Information," 132.

12. Joseph Fielding Smith, comp., *Life of Joseph F. Smith: Sixth President of The Church of Jesus Christ of Latter-day Saints* (Salt Lake City: Deseret News Press, 1938), 474.

13. For an excellent discussion of the personal and global contexts for Joseph F. Smith's vision, see George S. Tate, "'The Great World of the Spirits of the Dead': Death, the Great War, and the 1918 Influenza Pandemic as Context for Doctrine and Covenants 138," *BYU Studies,* vol. 46, no. 1 (2007), 4–40.

14. Editors' Table, *Improvement Era,* vol. 22, no. 1 (Nov. 1918), 80. This same report said that "over fifteen thousand men holding the Priesthood were in the military service."

15. Joseph F. Smith, in Conference Report, Oct. 1918, 2. According to Susa Young Gates, President Smith would have told of his vision at general conference "if he had felt strong enough to do so without being overcome with emotion" (Susa Young Gates letter to Elizabeth C. McCune, Nov. 14, 1918).

16. Joseph F. Smith, in Conference Report, Oct. 1918, 2. The report noted that "at the close of President Smith's remarks the organist struck a chord of 'We thank thee, O God, for a prophet.' The congregation arose in unison, and without announcement, and under strong emotion, sang that sacred song so dear to the Saints" (Conference Report, Oct. 1918, 3).

17. Doctrine and Covenants 138:11, 27, 30, 36.

18. "I wrote, at my father's dictation a revelation or vision, he received on the 3rd," Joseph Fielding Smith recorded in his journal on October 17. In *Life of Joseph F. Smith,* Joseph Fielding Smith wrote that his father had his vision written down "immediately following the close" of general conference, which was held October 4–6, 1918 (466). These dates are consistent with those given in subsequent discussions of the vision and in the current section heading in the Doctrine and Covenants. However, Joseph Fielding Smith's journal indicates that he did not record the vision at his father's dictation until almost two weeks after general conference (see Joseph Fielding Smith journal, Oct. 17, 1918, Church History Library, Salt Lake City).

19. Joseph Fielding Smith journal, Oct. 31, 1918, Church History Library, Salt Lake City, Utah. See "Vision of the Redemption of the Dead," *Improvement Era,* vol. 22, no. 2 (Dec. 1918), 166–70. The vision was also published in the *Deseret News,* the *Relief Society Magazine,* the *Young Woman's Journal,* and the *Millennial Star.* It was included in *Gospel Doctrine: Selections from the Sermons and Writings of Joseph F. Smith, Sixth President of the Church of Jesus Christ of Latter-day*

Saints, ed. John A. Widtsoe (Salt Lake City: Deseret News, 1919), which was a widely read reference work among Latter-day Saints throughout the 20th century. The vision was included in the Pearl of Great Price in 1976 and then added to the 1981 edition of the Doctrine and Covenants. See N. Eldon Tanner, "The Sustaining of Church Officers," *Ensign,* May 1976, 19.

20. This account is reconstructed from two sources: Susa Young Gates diary, Nov. 5, 1918, Church History Library, Salt Lake City, Utah; and Susa Young Gates letter to Elizabeth C. McCune, Nov. 14, 1918.

21. Susa Young Gates diary, Nov. 5, 1918.

22. Susa Young Gates diary, Nov. 5, 1918; see also Doctrine and Covenants 138:39.

23. Susa Young Gates diary, Nov. 5, 1918.

24. Susa Young Gates letter to Elizabeth C. McCune, Nov. 14, 1918.

25. "In Memoriam: President Joseph F. Smith," *Relief Society Magazine,* vol. 6, no. 1 (Jan. 1919), 21.

26. "In Memoriam," 21.

27. Susa Young Gates letter to Elizabeth C. McCune, Nov. 14, 1918.

28. Doctrine and Covenants 128:22

29. "In Memoriam," 21.

The Messenger and the Manifesto

Official Declaration 1

Jed Woodworth

One crisp fall morning, Monday the sixth of October 1890, seven thousand Latter-day Saints sat in silence on the long wooden benches in the large oval tabernacle on Temple Square. The event was the semiannual general conference of The Church of Jesus Christ of Latter-day Saints, and the assembly had come to listen to instruction from men who they revered as prophets, seers, and revelators.

At that time, conference speakers were not informed in advance when they would speak. The President of the Church made assignments in the moment as he felt impressed. No one prepared talks beforehand. Several of the speakers came to the conference with a brief outline tucked into their scriptures, but many others came with no notes at all, counting on the Holy Spirit to fill their minds when they heard the prophet call their name.

As the crowd awaited the session's first address, President Wilford Woodruff turned to his right, looked at the man seated next to him, and asked him to stand and address the audience. That man was President George Q. Cannon, First Counselor to President Woodruff in the First Presidency. The request caught President Cannon off guard, for he had supposed that President Woodruff would take the lead in this historic moment. Just a few minutes earlier, Orson F. Whitney, a Salt Lake City bishop, had read the Manifesto, the momentous document (known today as Official Declaration 1) in which President Woodruff declared his intention to submit to laws prohibiting plural marriage. President Woodruff had released the document to the press two weeks earlier, without comment. President Cannon stared out into a sea of pensive and eager people, with one thing on their minds.

"I felt to shrink very much from it," President Cannon wrote, speaking of the request to speak. "I think I never was called upon to do a thing that seemed more difficult than this."[1]

The Saints had practiced plural marriage for half a century. Women and men had anguished over the decision to enter a principle that was alien to their religious upbringings and inclinations. They had suffered personal and collective isolation, harassment, and imprisonment for the principle. But they had also accepted plural marriage as God's command to the Church. They believed the practice refined their souls and defined their peculiarity in the eyes of the world. What would define them now? President Cannon surely knew that wholesale changes in self-definition would not be easily made. The anguish of exiting plural marriage would rival the challenge of entering into it.

After Bishop Whitney read the document, the conference had voted with uplifted hand to sustain it as "authoritative and binding" upon the Church. Most voted in the affirmative, but some kept their hands in their laps, unready to accept the Manifesto as the will of God. From the stand, Church leaders looking out on the audience saw husbands and wives weeping, anxious and uncertain, not knowing what the Manifesto meant for them going forward.[2]

President Cannon raised his hand in support of the Manifesto along with most others in the crowd. But the weight of unifying a divided audience on what he called this "exceedingly delicate subject" seemed almost too much to bear. The message could go in a thousand different ways. As he stood and walked to the podium, his mind raced. "There was nothing in my mind that seemed clear to me to say upon this subject," he wrote of that moment. "I arose with my mind a blank."[3]

The Counselor

George Quayle Cannon was rarely at a loss for words. Friendly and gregarious by nature, he had been immersed in words all his life. As a teenager in Nauvoo, he apprenticed at the print shop of the Church's newspaper.[4] He went on to found one of the most powerful publishing houses in all of Utah and spent much of his adult life writing editorials in the Church newspapers and periodicals he published.[5]

Recognizing both Cannon's gifts and his powerful platform, President Brigham Young called him to the apostleship in 1860 and later to the First Presidency as a counselor. President Cannon would serve as a counselor to four Church Presidents over the course of nearly three decades.

George Q. Cannon was known during his lifetime for his powerful intellect. His fellow Apostles acknowledged him as a man without peer among the Church's leadership. He was usually the Apostle who was asked to give the sensitive speech or write the delicate letter. The non-Mormon press called him "the Mormon Richelieu" because he was thought to have been the genius behind all Mormon movements.[6]

But the reputation for genius also burdened George Q. Cannon. It bothered him to be credited as the source of ideas he did not invent and movements he did not initiate. He resisted being seen as the man behind the curtain. He well knew that his role was advisory. He was not the President of the Church, not the man who held the priesthood keys that led the Church. He humbly deferred to authority even if others could not see it.

The Crusade

The federal crusade against the Mormon practice of plural marriage was one of the great trials of George Q. Cannon's life. After eight years as Utah Territory's lone delegate in the United States House of Representatives, Cannon was expelled from Congress after he was deemed in violation of the federal law banning polygamy.

Cannon entered into plural marriage when in his early thirties, convinced it was a practice God would have him live. All told, his family eventually numbered five wives and 43 children.[7] He adored these family members. He was grieved that, between 1885 and 1888, he was frequently away from them, moving from place to place, often in disguise, trying to avoid federal marshals who sought to arrest him for violating federal marriage law. He nurtured the best he could by writing family members long, personal letters and by holding family councils whenever he could convene them. Eventually he surrendered to authorities and submitted to five months in the Utah penitentiary between September 1888 and February 1889.[8]

Government officials had long urged Church leaders to issue a statement ending plural marriage. President Cannon resisted that direction. The greatest speech of his career, colleagues later recalled, took place on the floor of the United States Congress, where he stood before his colleagues and defended plural marriage on grounds of religious conscience.[9] His inclination was to defend the practice despite all opposition. "I, for one, have not seen my way clear" to issue any statement calling an end to plural marriage, he reflected at a time when persecution roiled the Church. "President Woodruff has the same feeling. We shall have to trust to the Lord, as we always have done, to help us."[10]

A humble, simple, unassuming man, with little of President Cannon's learning, President Woodruff arrived at the conclusion that a change had to be made long before Cannon did.[11] In the fall of 1889, a stake president came to President Woodruff and asked whether he was obliged to sign a recommend for a man to enter into plural marriage, considering the law forbade the practice. President Cannon, who was in the room, was surprised to hear President Woodruff's answer. "It is not proper for any marriages of this kind to be performed in this [Utah] Territory at the present time," Woodruff counseled.[12]

President Woodruff reasoned by analogy: when persecutors blocked the Saints from building a temple in Jackson County, the Lord accepted the Saints' offering and suspended the original command. He said it was now the same with plural marriage. After making this explanation, President Woodruff turned to his counselor for comment. Ever cautious and prudent, President Cannon hesitated to launch out in a new direction. To this point in time, the Church had conscientiously objected to federal laws forbidding plural marriage. It was, Cannon wrote in his journal, the first time he had ever heard a President of the Church express himself so plainly on the subject of curtailing plural marriage. "I made no reply," Cannon wrote, "not prepared to fully acquiesce in his expressions."[13]

The Manifesto

On the morning of September 23, 1890, President Cannon appeared as usual at the First Presidency's office at the Gardo House, a large Victorian-style home just south of the Beehive House in Salt Lake City. "I found President Woodruff quite stirred up in his feelings concerning the steps taken by our enemies to malign us before the country and to make false statements concerning our teachings and action."[14] The Utah Commission, the small group of federal appointees charged with overseeing the execution of antipolygamy legislation in Utah, had issued a report claiming that Church leaders continued to teach polygamy and sanction plural marriages in Utah. Cannon felt the Church should issue a denial. President Woodruff had something stronger in mind.[15]

President Woodruff found the First Presidency's secretary, George Gibbs, and the two walked into a room adjoining the First Presidency's office, where the Church President dictated his thoughts while Gibbs took them down. When President Woodruff emerged from the room, his "face shone with pleasure and he seemed very much pleased and contented."[16] He asked to have the dictation read to President Cannon, which was done. "While it was not in exactly the proper shape to publish," Cannon felt "it contained the ideas and was very good. I told him I felt it would do good."[17]

At President Woodruff's request, the members of the Quorum of the Twelve Apostles who were not traveling on assignment were called to come to Salt Lake immediately to hear the document read. Three Apostles, along with George Q. Cannon and Joseph F. Smith of the First Presidency, met that afternoon to suggest edits. These revisions were then incorporated, and the document was submitted to the press for immediate publication.[18]

In his journal account of the day, Cannon included Woodruff's original dictation along with the edits he himself suggested.[19] He did this, he said, to set the record straight for future generations: "I have been often credited with saying and doing things which I did not say nor do." He wanted it on record that the President of the Church, not his counselor, had led out with the Manifesto. "This whole matter has been at President Woodruff's own instance," Cannon explained. "He has stated that the Lord had made it plain to him that this was his duty, and he felt perfectly clear in his mind that it was the right thing."[20]

The Speech

George Q. Cannon was sure of one thing as he stood at the podium of the Tabernacle to address the conference assemblage on that October day in 1890. "I felt that whatever was said must be dictated by the Spirit of the Lord."[21]

As President Cannon faced the audience, he discovered his blank mind suddenly filled with the words of scripture. It was the passage from Doctrine and Covenants 124 that President Woodruff had quoted in his meeting with the stake president the year before. Cannon began his talk by reading from verse 49: "When I give a commandment to any of the sons of men to do a work unto my name, and those sons of men go with all their might and with all they have to perform that work, . . . and their enemies come upon them and hinder them from performing that work, behold, it behooveth me to require that work no more at the hands of those sons of men, but to accept of their offerings."[22]

George Q. Cannon seemed to realize that reassurance came by knowing that the Manifesto was anchored in scriptural precedent. The President of the Church felt inspired to apply the word of the Lord given in one context, to another, just as prophets had done from the beginning. "It is on this basis"—Doctrine and Covenants 124:49—Cannon said, "that President Woodruff has felt himself justified in issuing this manifesto."[23]

Cannon's tongue began to loosen, and for the next half hour, he held his audience spellbound. "I did get great freedom and spoke with ease, and all fear was taken away," he later wrote in his journal.[24]

He admitted at the outset of his speech in the Tabernacle that he had been a great defender of plural marriage. "In public and in private I have avowed my belief in it. I have defended it everywhere and under all circumstances." This belief, of course, was rooted in the belief that God wanted him to practice plural marriage. "I considered the command was binding and imperative upon me," he said, speaking only in the first person.[25]

Nor had it been Cannon's personal inclination to have the Manifesto issued. "I can say for myself, that I have been appealed to many scores of times to get out something" that put an end to the practice. "But at no time has the Spirit seemed to indicate that this should be done. We have waited for the Lord to move in the matter."[26]

But the spirit surrounding the Manifesto was different. Cannon was positive the Lord had now moved. President Woodruff "made up his mind that he would write something, and he had the spirit of it. He had prayed about it and had besought God repeatedly to show him what to do." The document had Cannon's full support. "I know that it was right, much as it has gone against the grain with me in many respects."[27]

He told his audience that he had observed two reactions to the Manifesto among the Latter-day Saints. One reaction came from those who "feel to sorrow to the bottom of their hearts because of the necessity of this action that we have now taken." The other reaction was one of smug self-congratulation: "Did I not tell you so? Did I not tell you it would come to this?" This latter group reprimanded Church leaders for taking so long to come around. Had the leaders acted more expeditiously, they argued, Church members could have been saved from years of suffering and heartache.[28]

Cannon said his own view differed from this second group. "I believe that it was necessary that we should witness unto God, the Eternal Father, unto the heavens and unto the earth, that this was really a principle dear to us—dearer, it might be said, in some respects, than life itself. We could not have done this had we submitted at the time that those of whom I speak suggested submission." No one could question the Saints' willingness to espouse the principles they held dear. The "unmentionable" sufferings of men, women, and children was credited to them in the heavens.[29]

Conclusion

After President Cannon sat down, President Woodruff again surprised his counselor—by standing to deliver his own speech. "Brother George Q. Cannon has laid before you our position," President Woodruff said, affirming his counselor's words, making them his own. "I say to Israel, the Lord will never permit me nor any other man who stands as the President of this Church, to lead you astray. It is not in the programme."[30]

Cannon thought the abundance of the Holy Spirit at the conference provided proof that the Manifesto stood approved of God. "The Spirit of the Lord was powerfully poured out, and I think every faithful Saint must have had a testimony from the Lord that He was in this movement, and that it was done with His approval."[31]

"I am not able to tell my thoughts concerning our action," Cannon reflected in his journal entry for that day. "I know, however, that it is right. It is clear to me that this step taken by President Woodruff is a correct one." President Woodruff was the messenger of revelation, and Cannon's role as counselor was to support and defend the revelations of God, just as he had done his entire life. "I have a testimony from the Lord," Cannon said, "that our sacrifices in regard to this and our firmness up to the present time in resisting every attempt to extort from us the promise to stop the practice are accepted of the Lord, and He virtually says to us, 'It is enough,' and we leave the case in His hands."[32]

1. George Q. Cannon journal, Oct. 6, 1890, Church History Library, Salt Lake City.

2. Marriner Wood Merrill journal, Oct. 6, 1890, Church History Library, Salt Lake City. Heber J. Grant, who was on the stand that day, noticed many "wet eyes" in the audience when the vote was called, but whether they were tears of joy or sorrow, he did not say (see

Heber J. Grant journal, Oct. 6, 1890, Church History Library, Salt Lake City).

3. George Q. Cannon journal, Oct. 6, 1890.

4. On Cannon's conversion, see Davis Bitton, *George Q. Cannon: A Biography* (Salt Lake City: Deseret Book, 1999), 33–34. Cannon's family was converted to the Church by his uncle John Taylor, future President of the Church. Taylor

edited the Church's newspapers in Nauvoo, and Cannon learned the printing business by working under him.

5. These newspapers and periodicals included the *Deseret News,* the *Western Standard,* the *Millennial Star,* and the *Juvenile Instructor.*

6. Arthur I. Street, "The Mormon Richelieu," *Ainslee's Magazine,* vol. 4 (1899), 699–706.

7. Cannon's wives bore 33 children. He adopted two other children. He sealed to himself eight additional children, the children of Caroline Young and Mark Croxall, after Young and Croxall divorced. Cannon subsequently married Caroline Young. On Cannon's wives and children, see Bitton, *George Q. Cannon,* 373–85, 463–64.

8. See Bitton, *George Q. Cannon,* 373–90. The family councils are mentioned throughout Cannon's journal. For one example, see George Q. Cannon journal, Mar. 17, 1891.

9. Bitton, *George Q. Cannon,* 291–96.

10. Journal History, Apr. 13, 1901, 3, Church History Library, Salt Lake City; George Q. Cannon journal, Nov. 24, 1889. The speech was probably his valedictory speech in the House of Representatives. For a summary, see Bitton, *George Q. Cannon,* 254–57.

11. George Q. Cannon journal, Aug. 15, 1889.

12. Cannon once described President Woodruff as "a humble, plain, unassuming man, as free from all assumption of authority as any man I ever knew" (George Q. Cannon journal, Mar. 3, 1889).

13. George Q. Cannon journal, Sept. 9, 1889.

14. Doctrine and Covenants 124:49.

15. George Q. Cannon journal, Sept. 9, 1889.

16. George Q. Cannon journal, Sept. 23, 1890.

17. George Q. Cannon journal, Sept. 23, 1890.

18. Elder Franklin D. Richards, as quoted in Heber J. Grant journal, Sept. 30, 1890.

19. George Q. Cannon journal, Sept. 23, 1890.

20. George Q. Cannon journal, Sept. 24, 1890.

21. Cannon suggested nine edits, while the other members of the Twelve suggested two. Perhaps the most important of Cannon's edits was to suggest that the words "and to use my influence with the members of the Church over which I preside to have them do likewise" be added to the fourth paragraph (see George Q. Cannon journal, Sept. 24, 1890).

22. George Q. Cannon journal, Sept. 24, 1890. For more information on the conditions surrounding the reception of the Manifesto, see "The Manifesto and the End of Plural Marriage," Gospel Topics, topics.lds.org.

23. George Q. Cannon journal, Oct. 6, 1890.

24. Doctrine and Covenants 124:49. Cannon's speech is reproduced in *President Woodruff's Manifesto: Proceedings at the Semi-Annual General Conference of The Church of Jesus Christ of Latter-day Saints, Monday Forenoon, October 6, 1890* (Salt Lake City: 1890).

25. *President Woodruff's Manifesto,* 3.

26. George Q. Cannon journal, Oct. 6, 1890.

27. *President Woodruff's Manifesto,* 3. Elsewhere, Cannon said that "the people of Utah do not believe that plural marriage ought to be or can be universal. In Utah itself it is not possible, for the males outnumber the females" (Bitton, *George Q. Cannon,* 256–57).

28. *President Woodruff's Manifesto,* 6.

29. *President Woodruff's Manifesto,* 6.

30. *President Woodruff's Manifesto,* 4–5.

31. *President Woodruff's Manifesto,* 4–5.

32. *President Woodruff's Manifesto,* 9–10.

33. George Q. Cannon journal, Oct. 6, 1890. "I am thankful that so many manifestations of the Lord's approval and favor have been shown unto us, for if this had not been the case, there might have been doubtful ones, who might have felt that the Lord had withheld His Spirit because of our action. As it is, all testified that they never attended a better Conference" (George Q. Cannon journal, Oct. 6, 1890).

34. George Q. Cannon journal, Oct. 6, 1890.

Witnessing the Faithfulness

Official Declaration 2

James Goldberg

The Bible tells the story of a people who knew trouble and grief. In the Old Testament, the children of Israel were dragged away from their homes as captives and enslaved in distant lands. Later, the Israelites' homeland was occupied by foreign powers that ruled with a heavy hand. The people waited for salvation in part because they knew what it is to endure bondage.[1]

The experience of countless black Africans over the past five centuries has echoed the experience of the ancient Israelites. From the early 1500s to 1888, generations of black Africans were taken from their homelands and enslaved in the Americas. By the early 1900s, almost all of Africa was occupied by foreign powers.

On both sides of the Atlantic, slavery and imperialism led to deep divisions between white and black populations. Laws typically treated white people as superior. After The Church of Jesus Christ of Latter-day Saints was organized in 1830, some black people embraced the restored gospel and a few black men were ordained to the priesthood. However, the racially divided culture of the time and threats of outside persecution posed challenges to racial integration in the Church.[2]

Starting in the 1850s, the Church followed a policy that restricted black members' access to full participation in the Church by declaring them ineligible to be ordained to the priesthood or receive temple ordinances.[3] For several generations, many black Latter-day Saints, like many black people around the world, made the most of difficult circumstances while hoping for a better future.

As the Church began to expand globally in the decades after World War II, a growing number of black people converted to the restored gospel. In Africa and in the Americas, a new generation of black pioneers placed their trust in the Lord to open up a way for them to one day participate fully in the Church. Although there were encouraging signs of a change in racial attitudes both inside and outside of the Church, racial discrimination continued to be widespread, and the priesthood and temple restriction on black Saints remained.[4] The experiences of three couples—Charlotte Andoh-Kesson and William Acquah in Ghana, Helvécio and Rudá Tourinho Assis Martins in Brazil, and Joseph and Toe Leituala Freeman in the United States—shed light on what it was like to be a black Latter-day Saint in the years leading up to the 1978 revelation that made priesthood and temple blessings available to members of the Church regardless of race.

Charlotte Andoh-Kesson Acquah and William Acquah, Ghana

As a child, Charlotte Andoh-Kesson attended an Anglican church with her parents and 12 siblings. A naturally religious person, Charlotte memorized all the hymns and even the words of the mass.

When Charlotte was about 11 years old, her mother met a local pastor named Joseph William "Billy" Johnson. Johnson wasn't like other pastors—in addition to the Bible, he preached from another book of scripture called the Book of Mormon. Charlotte grew up hearing names such as Moroni, Nephi, and Ammon as well as names such as Moses and Mark. Alongside older hymns, she sang Latter-day Saint hymns about Zion and the Restoration of the gospel. At times, she and others from her church would travel down to the beach to wrestle with the Lord in prayer as Enos had done in the Book of Mormon.[5]

The congregation Charlotte attended met in a run-down building with a large crack in the roof, but they decorated the building with a statue of the angel Moroni to remind them of faraway temples. Some members of the congregation dreamed and prophesied of a day when they would be dressed in white, standing in a beautiful temple in Ghana.[6] Before that day came, though, they knew that representatives from Church headquarters would need to come and officially make them part of the worldwide Church.

In 1978, the year Charlotte finished college, she began to feel pulled between different forces. On the one hand, Brother Johnson became increasingly convinced that the day was coming when the predominately white Church, headquartered in the United States, would recognize the black LDS congregations in Ghana, and he led multiday fasts to hasten its coming. At the same time, Charlotte began dating William Acquah. William was happy to embrace her Latter-day Saint relatives and friends but was skeptical of the Church's teachings, critical of its poor physical facilities, and suspicious of white people in general, including those whom Ghana's Latter-day Saints were praying would come to their country.

Helvécio Martins and Rudá Tourinho Assis Martins, Brazil

In the early 1970s, Helvécio and Rudá Martins were searching for religious truth in Brazil. At the encouragement of Rudá's family, the couple had spent several years practicing Macumba, a faith that mixed African traditions, Catholic teachings, and spiritualism. Gradually, however, they began to feel that Macumba was not fulfilling their spiritual needs or bringing them closer to deceased family members and ancestors.[7]

In 1972, two LDS missionaries knocked on their door. Helvécio was interested but had one pressing concern. "Given that your church is headquartered in the United States, a country with a history of racial conflict," he asked, "how does your religion treat blacks? Are they allowed into the church?"

Helvécio remembered the older missionary "nervously squirm[ing] in his chair" in response.[8] Before answering, the missionaries asked to pray with Helvécio, Rudá, and the children. They then shared the story of the Restoration and explained the priesthood and temple restriction to the best of their understanding. Helvécio felt satisfied enough by their answer to focus on their other new teachings. Within a few months, encouraged by "the spirit of the talks . . . and the love of the members" at church, Helvécio and Rudá were baptized.[9] At the time, they were happy to let the gospel improve their lives and to wait—they assumed until the Millennium—for some priesthood-related blessings.

About a year after their baptisms, though, the Martins family was surprised when their patriarchal blessings suggested that they would be sealed together as a family in this life and that their son Marcus would serve a mission. Not wanting to be disappointed, they held to their understanding that they would wait for such blessings until Christ's return. At the same time, wanting to be prepared for whatever the Lord had planned, they opened a mission savings account for Marcus.[10]

Over the next few years, as the Martins family grew in the Church, members gave them support—and sometimes uncomfortable expressions of sympathy. On one occasion, a bishop said he felt Helvécio's greatest challenge was to remain faithful in the Church without being ordained to the priesthood. "Bishop," Helvécio replied, "I would be grateful if it were my greatest trial."[11]

In 1975, Helvécio and Rudá were invited to tour the construction site of the São Paulo Brazil Temple because of Helvécio's calling as the Church's regional public relations director. During the tour, both Helvécio and Rudá stopped at what they later learned was the site of the celestial room. "A powerful spirit touched our hearts," Helvécio recalled. "We hugged each other and cried, not really understanding why."[12]

Two years later, at the temple's cornerstone ceremony, President Spencer W. Kimball called Helvécio to his side. "Brother Martins," he counseled, "what is necessary for you is fidelity. Remain faithful and you will enjoy all the blessings of the gospel."[13]

But how could the Martins family receive all the blessings of the gospel without holding the priesthood or receiving temple ordinances? The next year, Marcus became engaged to a Church member who did not have black African ancestry. While she was content to rely on promises that all blessings would someday be available to all members, the prospect of not having a temple wedding was painful.

Joseph Freeman and Toe Leituala Freeman, United States

Long before he heard about The Church of Jesus Christ of Latter-day Saints, Joseph Freeman had sworn to give his life to Christ. His family was active in the Holiness movement, and he became a lay minister. In 1972, Joseph also enlisted in the army and was assigned to a base in Hawaii. His days were filled with military service, while his free time was filled with preaching and prayer.

But Joseph felt something was missing. Seeking guidance, he requested a week's leave, drove to a secluded section of beach, and fasted for five days. "I literally pleaded with the Lord," Joseph recalled, "that I would know what to do to gain the strength and spiritual power to teach the gospel as it ought to be taught."[14] He also expressed a second wish: to find a wife who would love God as much as she loved him.

Joseph's prayer was soon answered. While visiting the Polynesian Cultural Center in Laie, he met several Latter-day Saints whose gospel insights impressed him. In particular, a returned sister missionary named Toe Isapela Leituala struck him as the kind of woman he had always been looking for. Through conversations with new friends, missionaries, and Toe, Joseph became convinced he had found Christ's restored Church. He was baptized on September 30, 1973.

As a new member, Joseph's feelings about race and the Church were mixed. He was nervous about being the only black member in his ward. In addition, the priesthood and temple restriction stood between him and two of his deepest desires: he couldn't be a minister in the Church, and he couldn't have the marriage he wanted. Toe, who wanted a temple marriage, broke off contact with Joseph as she felt her attraction to him growing.

It disturbed Joseph that he couldn't find scriptural support for common justifications for the restriction, most of which involved speculation about the premortal life. At the same time, he found comfort in the promise that someday, at least in the Millennium, black men would hold the priesthood. "My concept of the Millennium was not of some faraway thing that was beyond comprehension," Joseph recalled. "I really felt it might not be very many years before 'that great and dreadful day.'"[15]

Even with the dilemmas he faced as a black man in the Church, Joseph remained grateful for the gospel. "With each day the gift of the Holy Ghost became a greater source of guidance and peace and a more permanent part of my life," he remembered.[16] Soon after his conversion, it was difficult for him to imagine how he had lived without it.

It also became difficult for Toe to imagine living without him. Though marrying Joseph would keep her from the temple sealing she had long hoped for, she felt prompted to pursue the relationship. The two began dating and soon counseled with their bishop about getting married. The bishop first expressed the typical concerns of the time about interracial and intercultural marriage but promised that if they would fast and pray, the Holy Ghost would tell them what to do. Joseph and Toe fasted, prayed, and felt the Spirit's confirmation of their choice. Others pressured them to break off their relationship, but they remained true to the answer they had received. They were married on June 15, 1974.

The marriage was soon blessed with a child, and Joseph and Toe decided to leave army life. They moved to Salt Lake City, where they had more children. One factor in their decision to settle in Salt Lake City was the Genesis Group, a Church-sponsored social and spiritual group for black Saints.[17] For the most part, he found himself content with his life in the Church. He worried, though, about how to raise his sons with enough self-esteem to weather being singled out in their teens for not being allowed to receive the priesthood along with their peers.

The Long-Promised Day

As congregations of believers grew in Ghana and Nigeria and people such as the Martins family and Joseph Freeman joined the Church in the Americas, President Spencer W. Kimball witnessed their faithfulness and became increasingly preoccupied with how to help them grow in the faith. On one occasion, he was moved to tears by a letter from Emmanuel Bondah, a sixth-grader in Ghana, asking for his own copy of the Book of Mormon and for help to become "a pure Mormon." [18]

By early 1978, President Kimball was regularly praying in the temple for revelation about extending priesthood ordination and temple blessings to black members of the Church. He spoke at length with his counselors in the First Presidency and with members of the Quorum of the Twelve Apostles on the subject and invited them to make it a matter of study and prayer.

On June 1, 1978, President Kimball met with the First Presidency and Quorum of the Twelve Apostles in the temple. He asked once again for their thoughts and counsel concerning the restriction and then prayed for revelation. "I had had some remarkable spiritual experiences before," Elder Bruce R. McConkie recalled, ". . . but nothing of this magnitude. All of the Brethren at once knew and felt in their souls what the answer to the importuning petition of President Kimball was." [19] A week later, the First Presidency sent word to Church leaders throughout the world announcing that the restriction had been lifted. This statement was later canonized in the Doctrine and Covenants as Official Declaration 2.

The day after the announcement, Joseph Freeman received a phone call from his bishop. As it happened, their stake conference was to be held that weekend: Joseph was interviewed, was sustained, and on June 11, 1978, became the first black man ordained to the Melchizedek Priesthood after the revelation. At last, he would be able to minister with the authority he had prayed to find. Two weeks later, Joseph and Toe took their children to the temple. As Joseph and Toe's family knelt at the altar, Elder Thomas S. Monson spoke the words of the ordinance and then sealed them together for time and all eternity. [20]

For the Martins family in Brazil, the news led their son Marcus to delay his wedding to serve the mission that his patriarchal blessing had spoken of and that his parents had saved for. Just after being ordained an elder himself, Helvécio stood in the circle to ordain Marcus to the same office. "I felt I would explode with joy," Helvécio recalled.[21] Just a few weeks later, he gave his maid's son a priesthood blessing and witnessed the boy's miraculous healing. That November, the São Paulo Brazil Temple opened and the Martins family—including Marcus, who was serving a mission in São Paulo, Brazil—was sealed.[22]

In Ghana, the revelation on priesthood at last opened the way for missionaries to come and officially organize congregations there. For members such as Charlotte, it was a clear answer to the extended fasts and many prayers of the local Saints. Her husband, William, was less impressed. In his studies, he had absorbed a mistrust of white people and their narratives about history and faith. His personal interactions with white people had only served to increase that distrust, and he was skeptical about the prospect of white missionaries bringing anything good to his country.[23]

What he actually experienced, though, surprised him. A senior missionary couple, Reed and Naomi Clegg, brought him the gospel through their actions and words. They were warm and straightforward. They not only taught that all people are children of God but also extended respect to everyone they met. "They welcomed me in the way that no white has ever welcomed me," William recalled.[24] Once his guarded attitude about the white messengers evaporated, it wasn't long before William felt the gospel message sinking deep into his heart. He was baptized, was ordained to the priesthood, and helped build up the Church in Ghana from its small beginnings until the day in 2004 when the visions of the first members were fulfilled and Ghana had a temple of its own.

Pressing Forward in Faith

As Helvécio Martins had expressed to his bishop in the mid-1970s, the priesthood and temple restriction was one of many trials in black members' lives. In addition to their own personal trials, many have faced and continue to face cultural misunderstandings and prejudice, even in their own wards or branches. And members of all races struggle to understand the restriction.

As a result of the revelation ending the restriction, Church members around the world experience real and meaningful integration with their fellow Saints. Through home and visiting teaching, Church callings, service, and fellowship, members with different racial backgrounds often become deeply involved in each other's lives. Members learn from each other, take counsel from each other, and have opportunities to better understand each others' perspectives and experiences.

Latter-day Saints still wrestle with the problems created by centuries of slavery, colonization, suspicion, and division. But Church fellowship offers them the chance to become of one heart and one mind as they minister to each other in love. As they press forward in humility and faith, members of the Church find healing and strength through Jesus Christ, the Savior of us all.

1. The Old Testament records that the Israelites were slaves in Egypt, and then many became captives in Assyria and Babylon. Some books in the Apocrypha are set during the time Israel was ruled by Greek forces; during New Testament times, Romans occupied Israel.

2. Peter Kerr, a former slave living in Ohio, likely became the first black person to embrace the gospel when missionaries visited the Kirtland area in 1830 (see Mark Staker, *Hearken, O Ye People: The Historical Setting of Joseph Smith's Ohio Revelations* [Salt Lake City: Kofford Books, 2009], 3). Elijah Abel, Jane Manning James, Q. Walker Lewis, and Green Flake are other examples of early black Latter-day Saints. The Latter-day Saints' early neighbors often saw the Saints as dangerously comfortable with black Americans, a perception that contributed to violence against the Saints as early as 1832, when people in Jackson County accused the Saints of tampering with their slaves (see William W. Phelps, "To His Excellency, Daniel Dunklin, Governor of the State of Missouri," *The Evening and the Morning Star,* vol. 2, no. 15 [Dec. 1833], 226–31).

3. See "Race and the Priesthood," Gospel Topics, topics.lds.org.

4. In the United States, the legal gains made by people of color during the 1950s and 1960s slowed in the 1970s, as many who had supported the end of discriminatory laws in the South resisted efforts to increase racial integration in the North. In Africa, too, the 1950s and 1960s saw many countries gain independence, only to realize in the 1970s that barriers to participation as equals in the international community remained.

5. William E. D. and Charlotte A. Acquah, interview by Matthew K. Heiss, Cape Coast, Ghana, Oct. 16, 1999, transcript, 26, Church History Library, Salt Lake City.

6. Acquah, interview, 22.

7. Helvécio Martins and Mark Grover, *The Autobiography of Helvécio Martins* (Salt Lake City: Aspen Books, 1994), 39–40.

8. Martins, *The Autobiography of Helvécio Martins,* 44.

9. Martins, *The Autobiography of Helvécio Martins,* 45.

10. Martins, *The Autobiography of Helvécio Martins,* 46.

11. Martins, *The Autobiography of Helvécio Martins,* 57.

12. Martins, *The Autobiography of Helvécio Martins,* 64.

13. Martins, *The Autobiography of Helvécio Martins,* 66.

14. Joseph Freeman, *In the Lord's Due Time* (Salt Lake City: Bookcraft, 1979), 43.

15. Freeman, *In the Lord's Due Time,* 67–68.

16. Freeman, *In the Lord's Due Time,* 66.

17. Freeman, *In the Lord's Due Time,* 87, 100–101. The Genesis Group had been formed in response to a request from three black members—Ruffin Bridgeforth, Darius Gray, and Eugene Orr—for help in serving and reactivating the few black Saints in the area. Elders Gordon B. Hinckley, Thomas S. Monson, and Boyd K. Packer of the Quorum of the Twelve Apostles met with the three and helped organize the group (see Edward L. Kimball, "Spencer W. Kimball and the Revelation on Priesthood," *BYU Studies,* vol. 47, no. 2 [2008], 30).

18. Janath Russell Cannon and Edwin Q. Cannon Jr., *Together: A Love Story* (Salt Lake City: Desktop Publishing, 1999), 153.

19. Kimball, "Spencer W. Kimball and the Revelation on Priesthood," 56.

20. Chris Peterson, "Black Priesthood Holder Recalls Historic Day," *Deseret News,* Apr. 23, 2010, deseretnews.com.

21. Martins, *The Autobiography of Helvécio Martins,* 70–71.

22. Martins, *The Autobiography of Helvécio Martins,* 78.

23. Acquah, interview, 8, 12–14.

24. Acquah, interview, 14.

Index by Section Number